Challenges to New Testament Theology

Challenges to New Testament Theology

An Attempt to Justify the Enterprise

PETER BALLA

Hendrickson Publishers, Inc.
P. O. Box 3473
Peabody, Massachusetts 01961-3473

ISBN 1-56563-394-6

Challenges to New Testament Theology: An Attempt to Justify the Enterprise, by
Peter Balla © 1997 by J. C. B. Mohr. All rights reserved.

Hendrickson Publishers' edition reprinted by arrangement with J. C. B. Mohr
(Paul Siebeck), P. O. Box 2040, D-72010 Tübingen.

Printed in the United States

First Printing — November 1998

Library of Congress Cataloging-in-Publication Data

Balla, Peter.
    Challenges to New Testament theology: an attempt to justify the
enterprise / Peter Balla.
    Originally published: Tübingen: Mohr Siebeck, ©1997, in series:
Wissenschaftliche Untersuchungen zum Neuen Testament. 2. Reihe; 95.
    Originally presented as the author's thesis (Ph. D.)—University of
Edinburgh, 1994.
    Includes bibliographical references and index.
    ISBN 1-56563-394-6 (paper)
    1. Bible. N.T.—Theology. 2. Bible. N.T.—Canon. I. Title.
[BS2397.B34   1998]
230'.0415—dc21   98-43246
                                                        CIP

To My Wife, Gyöngyi

Preface

In recent years, New Testament Theology has become a major subject of interest for New Testament scholars. Some have questioned the possibility of the enterprise. Others have written works that are related to the discipline and that even have the term *New Testament Theology* in their titles.

It seemed timely to attempt to assess the arguments for and against. Out of that study grew a thesis that was accepted for the degree of Doctor of Philosophy by the University of Edinburgh in 1994. This book is a version of that thesis brought up-to-date.

I would like to express my gratitude to my supervisor, Professor J.C. O'Neill, for raising the possibility of tackling this topic and then for guiding my studies with care, patience and wisdom. I am most grateful to him for the regular supervisory meetings and for his suggestions concerning possible focuses of attention. This greatly helped me to complete the research within the period of three years between 1991 and 1994. I am also greatly indebted to my second supervisor, Dr. D.A. Templeton, for making time for discussion and for his comments on everything I wrote. I am very much indebted to Dr. D.L. Mealand, the Reverend Robert Morgan, Professor Hans Hübner and Professor Gerd Theissen for their helpful comments on the manuscript.

I am most grateful to Professor Martin Hengel and Professor Otfried Hofius for accepting this work into the series *Wissenschaftliche Untersuchungen zum Neuen Testament*. My special thanks are due to Professor Ulrich Luz who suggested that I should seek a place in this series.

I should like to thank the Church of Scotland for granting me the exceptional privilege of a second bursary which enabled me to return to New College, Edinburgh, for another period of postgraduate research in addition to my MTh year in 1987-88. I would also like to thank the Hope Trust for their generous support.

It is fitting that I should also mention my indebtedness to my home church, the Reformed Church in Hungary, and its earlier leaders who gave me permission to take extended study leave. I also thank Dr. Loránt Hegedűs, my father-in-law, who as the then newly elected bishop allowed me to be absent at such an important time as the years between 1991 and 1994 when Hungarians had a great deal to accomplish by making good use of the opportunities afforded by the recently gained democracy.

Last but not least, I thank my wife Gyöngyi for all her support. She has cheerfully taken upon herself the extra burden of being far away from home and giving ceaseless care to a growing family. It is, therefore, my joy to dedicate this work to her.

Easter, 1997   Peter Balla
Ráday College
The Faculty of Theology of the
Károli Gáspár Reformed University
Budapest

Table of Contents

Abbreviations

AV	Authorised Version
EKK	Evangelisch-Katholischer Kommentar zum Neuen Testament
ET	English translation
ICC	The International Critical Commentary
JSOT	*Journal for the Study of the Old Testament*
LXX	*Septuagint*
NA^{26}	Nestle-Aland, 26th edition (of *Novum Testamentum Graece*)
RGG	*Die Religion in Geschichte und Gegenwart*
RSV	Revised Standard Version
SNTS	Studiorum Novi Testamenti Societas

In this work, references are made by giving the year of publication and the page number in brackets in the main text. If the same work is referred to in the same context more than once, after the first reference giving both year and page, page numbers alone are given in subsequent references. If more than one reference is made to the same page in the same context, then the page number is not repeated. The next occurrence of a page number indicates that the reference is made to another page. On occasion I repeat the page number for the sake of clarity (for example, in the case of a reference to a new theme). The page number is introduced by "p." if it is necessary in order to avoid a possible misunderstanding (for example, when there is a figure in the same context referring to a year or to a bible verse).

Italics in quotations are always those of the author quoted.

When I use "he" for a non-specific pronoun in the third person, "he or she" should be understood. (As a justification for my usage I note that there is only one word for "he" and "she" in my native - Hungarian - language.)

Introduction

In 1990 Heikki Räisänen published a work entitled *Beyond New Testament Theology*. The very title of the book points in a marked way to the main thesis of Räisänen: New Testament scholarship has reached a state where the discipline of New Testament theology should be abandoned and replaced by another discipline. To quote Räisänen (xviii):

> 'New Testament theology' may be a legitimate part of self-consciously *ecclesial* theology. By contrast, those of us who work in a broader *academic* context should abandon such an enterprise (and, *a fortiori*, any dreams of a 'biblical theology' which would cover both Testaments).

In a more recent article Räisänen affirms that his use of the quotation marks around the term New Testament theology points to the proposal that the name of the discipline is a "misnomer" (1992, 252). The quotation marks allude to an essay put forward by William Wrede in 1897, the title of which speaks of a "so-called" New Testament theology. Räisänen has re-affirmed his thesis of 1990: "It is my conviction that Wrede was right and that a synthesis of early Christian thought, rather than of NT theology proper, is called for" (1992, 252).

The programmatic essay of Wrede in question was entitled *Über Aufgabe und Methode der sogenannten Neutestamentlichen Theologie*. In this essay Wrede argued that (1897, 79-80; ET: 1973, 116):[1]

> ... the name New Testament theology is wrong in both its terms ... The appropriate name for the subject-matter is: early Christian history of religion, or rather: the history of early Christian religion and theology.

These quotations show that the enterprise of New Testament theology is under considerable challenge.[2] Räisänen's and Wrede's programmatic works call for a discussion. The scholarly challenge should not remain without some examination of the matters that are involved in the call to move "beyond" the enterprise.

---

[1] Throughout my thesis the first page reference is made to the original German edition, 1897; then after a semi-colon there follows the reference to the English translation (=ET) made by R. Morgan, 1973, which I adopt.

[2] For a more recent summary of his main theses, see Räisänen, 1995 and 1997.

My thesis takes Räisänen's and Wrede's works as a starting point for the discussion. However, it does not aim at discussing the works of these two great scholars comprehensively. Rather, I look out - often with the help of their programmatic works - for arguments and theses that are in connection with their general challenge. In doing so, I also must discuss works of scholars other than Wrede and Räisänen.

My thesis is an attempt to answer the challenges that have been put to the enterprise of New Testament theology. In my work I focus on major problems that have to be dealt with, if one maintains that the enterprise of New Testament theology may be justified. I do not focus on one area of problems only - in order to avoid the danger that while the enterprise is justified on one ground, there may be other grounds which make it impossible to justify the enterprise.

However, since the challenges cover a very wide range of problems and themes, I have to observe certain limits. When I focus on arguments that seem to play a key role in the cases of the major theses, I do acknowledge that there are numerous arguments - related to our theme - that do not surface in this thesis. My discussion of the themes includes some exegetical remarks - but only by way of examples.

In a way similar to the limitation in terms of themes, my thesis does not claim to discuss all the available - extraordinarily extensive - literature. Rather, I focus on the works of scholars who can be generally seen as representing a consensus of opinion. At other times, I refer to scholars who may have contributed to our theme - although they may not have been followed by others. On occasion, reference is made to articles of a survey type on individual matters. I try to summarise theses by referring to one or two key figures in scholarship - without following up the history of scholarship on that particular matter. As we shall see, my study involves references to scholars from the nineteenth century - without listing the names of all the scholars who hold the same view up to the present day.

Apart from these general delimitations, one particular theme has to be named which is not addressed in this thesis: the theme of the relationship between the Old Testament and the New Testament - or, in other words, the problem of justifying the enterprise of a biblical theology that covers both Testaments. This theme in itself could be a topic of research.

However, it is not simply the extensive character of this theme that provides a reason for not including it in this thesis. The problem of justifying biblical theology is a problem that overarches the problems of the justification of the individual Testaments of the Bible. It is true that arguments for justifying biblical theology would strengthen the case for justifying the enterprises of

Old Testament theology and New Testament theology. However, if it turned out to be the case that biblical theology cannot be justified, this - in itself - would not disprove the possibility of justifying New Testament theology as a separate enterprise.

My thesis is that the enterprise of New Testament theology may be justified. In order to support this thesis, I shall examine questions related to the two constituent parts of the name of the enterprise - in accordance with Wrede's challenge seen above. The term "New Testament" has to be argued for; this requires an examination of questions related to the process that led to the canonisation of the writings of the New Testament. These questions are addressed in the second and the third chapters.

The term "theology" in the name of the enterprise raises numerous problems. Some of the problems are related to the relationship between theological and historical enterprises; others are related to the definition of the term. The first and the last chapters address these issues.

"Theology" also raises another type of a problem: the question of the unity of the theology of the New Testament writings. If there are contradictory theologies in the New Testament - with an emphasis on the plural, theolog*ies*, - then the enterprise can also be challenged on this ground. In this case, perhaps, one would not have to call for abandoning the enterprise, but at least for renaming it accordingly: works in this field would be written only with the title *The Theologies of the New Testament*.[3] Chapter four examines the issues related to the diversity of the theological content of the New Testament.

My thesis has a twofold character. On the one hand, I attempt to show that the challenge has not succeeded in proving that the enterprise of New Testament theology cannot be maintained. On the other hand, I attempt to put forward arguments in favour of the two theses that a historian can justify limiting the focus of the enterprise to the canonical writings of the New Testament and that the enterprise can set itself the aim of describing the theological content of the New Testament.

By referring to "a historian" I anticipate here a central argument in this thesis: New Testament theology is a historical enterprise. As a starting point, it may be appropriate to mention two major implications of this statement.

First, I make the claim that New Testament theology may be justified even in an academic context - and not only in an "ecclesial" context as Räisänen

---

[3] Cf. F.W. Horn's quotation from Georg Strecker in the foreword of the posthumously published *Theologie des Neuen Testaments* of Strecker (1995, V-VI): "Es soll der hier vorzustellende Entwurf von der Endfassung der neutestamentlichen Texte ausgehen, also eine redaktionsgeschichtliche Theologie des Neuen Testaments intendieren. Dies meint, daß die einzelnen neutestamentlichen Schriften nach ihren individuellen theologischen Konzeptionen gewürdigt werden sollen, so daß der Begriff 'Theologie des Neuen Testaments' präziser die Komplexität von Theologien im Neuen Testament bezeichnet".

has affirmed. The enterprise of New Testament theology can - of course - be carried out in the church. However, I attempt to discuss Räisänen's challenge in a way that the discussion could also be "tested" and examined by scholars outside a church context. For this purpose I adopt some of Räisänen's proposals - for example, that New Testament theology should be a historical enterprise. I also agree with Räisänen that any attempt to justify the enterprise would have to use arguments understandable to people without a commitment to faith who do not accept the truth claims of the Bible. We only disagree about whether or not such arguments would succeed: whether or not the enterprise can be justified.

Secondly, my thesis differs from Heinrich Schlier's approach which is summarised in his essays entitled "Über Sinn und Aufgabe einer Theologie des Neuen Testaments" (1964, 7-24) and "Biblische und dogmatische Theologie" (25-34). Schlier's thesis is not argued but presented as a set of presuppositions and axioms. For example, he affirms that the New Testament canon is a theological fact (10). New Testament theology builds on this fact. In Schlier's opinion, from the point of view of a history of early Christian religion it is absurd to speak of the theology of the New Testament and also to limit the task to the New Testament writings.

In distinction from this approach, I do not start with the axiom that we have to accept the limitation of the canon on theological grounds provided by the church. My question is whether or not historians can justify their focus on the canonical New Testament within the enterprise of New Testament theology.

Schlier also affirms that the theology of the New Testament is a collection of different theologies (9-10). However, he maintains that the task of New Testament theology should not be the presentation of a historical development (10). Rather, the very name of the discipline expresses the basic theological decision that there is unity in the New Testament. Accordingly, New Testament theology has to deal with a, or: *the* theology of the New Testament (11, 19). Again, the presupposition of a unity of theology - which includes the view that there is no final contradiction among the various basic theological ideas - is in connection with the view that the New Testament is inspired and canonical (19).

I differ from this approach in as much as I do not presuppose that there is a unity in the theology of the New Testament. It may be the case that historical investigation finds that there is a unity in the theology of the New Testament. This can only be the result of inquiry, exegetical discussions - and argumentative study.

I should like my thesis to be a contribution to the on-going debate in this broad field of biblical scholarship.

Chapter One

The Relationship between Historical and Theological Interpretation in New Testament Studies

When Räisänen mounts his challenge to the enterprise of New Testament theology, he affirms as his main thesis that the historical investigation of the Bible and theological reasoning on it must be kept apart (see e.g. 1990, 90). The proposal concerning the separation of the historical task from the theological one is also in some way related to the idea that the theology of the New Testament should not be searched for within the discipline of the study of the New Testament. In this chapter we shall consider the various problems which may emerge in relation to the historical investigation of the New Testament if one attempts to maintain New Testament theology as an enterprise.

Since it is Räisänen who argues for the thesis of the separation of the tasks with full emphasis and in the most detailed way, most of the themes I will focus on in this chapter originate in his arguments.

Räisänen holds that the fusion of the tasks of historical and theological interpretation does not make the understanding of the New Testament clearer (xvii). He puts forward his suggestion (xviii):

> ... 'New Testament theology' ought to be replaced, in this context, with two different projects: first, the 'history of early Christian thought' (or theology, if you like), evolving in the context of early Judaism; second, critical philosophical and/or theological 'reflection on the New Testament', as well as on its influence on our history and its significance for contemporary life.

He points to two major predecessors of his in this emphasis: "Gabler made a helpful theoretical distinction between historical and theological interpretation of the Bible" (xv); so did Wrede (xvi). Räisänen (89) is dissatisfied with the scholarship of our century, because it has not realised Wrede's programme.

Let us turn to the questions, What is this programme in greater detail?; and, What are the major premises it builds upon?

1. The separation of the enterprises

Räisänen proposes that the primary task of a New Testament scholar should be an exegetical one. Scholars and students of the New Testament should understand themselves as historians. In his summary of the history of the discipline the first aspect he is looking for in other people's work is: "Awareness of the problems involved in relating historical study to theology" (1990, xiv). One of the most important criteria for Räisänen whether or not to agree with another scholar is the scholar's consistency in carrying out a historical enterprise. For example, Bultmann is criticised because his historical understanding "is overwhelmed by actualizing interpretation" (42).

Räisänen is cautious, however, not to oversimplify his emphasis on the historical character of the enterprise. The question mark in the title of the relevant section of his programme, "Purely historical?", already indicates his opinion that "the person of the scholar cannot be wholly bracketed out in historical work" (106). Even the historical reconstruction involves interpretation. The work of the modern interpreter is not independent of his situation. Thus Räisänen proposes "to talk of the relation between two sorts of interpretation: historical and actualizing" (108). The work of the New Testament scholar should move "on the level of historical interpretation" (109).

I agree with Räisänen's refined emphasis on the importance of the "historical" side of New Testament studies. I also accept his proposal concerning the separation between New Testament theology as a historical enterprise and an "actualizing interpretation" - that would be, in my understanding, a systematic theological enterprise. However, I should like to take issue with an implication of his thesis of separation: I argue that the historical study does not have to be "separated" from the study of the theology contained in the New Testament.

Since Räisänen largely bases his view on those of Gabler, Strauss and Wrede, it is appropriate to look at the theses of these scholars and so to discuss Räisänen's thesis (see e.g. xvii).

a. J.P. Gabler

Gabler's inaugural address from 1787 used the terms "biblical theology" and "dogmatic theology".[1] Since his terms differ from the ones discussed in this chapter of my thesis, we have to see what he understands under these terms.

---

[1] In my thesis Gabler's address is referred to after Sandys-Wunsch, 1980, 134ff.

Gabler used "biblical theology" for what we now discuss as "historical interpretation"; and "dogmatic theology" for what we would nowadays call systematic theological reflections, or, in Räisänen's term, "actualizing interpretation". In Räisänen's thesis Gabler's first term would cover what a scholar of
the New Testament should study.

Gabler distinguished between "religion" and "theology". Religion is "what
each Christian ought to know and believe and do" - we may say: what can be
easily understood as the content and meaning of the Bible. On the other hand,
theology is the view of the scholar who studies the Bible: "theology is subtle,
learned knowledge, ... derived not only from the sacred Scripture but also
from elsewhere, especially from the domain of philosophy and history" (136).

Gabler then distinguishes between the method with which one can ascer-
tain the "religion" of the Bible, i.e. "biblical theology", and the study which is
built upon biblical theology, i.e. "dogmatic theology". The first is "of historical origin, conveying what the holy writers felt about divine matters"; while
the second is "of didactic origin, teaching what each theologian philosophises
rationally about divine things" (137). Although Gabler sets out the first
method at length, it is clear from his address that the aim of the first type of
study is to provide solid, reliable material for the second (e.g. 143).

I find it problematic that Räisänen should stress the importance of Gabler's
thesis for Räisänen's own. Gabler's inaugural address is often referred to by
scholars who engage in Old Testament theology, New Testament theology,
or "biblical theology", as the decisive point in the history of biblical studies
when these new "biblical" disciplines originated. Most scholars view Gabler's
distinction to be what it actually claims to be: an emphasis on studying the
theology contained in the Bible distinctively from the theological systems of
the scholars.

In my opinion, Räisänen might refer to Gabler as the predecessor of his
own thesis in three points: 1) although Gabler repeatedly refers to the
"Sacred Scriptures" as the field of his study, he does point beyond the
boundaries of the canon when he urges the need to include the apocryphal
books in the collection and classification of the ideas of biblical figures (140);
2) Gabler describes biblical theology as a historical discipline; 3) Gabler uses
the term "interpretation" in relation to biblical theology.

But if Räisänen rightly endorses these points in Gabler's lecture, he would
surely have to disagree with a fourth point, for we have to see clearly that in
Gabler's opinion the result of "exegetical observation" is that "a clear sacred
Scripture will be selected" (143). This selected sacred Scripture - also called
by Gabler *dicta classica* - contains "universal ideas", or, "passages which are
appropriate to the Christian religion of all times". In other words, Gabler's

thesis seems to ascribe more to the historical, exegetical task than Räisänen's thesis would suggest. According to Gabler, biblical theology "in the stricter sense of the word" is achieved only (143-144):

> ... if these universal notions are derived by a just interpretation from those *dicta classica*, and those notions that are derived are carefully compared, and those notions that are compared are suitably arranged, each in its own place, so that the proper connexion and provable order of doctrines that are truly divine may stand revealed ...

One may argue that the reference to divine revelation is simply due to the language of the age in which Gabler lived. However, to work out the "order of doctrines" implies an understanding of the discipline different from Räisänen's view about the task of the discipline. In my opinion Gabler's thesis rather points in the direction in which I should like to define New Testament theology: the study of the theology contained in the New Testament.

b. D.F. Strauss

Strauss's *Leben Jesu* from 1835 is a historical examination of the Gospels. Strauss set himself the task in the Preface: "... the inquiry must first be made whether in fact, and to what extent, the ground on which we stand in the gospels is historical" (1906, xxix). He gave his own definition of myth and of what can be regarded as legendary (86-87). In the final section of his introduction he described in a detailed way the criteria "by which to distinguish the unhistorical in the gospel narrative" (87ff).

The long historical part of his thesis is followed by a short "concluding dissertation" which summarises "the dogmatic import of the life of Jesus" (757ff). Strauss struggled with the problem of justifying his attempt "to re-establish dogmatically that which has been destroyed critically" (757). He had a twofold answer. 1) Even an honest historian, a thoroughgoing "critic is intrinsically a believer". The critic - "in the spirit of the nineteenth century" - reveres religions (757); and Christianity is "the substance of the sublimest of all religions" (758). 2) The "ultimate object" of historical criticism "can only be arrived at by dogmatical criticism as a sequel".

Strauss affirmed that "the essence of the Christian faith is perfectly independent of his [the author's] criticism" (xxx). He distinguished between "eternal truth" and "reality as historical facts". For example, Christ's birth, his miracles, his resurrection can be the former while not the latter. The question is: Did Strauss succeed in confirming this statement of his in his "concluding dissertation"? O. Pfleiderer made the following evaluation in his "Introduction" to the same fifth English edition I am referring to (1906, xviii-xix):

> In all this Strauss was led astray by the influence of the Hegelian philosophy, which looked for the truth of religion in logical and metaphysical categories instead of in the facts and experiences of moral feeling and volition. But as there is no essential relation between these metaphysical ideas and the person of Jesus, he is made arbitrarily, as any one else might have been, an illustration and example of absolute ideas to which he stands in no more intimate relation than the rest of the human race ...

A similar criticism of Strauss's two-part thesis has been made recently by Robert Morgan. This criticism is important since it comes from a scholar who does empathise with Strauss's thesis to a very large extent. In an earlier essay Morgan approved of Strauss's "separation" model (1976-77, 260): New Testament theology should not be "simultaneously a historical and a doctrinal discipline"; the two tasks should be separated. Morgan shares Strauss's "radical historical criticism of the Gospels" (243). In Morgan's opinion Strauss's critical conclusions are "inescapable". Morgan seems to share the view with Strauss that supernaturalism is "impossible in the modern world"; and also to share the "refusal to believe that the miracles actually happened" (244, see also 260).

In the same 1976-77 article, Morgan pointed to the failure of Baur's and Bultmann's attempts to combine historical investigation with theological interpretation. These are not satisfactory for someone who does not want to stretch "history" so wide that it can include "a metaphysical view of God, man and the world" (Baur) or does not want to narrow theology so that it only discusses the existence of the individual (Bultmann) (245). This failure of two of the greatest scholars supports Strauss's separation model.

However, in a recent detailed study of the problems I am concerned with in this thesis, *Biblical Interpretation* (1991, orig. 1988), Morgan expresses his view differently. There he discusses the question which is only stated in a footnote in the 1976-77 article (249, n.1): "whether historical work alone can adequately perform theology's ... task of interpreting human existence". In *Biblical Interpretation* Morgan uses the term "separation" with reference to those who want to see only a historical task in New Testament studies, and to leave the theological part to systematic theologians. Morgan opposes that view (1991, 74-75, 90, 184-185). He speaks of "the necessity of combining" the "historical and theological tasks" (275). He clarifies this task but does not attempt to perform it (274). We may note that Morgan maintains that historical investigation has a controlling role in New Testament theology.[2]

---

[2] We shall return to this work of Morgan in the final chapter.

In this context it may suffice to make two observations. 1) The way Morgan criticises Strauss's thesis can be used as an argument against Räisänen's thesis: Strauss has not succeeded in providing a good example of separating the tasks of historical and theological interpretation in New Testament studies. It may be argued, of course, that an unsuccessful attempt does not prove that the task of separation is impossible. I propose that the historical and theological tasks should be kept apart if the "theological task" means "systematic theology".

2) If we adopt the separation of the historical task in New Testament theology from a systematic theological study of the New Testament, then another question arises: How successfully is the historical task carried out by Strauss? Since Strauss did not address the question of describing the theology contained in the New Testament, we cannot give a direct answer to this question. It may suffice here to emphasise that Strauss's historical work - and its possible implications for New Testament theology - can be discussed by someone engaging in New Testament theology as a historical enterprise. In other words, historians can argue with historians. In my understanding of the enterprise, New Testament theology should be based on historical arguments. Strauss's work does not refute this definition of the enterprise.

c. *William Wrede*

As we have already seen, the programmatic essay of Wrede has been very influential on Räisänen's thesis. Wrede's work, *Über Aufgabe und Methode der sogenannten Neutestamentlichen Theologie*, has only quite recently been translated into English. It is of great importance for any discussion of the problems of New Testament theology. I shall discuss various points of it in the chapters of my thesis. Here I shall simply summarise the way Wrede puts his thesis.

Wrede presupposes the "strictly historical character" of New Testament theology (1897, 8; ET: 1973, 69). It has to be treated in the same way as any of the branches of "intellectual history in general or the history of religion in particular" (10; ET: 70).

In his opinion, the task of New Testament theology has to be separated from that of systematic theology. The latter could not help the former; it could only control it which is contrary to the aim of New Testament theology (9-10; ET: 69-70).

I think it is Wrede who has set out in the most consistent way the programme Räisänen is arguing for. Most of Räisänen's points are there in Wrede's essay. It is a sad fact in the history of scholarship that Wrede did not live long enough to make an attempt at carrying out his own programme. So far Räisänen has only enlarged on the presentation and argumentation of the programme but he himself has not made more than a few tentative attempts to carry it through, either.[3]

It is difficult to argue over a programme in a purely theoretical way without being able to judge it from its fruits. One way of arguing against a programme is to provide another programme. Thus it is significant that recently new attempts are being made to construct theologies of the New Testament.[4] I shall discuss arguments underlying Wrede's programme later. First, let us see two recent rival programmes.

d. Criticisms of the "purely" historical approach

Hans Hübner and Peter Stuhlmacher engage in their enterprise in the knowledge of Räisänen's thesis. Their criticisms of Räisänen are as follows.

Stuhlmacher (1992, 34) has two major arguments against Räisänen's thesis: 1) "the particular kerygmatic claim of the books of the New Testament" can only be perceived and presented in a systematic order in the enterprise of New Testament theology; 2) acknowledging the diversities among the witnesses of the New Testament, there still remains a question to be answered: "warum gerade die 27 neutestamentlichen Bücher zum zweiten Teil des Kanons zusammengefaßt werden konnten, in dem die Alte Kirche ihre eine 'regula fidei' bezeugt fand"? To answer this question means to set the task of presenting "lines of theological unity in the kerygma". This calls for maintaining the enterprise of New Testament theology.

I accept this criticism. However, I should like to modify it by suggesting that New Testament theology may fulfil the tasks ascribed to it by Stuhlmacher, even if it retains a "historical", descriptive character: if it summarises the theology which can be found in the New Testament by historical analysis and investigation.

Hübner (1990, 27, n.60) criticises the "ecclesiological deficit" of Räisänen. In Hübner's opinion, Räisänen's emphasis on the separation of the historical and theological tasks originates in Räisänen's conviction that the latter im-

---

[3] Apart from the programmatic work from 1990, see also his articles from 1995 and 1997. For a fuller list of Räisänen's writings see the literature given at the end of the 1995 article, p.265.

[4] For an excellent summary of the main points of the major recent contributors to the theme of biblical theology, see the articles in Dohmen - Söding, 1995.

plies a commitment to the church. Such a commitment, in turn, makes it impossible to carry out an unbiased, unprejudiced work. Over against this view Hübner asks:

> Was ist für *Räisänen* die Wirklichkeit der Kirche? Ist es für ihn noch eine *geistliche* Wirklichkeit? Natürlich, und das ist das Wahrheitsmoment des Engagements *Räisänens*, kann und darf das, was das Neue Testament zu sagen hat, nicht introvertierte, nur in den Innenraum der Kirche gerichtete Botschaft sein. Aber die Kirche kann als Kirche nur nach außen wirken, wenn sie ihre missionarische Energie aus ihrem "Sein in Christus" gewinnt.

Hübner is probably right in this criticism. However, in my approach to the enterprise this criticism in itself would not be enough to be put against Räisänen's thesis. I should like to argue for the enterprise of New Testament theology even if it is carried out in a non-church environment. In an academic study, detached from the mission of the church, New Testament theology still could retain its validity in describing the missionary claim the New Testament shows. I should like to distinguish between a New Testament theology carried out in order to fulfil a missionary task and a New Testament theology which reports as a historical finding the fact that the early church emphasised mission. What the reader will do with this finding: reject it, or regard it as authoritative and follow it in the present, may be left as an open question. I can accept both possibilities as valid and justifiable.

I should like to argue with Räisänen in such a way that I try to go along with his suggestion as far as possible. Thus, in this case, I would adopt that understanding of New Testament theology in which the aim is a description of historical findings and would still claim that Räisänen's call for moving "beyond" the enterprise should not be maintained. His emphasis on history is right. However, that emphasis does not exclude the possibility of New Testament theology.

In Wrede's and Räisänen's theses the call for the separation of historical and theological tasks in New Testament theology is followed by the demand that a history of the early Christian literature should be written. At this stage I am still concerned with the emphasis on history. Now I turn to a discussion of the problem: Does an emphasis on history challenge New Testament theology? The question of the canon as opposed to all early Christian literature will be discussed in the following two chapters.

2. A history of early Christian literature

Wrede is interested in the beginnings of the Christian religion. In his introductory work (1909, 3) he affirms that we are concerned with a "purely historical question" when we are seeking to establish the origin of the New
Testament. He proposes the following: "the discipline has to lay out the history of early Christian religion and theology" (1897, 34; ET: 1973, 84). I
note here that Wrede does mention "theology". The same applies to the
summary of the programme of Räisänen quoted above (1990, xviii). We shall
see later in what sense they use this term.

The use of the term "history" in the context of New Testament theology is
somewhat problematic. We have to discuss the question: What do the basic
characteristics of history as a science imply for biblical studies? I shall focus
on three main thinkers whose understanding of history is of great influence in
our century: Troeltsch, Collingwood and Harvey.

a. Ernst Troeltsch

Biblical scholars in our century make considerable use of historical methods
summarised by Troeltsch.[5] It is worth looking at his theses and arguments because of his great influence up to our present day.

In an article in 1913 Troeltsch defined the historical task as a strictly descriptive summary of phenomena. He argued for a science which can only
study things and events that are in a causal relationship to one another. Consequently, God's intervention in the lives of people or in natural events cannot be spoken of in historical study. His main affirmations are as follows:
1) "the modern conception of Nature ... demolished the cosmology of the
Bible" (716); 2) modern history writing views history as a "concatenation of
things" or that of events (716-717); 3) the "earliest manifestations of historical reflexion" of the Greeks "were extinguished by Christianity" which revived the "mythological representation of history" (717); 4) our methodology
in historical inquiry is that of looking for an analogy in the events which we
know; from that point we criticise the tradition; and we seek a "causal expla-
nation of all that happens" (718); 5) our results show "at all points an absolute contrast to the Biblico-theological views of later antiquity".

Troeltsch emphasised, however, that there is a "difference between the
causality of natural science and that of historical science" (719). The differ-

---

[5] See Morgan 1973a, 21.

ence lies in the fact that natural science works with a changeless, always identical law of reciprocity. Historical causation has to include the "irrational quality and initiative of the individual consciousness". This means that the psychological motivation "gives a special and peculiar character to every particular case".

Historical science also has to deal with things that are "new". This "new" is not simply the "transformation of existent forces, but an element of essentially fresh content". However, this "new" is also "due to a convergence of historical causes" (719).

A clear distinction between "empirical and philosophical history" must be made. The former is "history proper", the latter can discuss metaphysical matters as well as ethical implications one may learn from the study of history (721).

Troeltsch put forward his major axioms for the understanding of modern historiography, the principles of criticism, analogy, and correlation, in his programmatic article in 1898 (my references: 1922²).

The first principle is that of criticism (731). All tradition has to be put under criticism which will analyse, correct and change the traditional material. This criticism only allows for judgments of likelihood. Religious traditions have to be viewed together with all other traditions which have to be criticised. Religious traditions share the same essence and nature as all other traditions (732).

This criticism is carried out by the application of the principle of analogy (732). We may judge something to be likely if it conforms to what we consider as normal, usual procedures or states, or to what has been testified several times. Even what is not known in one procedure from the past may be interpreted from what we know in another procedure, because all historical events share a principal core which is common to all of them.

The common core of all historical events points to the third principle of historical study: correlation or reciprocity (731, 733). This means that a change at any point can only occur if there occurs a change at the preceding and the following points as well. All events form a flow where all parts belong together and every procedure is in relation to another one (733).

These principles of Troeltsch exclude any acknowledgement of an act or intervention of God in human history by definition. One of the most prominent Christian traditions which cannot be dealt with on these principles of history is the resurrection of Jesus to which there is no historical analogy. The stories of dying and rising gods are an analogy to the story of Jesus' resurrection. But the historicity of the resurrection itself cannot be affirmed by historical methods. There is no analogy to someone's actual rising from the dead. Troeltsch notes that by his time many people have learnt to be satisfied with the fact that out of the Judaeo-Christian history they can exclude from the operation of the analogy principle only the moral characteristics of Jesus and his resurrection (732-733). This implies that Troeltsch thought nothing should be made exempt from those principles; not even these latter themes.

I think that the definition of historical study expressed by Troeltsch may be regarded as a consensus of opinion held by the majority of historians today - even if in modified forms.[6] Robert Morgan stands in this line when he affirms that to try to stretch the "historical methods to make them speak of God" means the failure to acknowledge "the limits set on historical method by the intellectual community of historians" (1991, 186). Morgan affirms that "acts of God cannot be spoken of, let alone established, by historical research. That is a presupposition or axiom: it defines what is meant by historical research" (70).

It is significant that Morgan also points to some limits of Troeltsch's historical method. He affirms that (1973a, 26):

> ... it is one thing to say that theological interest in the New Testament must not contravene the canons of modern historical method, and quite another to imply that these prohibit any theological interest in it or interpretation of it by a historian while he is wearing his historian's hat. No doubt some types of theological interpretation do contravene historical methods. Perhaps, too, the rules of historical method are less absolute than Troeltsch suggested. But in any case the possibility of a new synthesis must not be ruled out in advance, and theologians at least will be concerned to explore it.

I accept Morgan's emphasis on the role of historical criticism in ruling out implausible interpretations, because, as Räisänen insists, "the number of legitimate interpretations of a text are limited" (1990, 107).[7]

Here I point to another possibility of supplementing Troeltsch's principles. Stuhlmacher suggests that Troeltsch's principles should be "opened up and developed" in order to gain new insights into history (1979, 220). Stuhlmacher numbers "die schaffende Bedeutung der die großen Lebenskomplexe beherrschenden Persönlichkeiten" among Troeltsch's principles (153). He formulates accordingly (220):

> Ich schlage deshalb vor, das von guter und weiterführender Arbeit an der Historie implizit schon längst praktizierte Prinzip des "Vernehmens" (Schlatter: der Wahrnehmung) von Phänomenen und Aussagen, die jenem klassischen Geviert von Kritik, Analogie, Korrelation und Subjektivität zu widerstreiten scheinen oder wirklich widerstreiten, ausdrücklich in die Prinzipienlehre der historischen Kritik aufzunehmen.

---

[6] See Stuhlmacher 1979, 24; 1992, 10, 28.
[7] I shall discuss Morgan's proposal in my final chapter.

In his recent *Biblical Theology* Stuhlmacher acknowledges the need to prac-
tise the historical critical method in New Testament theology. He subscribes
to the principles of Troeltsch: criticism; analogy; correlation (1992, 10).[8]
However, he suggests a modification. Because of the claim of revelation of
the New Testament writings, it is not wise to adopt a method which by definition doubts talk about God (10-11). If we want to interpret the New Testament writings in accordance with their own intention, then we have to
adopt a method which is open to accepting the biblical texts as having sense
in themselves. We also have to interpret them in a way that leaves open the
possibility of their kerygmatic affirmations becoming transparent ("durch-
sichtig") (11). Thus Stuhlmacher calls for "Einverständnis". This involves a
willingness to enter an open-minded dialogue with the texts.

At this point it is appropriate to affirm that I do agree with the scholars
referred to in this section - and with many others - that historical criticism is a
useful tool to be exercised in New Testament scholarship. Since I argue for
retaining the historical character of the enterprise of New Testament theology, I hold that New Testament theology has to make use of the method(s)
of historical criticism.[9] I note that I agree with Stuhlmacher that for those
who engage in New Testament theology, a definition of history is preferable
which leaves room for discussing reports about God's acts in human history.
However, New Testament theology can be maintained as a historical enterprise even if one retains the definition of history as it was expressed by
Troeltsch. In this case, too, the historian can report what the biblical authors
or figures believed about God's intervention in history, although the historian
may choose not to accept their claim to be true.

b. R.G. Collingwood

In his *Autobiography* Collingwood summarises his philosophical view which
is in close relationship with his view on historical study. He rejects the various "theories of truth" (1982, 36). He summarises his own criteria for a
proposition to be called true, as follows (38):

> (a) the proposition belongs to a question-and-answer complex which as a whole is
> 'true' in the proper sense of the word; (b) within this complex it is an answer to a
> certain question; (c) the question is what we ordinarily call a sensible or intelli-

---

[8] P. Stuhlmacher, *Biblische Theologie des Neuen Testaments.* I note that here (1992,
10) he only mentions these three principles.

[9] For a recent example of making excellent use of the historial critical methods see
G. Theißen - A. Merz, 1996.

gent question, not a silly one, or in my terminology it 'arises'; (d) the proposition is the 'right' answer to that question.

I do acknowledge the strength of these definitions in terms of aiming at high probability in our quest for truth. In other parts of my thesis I shall rely on them when I argue against alleged antitheses within the New Testament. Some of the antitheses may turn out not to be antagonistic ones, because the antithetical proposals may not be meant to be answers to the same questions.

In *The Idea of History* Collingwood summarises the four characteristics of modern history-writing which, in Collingwood's opinion, would be shared by most, if not all, historians of his day (1961, 9).

a) History is research or inquiry (9). History, being a science, has to proceed from the yet unknown by asking questions and trying to answer them. Even when it starts from things already known, "it is scientifically valuable only in so far as the new arrangement gives us the answer to a question we have already decided to ask".

b) History wants to find out "actions of human beings that have been done in the past" (9).

c) The historical method "consists essentially of interpreting evidence" (10). This evidence has to exist in the time of the historian. The evidence must be of such a kind that the historian can find answers to his questions about past events.

d) The final purpose of historical investigation is to gain a better "human self-knowledge", a knowledge of the nature of man (10).

In my opinion, these definitions limit the possibility of seeing "history" in the New Testament to a large extent. Parts of the New Testament where God's presence or action is claimed cannot be regarded as historical; and these parts are numerous. At most, we can use the New Testament as evidence in the sense of gaining insight into the life of early Christians.[10]

These criteria do not exclude the possibility of studying someone's faith in God as a historical study, but they regard the beliefs held by New Testament writers as unhistorical. Collingwood wants to study mainly things and actions of human beings, but he has also room for studying the thoughts of people whose beliefs he does not share.

For the purpose of my thesis Collingwood's understanding of history is not a real threat. Remaining within the boundaries of his definition of what is historical, one can still study the theology of the New Testament, but, in that case, one does not regard as historical what is being studied. This would also apply to Troeltsch's definition. However, as I have mentioned in the previous

---

[10] Cf. Collingwood's example in relation to Sumerian religious writings, 1961, 12.

section, I should like to stretch these definitions in a way that they leave open the possibility that what is being studied in New Testament theology may also be historical.

Whether or not my suggestion is accepted, it is important for my thesis that as a historian one does not have to investigate whether or not God inspired the canon. One can still turn to the historian's task of seeing whether the attempt to present a New Testament theology is justified.

c. Van A. Harvey

Harvey (1967) discusses "the problem of faith and history" in an important work of the second half of our century. He is concerned with the historian's commitment to "an ideal of judgment" (xiii). He acknowledges that he owes much to Troeltsch (33). He makes an attempt to "reformulate his [Troeltsch's] most important insights in a fashion that is less heavy-handed" (34). Harvey calls his own historical method "the historian's morality of knowledge, or ethic of assent" (33). He discusses four "basic elements of this new morality" - the "ideal of critical judgment" (38):

> the radical autonomy of the historian; the responsibility he has for making his arguments and statements capable of rational assessment; the need to exercise sound and balanced judgment; the need to use his critically interpreted experience as the background against which sound judgments are made about the past.

Harvey proposed these "interrelated aspects" of this "ideal", because in his opinion Troeltsch was right in seeing that after the Enlightenment scholars in the Western world cannot work any longer "with the ethic of belief that has dominated Christendom for centuries" (38; see also 104ff).

Following Collingwood, Harvey (40) affirms with regard to the "new spirit of autonomy" that it is "the Copernican revolution" of historiography. The historian cannot simply accept a witness as authority (42). Rather, the "historian *confers* authority upon a witness" by establishing his own judgment on the basis of "a rigorous cross-examination".

This autonomy cannot become a "mere subjectivism". The historian has to be able to communicate his "conclusions to others in such a way that these conclusions can be assessed by those who have competence to do so" (43). Harvey is mainly concerned with the problem of "the justification of the explanations historians offer when these explanations are challenged" (44).

The justification of certain conclusions is based on "diverse kinds of arguments making use of correspondingly diverse data and warrants" (55). Thus "there will also be diverse kinds of verification, and no one can anticipate in advance how one can go about ascertaining their truth". Reasons given for any responsible claim should be "commensurate with the degree of assent they solicit from us" (64).

Following Bradley, and incorporating Collingwood's criticism on Bradley, Harvey argues "that the historian's present standpoint should determine his belief about all past events" (74). He affirms that (98):

> the historian's canon for judgments about the past is the same canon he uses in making judgments about the present. It presupposes his present, critically interpreted experience ...

Harvey's thesis is very much in line with those of Troeltsch and Collingwood. His own proposal is a very constructive one, since it criticises other theses in a way that keeps the elements of truth he can find in them (see e.g. 249-250). In my opinion, the great strength of Harvey's thesis is his complex view in which truths of opposing propositions can be appreciated. His emphasis on understanding and defining history in a wide way as a "field-encompassing field" (e.g. 55) does leave room for discussing theology as a historical discipline. His study about Jesus may be an example of this.

Harvey distinguishes four "levels of meaning" in relation to "Jesus of Nazareth" (266-267): a) Jesus as "a man who lived two thousand years ago"; b) "the historical Jesus" in the sense of what is "now recoverable by historical means"; c) "a memory-impression of Jesus", or, the "perspectival image" the earliest Christian community had of him; d) "the Biblical Christ", by which Harvey means "the transformation and alteration of the memory-impression (or perspectival image) under the influence of the theological interpretation of the actual Jesus by the Christian community".

In my opinion, Harvey's distinction "between the memory-impression and the Biblical Christ" (276) opens up the possibility to study the theology of the New Testament in a historical context. As he puts it: "the historian *can compare the perspectival image with the Biblical Christ*". Since there are "unintentional data" that the witness "reveals in the process of telling us" (277), the historian can *test the perspectival image to see to what degree it says something which the historian can accept as true*". Through these two steps the historian can work backwards from the theological picture to the "historical Jesus". It is a historical activity, yet it includes the study of the theology of the New Testament.

It is true that, on the basis of his method described above, Harvey holds that very little of the New Testament can be regarded as historical.[11] This is

---

[11] See e.g. concerning the historical Jesus, Harvey 1967, 268.

not a real problem for my thesis. Important is the fact that New Testament theology can be defined as a historical study.

Having emphasised this fact itself, I repeat my own opinion (made in the previous sections): I differ from Harvey on the point concerning what one might hold to be historical in the New Testament. However, this is only a matter of judgment concerning individual texts; it is a matter of the quantity of what may be regarded as historical. How little or how much, this does not challenge the suggestion that the theology of the New Testament may be studied by historians.

In summary, on the basis of important and influential definitions of historical study, I do agree with Räisänen that the characteristic of a New Testament theology should be a historical one. I do not think, however, that this would force us to give up the theological aspect of the study of the New Testament. A historian can study the theology of the New Testament.

3. Religious experience instead of doctrine

Another reason why New Testament theology as an enterprise should be abandoned is given in the suggestion that it is early Christian "religion" that should be studied instead.[12] I shall focus here on one aspect of this challenge: How does religious study relate to the study of doctrine?

a. History-of-religion

Wrede belonged to the "history-of-religion school" (see 1897, 10; ET: 1973, 70). Wrede's emphasis on the history-of-religion approach results in his rejection of the "theological character" of New Testament theology. In his opinion, retaining the theological character of New Testament theology necessarily involves "the personal theological viewpoint of the scholar, and that could obscure things" (10; ET: 70).

This affirmation is problematic in two ways. On the one hand, it may be argued that some kind of a viewpoint of the scholar is inevitably present; so it is better to analyse it than to deny its presence. On the other hand, there are not only these two alternatives: with or without the theology of the scholar. I should like to argue for a third possibility: the scholar clarifies his own standpoint and studies the theology of the New Testament writings in a constant

---

[12] See e.g. the quotation from Wrede (1897, 79-80; ET: 1973, 116) in my Introduction.

awareness of his own stand-point. In this way the scholar may be critical of his own position and aim at an analytical study of the New Testament.

Räisänen has taken up the emphasis of the history-of-religion school on the fact that "religious thought is only one, relatively small, part of religion" (1990, 105).[13] However, for pragmatic reasons he suggests that a "comprehensive history of early Christian religion" should begin with the study of religious thought. He qualifies his statement lest he should repeat mistakes he has criticised in New Testament theologies (106):

> A history of early Christian thought as I see it ought to make abundantly clear the connections of the thoughts and ideas with the experiences of individuals and groups. The development of thought is to be analysed precisely in the light of the interaction between experiences and interpretations.

It is significant that Räisänen approves of the history-of-religion approach in principle, but he also qualifies the way he wants to use it. It is therefore necessary to discuss what that approach means for New Testament theology. This we may study through the example of Wrede.

Wrede argued against the theological character of New Testament theology by attacking the dominant method of New Testament theology of his day: the method of doctrinal concepts, *Lehrbegriffe* (1897, 17; ET: 1973, 73). Before I discuss his major counter-arguments in turn, I stress that the theology of the New Testament and the doctrinal concepts of the New Testament are not identical. It is not only doctrinal concepts that contain theology. Theology is a wider concept. I propose to define theology in a wide sense: all affirmations and actions which are in relationship with God. Furthermore, the "method of doctrinal concepts" as it is criticised by Wrede is not the only possible way to study doctrine in the New Testament. Wrede affirms that in the method he criticises there is an "unspoken assumption that these [biblical] concepts must be of similar character to those of dogmatics" (25; ET: 79). I suggest that the student of biblical doctrinal concepts may keep this warning in mind and resist this temptation. The "unspoken assumption" may be brought to light and then kept under control during the carrying out of the enterprise of New Testament theology.

Now I turn to Wrede's theses concerning *Lehrbegriffe*.

1) He points to the brevity of some of the books of the New Testament: "Writings like I Peter, II Peter with Jude, and James, are simply too small to extract doctrinal positions from". Consequently, one can come to false conclusions by "regarding as characteristic what in fact is not" (1897, 17-18; ET: 1973, 74).

---

[13] See also Räisänen's reference to Kaftan on p. 29.

This warning is an important one. However, one may add that it may be possible to find out which "circle" a short writing belonged to. If there are other writings in the New Testament which can be brought in relation to them, then we have a wider basis to work out a certain theological position of a short writing.

2) Wrede claims that it is a mistake to discuss only doctrine in New Testament theology. He even disapproves of the usage of the term "doctrinal concept" in New Testament theology. He affirms: "It is only justifiable to speak of doctrine when thoughts and ideas are developed for the sake of teaching. That happens only rarely in the New Testament" (19-20; ET: 75).

Here it becomes significant to distinguish between doctrine and theology as I have suggested above. Wrede's criticism may attack the narrow focus on doctrine, but it cannot be applied to theology in a wider sense of the word: everything which is in connection with the thoughts of the early Christians about God.

Wrede suggests further that "the significance and power of the religious tone" should not be neglected. New Testament theology can be accused of lacking "any feel for the variety and special character of all the elements of what we call religion" (21; ET: 76).

We have already seen how Räisänen supports this point, yet how he maintains his preference for discussing doctrine - even if only as a "beginning" in the enterprise of New Testament theology (1990, 105). In my opinion, there is no need to exclude from the field of "theology" what Räisänen refers to as aspects of religion or branches in the study of religion: "cult, rite, myth, communality" including "historical, psychological and social realities" (105). In as much as these are in relation to the early Christians' beliefs about God they do belong to a theology of the New Testament.

3) Wrede's next objection is of a more practical nature. He suggests that one should not go into a detailed analysis of notions. The biblical authors did not develop systematic constructions based on single notions (22; ET: 77). Wrede expresses his disappointment: "One might with some justification call New Testament theology the science of minutiae and insignificant nuances" (23; ET: 78).

Wrede further affirms that literary criticism - although it has its merits - contributes to this character of New Testament theology. Wrede addresses a "widespread type of literary criticism which finds connections of thought and expression between the documents at every point ..." (25-26; ET: 79). This type of literary criticism has its limits when it fails to take into consideration relationships due to historical developments. It is too much restricted to visible literary relationships (26-27; ET: 80). This warning is as valid as his first point was. However, I have the same remark to make: this only calls for caution on the side of the scholar but does not essentially challenge the study of the theology contained in the New Testament.

4) Wrede stresses as a final argument that New Testament theology is not simply a "succession of individual doctrinal concepts" (28; ET: 81). He criticises B. Weiss's textbook, but he thinks his criticism does not apply to Baur's *Lectures on New Testament Theology*. In Wrede's opinion, a "New Testament theology must show us the special character of early Christian ideas and perceptions, sharply profiled, and help us to understand them historically" (30-31; ET: 83). Even Holtzmann's work is criticised because of "a shortage of really historical grasp and reflection that is truly history of *religion*" (33; ET: 84).

In my opinion, this point shares several of the problems I have indicated above. Firstly, to attack the presentation of the succession of *Lehrbegriffe* does not amount to denying the validity of New Testament theology as an enterprise. The warning is justified not to claim a succession where there is none. However, where there are connections, or "successions", it can be discussed in a theology of the New Testament. Secondly, a theology of the New Testament can include a wide range of religious phenomena, not only doctrine.[14] Thirdly, the emphasis on the historical character does not exclude the study of theology in the New Testament writings, as we have seen in the previous section. Finally, it may be noted that it is difficult to understand: Why should Baur be exempt from Wrede's criticism if Holtzmann is not? Baur does present a certain kind of "succession" of *Lehrbegriffe*. He also writes a highly theological work, albeit in a historical framework. It is, it seems to me, worth discussing Baur's thesis itself at some length.

b. F.C. Baur's study of Lehrbegriffe

I shall summarise Baur's views on the basis of his *Vorlesungen über Neutestamentliche Theologie* (1864). This work summarises the lectures Baur delivered in Tübingen between 1852-1860. They have been published posthumously by his son (iii).

Baur organises his New Testament theology in the order of his reconstruction of the history of the canonical writings. This is probably the reason why Wrede does not want to criticise him. Baur's work is not a succession of *Lehrbegriffe* in the sense that the actual concepts would be linked with each other. The succession follows a historical development. He describes New

---

[14] See also point "f" later in this section.

Testament theology as a "living organism", and as a part of "historical theology". Its task is to present the teaching of Jesus as well as the concepts of doctrine based on it. It has to take into consideration the "historical development" of these doctrines (28).

Baur stresses that in New Testament theology one is only interested in the question of doctrine. However greatly he differs from the approach Wrede criticises, this emphasis on doctrine also differs from Wrede's approach. For Baur non-canonical writings are of interest in principle, but in reality the doctrine of the New Testament can only be derived from the canonical writings (30, 33). We shall consider later Wrede's thesis concerning the necessity of studying non-canonical writings.[15] Here I simply note that Baur is in sympathy with that thesis, yet he also differs from it.

Baur discusses the development of doctrine in accordance with his classification of the various periods of that development. He first affirms that although the teaching of Jesus is, as a matter of course, part of New Testament theology (39), it cannot be viewed in one line with the rest of New Testament concepts of doctrine ("Lehrbegriffe"). It is of primary nature, while the others derive from it. Jesus' teaching "is not theology at all, but it is religion" (45).

The first period in the development of the concepts of doctrine began with the death of Jesus. Concerning Jesus' death Baur affirms: "Durch ihn erst gewann die Person Jesu die hohe Bedeutung, die sie für das christliche Bewusstsein hat" (123). Paul and the author of Revelation belong to this period. Baur's famous and highly influential thesis is largely based on a view concerning the validity of the Old Testament law in early Christianity. In Baur's opinion, Paulinism means a decisive break with the law and with Judaism (128). By this, Paul states openly what was already there "*implicite*" in the teaching of Jesus. For Paul, all signs of particularism of Judaism disappear in the universalism of Christianity (131).

The Pastorals contain a modification of the Pauline concepts of doctrine (339). They fight against the Gnostics (341). "Faith" has become an expression for true statements, which have developed into a system of "dogma" by this time (342).

The Johannine concept of doctrine is the highest grade and most complete form of the development in New Testament theology (351). This doctrine comes to the borders of Gnosticism, but is not to be identified with Gnosticism (367). Judaism is so far from the stand-point of the Fourth Gospel that we have to date the Fourth Gospel late (389). Love (400) and Spirit (403) are the most important notions for Christians. Eternal life has become a pres-

---

[15] See chapter two and chapter five (section 7) in my thesis.

ent reality (404, 406). In this idealism the historical reality is merely a mediating form of that which is true in itself (407).

I point to the following areas where Baur's thesis may be criticised. Firstly, Baur seems not to be clear in his thoughts on the relationship between Jesus and Judaism. In his section on Jesus, he seems to struggle with the problem: Can he establish that the anti-Judaising doctrine was present in the teaching of Jesus? In Baur's opinion Jesus does not require a new attitude over against the commandments, but the law has to be expanded toward a normative character for one's thinking ("das Gesetz auf die Normirung der Gesinnung ausgedehnt werde", 50). However, the mosaic law has "no absolute binding authority" for Jesus (57). Jesus has an affirmative attitude toward the law, but a polemic one toward Pharisaism (60). Baur then finds the anti-Judaising doctrine firmly represented by Paul. However, in my judgment, Baur did not succeed in establishing that this doctrine was "implicitly" there in Jesus' teaching.

Secondly, his thesis that in the apostolic age there was not any harmony and unity, but there was a difference in doctrines and opinions (25), is in a strong connection with a Hegelian view on history. The "antitheses" of Judaising and anti-Judaising tendencies, and the development toward a "synthesis" is a scheme that came under criticism once Hegel's influence started to weaken.

Thirdly, the actual historical picture in which Baur placed the New Testament writings has been modified and criticised since his time. It is interesting to note that Baur's influence does reach to the scholarship of our own day, although parts of his "picture" started to come under criticism as early as Baur's own era.[16] We shall discuss these questions in more detail in the chapter on the unity of the theology of the New Testament.[17]

Thus I suggest that we may draw three conclusions from Baur's thesis for our present discussion. 1) Baur's New Testament theology may not be a successful one in terms of describing the beliefs of early Christianity. This failure is due to his historical affirmations which are open to criticism. 2) Yet his work may be used as an argument for the following suggestion: It is a legitimate and justifiable enterprise within New Testament theology to study doctrine in the New Testament. 3) This study may be carried out in a historical framework.

---

[16] See Meyer's article, "Bibelwissenschaft: II. Neues Testament", in *RGG*[1], 1909, col. 1220.

[17] See chapter four in my thesis.

c. *Wrede's criticism of Holtzmann*

As we have seen, Baur's work, which is based on the history of *Lehrbegriffe*, is not criticised by Wrede. Why is it that another work which follows a historical order, the textbook of Holtzmann, is criticised by Wrede in detail in his 1897 article? H.J. Holtzmann's *Lehrbuch der Neutestamentlichen Theologie* was very influential in the first half of our century. Its two editions were widely used as textbooks in German universities. It is worth discussing Wrede's criticism of Holtzmann's approach, because this criticism is directed against a concrete realisation of the enterprise of New Testament theology. Accordingly, it may be regarded as a challenge to New Testament theology in general.

The first edition of Holtzmann's textbook was published in the same year as Wrede's article. Perhaps this is the reason why Wrede felt it necessary to put forward his thesis distinctively against Holtzmann's approach. In Holtzmann's opinion, the task of New Testament theology is to give a scientific presentation of the religious and moral contents of the New Testament. The main interest of the enterprise is the world of ideas, the doctrine in the New Testament (1911, 20). The New Testament writings are of importance to Holtzmann only from the point of view of how they are witnesses to a world view, a faith and a doctrine (XI).

Wrede cannot accept this. He puts forward his counter-thesis (1897, 34; ET: 1973, 84): "Against this, I would say that the discipline has to lay out the history of early Christian religion and theology". He acknowledges that the two programmes "might sound virtually identical". However, he formulates the difference in this way: "... one approach looks closely at the content of *writings* whereas the other simply considers the *subject-matter*". In Wrede's approach the aim of the enterprise is "to know *what was believed, thought, taught, hoped, required and striven for* in the earliest period of Christianity; not what certain writings say about faith, doctrine, hope, etc." (35; ET: 84-85).

In the background of Wrede's thesis lie his views about the problems of canonicity and inspiration. Although problems related to the canon are discussed in the following two chapters of my thesis, some of Wrede's arguments have to be mentioned here, because they are in strong connection with his differentiation between "the content of writings" and "the history of faith and doctrine itself" (35; ET: 85). Wrede's arguments imply that, in his opinion, one should "give up the doctrine of inspiration, i.e. the *a priori* concept of revelation" (9, n.1; ET: 183). One's aim should be "to find out the content of the biblical religion". This aim, then, requires that one should not restrict this enterprise to the canon. We have to discuss together all early Christian writings which belong together from a historical viewpoint (12; ET: 71).

It seems that for Wrede the key term in this argumentation is "history". He thinks that if the enterprise is a historical one, then it should not focus on certain writings for the sake of finding out the content of those writings. To write a history of early Christianity would mean that for the historian *"the writers' personalities and the writings as such are not important, but very subsidiary matters"* (35; ET: 85). Wrede proposes criteria for including an individual writer's point of view in the discussion. A writer's views should be included: 1) if he has an epoch-making influence; 2) if he is an intellectually outstanding personality; 3) even if he may not be a significant intellectual, if he has a "very distinct character".

These criteria lead to a very radical position. Because of the fact that we know "virtually nothing" about the authors of 1Peter, the Lukan writings, Mark, Matthew, 1Clement, James, Didache, the Pastorals, 2Peter, Jude, the Epistle of Polycarp and the Shepherd of Hermas, "these writings and their authors are of no interest to New Testament theology" (36; ET: 85-86). Setting out the content of these writings means only the *"gathering of raw material*, not in itself the real historical fashioning of it" (36; ET: 86). What deserve independent treatment are: the preaching of Jesus; Paul's theology; and the Johannine writings.[18]

I have already argued the case that the historical character of the enterprise does not make it impossible to study New Testament theology. Here I have to add that, in my opinion, Holtzmann's approach can be justified in as much as it studies the content of writings. Wrede's usage of the term "raw material" implies that we should not look for the "theology" of the early Christians in their writings. In a similar way, Morgan affirms that the task of New Testament theology as a historical study is not that of "gathering together the material contained" in the New Testament, but rather that of ordering "the various traditions which have provided raw material for Christian proclamation in the New Testament period" (1974, 399). Against this opinion I ask: What is the relationship between that "raw material" and the content of the New Testament? In what sense would Wrede's history of the "raw material" be more than or different from what he can find in those writings? I can only think of one answer to these questions: Wrede wants to criticise these writings in order to find the "real" theology of the early Christians; this theology lies "behind" the writings: we have to recover it. I have already affirmed that the historical critical method may be maintained in New Testa-

---

[18] Cf. the full title of Kümmel's *Die Theologie des Neuen Testaments*, 1987, which names these three as "Hauptzeugen".

ment theology. But this method only has as its object the writings themselves. Even after the completion of a critical analysis, it is still the theology in those writings one can "gather", and not something behind or above those writings as raw materials.

Thus I do not accept Wrede's criticism of Holtzmann. For my thesis I conclude that it is a justifiable aim to study writings for the sake of finding out the content of those writings. I note that here I use "writings" in a wide sense: early Christian writings. The problem of the relationship between canonical and non-canonical writings is discussed in the following two chapters of my thesis.

d. The relationship with systematic theology

In my opinion, the history-of-religion school's aversion to studying doctrine may be in connection with the view that the study of doctrine in the New Testament is necessarily bound to systematic theology. If New Testament theology is in this way connected to systematic theology then the view may arise that doctrine in the New Testament is the first period in the history of dogma. New Testament doctrine, in this case, may not be studied without presupposing a dogmatic value of that doctrine. This view about doctrine is criticised by the history-of-religion school.

I acknowledge that it may happen that New Testament theology comes under the control of dogmatic theology; or, the aim of doing New Testament theology may become to provide a preparatory, preliminary service for systematic theology. Wrede argues against this interference of systematic theology in New Testament theology (1897, 9-10; ET: 1973, 69-70):

> ... New Testament theology has its goal simply in itself, and is totally indifferent to all dogma and systematic theology. What could dogmatics offer it? Could dogmatics teach New Testament theology to see facts correctly? At most it could colour them. Could it correct the facts that were found? To correct facts is absurd. Could it legitimize them? Facts need no legitimation.

I fully accept this warning. As far as "facts" can be established in history, those facts have to be respected, otherwise theology would become "ideology" in the sense that it wishes to superimpose itself on facts. The scientific character of the enterprise of New Testament theology, or, in other words, the demand for intellectual honesty precludes this kind of interference in our field of study.

However, I should like to distinguish between studying "theology" in the New Testament and studying the New Testament as an enterprise of systematic theology. I accept Wrede's point that systematic theology should not interfere with New Testament theology; these two are two different disciplines. K.H. Schelkle's differentiation is helpful here (1973, 14).

He finds the following points in which systematic theology (in Schelkle's terms: "dogmatics") differs from New Testament theology. 1) They differ in the "range of their sources". Dogmatics studies "Scripture and Tradition". Tradition includes "the modern ecclesiastical announcement of doctrine". New Testament theology studies only the biblical writings. The study may include apocryphal writings. The emphasis here lies on the "biblical times" as opposed to the "conditions" prevailing in the day of the scholar. 2) The two disciplines differ in "the goal of their scientific endeavors". Dogmatics systematises doctrine in a way that it also gives a "fresh development to the teachings of faith". New Testament theology "writes principally about the findings of exegesis".

Thus, accepting Wrede's arguments against systematic theology's interference in New Testament theology, I still argue that doctrine and theology may be studied in the enterprise of New Testament theology.

If not on the face, then on a deeper level, these observations are also related to another problematic area: How does structure relate to the possibility of the enterprise of New Testament theology?

e. The problem of a thematic structure

Baur's and Holtzmann's New Testament theologies are structured on the basis of the history of doctrine. Another possibility in New Testament theology is to structure the material on the basis of the doctrines or themes themselves. This latter is often referred to as the "thematic approach". We may note that the thematic approach was often represented in the earlier periods of biblical studies. It was a consequence of the dominance of the *dicta probantia* method which looked for proof-texts in the Bible for certain dogmatic propositions.

It may be fruitful to discuss questions which arise for New Testament theology if its structure is based on themes.

It is significant that Räisänen holds that in New Testament theology both the historical and the thematic structure "are possible in principle" (1990, 116). He even suggests that a combination of the two would be desirable. Since it is impossible to do both in a single work, Räisänen is "inclined to favour slightly a thematic structure". In his opinion, it is good if authors who decide for one particular structure also give "at least some hints as to what their discussion would look like if organized differently". In his own favoured case the "thematic treatment must ... be prefixed with a short diachronic survey of the various groups in the early church and of the main lines of their thought".

Räisänen acknowledges that the thematic approach has been carried out with some success by others. Even Bultmann, whose *Theology of the New Testament* is organised in a chronological order, "treats parts of his material (the Hellenistic church, post-Pauline developments) thematically, not without success" (116).

Räisänen approves of the starting point of Schelkle as being a "fruitful" one (55). Since Räisänen criticises other works with a thematic structure (116), it is significant that he praises the work of this Catholic scholar in spite of the fact that "the work is theological and orientated on the church" (55). This latter orientation is criticised by Räisänen - as we shall see in the final chapter of my thesis.

Räisänen agrees with Schelkle in as much as the latter "manages to draw traditio-historical lines concerning different themes and concepts" in a work that is structured thematically (55). Schelkle's study of the various themes includes treatments of the Old Testament, early Judaism, and the writings of Qumran. Räisänen criticises Schelkle for "the lack of sufficient differentiation between the different writings". However, Räisänen affirms: "This deficiency is not ... due to the thematic method itself, but to the particular manner in which it has been carried out".

We have seen some aspects of the complex character of the relationship between structure and view about doctrine in New Testament theology. On the one hand, New Testament theology may be structured on the basis of the historical development of doctrine. This may not be acceptable for the history-of-religion school - as we have seen in Wrede's criticism of Holtzmann. On the other hand, New Testament theology may be structured on the basis of themes. It is not acceptable if it takes no interest in historical relations. It is, however, possible to construct New Testament theology on the basis of themes if the individual themes are discussed in a historical framework - as Schelkle's attempt may show. Thus the problem posed to New Testament theology by structure does not prevent one from engaging in the enterprise.

f. Experience

I have already indicated that the demand for studying experience instead of doctrine challenges New Testament theology mainly in the rejection of studying doctrine. The positive affirmation that experience should be studied does not challenge New Testament theology if we accept a wider definition of theology: a definition which includes experience, experience being related with one's belief in God. I support this wider definition.

There is, however, one aspect of the emphasis on experience that has to be discussed here, because it may challenge New Testament theology. Connected with Räisänen's understanding of the term "experience", is a certain ranking of the notions. This can be seen when Räisänen praises in the work of the "old liberals" and of the history-of-religion school "their willingness to assess religious and theological ideas as secondary theories devised to interpret underlying *experiences*" (1990, xv). The idea that religious experience "underlies the texts" meant that "theological theories (e.g. of Paul) were described as interpretations of those experiences" by these scholars at the turn of the century (86). Räisänen criticises some scholars for their "one-sidedness" (xv), and others for a too narrow definition of experience (87, 124). He himself put forward a wider model (125ff). However, at this point I am interested in his approval of "distinguishing between experience and interpretation" (123; see also 125).

I find two areas of problems in this view of experience. 1) It is true that when biblical figures or authors affirm something about God, that affirmation is based on something: it does not come out of nothing. We may call that something "experience". However, we only have access to that experience through the affirmation. For us, the affirmation is what should be viewed as "primary"; most of our work as historians has to deal with the affirmation. It may also be the case that the experience lying behind the affirmation is not at all accessible. It may be the case that different experiences may result in the same affirmation; so the inquiry into the experience may yield ambiguous results. All these problems suggest that theological affirmations should be made our primary field of study. We should recognise the extreme difficulty of studying the experiences that lie behind the affirmations.

2) Räisänen does not explain what he understands under the term "interpretation". I think, for him interpretation in this context may be seen as theological reflection within the Bible: biblical figures or authors were thinking through something that had happened to them. Interpretation is in close connection with the (biblical) personage who does the interpreting. We may see an example of this in Räisänen's discussion of Paul's relationship toward the Law. He argues that Paul is basing his theology on a break with the Law (1987, 200) and that Paul then engages in "*secondary rationalization*" in arguing that he is the real upholder of the Law (201, cf. also 266ff).

This interpretation, the theology of the interpreter in the Bible, is called "secondary" by Räisänen. In Räisänen's opinion, the liberals and the history-of-religion exegetes used experience "to relativize the interpretations" (1990, 81). However, I would argue that the first thing the historian has to be interested in, is that particular interpretation. If an experience lying behind the interpretation can be recovered, that may contribute to the proper understanding of that interpretation. However, the "theology" we are looking for in the New Testament should include both. Experience and its interpretation should be described in New Testament theology. Thus I do not accept Räisänen's attempt to separate the study of experience from the study of the interpretation of the experience. The demand for studying experience does not challenge New Testament theology.

4. Against normativeness as a presupposition

The suggestion of Wrede and Räisänen to put an emphasis on studying experience is in logical connection with another demand of theirs. They propose that no normative nature of the New Testament should be presupposed in New Testament theology.

In a footnote Wrede rejects B. Weiss's proposal, according to which New Testament theology should presuppose that the "normative character of the New Testament writings has been demonstrated by dogmatics" (1897, 9, n.1; ET: 183).[19] Wrede first of all asks: which dogmatics? - referring probably to the diverse character of the opinions within systematic theology itself.

He argues against New Testament theologies where the writings are not simply viewed as documents, but "are burdened with definite dogmatic predicates like 'normative'" (1897, 8; ET: 69). His main reason for this rejection is that if the normative character of the writings is presupposed, then "it is at least psychologically probable that New Testament ideas which go contrary to expectation will be worked on and arranged till they fit those predicates". Furthermore, scholars working with this presupposition will not be open to allow for "serious contradictions within the New Testament".

I agree with this proposal of Wrede. I should like to understand New Testament theology as a historical enterprise. In historical study we cannot presuppose the normative character of the Bible. We have to study what it says about itself. If we find as historians that the Bible makes claims concerning its normativeness for the reader, then we have to point to this claim. To report this claim as a historical finding does not mean to state whether or not that claim is true. The historian and the reader for whom the historian

---

[19] Cf. Räisänen 1990, 17.

summarises the theology of the New Testament are free to make a decision whether or not they accept that claim.

I hold that New Testament theology can be studied with the aim to help people to accept that claim. However, for the purpose of a fruitful dialogue with Wrede - and Räisänen - I suggest that New Testament theology should not set the aim to promote the claims made by the Bible. Thus I agree with Räisänen (1990, 98): "Exegesis cannot impose a normative interpretation of the Bible on a society". My thesis here is that New Testament theology may be justified even if it does not engage in the debate whether or not the claims of the Bible concerning its normativeness are true.

Let us turn to the arguments concerning the proposal that normativeness should not be presupposed in New Testament theology in a little more detail.

Wrede's own arguments referred to above are true with a certain qualification. The danger exists that the scholar adjusts his findings to produce certain results expected on the basis of dogmatic interests. This inappropriate handling of the material can be overcome, at least in principle, if the scholar is conscious of the danger, and checks his own intellectual honesty repeatedly. This is in connection with the necessary openness to accept contradictions in the New Testament documents. However, caution is due lest one should go to the other extreme: looking everywhere for contradictions. This may endanger the exegesis of certain passages: one may "find" contradiction where there is not any. This attitude may also result in major hypotheses, as, for example, in the thesis that what we have now in the New Testament, is the end-product of a development which started from a contradiction among Christians in the earliest period (cf. Baur's "tendency" theory). This thesis may also result in misunderstanding certain passages which would support it only on a surface level. I shall return to this problem when I discuss the problem of the unity of the theology of the New Testament.[20]

Robert Morgan gives another reason why New Testament theology should not presuppose the normative nature of the New Testament writings. If we accept the proposal that New Testament theology should be a historical discipline - and I have suggested we ought to accept this - then it follows that historical descriptive work "cannot deliver normative theological judgements" (1976-77, 246, 253). Morgan emphasises this even against scholars like Troeltsch and Schleiermacher (1973b, 59). This point of Morgan strengthens my approach to the enterprise. In my understanding, New Testament theology does not aim at making decisions concerning the truth of its findings. I agree with Morgan (1973b, 61-62) when he adopts a "purely descriptive or

---

[20] See chapter four in my thesis.

phenomenological platform" in his contribution to comparative religious studies.[21] Some more discussion of this matter will follow in the final chapter.

Another argument of Morgan leads up to the question of the canon (which I discuss in chapter three). Since the argument relates to our present discussion, it is appropriate to mention it here. Morgan affirms that one of the axioms of modern thinking is that texts do not have "rights" to authority in themselves: "Where texts are accepted as authoritative within a community it is the community's authority that is invested in them" (1991, 7; cf. 258). I think we may make a distinction here. On the one hand, I accept that texts in themselves should have no "rights" in the sense that we have to study them without presupposing their normativeness. On the other hand, I suggest that we have not only an "invested" authority of the texts which we can discuss. Authority may be recognised and not only invested. It may be the case that a community invests authority in a text because the community recognises an authority (or claim of authority) in the text.

One way of pointing to the importance of the biblical writings is to hold that God gave them as his revelation. I have to note here that Morgan is proposing the above axiom against a "biblicist" view of revelation (see 272). I agree with Morgan that we should not adopt this view of revelation as a starting point in New Testament theology.

However, this is not the only possibility of pointing to the canon as the locus of New Testament theology. I argue in the following two chapters that New Testament theology may be justified in its insistence on the canon on another ground. It may be possible to show that the writings and their authors claim authority. New Testament theology has a right to deal with them as canon, independent of the question whether or not a community invests authority in those texts.

Thus I may summarise the results of the above discussion for my approach in this way. 1) We should not presuppose a normative character of the New Testament writings. This starting point does not make it impossible to engage in New Testament theology. 2) As historians we have to report what these writings say about their claim of being normative. New Testament theology may be maintained even if one does not set the aim of convincing readers about the truth of the claim of the biblical writings. 3) We have to clarify later: Is it possible to argue for the justification of the canon even if one does not presuppose the normative and revelatory character of the biblical writings?

---

[21] See also Morgan 1974, 401ff, where he approves of a "phenomenological approach" when discussing the place of New Testament theology in general religious studies departments of modern universities.

5. How much theology is there in the New Testament?

To engage in the enterprise of New Testament theology may be shown to be without much sense or to be even impossible if it can be claimed that there is little theology in the New Testament.

We have already seen that Wrede related the term "theology" to that of doctrine, *Lehre*. He affirms that there is little "doctrine" in the New Testament. He argues (1897, 20; ET: 1973, 75):

> Most of it [i.e. the New Testament] is practical advice, direction for life, instruction for the moment, the stirring up of religious feeling, talk of faith and hope for believers and hopers ... New Testament theology makes doctrine out of what in itself is not doctrine, and fails to bring out what it really is.

The affirmation that there is little theology in the New Testament can only be made on the basis of much exegetical study. Similarly, to argue against this affirmation can only be possible if the results of exegesis are different from those of the challenging side. Since my thesis is not an attempt to write a New Testament theology, the exegetical arguments cannot be carried out in detail here. My thesis is to argue that the enterprise is justifiable. At this point I shall briefly discuss the challenge posed by this thesis.

To argue the thesis that there is little theology in the New Testament is strongly bound up with the question of the definition of theology. I have already proposed that "theology" should be used as a wide concept. It should include what is listed above by Wrede as well as what is "doctrine" in Wrede's term. Thus New Testament theology does not make doctrine out of what is not doctrine, but discusses under the term "theology" everything that is connected with the New Testament people's belief in God. Their religious feelings as well as practices are bound up with their theology. Accordingly, these should be studied under the term "theology".

Further, Wrede affirms in the same context that (20; ET: 75):

> Ideas, notions and credal statements play a part here, but are touched on in passing or presupposed, rather than consciously developed. Where there is deliberate development this normally happens under the control of some practical impulse or purpose.

I would argue that the presence of practical aspects does not make the study of theological ideas in connection with those practicalities unnecessary. Rather, New Testament theology should discuss the theology underlying practice. I note that Wrede acknowledges the significance of credal statements. This is important for my thesis - as we shall see in chapter four. Here it may suffice to point to the significance which credal statements retain for New Testament theology even if they are only "presupposed" by the New Testament figures or writers.

Räisänen seems to share the view of Wrede that there is little theology in the New Testament. Räisänen implies this when he discusses the work of Kaftan with much sympathy and approval. In Räisänen's opinion, Julius Kaftan's *Neutestamentliche Theologie* is a "mature synthesis" that was unduly ignored because of "the ascent of Barthianism" (1990, 27). According to Räisänen (28), Kaftan's view may be summarised in this way: "the New Testament contains little reflection that could be called theology".

Kaftan (1927, 8) agrees with Wrede that the discipline of New Testament theology should set itself the aim: "in erster Linie die Religion, den Glauben zu schildern, die Anfänge der Theologie nur daran anschließend in zweiter Linie". Then Kaftan adds his own proposal: "Die neutestamentliche Theologie hat die *Motive* der Entwicklung in der *Religion* und nicht im Begrifflichen als solchem zu suchen".

I think that much depends on definitions. For Kaftan, theology means "Dogmatik" (8). Theology is a later development; it follows religion (or religious experience). Thus my argument here is similar to what I have said with regard to Wrede's affirmation above. I should like to define theology in a way that includes religious experience. Theology in the New Testament does not have to equal "dogmatic ideas", nor does it have to imply a connection with systematic theology. How much theology there is in the New Testament can only be established by exegetical work. I argue against the view that there is little theology in the New Testament by arguing against a narrow definition of theology.

This problem of definition can be seen in an important article of Gerhard Ebeling, entitled "The Meaning of 'Biblical Theology'", and Claus Westermann's answer to it. Ebeling argues that "theology arises from the meeting of the biblical testimony of revelation with Greek thinking" (1963, 93). On this basis one can say that there is theology in the New Testament "above all in Paul and the author of the Fourth Gospel" (94). Ebeling concludes "that although the Bible for the most part does not contain theology in the strict sense, yet it does press for theological explication". Accordingly, the term "theology" should not primarily "denote the content of the Old or New Testament, but rather the scientific explication of the content of the Old and New Testament".

Westermann does not follow Ebeling in "starting from an understanding of the word 'theology' which is pre-determined" ("vorher festgelegt") (1986, 13). Ebeling affirms that it is "a doubtful proceeding to use the concept

'theology' in such a wide sense that any talk of God and any religious statement whatever may be designated as theology" (1963, 93). Westermann does
maintain against this view that he takes the term "in einem verbalen, sehr
weiten Sinn als Reden von Gott" (1986, 13). He argues against the proposal
that Greek thinking is a constitutive element of theology in the following
way. 1) It is not to be denied that it was unavoidable that the Christian proclamation had to meet with Greek thinking (16). However, this connection
does not have an "absolute significance" that would be valid for ever.
2) Ebeling's proposal would have as a consequence that the interpretation of
Old Testament texts should be carried out from the point of view of Greek
thinking if it wanted to be a theological interpretation (16). This would support an allegorical interpretation of the Old Testament (17). Ebeling's thesis
also implies "daß es eine im strengen Sinn theologische Auslegung des AT
vor dieser Begegnung nicht geben konnte". 3) It is a widely held view in the
Western Christian tradition that the meeting between the Christian proclamation and Greek thinking is something beneficial ("förderlich"). This is problematic from the point of view of the "religious roots" of Greek thinking (17).
A comparison between the monotheistic view of the First Commandment and
the polytheism of Greek thinking may reveal this problematic:

> Wo Gott *einer* ist, unbedingt nur einer, geschieht alles, was geschieht zwischen
> Gott und seinem Volk und in einem weiteren Sinn der Welt und der Menschheit.
> Wo aber von Göttern in einer Vielheit gesprochen wird, ergibt es sich von selbst,
> daß das Schwergewicht des Geschehenden auf das zwischen den Göttern Gesche-
> hende fällt, was seinen sprachlichen Ausdruck im Mythos erhält.

In my opinion, Westermann's counter-arguments are convincing. It is problematic to define "theology" in the way Ebeling does. If we adopt a wider
sense, as Westermann does, then we do not have to affirm "by definition" that
there is little theology in the New Testament. It is by historical methods that
theology may - or may not - be found in the New Testament, and not by definitions.

6. Overbeck's thesis against New Testament theology

Franz Overbeck examined the character of the theological trends of his own
day: the end of the nineteenth century and the turn of the century. In his
work, *Über die Christlichkeit unserer heutigen Theologie*, he challenges the
Christian character of the work of theologians. It is not easy to derive his thesis
from his work which is written in complex German. However, his arguments

amount to a challenge to the possibility of the enterprise of New Testament theology. Since Overbeck's thesis is based on the relationship between history and theology, it is appropriate to discuss it in this chapter.

I think it may be helpful to mention as background knowledge that Overbeck did not regard himself as a believing Christian.[22] His analysis of early Christian literature and of church history is the more important since he cannot be accused of a bias or personal commitment for Christianity that may have distorted his results.

Overbeck first published his work in question in 1873. He wrote an introduction and an epilogue to it and published his work unchanged thirty years later in a second edition.[23] In 1873 he was a university teacher in Basel who had five years' teaching experience in Jena and three years' professorship in Basel behind him (1-2). By 1903 he had six years' retirement behind him (193). His second edition extends the discussion of theological "parties" or trends to include "modern theology", i.e. the theology of the day of the second edition, but even here he maintains the main thesis of the original work (217).

The main thesis of Overbeck is to show that theology contains an "irreligious" element and Christianity contains a "non-Christian" ("unchristliches") element (41). In the hands of theologians, Christianity can become a thing which is not Christianity any longer (42). His main arguments are as follows.

a. Scientific knowledge

Christianity reached the modern nations not only as a religion but also as a culture (22). Christianity has become intertwined with the end-period of Graeco-Roman antiquity: "das Christenthum sei die Einbalsamirung, in welcher das Alterthum auf unsere Zeiten gekommen ist". Due to this fact, Christianity contains science incorporated in itself. However, every religion has an aversion ("Abneigung") against science; so did Christianity in its original form.

Every religion exists in the realm of the world (23). Religion takes its "forms" from the material of the world. With these forms religion is subject to knowledge. When a religion is strong, it can keep away science from the problematical points ("Angriffspunkte") of that religion. When faith becomes weak, it surrenders some of its territory to knowledge. In doing so, faith either abandons elements of itself or expects knowledge to confirm those elements.

---

[22] See Räisänen 1990, 192, n.66.
[23] Here I shall refer to this latter edition, 1903, reprinted in 1981.

In both cases faith has become superfluous (24). Knowledge will always remain something different from faith. There is an antagonism between faith and knowledge (22).

Thus theology is "irreligious" in as much as it connects faith with knowledge (25). To support this thesis Overbeck argues that every religion holds that it is the only true religion; science "robs" every religion precisely of this conviction.

Overbeck affirms that both the "apologetic" and the "critical" theology of his day share the same character; in as much as they are theologies employing scientific methods, Christianity as a religion is a problem for them (35). This means that "die Theologie das Christenthum als Religion problematisch macht, d. h. als solche überhaupt in Frage stellt". Even if "apologetic theology" succeeded in proving Christianity in a scientific way, even then Christianity would be ruined as religion.

These arguments of Overbeck challenge New Testament theology in as much as they challenge theology in general. I think that the key term in this line of argumentation is that religion is "subject to" ("unterliegt") knowledge. Why is knowledge so destructive of faith? This view of Overbeck betrays a highly critical opinion about the contents of the Bible. Overbeck seems to imply that if the Bible is scrutinised by critical knowledge, the result will be that the Bible does not contain truth (cf. the last part of the quotation below from his p.34).

I think that scientific knowledge does not have the role of verifying biblical affirmations. New Testament theology should study the Bible; then it should present its results, and leave the question whether or not what is presented is held to be true by the reader or the author of a New Testament theology. I have argued that historical criticism may be used in New Testament theology. The fact that it is used does not deny the possibility of New Testament theology. In a similar way here I propose against Overbeck's thesis that "knowledge" does not ruin "religion".

Overbeck is right in saying that religion is strongly connected with the world that surrounds it. However, I think Overbeck wants to draw from this fact conclusions that are too exaggerated. He rightly emphasises that theology as science does not have its own epistemological principles (34). I accept his description of the relationship between the church and scientific methods:

Die Wissenschaft hat sich von der Kirche völlig emancipirt, ihre Beweismethoden schafft sie sich selbst und wendet sie ohne alle Rücksicht auf Zwecke, die ausserhalb ihrer selbst liegen, an, keine einzige ihrer Disciplinen ordnet sich bei ihrer Arbeit den Bedürfnissen des Christenthums unter, völlig unbekümmert sind alle um etwaige Collisionen mit Vorstellungen der christlichen Tradition und am Wenigsten schrecken sie vor der thatsächlichen Häufung dieser Collisionen zurück.

However, it is too much to affirm on this basis that theology is not a Christian science (34). The Christian character of theology should not be measured on the basis of the method of theology, but on the basis of its content. New Testament theology, when it describes the content of the biblical writings, may be justifiably called theology if it finds theology in the New Testament. New Testament theology does not cease to be theology because of the fact that it makes use of scientific methods which are non-Christian by definition.

b. Apologetic theology

On the basis of this general point, Overbeck discusses the main trends in theology of his day in particular. First he shows that the "apologetic" theology of his day was not successful. The apologetic theology wishes to use historical means to prove the truth of Christianity. Overbeck holds that among the proofs of religions the historical proof is of least value (44). He affirms that the origins of religions always contain "unhistorical and unscientific" elements. For example, early Christianity shows its power "indem es über den wissenschaftlich augenscheinlichen Widerspruch sich wegsetzend, neben das synoptische das johanneische Christusbild setzt". As soon as that early "power" decreases, historical proof is not strong enough to maintain the "courageous" juxtaposition of the Synoptics with John's Gospel.

As a further argument, Overbeck proposed that the "apologists" could only claim to prove that there existed miracles in biblical times if they could perform miracles themselves (51). If they agree that there are no miracles in their own day, they should also acknowledge that something which does not function ("wirkt") is dead (52). Science asserts theoretically that there are no miracles in this world (53). If theologians want to argue against this theoretical proof, then they should first refute "in practice" that there are no miracles.

To conclude, Overbeck affirms that the apologetic theology has no specific "character" and no "effect" (68). Even apologists themselves acknowledge that they preach an ideal view that cannot be put fully into practice (70). They should acknowledge that they have no right to urge others to share their belief (71).

Christianity can only be founded on the absence of salvation ("Unseligkeit") of the world. The apologetic theology does not have the "power" of the early stages of Christianity any longer. The apologetic theology has abandoned the original Christian understanding of the world and of life ("Welt-

und Lebensbetrachtung"), so Overbeck denies that the theology of the apologists can be called a Christian one (71).

These arguments are concrete applications of the first general point made by Overbeck. I think that much of his critical report about the apologetic theology of his day is true. However, I should like to point to the following areas where I find difficulties in Overbeck's argumentation. 1) I should like to raise as a main counter-question: Do we have the right to expect the same "power" in a religion at a later stage as it had in the earlier stage in order to maintain that that religion is still a "living" one? 2) I find it also problematic to accept that a religion that cannot perform miracles in the present should acknowledge that there are no miracles in general so there were no miracles in the past either. 3) What does it mean that the church cannot put its "ideals" into practice? What are we to call "ideals" in Christianity: Jesus' example, or, the early church's life? Did Jesus mean that his followers should fulfil "ideals"? In what sense was the early church "ideal"? In other words, I do not think that it is a justifiable claim that the church should fulfil ideals if it wants to have a right to mission; or if it wants to call itself "Christian".

c. *Liberal theology*

Overbeck examines the results of the "liberal theology" of his day and affirms that liberal theology entertains the illusion that it can first analyse - "critically dissolve" - then re-build Christianity by historical means (73). As one concrete example, Overbeck criticises the concern of liberal theology to examine the "Christianity of Christ". Already the very term itself is problematic. According to the etymology of the word, Christianity is faith in Christ: so it cannot mean the faith of Christ (74). On the basis of Lessing's arguments Overbeck affirms (75):

> Die Vorstellung einer "Religion Christi" dagegen beruht auf der historischen Entdeckung des menschlichen Wesens Christi, d. h. auf der Entdeckung, dass die christliche Religion, wenn sie auch schon im ersten Moment ihres Auftretens als Universalreligion Christus zur Würde eines göttlichen Wesens erhoben hat, doch mit Unrecht diese Vorstellung von ihm in die vorausgegangene Urzeit zurückverlegt und mit besonderem Unrecht auf das eigene Zeugniss des Stifters begründet hat.

Overbeck argues that Christianity never existed without that move that it attached to Christ its own view about the deity of Christ. If we find out that they did attach to Jesus what he did not think of himself, then Christianity cannot be based on the "religion of Jesus" (76). Overbeck concludes:

> Wir gelangen also, wenn wir uns der eigenen menschlichen Religion Christi gegenüberstellen, nur zu einer vom Christenthum aus betrachtet dahinter liegenden aber für dessen Begründung gleichgültigen Thatsache, da in Wirklichkeit nicht diese Religion das Christenthum begründet hat ...

Overbeck further holds the view that the true nature of Early Christianity was self-denial ("asketische Lebensbetrachtung"). The martyrs represented it fully, and later on monasticism kept the idea safe in a society where the state acknowledged Christianity (84). Paul represented a "world-denying" character of early Christianity. This asceticism helped Christianity to overcome the problem created by the fact that Jesus had not returned (86-87). Asceticism is "in der That eine Metamorphose des urchristlichen Glaubens an die Wiederkunft Christi ... sofern sie auf der fortwährenden Erwartung dieser Wiederkehr beruht ..." (87).

Liberal theology failed to find this true essence of Christianity (87). To replace the world-denying character of the Christian religion (91) by a world-accepting view means to destroy the religion of Christianity (93). Also on a practical level, liberal theology proves to be ineffective in reaching out to its addressees (99-100). Liberal theology should turn back to science in a more unconsiderate ("rücksichtsloser") way instead of presenting itself in a "popular" way (109). Liberal theology should consider in what sense its efforts can be called Christian.

In my opinion, Overbeck's criticism of the liberal theology of his day is only justified with regard to the actual views he refers to. If Jesus is found not to have thought of himself as anything other than a human being, then it is true that Christianity cannot claim that it followed Jesus when it thought of him as Son of God. In this case Overbeck may be right that liberal theology "mit dem Kern auch die Schalen des Christenthums von sich geworfen hat" (73). The question arises: Is liberal theology bound to arrive at this result? Is another result not possible at which one may arrive by using liberal principles and methods?[24]

With regard to Overbeck's description of early Christianity as an ascetic movement one may ask: Is this not an over-simplified picture? Has Christianity not shown a considerable interest in the life and the fate of the "world"? Perhaps it is too much to claim, but it may be argued that even the ascetic character of early Christianity could be exercised as a way of life which could still find much place for the service of the world. Overbeck's hard criticism on liberal theology would stand its ground only in the case if liberal theology

---

[24] See as an example J.C. O'Neill's remark concerning his own work (1995, 6): "Radical criticism, but conservative conclusions that tend to show that orthodox Christianity is based on what Jesus himself held to be true".

could take only the shape which he criticises, and if he would be right in his one-sided picture of an ascetic early Christianity. I think he may be challenged at both points, but that would go beyond the limits of my thesis.

d. Critical theology

Overbeck proposes that a "critical" theology would be preferable over against the apologetic and liberal ones, because critical theology makes it clear that it does not have a purely religious character in its aims (109). However, Overbeck is not satisfied with the work of Strauss. The culture Strauss proposes would be like going back to the times previous to Christianity (116). It is highly individualistic (118). It is a "cult of the universe" (119).

I agree with Overbeck that New Testament theology should have a "critical character". I would argue that Strauss's criticism is not the only possible one; that "apologetic" theology and "liberal" theology may also be carried out in better ways than the ones criticised by Overbeck. Both these theologies may be exercised in a "critical" manner.

On the basis of Overbeck's "autobiography" in the epilogue, I have the impression that Overbeck was consistent with what he held on theology. On the one hand, he wanted to be a "theologian", i.e. to teach a "critical-historical understanding of Christianity" (8). On the other hand, he did not think of himself as a theologian at all. As he confesses: "was ich in meinem Auditorium verbarg, nämlich dass ich gar kein Theologe war" (188). He was convinced, however, that to do theology means to abandon the "predicate" Christian (cf. 21).

e. Christianity - dead?

I think that the following - more general - argument of Overbeck may be the key to his whole thesis. He affirms that a religion can only be safe from the attacks against its "forms" if it has a living power to build up myths (35). Overbeck's point here must mean that science cannot successfully demolish myths in a religion if that religion is able to produce new myths. Overbeck gives an example: a living religion is one that has "Wunderkräfte". Christianity has lost these living, effective powers "im Grunde seit es eine christliche Theologie giebt". The early church saw that "der christliche Mythus in das Stadium einer starren Tradition trat" (35-36). That is why the church developed a "historical interpretation" (36). However, historical interpretation is not strong enough to maintain the canonical status of certain writings, so the church developed the allegorical interpretation as a kind of "Surrogat für den nicht mehr selbst lebenden Mythus".

Theologians of Overbeck's day thought they could re-establish ("wieder gewiss werden") Christianity on a historical level only. Overbeck affirms that this would result in a theoretical religion ("Gelehrtenreligion", "Denkreligion") which has nothing in common with real religion (36).

On the basis of these arguments we have an insight into Overbeck's views. On the face of it, he challenges the Christian character of theology from different aspects: the presence of science; the weaknesses of the trends in theology in his own day. However, his basic thesis can be seen in the clearest form at this point. Overbeck's thesis can be put in this way: the very fact that theological reasoning on the biblical texts had started, shows that Christianity was no longer a living religion. For our thesis, this implies the following: the very fact that we are engaging in New Testament theology shows that we deal with a dead religion.

In my opinion, this thesis is in connection with a certain definition of theology. I do not separate the notion of religion from that of theology as sharply as Overbeck does. He understands theology as a development that follows religion. Religion is the belief of people (cf. Overbeck's term: "Glaubensreligion", p.36). Theology is reflection on religion at a later stage when that religion does not have its living power any longer and needs scientific defence in order to maintain itself. In my terminology theology would be very close to what is understood by Overbeck as religion: people's belief about God - and whatever is in connection with this belief.

However, I think that my disagreement with Overbeck is not only on the level of definitions. I argue against him on the basis of what is in fact inherent in his own arguments. I accept his point about the change in a religion's character when it loses its "myth-creating" power. However, that change does not necessarily mean the death of that religion. On the one hand, old "myths" may exercise powerful effects even in times when there are no new "myths" to be born in a religion. On the other hand, Overbeck himself implies that the emergence of theological reflection is a certain type of continuation of that religion, albeit with different characteristics from its original form. Apart from this counter-argument, I do not investigate the problem: What are the necessary changes in a religion after which one can say that it is not the same religion any longer: the old form has died, and the new one is not in a real continuity with the old?

Applied to the problem discussed in my thesis, these points of Overbeck do not prevent us from doing New Testament theology. I point to the following reasons. 1) If there are bad theologians and unsatisfactory New Testament theologies, this does not mean that the enterprise should be abandoned. Instead, it has to be improved. 2) Strictly speaking, it would be possible to describe the theology contained in the Bible even if Christianity was dead. In this case the presentation of a New Testament theology would have no "answer" from its present reader, but that may not be its aim at all. I note that in my opinion Overbeck's thesis is not convincing. Christianity is not "dead". 3) If Christianity is not dead, then two things are possible. a) New Testament theology may describe the content of the New Testament without the aim of convincing its readers that the claims made by the New Testament are right ones. Even in this case it may happen that some readers will decide that they do accept the message of the New Testament and wish to lead their lives in accordance with that message. b) It is also possible to maintain the following view of New Testament theology: the theologian has the aim to promote the message of the New Testament among modern readers. Although in my thesis I adopt the first view (3.a), I emphasise here that the possibility of the second could also be maintained, in spite of the challenging thesis of Overbeck.

7. Conclusion

In this chapter I have discussed challenges which are brought against New Testament theology from the point of view of historical studies.

The most radical of these challenges is to argue that historical study excludes studying theology. I have argued that the major challenges are related to definitions. We may encounter two problematic areas: 1) our definition of history may cause us not to speak about God's acts in history; 2) our definition of theology may require that we should not study New Testament theology as a historical enterprise.

I have argued that Gabler did not separate the enterprises in the same way as Räisänen would propose. After Gabler's "separation" there still remains the possibility of a historical enterprise that studies the theology contained in the New Testament.

Against Wrede's and Räisänen's theses in general one may argue that the very fact of the existence of a canon calls for studying that which unites the canon. This involves studying theology (Stuhlmacher). It may also be argued that the environment that treasured the New Testament writings, i.e. the church, needs a theological understanding of its Scriptures (Hübner). However, I do not think this argument is essential for making a convincing case against Räisänen's challenge to the enterprise. I propose that New Testament theology should be a historical enterprise. The theology of the New Testament should be studied historically.

We may take two main lines in relation to the character of historical study. A "narrow" definition of history excludes the possibility of accepting biblical affirmations that include talk about God acting in history, as true. In this case historical work may report as "theology" things that biblical figures and authors have asserted in relation to God. This activity does not raise the question of truth with regard to what is reported. At this point it is only important for my thesis that New Testament theology is possible with this view of history. I have to note, however, that there may be no unity in what is reported as theology. This challenge is the theme of chapter four in my thesis.

In this thesis I propose to adopt a "wider" view of history. A historian should be allowed the possibility that he can think something to be historically true even if it is reported about people's beliefs in God. This "stretching" of the definition of history may be fruitful in the study of a field that has the talk about God as its main characteristic. This view does not "prove" biblical ideas; it cannot do so, because the "critical" character of the historical enterprise is retained. However, it may find things to be historically likely, or not likely, which are not discussed under a narrow view of history by definition.

From the point of view of a history-of-religion approach the main challenge against New Testament theology turns out to be a matter of definitions. I propose that theology should include every thought and action that is in relation to New Testament people's belief in God. This includes their religious experiences. This definition also avoids the difficulty of finding little theology in the New Testament because of our definition of theology.

Theology does not equal doctrine; theology is a concept with a broader meaning. However, doctrine does belong to the content of the New Testament, thus it also belongs to New Testament theology (see Baur's study of *Lehrbegriffe*). I have also argued that we have access mainly to the content of the biblical writings. Consequently, it is valid to study the content of these writings primarily (see Holtzmann's approach), and the experiences lying behind the affirmations of these writings only secondarily, whenever possible.

We have met arguments against New Testament theology which were in relation to the view that "theology" means the modern interpreter's theology. Against this view I propose that the term "theology" should be understood as referring to the theological content of the Bible. New Testament theology differs from systematic theology mainly in the realm of age-relatedness. The former is confined to biblical times whereas the latter includes theological thoughts up to the present. The latter should not "direct" or "control" the former.

I have further argued that New Testament theology may be maintained even if it adopts a thematic structure. In this case the historical character of the enterprise has to be maintained while handling certain themes.

New Testament theology may be justified even if the normative character of the biblical writings is not presupposed. In fact, this decision is desirable in order to retain the historical character of the enterprise.

Finally, I have argued that Overbeck is not right in implying that the fact that one engages in the enterprise of New Testament theology shows that one regards the religion of the New Testament as dead. The discipline may be maintained as a historical discipline. On the one hand, it is not impossible. On the other hand, to study Christianity is not necessarily un-Christian: the enterprise does not dissolve itself.

If New Testament theology is defined to be a historical enterprise, how does it find its field of study? How does it distinguish between the study of the New Testament and that of the rest of early Christian literature? Our next problem may be put in this way: Do we have historical grounds for confining our study to the canonical writings of the New Testament?

Chapter Two

Early Christianity and Its Writings

According to the challenge put to New Testament theology by Wrede and Räisänen, one area where the enterprise is problematic is the relationship between early Christianity and Christianity as it is reflected in the canonical New Testament. New Testament theology is problematic with regard to the first part of its title: we should not confine our study to the canonical writings, the "New Testament".

This challenge is supported by substantial arguments. In this chapter I shall focus on challenging theses which have been put forward in this area by Walter Bauer and Helmut Koester. I think that they have summarised the problems in argumentative, historical studies which deserve detailed discussion. I agree with Räisänen who affirms with reference to Koester: "his contribution is a massive challenge to New Testament study" (1990, 84).

One of the arguments may be the application of the theme discussed in the previous chapter: historians have no right to limit the scope of their study. They should discuss all evidence - in our case, all early Christian literature. We have to discuss this general question briefly before we turn to more particular theses and arguments.

1. The historian and his sources

Räisänen asserts that it is "arbitrary" in a historical work to confine one's task "essentially to the interpretation of the canonical New Testament writings" (1990, 100). Räisänen refers to Schlier as a support for his own view. Schlier affirms (1964, 10 = Strecker, 1975, 327):

> Vom Standpunkt einer urchristlichen Religionsgeschichte aus und überhaupt vom bloßen "historischen" Standpunkt aus ist eine Theologie des N. T. eine Absurdität, einmal als Theologie überhaupt und dann durch ihre historisch durchaus nicht zu rechtfertigende Beschränkung auf die im N. T. gesammelten Schriften.

Since Schlier himself opts for New Testament theology as a matter of "faith decision", his acknowledgment with regard to the historical enterprise is important to Räisänen (101). However, I cannot accept Räisänen's and Schlier's affirmations because they emphasise one good argument without taking into consideration another possible argument which in turn may modify the first one.

They are right in holding that a historian has to deal with all his sources. A historian starts his work by studying all the documents and sources available for him. This also applies to New Testament theology, in the way I argue we should understand the enterprise. A New Testament theologian should be a historian and should study all the evidence which may have a connection with early Christianity.

However, the historian may be faced with the result in his study that the sources may show different characteristics. On the one hand, some documents may turn out to be dependent on other sources to an extent that they may be regarded as secondary. They do not shed new light on early Christianity. Some documents may turn out to be "forgeries", i.e. they provide false information about an aspect of early Christianity. These writings, like all evidence, should be criticised by the historian. The result of criticism may be that they do not contribute to our knowledge of early Christianity.

On the other hand, other writings may show a higher degree of reliability as regards information about early Christianity. Furthermore, it may be theoretically possible that certain writings show signs that they belong to a group of writings whose authors thought they shared a common theology. It is possible that they thought they were writing a "canon". In this case the historian is justified by the results of his study in separating a group of writings from other writings in order to study the theology of those writings *as historian*. This possibility should be explored by detailed historical study. However, this possibility should be acknowledged, and should not be ignored by simply presupposing it does not exist. My thesis is an attempt at clearing away some obstacles in the way of this possibility.[1]

2. "Heresy" earlier than "orthodoxy"? (Walter Bauer's thesis)

One major argument against the separation of canonical writings from non-canonical ones arises from the area of distinguishing between orthodoxy and heresy. Walter Bauer, the scholar renowned for his Greek lexicon, wrote an important study in 1934, entitled *Rechtgläubigkeit und Ketzerei im ältesten Christentum*. Strecker summarises Bauer's thesis in the preface of the second

---

[1] See especially the following chapter.

edition of Bauer's work as follows: "In earliest Christianity, orthodoxy and heresy do not stand in relation to one another as primary to secondary, but in many regions heresy is the original manifestation of Christianity" (1972, xi). This thesis would have as its consequence that for a historian the distinction between heresy and orthodoxy is not a relevant one.

Accordingly, for a historian it is not relevant what was regarded as orthodoxy in the first few centuries of Christianity when they created their canon. The irrelevance of the distinction between orthodoxy and heresy is an argument against the distinction between canonical and non-canonical writings in a New Testament theology. Because of this implication of Bauer's thesis it is appropriate to discuss it in some detail.

According to Bauer, the church in the second century held that there was the following sequence of events during the spreading of the Gospel: "unbelief, right belief, wrong belief" (3; 1972, xxiii).[2] This would indicate that "where there is heresy, orthodoxy must have preceded". Bauer wants to examine and challenge this view. For his study he retains the usage of the terms "heresy" and "orthodoxy" as they are "customarily and usually" understood, i.e. from the view-point of the church in the second century (2-3; 1972, xxii-xxiii).

As a methodological decision he does not start his study with the New Testament, because the "majority of its anti-heretical writings cannot be arranged with confidence either chronologically or geographically" (5; 1972, xxv). In line with this argument, first Bauer examines Edessa and Egypt in order "to obtain a glimpse into the emergence and the original condition ("Beschaffenheit") of Christianity in regions other than those that the New Testament depicts as affected by this religion".

a. Edessa, Mesopotamia

Bauer argues that there was no Christian prince or state church in Edessa around the year A.D. 200 (pp. 13, 19). Eusebius's story of King Abgar V Ukkama's letter to Jesus and the subsequent conversion of Edessa "can in no way and to no extent be traced back as a report that is earlier than the beginning of the fourth century, when Eusebius' *Ecclesiastical History* originated" (8; 1972, 3). Bauer not only argues against the historicity of this report, but also against the suggestion that the Abgar of the story is Abgar IX, A.D. 179-214 (p.9). Eusebius was misled through false stories presented to him by others ("Fälschung", 15).

---

[2] In my thesis references without the year of the publication are made to the second German edition, 1964.

On the other hand, Bardesanes represented the non-orthodox form of Christianity at an early stage (17, 21). Even prior to his appearance, Christianity existed in Edessa in the form of Marcionism, not later than A.D. 150 (p.34). Bardesanes, who appeared well before A.D. 200, attacked Marcion's views. Bardesanes wrote his own psalms for his congregation. Bauer concludes that Bardesanes's community must have had its own Scripture because they did not accept Marcion's Bible. Their Gospel must have been Tatian's Diatessaron (35).

I point to the following problems in connection with these arguments of Bauer.

If Bardesanes had the Diatessaron, which was prepared before the appearance of Bardesanes (36), this may be used as an argument for the view that there must have been orthodox Christians in Edessa prior to Bardesanes's time. Bauer asserts that Tatian prepared the Diatessaron for Syriac-speaking Christians. If these are people who lived far from Edessa, then it remains to be shown how the Diatessaron reached Edessa. Bauer argues that there were Marcionite Christians in Edessa prior to Bardesanes's appearance. However, the Marcionites could not have received the Diatessaron, because of two reasons: a) they had their own New Testament canon; b) Tatian or his followers were critical of Marcion's movement, as Bauer affirms.

Thus it remains possible that Tatian prepared the Diatessaron for orthodox Christians and that orthodox Christians received it in Edessa. Bauer comes near to acknowledging this point when he argues that the little group of orthodox Palutians had no other choice than to accept the Diatessaron which had been introduced in Edessa by the leading figure, Bardesanes (36-37).

As another counter-argument I refer to what Bauer himself gives as evidence (e.g. 13). There are some short references in Eusebius to the presence of orthodox Christians in Mesopotamia in an early period. Bauer disregards these because he has disproved the reliability of the "strongest", detailed evidence of the Abgar story.

b. Egypt

From the silence concerning early Christianity in Egypt Bauer concludes that the lack of evidence is due to the fact that there was no strong orthodoxy in Egypt in early times. The fathers preferred not to report anything (49ff). Furthermore, the early form of Christianity in Egypt was non-orthodox (53, 62-63). Gnostic writings in the Coptic language support this view (e.g. the *Apocryphon of John*, the *Pistis Sophia*, the *Books of Jeu*, pp.53-54). The orthodox Demetrius's strength on the side of the orthodox was due to the influence of Rome (60).

Bauer affirms with regard to Demetrius, "ecclesiastical" bishop of Alexandria from 189 to 231, that he "lived long enough to achieve success and possessed a consciousness of his own power that was sufficient to take disciplinary action against even an Origen ..." (1972, 54). However, earlier Demetrius had not fought against Clement who "deviated from the teaching of the church far more" than Origen (60; 1972, 56). From this Bauer concludes that at that earlier time "there existed no prospect of successfully assailing ideas" like those of Clement (61-62; 1972, 58).

I find the arguments Bauer derives from silence weak. Bauer even acknowledges that there must have been "orthodox" Christians in Egypt very early, as a minority (57). Bauer does not answer the question: Why did the number of the orthodox Christians grow and become dominant later? In my opinion, it is historically unlikely that the power on the orthodox side could have grown so quickly in Demetrius's lifetime. It seems to me more plausible to think that Demetrius's opposition against Origen could not have happened without strong orthodoxy in Egypt prior to Demetrius's time.

I think Bauer weakens somewhat his own thesis when he adds that "even into the third century, no separation between orthodoxy and heresy was accomplished in Egypt and the two types of Christianity were not yet at all clearly differentiated from each other" (63; 1972, 59). If this is true, then Bauer should not attribute too much to his arguments from silence. He should rather acknowledge that views of both orthodox and heretical kinds existed in Egypt, but it was not until the later period of Demetrius that a clear differentiation appeared.

c. Asia Minor

Bauer argues against Harnack that Papias and Polycarp did not have the authority in Asia Harnack thought they did (74). For Bauer, Ignatius's data are not very reliable: "time and again [Ignatius] loses all sense of proportion" (65; 1972, 61). There is evidence for the presence of heresy in Smyrna shortly after the death of Polycarp (e.g. the patripassian doctrine of Noëtus; Marcionism was present in Smyrna even a hundred years later, p.75).

Bauer holds that the picture of early Christianity in Asia Minor and its neighbourhood is not a uniform one. In Ephesus, Magnesia, Tralles, and Philadelphia, the bishops Ignatius addressed in his letters led orthodox groups which were in the majority (73, 81), but in Antioch, Philippi, and Smyrna,

Bauer suspects the presence of strong heresy (81). For example, Gnosticism appeared in Antioch prior to the time of Ignatius (70). Bauer attaches significance to the fact that from among the churches John, the apocalyptic seer, had addressed in Rev 2-3, Ignatius did not write to those which were rebuked by the "seer": Pergamum, Thyatira, Sardis, and Laodicea (83). Bauer concludes that in these places "there was nothing Ignatius could hope for from the Christian groups" (1972, 79).

We have to notice that Bauer does not make an attempt to show that heresy was older than orthodoxy in Asia Minor. His aim is to show the presence of heresy in a place where one would expect strong orthodoxy. My criticism of Bauer is that he argues as if it were a condition of orthodoxy that it was strong and without opposition; otherwise it cannot be called orthodoxy. If this is the implication of Bauer's thesis with regard to Asia Minor, then he contradicts himself because he does assert in the beginning of his work that the question of majority and minority is not a decisive one with regard to the study of orthodoxy and heresy (2; see also 94).

Bauer does not acknowledge the importance of the fact (although he does discuss the question, e.g. p.86) that from the earliest New Testament periods on, the "orthodoxy" - for example, of apostle Paul - was strongly opposed. The presence of opposition does not necessarily mean that orthodoxy was weak in that particular place.

With regard to other regions, Bauer infers from the silence in Eusebius that there was no orthodoxy in Central and Eastern Asia Minor in the second century. In that period there were only heretics in that region (176).

Again, I think that Bauer allows himself to conclude too much on the basis of an argument from silence. As a counter-argument one might ask: Why did orthodox Christians from other regions not attack heretics in the discussed region?

d. Rome

Bauer affirms that there was a strong orthodoxy in Rome in the second century. It could develop to become strong, because it did not have heretical "disturbances up to a point well into the second century" (132; 1972, 128). Orthodoxy in Rome was able to overcome Marcion's attack (132). It could even influence churches in other places, for example, in Corinth, Antioch, and Alexandria (126; see e.g. 1Clement, pp.99ff).

Bauer's reference to the absence of heresy does not answer the question sufficiently: Why and how did the church of Rome become so powerful? Bauer himself points to the persecutions under Nero and Domitian as factors which had resulted in "that toward the end of the first century the believers of the capital city could no longer feel safe" (131-132; 1972, 128). For a later (Constantinian) period Bauer can point to the powerful support of the state (31). However, in the first and second centuries, we can only think of a "natural" powerful spreading of the orthodox views in spite of the hostility of the surrounding state.

Bauer's affirmation with regard to the influence of the church in Rome implies that heresy could have been stronger in other parts of the Mediterranean if it had not been suppressed by Rome. I would argue that the influence of Rome in other places would be more understandable if there were a sufficient number of orthodox-thinking people with whom Rome could build up relationships. I should like to suggest that the growth of orthodoxy in Rome in the first two centuries, which occurred in spite of persecutions, may be an argument for the proposal that there were other places, too, where the orthodox views had spread quickly and extensively.

e. Why so few heretical writings?

Bauer gives the following reasons why we do not have many heretical writings: 1) many heretical writings were lost (172); 2) heretical writings may have been altered by the orthodox (163); 3) wherever heretics saw themselves in the majority, they did not feel the need for writing polemical writings against the orthodox (173).

I agree that heretical writings are unlikely to have survived, since orthodoxy eventually won. However, it is worth noting that many heretical writings are known to us because they are mentioned in the writings of the orthodox. To argue against a view also meant that that view was repeated. This, of course, may not apply to later periods when there was not any longer a threat from certain heresies. When a dispute ended, it is understandable that the writings of the losers were not "treasured" by the winners. In this context Bauer affirms that "the 'church' is clearly in a privileged position insofar as it became authoritative bearer and custodian of the tradition" (1972, 169). He is right in this assertion. This privileged position on the side of the orthodox may account for the disappearing of heretical writings.

Bauer shows how Africanus altered a work of Homer (167). I think it is not a valid move to say that other Christians could have altered, just in the same way, writings of heretics (cf. 168). The claim that Irenaeus feared heretics would alter his writings does not imply that Irenaeus would have been prepared to alter the writings of heretics (see 169).

In itself, Bauer's third point seems to be a plausible argument. However, I must add, that it is in some tension with the first point. If both points are true, then it is unlikely that we should find any writing of any view: where the representatives of a view are in the minority, their writings are unlikely to survive; where they are in the majority, they do not feel it necessary to write at all. This, of course, would then be true of the orthodox views as well. However, we do have writings representing the orthodox view. Thus I do not find Bauer's third point convincing. The fact of the non-existence of writings should not be regarded as an argument for the strength of that particular group.

Bauer may have sensed this possible weakness in his arguments, because he felt the need for attacking the seemingly great number of orthodox writings. He wants to strengthen his thesis by showing that Eusebius's remarks concerning the strength of orthodoxy are not reliable (e.g. 153). Eusebius could not have had or known as many orthodox writings as he refers to (161). In many cases we only have the titles. These writings may have been written against heresies, and so these writings could give further evidence for the presence of heresies.

These observations may be right. Even if they are right, it does not follow that heresy may have been stronger or earlier at the places those writings refer to.

In summary, I think that Bauer's main aim with his arguments is to support the thesis that there is no valid distinction between orthodoxy and heresy. Concerning his thesis, I do acknowledge the presence of heresy from a very early point in time on and in many different places. However, Bauer cannot convincingly show that at certain places heresy might have been the first form of Christianity.

At this point I must note that I have deliberately avoided the question of truth in the discussion. I have looked at the spreading of different views from a historical point of view. I have used the terms heretical and orthodox as a convention without making any decision concerning the questions: Who was right? Which side represented the truth? I have found that Bauer's arguments do not have the strength of disproving the possibility of distinguishing between heretical and orthodox views (and writings expressing those views) on historical grounds. The second century view, which Bauer has attempted to disprove, can be maintained: it is possible that heretical views appeared where there had been an orthodox presence beforehand.

We have to consider one further possibility. It is plausible to hold that every Christian church thought of themselves as holding the truth, as "orthodox". It is even possible (as we have seen in Bauer's thesis) that in a certain geographical area different views existed together without dividing their representatives into two groups. What was regarded later as heresy, may have existed alongside orthodox views at an early stage. However, we have also seen that there came a point in history when ideas have been separated, and groups have been separated.

Thus as historians we find that there was a distinction between heresy and orthodoxy in the early period. There are, of course, great differences with regard to the questions: Which view could not be accepted as orthodox any longer? Where did that happen? What was regarded as heretical and as orthodox should be examined in a detailed way according to areas and periods of time. This cannot be done in my thesis. For my thesis, the important result is that historians may describe early Christianity in a way which accords with this finding: orthodoxy has been separated from heresy.

Accordingly, it is a historical phenomenon that orthodox groups collected their writings into a "canon" and heretical groups created their own writings. Perhaps heretics formed alternative canons themselves: they may have regarded some of their writings as canonical. Thus it is a valid historical enterprise to discuss the content of a canon in comparison with writings outside that canon. Without raising the question: Which canon should be accepted as containing the truth?, one has to acknowledge the historical phenomenon of the formations of canons. For my thesis, in particular, it means: as historians we are justified in our enterprise to summarise the theology of one particular canon in history: the New Testament.

Now we turn to arguments that are mainly taken from works of Helmut Koester. Since Koester is an influential scholar who has revived much of Bauer's thesis, and who has developed several of his own, it may be appropriate to turn to the question: Why does Koester deny the legitimacy of distinguishing between canonical and non-canonical books?

Koester has laid down the basic theses and arguments in relation to our question in his doctoral thesis (1957) and in a collection of articles which he has published together with J.M. Robinson (1971). Building on these studies, he has written two additional works, which are detailed historical summaries - a kind of working out in detail what had been proposed in the earlier works. One of them, entitled *Einführung in das Neue Testament: im Rahmen der Religionsgeschichte und Kulturgeschichte der hellenistischen und römischen Zeit* (1980), is meant to be a textbook. The other presents a historical picture as well: *Ancient Christian Gospels: Their History and Development* (1990). These historical summaries contain many exegetical decisions of Koester, sometimes put forward as a view without the supporting arguments. I do not enter into discussion with them in this thesis. I shall mainly focus on the major arguments of the first two works.

3. Were the Synoptic Gospels not known to the Apostolic Fathers? (Helmut Koester's thesis)

In his doctoral thesis, *Synoptische Überlieferung bei den apostolischen Vätern* (1957), Helmut Koester has put forward the thesis that passages in the Apostolic Fathers which are similar to passages in the Synoptic Gospels do not make it necessary to hold that the Apostolic Fathers used the Gospels in the form as we have them. It is possible to argue that the Apostolic Fathers used material which was also used by the Gospel writers, but the Apostolic Fathers did not use our Gospels (e.g. 239). Thus the history of "synoptic" traditions in the Apostolic Fathers has to be viewed as one running parallel alongside the history of the Synoptic Gospels rather than after it (e.g. 267).

This thesis implies that the evidence of "synoptic" traditions in the first half of the second century does not suggest that the Gospels were regarded by the Apostolic Fathers as Scripture in the second century.[3]

As an example, we may quote Koester's assertion concerning the Didache (240):

> Did. setzt also die Existenz der Synoptiker voraus, aber nicht ihre Geltung als maßgebliche Quelle dessen, was der Herr gesagt und seiner Gemeinde zu tun befohlen hat. In dieser Beziehung steht die Did. nicht hinter den synoptischen Evangelien, sondern neben ihnen.

Because of the importance of this challenging implication for my thesis, it is worth looking at Koester's arguments in more detail.

Koester's starting point is the affirmation that during the course of its transmission the "synoptic" tradition did not have a unified wording in the first half of the second century. The "Western text" is an example. Consequently, one has to be ready to see "free citations" in the Apostolic Fathers (pp. 1, 257-258). A further example is the "free" way in which Matthew and Luke used Mark (2).

Around the middle of the second century Justin Martyr quoted our Gospels. Thus the middle of the second century is the *terminus ad quem* by which time the written Gospels have established themselves over against the oral transmission. Thus it has to be noted that this process took place in the period when the Apostolic Fathers wrote their works (3).

In order to establish where the Apostolic Fathers received their "synoptic" traditions from, Koester adopts the following method (3): a) one has to examine

---

[3] I use the term "Scripture" here in the same way as Koester does, i.e. referring to a writing that had the same authority as the Old Testament Scriptures did for early Christianity. Problems related to the usage of the term "Old Testament" will be addressed in the next chapter.

the introductory formulae of the quotations in the Apostolic Fathers and the references which are made to a written authority; b) one has to distinguish whether the authority referred to is the "Lord" or it is a Gospel that had the authority of "Scripture"; c) if the reference is made to the latter, then it is likely that either our Synoptic Gospels, or apocryphal Gospels with the same status as the Synoptics, are referred to; d) if the tradition is quoted with reference to the Lord's authority then it can come from our Gospels only if one can find editorial work of an Evangelist in those passages. With regard to the last methodological point, Koester simply affirms that he presupposes the Two-Document-Hypothesis.

I think that these points are problematic. If that is so, Koester's thesis does not stand on a solid foundation. I have the following criticisms of Koester's method and thesis.

a. Introductory formulae

Koester argues that one can distinguish between references to Jesus' words and references to the writings of the New Testament as Scripture on the basis of the introductory formulae used by the Apostolic Fathers when they quote "synoptic" type traditions.

1Clement is the oldest among the documents Koester examines (4); thus it is the first among his discussions. Since he applies a method here which he then applies to all other documents, we can take Koester's analysis of the introductory formulae in 1Clement as a good case to present and discuss his views.

Koester lists the following types of quotations (4). 1) Jesus' words are quoted twice (1Clem 13,1f; 46,7f). On both occasions εἶπεν is used. 2) The Old Testament is regarded by the author of 1Clement as Scripture. The Old Testament is quoted by various introductory formulae: a) γέγραπται; b) λέγει ἡ γραφή (p.4); c) if the Old Testament is quoted by reference to a concrete person as speaker, then λέγει can be substituted by other verbs, for example, εἶπεν (p.5). From these Koester draws the conclusion that:

> λέγει is used specifically to quote 'Scripture' whereas εἶπεν is never said about γραφή. Because 1Clement introduces both its quotations of the Lord [Jesus] by εἶπεν, one can at least say: he does not quote them as γραφή.

I do not find these arguments convincing, for the following reasons. 1) Two quotations of the "Lord Jesus" may not be enough to establish a general rule how his sayings were quoted in Clement's day. However, I have to add that in the case of a living person of the past it is natural to use εἶπεν. It should not be surprising to find a formula that is different from formulae used in connection with an "impersonal" subject, the book of the Old Testament. Let us accept, then, that Jesus' sayings were introduced by εἶπεν generally.

2) Koester acknowledges that if God or the Lord is the subject of speaking in Old Testament quotations, then the verb may be εἶπεν and yet the Old Testament is quoted as "Scripture". Consequently, if Clement thought of Jesus as "Lord", he may have quoted him by εἶπεν and at the same time may have quoted him from a writing regarded as Scripture. By the time of Clement there is no reason to doubt that Jesus was thought of as God among Christians.

3) With regard to the affirmation of Koester that γέγραπται is used to quote the Old Testament, I note that the New Testament also uses this term to introduce Old Testament quotations. I suggest that the New Testament usage of the term may have influenced the Apostolic Fathers' usage when they quoted the Old Testament. The way the Apostolic Fathers quoted the Old Testament did not necessarily have to be the way they quoted the New Testament, even if they wanted to quote the New Testament as Scripture. Thus I do not accept the conclusion that the εὐαγγέλιον referred to in 2Clem 8,5 cannot be regarded as Scripture because γέγραπται is not used there (p.11).

In my opinion, Koester wants to build too much on the observation that γέγραπται is used by the Apostolic Fathers when they quote the Old Testament which they regarded as Scripture. It is true, his thesis seems to be strengthened by the evidence that it is only in Justin that we first meet γέγραπται and εὐαγγέλιον together (12). However, this observation can only be used as an argument for the thesis that the Synoptic Gospels were not regarded as Scripture prior to Justin, if it is certain that the absence of γέγραπται in a quotation formula excludes the possibility that what is quoted there is quoted as Scripture. Since I think I have been able to argue against this latter point, I cannot accept Koester's thesis as conclusive.

There is even one possible passage where γέγραπται may introduce a quotation from a Synoptic Gospel in the Apostolic Fathers: Barn 4,14 is very near in wording to Matt 22,14. Koester argues that 4Ezra 8,3 and 9,15 have a similar idea, so "Barn. könnte diesen Satz aus einer uns nicht mehr bekannten jüdischen Apokalypse entnommen haben, die für ihn kanonisches Ansehen hatte" (126). As another solution he suggests (157, n.1):

> Wenn dieses Logion nicht in irgendeiner apokryphen Schrift, die wir nicht kennen, gestanden hat, kann es dem Barn. nur über die mündliche Überlieferung zugeflossen sein; er irrt sich dann in der Zitation dieses Logions als "Schrift".

These suggestions are possible. However, they seem to be less plausible than to accept that the reference is made to Matt 22,14.

b. The "Lord" as authority

I think it is an arbitrary distinction to say that what is quoted under the authority of the "Lord" is not quoted under the authority of Scripture (e.g. 23, 65-66, 121, 241). I can accept this distinction only if the aim is to say with absolute certainty which quotation is taken from a writing regarded as Scripture.

However, we cannot exclude the possibility that a saying of Jesus is introduced by the formula "the Lord said" and at the same time it is a saying quoted from a ("Synoptic") Gospel as Scripture. It is well understandable and even probable that it was precisely the Jesus-logia tradition which was quoted most frequently from the Synoptic Gospels. Thus it is easy to understand - what even Koester had to acknowledge - that in Justin Dial 100,1 a saying of Jesus could be introduced by ἐν τῷ εὐαγγελίῳ δὲ γέγραπται εἰπών (p.12). It does not show that it is only from Justin on that we can say the written Gospel was regarded as "Scripture" - as Koester asserts (12). Rather, the very quotation shows that one cannot make a rigid distinction between the sayings of Jesus on the one hand and his sayings quoted from the written Gospels on the other.

c. When did εὐαγγέλιον first refer to a written Gospel?

Koester argues that in the New Testament and in the earlier writings of the Apostolic Fathers εὐαγγέλιον referred to the oral kerygma (6ff, 25, 126).[4] His method to prove this thesis has two key elements. First, he advances the argument concerning the requirement of the presence of γέγραπται if we want to accept that a reference was made to a scriptural authority. This argument has not proved compelling - as we have seen above. Second, Koester finds that a great majority of the early appearances of the term εὐαγγέλιον refers to the oral kerygma. The few passages where this is not obvious should be understood in the light of the overall picture. Thus even if there are passages where Koester contends that εὐαγγέλιον seems to mean a written Gospel, he decides against that option.

For example, he argues in relation to Ignatius: "Bezeichnet Ign. mit εὐαγγέλιον das Kerygma, so wird ihm der Gebrauch desselben Wortes zur

---

[4] See also his article from 1989.

Bezeichnung schriftlicher Evangelien fremd gewesen sein" (1957, 25). It is generally true that we do not regard it as probable that an author would use the same term with different meanings in the same context. However, we may not exclude the possibility that an author knew two different meanings of a word.

I also note that it happens repeatedly that Koester acknowledges an exception to his general statements. However, in these cases he seems to be willing to underestimate that one exception.[5] It is true that we normally look for "multiple attestation" for a phenomenon to be accepted as possible or real. However, one exception may be precisely this one case which refutes a generalising statement.

For example, in Ign Philad 8,2 εὐαγγέλιον may refer to a written Gospel, but on the basis of the majority of other usages Koester asserts (9): "Nach unserem bisher gewonnenen Ergebnis müssen wir annehmen, daß es sich auch hier um ein mündliches Evangelium handelt". It is, however, significant that Koester himself acknowledges that there are scholars who argue for the possibility that εὐαγγέλιον may refer to a written Gospel in this passage (p.9, in his n.1: Zahn, Klevinghaus).

In my opinion, Koester cannot prove convincingly that εὐαγγέλιον could refer to a written Gospel only from the time of Justin Martyr onwards.

d. Written Gospel(s) other than our Synoptics

When Koester finds passages that seem to refer to written sources, he tries to avoid the conclusion that εὐαγγέλιον may refer there to our Synoptic Gospels by arguing that a written εὐαγγέλιον may still be something other than a Synoptic Gospel. There are some important examples from the Didache and 2Clement where, in my opinion, Koester cannot convincingly disprove the possibility that εὐαγγέλιον may refer to a Synoptic Gospel.

Did 15, 3 and 4 employ the phrase: ὡς ἔχετε ἐν τῷ εὐαγγελίῳ. The term "you have" points to the likelihood of a written εὐαγγέλιον (Koester, 11). A problem arises from the fact that there are no actual quotations here. Rather, it seems that the author referred to a written document where the readers may look up certain practical guiding or warning statements of the Lord (211). Koester's own conclusion is that references here are made to the "free tradition" (240). The actual written "Gospel" may be a document containing "Anweisungen und Regeln" (11). Since εὐαγγέλιον up to this period

---

[5] See e.g. 1957, 65, 71; 125-126, 157, n.1 as we have seen above concerning a Barnabas passage; 172, 255.

normally refers to the "kerygma", it cannot mean one of the written Synoptic Gospels.

In my opinion, this is plausible. However, Koester's own remark may be used as an argument not only for his point, but also for the possibility that εὐαγγέλιον here refers to a Synoptic Gospel (11):

> Als schriftliches Evangelium kann das Evangelium der Did. nicht einfach das schriftlich fixierte Urkerygma gewesen sein. Solche Regeln und Anweisungen können erst im Evangelium gestanden haben, seit das schriftlich fixierte Urkerygma zu Berichten ausgebaut wurde, in die man auch die wichtigsten der dem Herrn in den Mund gelegten und als Worte des Herrn überlieferten Sprüche, Anweisungen und Regeln aufnahm, so daß die Schriften entstanden, die wir heute unter der Bezeichnung "Evangelien" kennen.

This leads me to ask: Could this process not be completed by the time of the Didache?

Concerning another important passage, 2Clem 8,5: λέγει γὰρ ὁ κύριος ἐν τῷ εὐαγγελίῳ, Koester proposes the following paraphrase (11): "Der Herr redet (gegenwärtig) aus einer vorliegenden Schrift, die Evangelium heißt". He proposes cautiously that the logion quoted after the introductory formula may originate in an "apocryphal Gospel" (101). Since the second half of the saying is identical with Lk 16,10a, Koester argues: "Auch wenn letzten Endes diesem Logion ein Evangelium, nämlich Luk., zugrunde liegt, so läßt sich der direkte Herkunftsort von 2. Clem. 8,5 doch nicht genauer bestimmen" (102).

Koester argues in a similar way concerning another passage: "Es ist nur eine einzige Stelle, an der im 2. Clem. ein Stück synoptischer Herkunft als 'Schrift' zitiert wird (2. Clem. 2,4)" (p.64). Here again he argues that a written "Gospel" may have contained sayings of Jesus. This was a "Gospel" that "was given the same respect as the Old Testament since it contained the words of the Lord" (65). Although he does not specify in detail which "Gospels" he has in mind here, he does say elsewhere in his thesis that he presupposes the existence of Q ("Spruchquelle", p.2). In other works of his he builds on the evidence of the Gospel of Thomas (1971, 1990).

I do acknowledge the possibility that churches in different geographical areas had different collections which they called "Gospels". It is perhaps even likely that one church normally had only one "Gospel" in the earlier periods. However, these written Gospels may have been regarded by them as "Scripture". If we accept that εὐαγγέλιον in the passages we have discussed refers to one of these Gospels, then we have to pursue the question further: How did the churches come to know more than one Gospel? What happened when they compared their own Gospel with that of another church? Since there came a point in history when these churches "surrendered" their Gospels to the authority of the four established ones, the historian does have a right to examine those four in contra-distinction from all other Gospels.[6]

All these theses of Koester can be maintained. However, I also have to point to another result of my discussion above: Koester's arguments do not exclude the possibility that the "Gospel" referred to in these passages as "Scripture" may have been a Synoptic Gospel.

e. Other examples for the "dissimilarity test"

Koester has found many examples for Jewish material used by the Apostolic Fathers.[7] In relation to 1Clement, Koester affirms: "Es wird an ihr deutlich, wie stark auch ein heidenchristlicher Verfasser der ersten Jahrhundertwende in der homiletischen und liturgischen Tradition der jüdischen Synagoge und der LXX stehen konnte" (1957, 4).

At another part of my thesis I should like to use this observation as an argument in the discussion whether or not the early Gentile Christians were anti-Jewish. Here this observation is used by Koester as a kind of "dissimilarity test": anything that can be found in Jewish tradition or writings could be known by the Apostolic Fathers without the knowledge of the New Testament. So if a "synoptic" tradition is Jewish, we do not have to hold that the Apostolic Fathers used the Synoptic Gospels at these points. Rather, it may be assumed that both used the same Jewish material (example from 1Clement on p. 20).

Here I have the same counter-argument as in the case of the distinction between Jesus-logia and the written Gospels. Just as it is possible that the Apostolic Fathers used Jewish sources independently from the Synoptics which also used those Jewish sources, it is in the same way possible that Jewish material was taken up by the Apostolic Fathers from the Synoptics.

What I have just observed concerning Jewish material in general can be said about Old Testament quotations, shared by the Apostolic Fathers and the Synoptics, in particular (e.g. Barnabas, p.157). An Old Testament quotation may have been known by the Apostolic Fathers independently from the New Testament's usage of that quotation. However, the Apostolic Fathers may have taken an Old Testament quotation from the New Testament (e.g. 1Clem 15,2 on p.21; see also 110).

---

[6] Cf. also G.N. Stanton, 1996.
[7] See e.g. concerning Barnabas: 1957, 136; Shepherd of Hermas: 254; in general: 258.

In a similar way to the handling of Jewish material, Koester uses a method, that I may call the "dissimilarity test", in the case of material of cultic, dogmatic, and paraenetic character.[8] Wherever he can think of the possibility of a tradition coming from sources earlier than the New Testament he argues that the Apostolic Fathers did not take that material from the New Testament (e.g. 60). However, he repeatedly acknowledges the possibility that material in the Apostolic Fathers may just as well go back to pre-synoptic tradition as it may originate in our Gospels.[9]

The "dissimilarity test" could be useful if we want to establish with absolute certainty that an idea does not come from a particular source. In as much as this is Koester's aim, I do acknowledge his use of this method. However, this test normally has to be exercised together with other tests.[10] The "dissimilarity test" has its limits. In our case, we cannot use it to exclude the possibility that the passages referred to above may have come to the Apostolic Fathers from the Synoptic Gospels.

f. "Changes"

If we accept this result, we still have to reflect on a point which is rightly emphasised by Koester in the beginning of his thesis. This regards the phenomenon that the Apostolic Fathers' texts do differ from the Synoptic Gospels at certain points. We have to face the problem: If they regarded their sources as Scripture, how could they change the text of the Synoptic Gospels?

Before I attempt an answer to this question, I point to the fact that Koester does list a number of sayings which have exact parallels in the Synoptic Gospels.[11]

In these cases Koester has to argue that in spite of the agreement in wording, the content makes it possible to hold that these sayings reached the Apostolic Fathers through ways other than the Synoptic Gospels. As an example I mention here that Koester holds that a "Christian interpolation concerning the ways" is contained in Did 1,3ff (p.217). He affirms (238): "Ein Teil der Sätze dieses Einschubs geht sicher auf Mt. und Luk. zurück" (238). He concludes that these sayings nevertheless "nicht vom Kompilator

---

[8] General method: 1957, 25; example: 209; see also 259.

[9] E.g. concerning Ignatius: 1957, 36; the case of sayings which have a general "gnomic" character: 42-43; Shepherd of Hermas: 255.

[10] As D.L. Mealand has shown in an article (1978) on this method applied to the sayings of Jesus.

[11] E.g. a part of 1Clem 13,2 - Matt 7,2b, pp.12f; 2Clem 2,4 - Mk 2,17b and Matt 9,13b, p.71; 2Clem 6,1 - Lk 16,13, p.75; part of 2Clem 8,5 - Lk 16,10a, pp.99-100.

selbst direkt aus schriftlichen Evangelien entnommen wurden, sondern innerhalb einer schon fertigen Logiensammlung auf ihn kamen" (240).

To answer the question above I draw on Koester's own views which do
leave room for the possibility that even Synoptic Gospels may have been referred to by the Apostolic Fathers from memory. Concerning 2Clem 13,4a
Koester raises the possibility that Q may be in the background (75). He also
remarks that a saying concerning love toward one's enemy may have been
familiar to a Christian even without any knowledge of a written Gospel (76).
However, Koester himself opts for the larger likelihood of a memory quotation ("gedächtnismäßige Zitation") from Lk 6, 32 and 27 here.

It is, of course, possible that the possibility of quotations made from memory may not account for all the evidence where we encounter a "change" in
the Apostolic Fathers as opposed to a Synoptic saying. In this context I have
to repeat that I have acknowledged the possibility that sayings may have
reached the Apostolic Fathers through "Gospels", treasured in different geographical areas, that were not canonised later when our four Gospels were
generally accepted as canonical. I cannot set myself the task to re-examine all
the evidence from the point of view of the "changes". For my thesis, it is significant that I have found possible weak points in Koester's arguments which
I have tried to challenge.

If Koester's thesis is right, then I would argue that my general thesis concerning the justification of the enterprise of New Testament theology can be
maintained on other grounds. However, I would lose one argument which
supports my thesis: the argument that the Synoptic Gospels can be shown to
have been regarded as Scripture from a very early period on, because they
were quoted as Scripture by the Apostolic Fathers.

To summarise my investigations up to this point, I do acknowledge that
Koester argues a plausible thesis: "synoptic" traditions could reach the Apostolic Fathers through sources different from our Gospels. However, at crucial
points the evidence he interprets is open to other interpretations. Thus Koester's
thesis does not prove to be compelling. I tentatively argue for the possibility
of maintaining another thesis: The Apostolic Fathers may have known our
Synoptic Gospels. They may also have regarded them as Scripture.

4. "Trajectories"

Koester's essays - published together with J.M. Robinson's essays - aim to
show how one can draw certain lines of development in the history of early
Christian traditions. These trajectories often start outside early Christianity

and often go beyond it. For example, with regard to the genre of the apocalypse Koester affirms (Robinson, J.M. - Koester, H., 1971, 271):

> A trajectory that will open up new perspectives has to encompass the whole range
> of literary activity from the Old Testament book of Ezekiel to the *Pistis Sophia*,
> and from the *Genesis Apocryphon* to the pre-Genesis speculations of the *Apocry-*
> *phon of John*.

I think that it is methodologically right that in a historical enterprise early
Christianity has to be seen as it was embedded in its environment and as it
was continued in later centuries. It is another question how we evaluate the
particular "trajectories" Koester proposes with regard to developments of
traditions in early Christianity. His theses are not only stated: the essays are
well argued. Thus I have to summarise Koester's main points and also to
look at his arguments.

a. Controversies in early Christianity

The essay entitled *"GNOMAI DIAPHOROI:* The Origin and Nature of Diver-
sification in the History of Early Christianity" (1971, 114-157) takes up the
1934 thesis of Walter Bauer. Koester (114) agrees with Bauer that "Christian
groups later labeled heretical actually predominated in the first two or three
centuries, both geographically and theologically". Koester works "on those
developments which begin in the earliest period" (119). With this focus on
"the apostolic age" he examines an era which "is seldom considered in Walter
Bauer's study". As I have discussed Bauer's thesis in a separate section, I
shall focus here on Koester's points.

aa) General affirmations
Basing himself on Bauer's study, which he has found to be convincing (114),
Koester asserts that the "conventional picture of early Christian history ... is
called into question" (114-115). In the beginning of his essay he makes the
following general affirmations.

   1) One has to be cautious with the labels "orthodox" and "heretical", because "they threaten to distort the historian's vision and the theologian's
judgment" (115).

   I fully accept this warning. However, there are views in early Christianity
which are closer to Jesus' teaching than others.[12] A difference does exist; and
a distinction has to be made. Historical study may find that traditions which

---

[12] See Koester's criterion below.

were labelled heretical by the orthodox in the second century were either later than the apostolic age or did not derive from Jesus' (or the apostles') teachings. The historian should not use these labels to prejudge what is right or wrong in the traditions. However, the historian may find distinctions made by people in the age that the historian is studying. In this case the historian has to report that distinction.

2) The term "canonical" cannot be used to set claims for normativeness, because the writings became "canonical" through "deliberate" collecting (115; see also 118).

I can accept this affirmation with the following qualification. As I have argued in the previous chapter, normativeness of the writings which have become canonical should not be presupposed by the historian when he embarks on his study. However, on the basis of Zahn's work I shall argue in the next chapter that certain writings were recognised as "canonical" - rather than made canonical by a deliberate, arbitrary decision - by collectors, editors, and church leaders from very early periods onward.

I propose a different definition of the term "canonical". For me the term not only designates the final "list" of books which are regarded as Scripture, but also refers to individual writings or short collections of writings which are viewed as having Scriptural authority, even prior to the date when the full "list" can be established. Canonical means: writings which were regarded as Scripture by a certain group. In accordance with this definition, historians may choose to study certain writings which were canonical in a certain period only and later lost that status. Canons of groups other than the orthodox group of Christians may also be studied. However, I have argued in connection with Bauer's thesis that historians may choose to study the canon of one particular group of Christians: the New Testament.

3) One cannot use the term "apostolic" as a criterion, because "Christian movements that were later condemned as heretical can claim genuine apostolic origin" (115).

One has to look at individual examples: In what sense do they claim to be apostolic? Do they rightly claim this? I refer to point 1): there may be a possibility of distinguishing between writings which claim to be in line with apostolic tradition; we may ask whether they are or are not in that line.

4) Christianity is a "thoroughly syncretistic religion". It follows that one should not use labels like, for example, "gnostic" with the implication that "heresies always derive from undue foreign influences" (115).

I agree with this warning. Here I simply note that the origin and often the content of Gnosticism is still a debated issue. As Koester himself writes (115-116):

There may be different opinions about the origins of Gnosticism, whether it antedated Christianity and arose out of Judaism, oriental syncretism, or Hellenistic philosophy, or whether it was an inner-Christian development in the second century.

With this just remark Koester turns, with a move significant for my thesis, to the "question of theological evaluation among such [i.e. gnostic] developments as well as elsewhere" (116).

bb) A criterion

As a criterion for the evaluation of orthodox and heretical tendencies Koester points to the "historical Jesus". The historian has to study "whether and in which way that which has happened historically, i.e., in the earthly Jesus of Nazareth, is present in each given case [of the tradition] as the criterion, not necessarily as the content, of Christian proclamation and theology" (117).

I agree with Koester that "the historical origin of Christianity lies in Jesus of Nazareth, his life, preaching, and fate" (117). Thus I accept his "criterion". However, the application of this criterion is not without problems. It leads to different results in the hands of scholars who hold different views with regard to what one can reconstruct of the "historical Jesus". It is also arguable that this criterion may not be sufficient in itself. One may add that Jesus may have shared beliefs with his disciples, for example, Jewish expectations concerning God's intervention in history. If some basic elements of these beliefs were regarded as some kind of a creed, or *regula fidei*, by a group of people, then this creed would count as a criterion.[13]

I note at this point that Koester's proposal concerning the usage of a criterion implies a theological element within the historical enterprise. Koester's thesis as a whole is similar to that of Räisänen. What Räisänen argues with regard to New Testament theology, Koester argues in relation to a related discipline, that of "introduction". Koester asserts (270):

> The distinctions between canonical and noncanonical, orthodox and heretical are obsolete. The classical "Introduction to the New Testament" has lost its scientific justification. One can only speak of a "History of Early Christian Literature."

In view of this overall agreement between their understanding of these enterprises, it is the more striking that Koester differs from Räisänen on the question of the relationship between the task of the historian and the theologian. Koester affirms that: "The theological search for the decisive criterion for distinguishing between true and false belief coincides with the historical quest

---

[13] Cf. my discussion of credal statements in chapter four.

for the essential characteristics of early Christianity as such" (116-117). As we have seen in the first chapter, Räisänen argues for a separation of the historical and the theological task.

As the title of the article indicates, Koester's aim is to look for debates and controversies in early Christianity. Following Bauer, Koester does this according to geographical areas (see also 273). I think that it is a good method. On the one hand, different cultural, ethnic, religious environments may have had an influence on the presentation of the gospel. On the other hand, we have different amounts of evidence from different areas. This calls for cautiousness not to make generalising statements about Christianity in the various regions.

cc) Palestine
With regard to Palestine Koester finds the following evidence of conflicts (120): 1) Stephen's martyrdom; 2) the Jerusalem council; 3) the incident between Paul and Peter in Antioch (Gal 2).

1) In Koester's opinion, we can detect that according to the source underlying Acts 6,1-8,5 Stephen's martyrdom led to the consequence that only the "Hellenists" were persecuted. The circle around Peter and James did not have to leave Jerusalem. This shows that "Stephen was martyred, not because he was a Christian, but because as a Christian he rejected the law and ritual of his Jewish past" (120).

However, one may argue that this latter statement may have been a false charge (cf. Acts 6,11.13). In Stephen's speech there is no indication that he did not honour Moses or the law. On the contrary, he accused his listeners of not having kept the law (Acts 7,53). If he criticises the temple, then his criticism is the same as that of the prophets - as Stephen refers to Isa 66,1. It seems to be unlikely that the reason why he was stoned would have been his rejection of the law. I do not find Koester's reconstruction of the original source behind Luke's composition convincing (see Koester, 1980, 523). I do not think that we may infer from Acts 8,1 that the reason why the apostles remained in Jerusalem was that they were not persecuted. Consequently, the passage in question does not support the distinction between law-rejecting and law-keeping Jewish Christians.

2) With regard to the Apostolic Council in Jerusalem, Koester affirms that it "could not eliminate all conflicts" (1971, 121). Koester argues from Gal 2,4 that there was a group at the council which "had not signed the agreement" (121). I think that Gal 2,4 does not necessarily mean that those people were present at the council: the council did not ask for the circumcision of Titus in spite of the fact that there were (somewhere) people who would have liked

that to happen. Acts 15 does not say that there were people who did not sign the letter. One may argue, however, that it is possible as an inference. Koester himself does not think that we can learn much about the council from Acts 15, because the passage is "stark überarbeitet" (1980, 537). He relies rather on Gal 2. I note that the relationship between these two passages is notoriously difficult to establish. We have to be careful not to build too much on what is extremely difficult to understand from the point of view of exegesis.

3) Koester affirms that what we find in Gal 2 was not simply a conflict over practice (1971, 121). There was a deeper theological disagreement. Paul could not approve of Peter's behaviour because Peter's "enlightened (Jewish-Hellenistic) attitude makes the demands of the law theologically irrelevant" (122). Peter could eat with Gentile Christians at one time and then he could "return into the observance of the law" at another (122). For Paul, "the road from law-observance to life 'in Christ' permits only one-way traffic" (121). This interpretation of Peter's behaviour seems to be in tension with what Koester asserts about him in the later part of this section. There Koester argues that Peter represents a law-observing Jewish Christianity. This can be seen in the Gospel of Matthew which represents a "development of traditions under the authority of Peter" (123).

I think that Koester's own words can be used as an argument against his interpretation of Gal 2. He acknowledges that: "Paul grants that Jews who become Christians may continue faithfully in their law observance" (122). We may add that Paul himself observed Jewish law on other occasions, for example, at the circumcision of Timothy in Acts 16,3. Thus the "one-way" argument of Koester does not stand. Perhaps, we may say that the issue at Antioch was about "hypocrisy", i.e. inconsistent behaviour on Peter's side, as Paul reported in Gal 2,13f (Koester himself mentions this, 121). We do not have to see a deeper theological disagreement here.

dd) Edessa

The study of early Christianity in Edessa has produced important results for Walter Bauer and Helmut Koester (126-127). It seems that "for several centuries Christianity in Edessa was dominated by the controversies between several major heresies". Koester has refined the picture drawn by Bauer by arguing that it was not the Marcionite Christians who came first to Edessa (127). Koester has put forward the thesis that the Thomas material preserved in Coptic (*Gospel of Thomas* and *Thomas the Contender*, found in Nag Hammadi) originated in Edessa (127ff). If this is true, then "the Thomas tradition was the oldest form of Christianity in Edessa", because these writings were known in Egypt by the second half of the second century, as the *Oxyrhynchus Papyri* testify (129).

I think that both Bauer and Koester put forward a strong case for showing that from ancient times on there were several movements in Eastern Syria which were heretical from the perspective of later triumphant orthodox views. However, they were not able to show convincingly that only the heretical movements arrived early in Edessa. Koester's main argument for this latter point is that the "Abgar legend" is "completely unhistorical" (143). It was propagated from the fourth century onwards only. Koester gives the following reason for its emergence: "the orthodox Christians invented the legend for no other purpose than to justify their claim that they had come to Edessa in apostolic times rather than around A.D. 200" (p.143, n.83).

It is generally possible that legends may arise with the purpose of legitimating a group's origin. However, this may not be likely in the case of a polemical situation. I think that it is unlikely that a "legend" invented and put forward in the fourth century could achieve the aim of showing the ancient origin of the orthodox over against the dominance of an old and strong heretical presence. The "Abgar legend" could only be a good argument in the hands of the orthodox if it had a long tradition behind it, if people were not able to refute it simply by showing that it was a "new invention". It is more likely that orthodox Christians must have been present in Edessa very early. It may also be true that they became dominant only later.

ee) Countries around the Aegean Sea
Koester argues that in the countries around the Aegean Sea there was an ongoing battle between Paul and his opponents about "the question of the continuing validity of several aspects of the religious inheritance of Judaism: the Old Testament, the law, the covenant, and Jewish tradition in general" (144). Koester holds that Paul's opponents in Galatia were "Judaizers" (144) who had a mythologized Old Testament covenant theology (145).

In Philippi Paul's opponents taught law obedience as a way "to otherworldliness and spiritual perfection" (147).

1Corinthians shows that: "The first disturbance among the Corinthians arose from a Jewish Hellenist wisdom teaching" (149). 2Corinthians displays a different controversy. Paul's opponents here "represent Jewish-Christian propaganda (2 Cor. 11:22) which understands the Christian message as the renewal of the covenant (2 Cor. 3). Christianity is the true Jewish religion" (151).

2Thessalonians (pseudepigraphical in Koester's view) testifies that a "new factor was introduced into Asia Minor" after A.D. 70: an apocalypticism of "Palestinian Jewish" origin (153).

Out of these controversies a "conservative" theology emerged in Asia Minor around A.D. 100 (p.156). This could be achieved only at a great price. The Pastorals "sell out" Pauline theology when they let the "eschatological tension of Paul's thought" disappear (156).

All these areas are discussed by Koester in a detailed, argumentative way. There can be no doubt that the above letters exhibit controversies. One has to note, however, that in each case our method can only be a reconstruction from the letters we have.[14] There is a great variety of reconstructions of what those "opponents" taught. The results are bound to be tentative. For me the question remains open: Do these controversies testify to irreconcilable theologies among the early Christians? The answer to this question can be given only on the basis of detailed exegetical work which lies outside the scope of my thesis.

b. The diversity of Gospel forms

In an article entitled "One Jesus and Four Primitive Gospels" (1971, 158-204) Koester analyses the stage of gospel tradition prior to the time when our four canonical Gospels were put into written form. He holds that the written "canonical" Gospel is a "genuinely Christian type of literature" (162). It was the credal formulations, e.g. 1Cor 15,1ff, that "have set the pattern for this literature" (161). Thus the "kerygma" of the suffering, death, and resurrection of Jesus shaped Mark and John, and the other two Gospels which were "dependent upon Mark", i.e. Matthew and Luke (162, see also 164).

Koester argues that at the oral stage, prior to the formation of Mark, there existed short collections which were not modelled after the death-resurrection pattern. These earlier forms of the "gospel" found their way into writings which are not included in the canon. However, the fact that they are early and were regarded as "gospel" material is an argument in favour of the view that there is no legitimate distinction between the canonical Gospels and non-canonical Gospels. The latter were not formed after the death-resurrection pattern; however, they were formed after a different early "gospel" material.

Like Koester, I find it very likely that there were collections prior to the formation of the canonical Gospels. I also accept that these collections had their own distinctive material. In the next chapter I shall discuss questions in connection with the developments that led to the inclusion of certain writings in a group of canonical Gospels - and to the omission of others. Here I shall summarise the points which I find problematic in Koester's article in question.

---

[14] See e.g. Koester 1980, 550-551.

1) The fact that early tradition apart from the "kerygma" of the death and resurrection of Jesus was used extensively in later non-canonical writings does not make those writings Scripture. Had those writings made use of the "kerygma" more extensively, this, in itself, would not exclude the possibility that they would have been regarded as heretical by the orthodox and therefore not included in the canon. The reason why writings were not accepted as Scripture may have been different in the case of each particular writing.

One possible reason why certain writings were not accepted as canonical may have been that those writings contained heretical material beside the traditions that were regarded as orthodox. Koester himself mentions a similar possibility. The difference between canonical and non-canonical writings may have been made on the basis of *how* this early material was used and not on the basis of the fact that it was used: "The church decided against the heretical tendencies that characterized these direct expansions of Jesus' works and words" (204).

2) In my opinion, it is not proved satisfactorily that the canonical Gospels were formed after one pattern: the kerygma of the death and resurrection of Jesus. Koester himself acknowledges that the various types of primitive collections which were "better preserved in the apocryphal gospels" also "influenced the canonical gospels" (166).

Thus Koester's detailed study of "prophetic and apocalyptic sayings" (168-175), "parables" (175-177), "I-sayings" (177-179), "wisdom sayings and proverbs" (179-184), "rules for the community" (184-187), "aretalogies" (187-193) and "revelations" (193-197) is useful for the study of the various "genres", but does not prove that there can be no distinction made in respect to canonicity among writings that have all made use of these materials. It is possible that the oldest examples of these genres had been regarded as true representations of the orthodox view. The problem of canonicity may have arisen when these genres were used extensively with heretical expansions. I do not find the view convincing that the presence or absence of certain types of traditions would account for the distinction between orthodox and heretical.

3) I do not agree with Koester's challenging view that: "The honor of having continued and developed the tradition about Jesus' original works and words must go to the more primitive gospel sources and to the apocryphal gospels" (203). If the canonical Gospels made extensive use of the kerygma, this does not prove that "theology" was more important for the orthodox Christians than "history". The presence of Christology in the canonical writings does not imply an indifference to the "historical Jesus".

c. The diversity of credal formulations

The next article in *Trajectories*, entitled "The Structure and Criteria of Early Christian Beliefs" (205-231), is related to the article I have just discussed. Its thesis is that one should not "understand the heretical diversifications of early Christianity as aberrations from one original, true and orthodox, formulation of faith" (205).

Koester points to "basic symbols of belief which, both in form and in content, are completely different from the generally known creeds" (207). According to his thesis, out of four distinctive types of beliefs and symbols, only one became "the nucleus of the orthodox creed" of the church: "the pattern of cross-resurrection" (229). However, because of the fact that the other "patterns" also go back to the earliest stages of the tradition, the "question of heresy and orthodoxy today" cannot be decided "upon the basis of any established creed as such" (230).

My criticism of Koester here would be similar to what I have said with regard to the diverging material at the stage prior to the written canonical Gospels. Again, I can refer to Koester's own counter-argument (230):

> Before it came to be what we know as the Apostles' or the Nicene Creed, various motifs from other creeds and symbols were partially incorporated ... Parallel to this development, the emerging gospel literature of the orthodox church did not restrict itself to a passion and resurrection narrative, but tried to incorporate materials which actually had heretical tendencies, according to the standards of that creed: the divine man type of miracle stories, and the future-oriented apocalyptic predications which Mark appropriated for his gospel, collections of sayings of the wise which Luke and Matthew incorporated, and the myth of Wisdom humiliated and glorified, which is a main theme of the Fourth Gospel.

If these other "patterns" were incorporated in the orthodox creed, then we might say that they were not regarded as heretical. The fact that three main motifs: "Jesus as the Lord of the future" (211-216), "Jesus as the divine man" (216-219), "Jesus as Wisdom's envoy and as Wisdom" (219-223) were developed in directions not acceptable by the orthodox, does not imply that the roots of those unacceptable developments were not shared by the orthodox.

Thus Koester's distinction among primitive beliefs and symbols does not prove that heretical beliefs are just as early as the "winning pattern", and therefore would have claims on having a place in the creed of the church: a place which would be just as legitimate as the place of the pattern "Jesus raised from the dead" (223-229).

One may rather argue that all the motifs discussed by Koester belong to early times. They became part of the creed of the orthodox and part of the canonical Gospels. It was only the heretical tendencies which developed later that were not acceptable for the orthodox. The fact that these developments could claim a connection to the early roots shared by the orthodox does not exclude that their *developments* were heretical. I would use this argument also against Koester's repetition of his thesis in 1990 (p.xxx) where he himself uses the term "developments" and "seeds".

In my opinion, it is understandable that the first three motifs discussed by Koester could more easily become the basis of heretical developments than the death-resurrection motif. However, this does not exclude the possibility that the origin of those three motifs was as orthodox as that of the death-resurrection motif. Thus, in spite of Koester's arguments, the view may be maintained that the tendencies which were later labelled "heretical" did develop from an earlier orthodox set of beliefs. I shall discuss in chapter four how far back in early Christianity we may trace the origin of an orthodox creed.

d. Koester's conclusions of the 1971 volume of essays

Apart from summarising the results of the other essays in the volume, Koester assesses "the prospect toward which these essays seem to point" (270). I refer to some of the observations that are of significance for my thesis.

1) Koester acknowledges the contribution of form criticism to our study of the "History of Early Christian Literature" (270). I agree with Koester that we have to study the "different genres of literature". However, Koester attaches too great an importance to the phenomenon that the gospel genre "has emerged more and more as a complex form to which non-Christian genres have made substantial contributions". For example, the "genre *logoi*" emerges out of the Jewish genre of the "words of the wise". The "aretalogy genre", or the "divine man literature ... appears in diverse cultural contexts" which include, for example, Philo and Philostratus. Concerning the investigation of the oral roots of this literature, Koester asserts that there is a "dependence upon pagan prototypes" on the side of the ancient church (271). These and other genres: for example, that of the apocalypse and of the apology, show Jewish and/or pagan parallels which have influenced the Christian gospel tradition.

These observations of Koester are based on studies of much non-biblical material. I can accept that Christian traditions made use of different, non-Christian, material. My problem with Koester's observations is the conclusion he wishes to build on them. He seems to imply that the phenomenon of using

these Jewish and pagan genres shows that orthodoxy and heresy were there
side by side in early Christianity. The difference between the Christian groups
was that some made use of the kerygma concerning the death and resurrection of Jesus primarily, while others drew more on Jewish and pagan genres
as mentioned above. Thus Koester concludes (273):

> It should become a general rule that the literature of the first three centuries must
> be treated as one inseparable unit. The genres of this literature and their develop-
> ment cannot be evaluated unless one is willing to work through the trajectory that
> traces the history of such a genre, both in its Christian form and in its non-
> Christian background, and regardless of the later more or less arbitrary traditional
> dogmatic, polemical, and theological classifications.

This seems to be a strong case. However, its strength is only due to the right
observations that there are diverse traditions in early Christianity and that
these traditions have made use of non-Christian genres. In my opinion, it is a
different matter whether or not Koester's actual trajectories are drawn in the
right way. They certainly form a good hypothesis.

I would argue that the presence of those non-Christian materials does not
mean that they were regarded as heretical by those Christians who first made
use of them. I argue against Koester for the thesis that orthodox Christians
may have made use of non-Christian genres. In the hands of the orthodox,
these genres served orthodox purposes. Later developments of these genres
could be labelled by the orthodox as heretical, because these developments
did not correspond to the orthodox origins.

2) Koester does not accept Overbeck's "distinction between primitive
Christian literature (*Urliteratur*) and patristic literature" (272). Koester's
main counter-argument is the role of the creeds which can be seen in the New
Testament writings as well as in later writings. Thus Koester concludes
(273):

> There is no justification for the division between "New Testament Introduction"
> and "Patrology". The same credal developments that formed the apologetic lit-
> erature also created the gospels of the New Testament.

I think it is important to note that Overbeck's main point is the distinction based
on the *genre of whole writings*. For example, he distinguishes between apostolic
letters and letters written by Christians after the apostles' time. In my opinion,
Overbeck's thesis is not refuted by the form critical affirmation that "credal
developments" formed the apologetic literature as well as the canonical Gospels, because the credal elements are smaller units than the New Testament
writings: they belong to a genre on a smaller scale. Rather, Overbeck's thesis

has to face another problem: How do canonical and non-canonical writings relate to one another when they share the same genre, for example the genre "Gospel"?

I shall discuss Overbeck's thesis in more detail in the next chapter. Here I simply put forward a counter-argument against Koester's affirmation quoted above. Koester's statement implies that the presence of "credal developments" in the earliest and in subsequent Christian theology makes it impossible to distinguish between the theology of the New Testament writings and later theology. I would argue that there is much material taken from the New Testament in later theology, not only the credal formulae, that played an important role in later theology. However, the church fathers of the third century (or the Reformers who produced new credal statements) did not think of themselves as writing canonical Scripture. I shall argue in the next chapter that, unlike these later theologians, the authors of the New Testament intended to write with an authority that was on the same level as the authority of the Old Testament.

3) Koester further argues that there was a "close relationship between distinct Christian developments and the particular cultural conditions in limited geographical areas" (276). For example, he tries to show that "Greek culture, mediated through Hellenistic Judaism and documented in its Scripture, namely the Greek translation of the Old Testament, played a much less significant role in North Africa than in Rome" (276). I agree with Koester (273) that Walter Bauer's method of discussing the history of Christianity according to geographical areas has been a good proposal. It may also be true that Christianity had to meet different environments in the different areas and had to respond to different problems. As Koester puts it: "New and different types of Christianity developed in areas in which either the Hellenization of Judaism was superficial or where there was no visible connection between the rise of Christianity and Jewish communities" (275). However, I find the term "different types of Christianity" challenging. It may imply opposing theologies in different geographical areas.

The differences between theological views may range from polarity to actual contradiction. To establish the presence of differences does not say much about controversies. It needs to be discussed in detailed exegetical historical studies whether or not the differences amount to contradictions. In the case of contradictions there is still another possibility: the contradictions may be views of the orthodox and those of the heretics. It is only the contradictions among orthodox Christians that would present a challenge to the possibility of New Testament theology as an enterprise. The major examples of these possible contradictions will be discussed in chapter four.

4) Koester's final thesis in his conclusion is that we have a hermeneutical problem when we try to test critically whether what has been said in Christian

theology actually corresponds to the historical Jesus. All theological formulations (including those which claim to be revealed truths) are subject to "historical conditioning" (277). So are "the historical life, words, and works of a purely human man, Jesus". Even "the language of the most primitive credal formulation is already historically conditioned" (278).

In Koester's view, this "conditioning" causes a "conflict between the historical particularity of Jesus' life, work, and death, on the one hand, and the cultural and religious expectations and ideologies available in a certain culture to express the meaning of that life, on the other" (279). I think Koester applies this to the earliest affirmations about Jesus in the kerygma as well as to later theological affirmations - perhaps up to the present day -, although he does not say so explicitly. Concerning his discussion of the criterion of the historical Jesus, I have two remarks.

On the one hand, I do acknowledge the difficulty of solving the "problem of the relationship between Jesus and early Christian history" (279). Whether or not the "problem" is actually a "conflict" may remain a matter of discussion. For my thesis it is significant that Koester can see a connection between the historical and the theological enterprises. He asserts (279): "The investigation of this history and the analysis of the structures of these conflicts and of the tendencies of its language is the place where the endeavors of the historian, the theologian, and the interpreter are identical". I think Koester would include scholars from the whole history of Christianity up to the present in the circle of "interpreters". For me it is important that he also includes the early Christian authors. Although I do not define New Testament theology as referring to the theology of the modern interpreter, this view of Koester lends some support to my thesis: the phenomenon of orthodoxy and heresy in early Christianity invites us to study the theology of the early Christians, as historians. I would differ from Koester, however, in one point. I hold that the enterprise of studying the theology of various canons of the early Christians, and thus also that of the New Testament canon, can also be justified.

On the other hand, I strongly disagree with Koester's position in regard to what we may say about the historical Jesus. When Koester wants to use the historical Jesus as a criterion to test theological affirmations, Koester seems to approve of the following trend of the work of historians (278):

> Historical scholarship tends to focus on those undigested blocks of information about Jesus which are relatively reliable precisely because they did not quite fit the perspectives and theological views of those Christian writers who, unwittingly, happened to preserve such traditions.

Here I have the same difficulty as I have pointed to in relation to Koester's doctoral thesis: the test of "uncensored information" (278) is good to find out what we can say about Jesus with certainty. However, material which does not pass the "dissimilarity test" may also be original Jesus tradition. As an illustration for his views, Koester suggests that the following could be said about the historical Jesus with reasonable certainty (278):

> Jesus had normal human parents, Joseph and Mary. He was baptized by John, whom he called the greatest among all men. He ate with prostitutes and tax collectors. He demanded that each man love his enemies. He was crucified under Pontius Pilate.

For me the question arises: As historians, are we not able to say anything about what Jesus thought about God? Or, about the relationship he thought he had with God? Koester insists that a believer should be held "accountable" for the "human dimension of Jesus" (278). He also asserts that Christian faith is "faith in Jesus" (279), but this can only mean in Koester's terms a faith in Jesus, the "purely human man" (277). Why should we have faith in someone who did not intend that we should have faith in him or who did not evoke faith in himself? We shall meet this problem again when we discuss the problem of the unity of the theology of the New Testament in chapter four.

Before I summarise the results of my discussion of Walter Bauer's and Helmut Koester's theses, I shall first point to a recent criticism of them by T.A. Robinson.

5. The Bauer Thesis re-examined

In a work based on his doctoral thesis, Thomas A. Robinson offers more than the title of his book promises. In *The Bauer Thesis Examined* (1988), he not only deals with the relationship of orthodoxy and heresy in early Christianity by testing Walter Bauer's thesis, but he also discusses the theses by which Helmut Koester has developed Bauer's ground-breaking work. Much of Robinson's critical observations strengthen the criticism I have presented in this chapter. Let us consider some further points which argue that the history of early orthodoxy and heresy may have been different from what Bauer's and Koester's reconstructions suggest.

a. Method

T.A. Robinson's starting point is to examine the view of Eusebius expressed in his *Ecclesiastical History*. Robinson summarises Eusebius's "view of the history of the primitive church" in this way (4): "orthodoxy had credible apostolic roots, whereas heresy lacked such primitive roots and credible parentage". To start with, Robinson has a negative and a positive critical remark concerning Eusebius's picture. On the one hand, Robinson generally agrees with the judgement of the scholarship of the last century (3). This criticism relates to two areas (2):

> First, the [traditional] view has been blind to the tolerated presence in the first century of views judged as heresy by the second-century orthodox church. Second, the view has been blind to the competing diversities in first-century theological interpretations of the Christian message ...

On the other hand, Robinson asserts that "with some fairness to Eusebius it must be noted that a similar view of the purity of the early church was held by every second and third century catholic writer whose writings are known to us" (5). Here he not only refers to Irenaeus and Ignatius (5), but also to Origen whom some would see as an exception (8). Robinson affirms: "Origen, as clearly as any church Father, denied to the heretics of the second and third centuries any right to their claim to authentic tradition or apostolic parentage ..."

Robinson then goes on to criticise Bauer's thesis on the following points. Firstly, Bauer was only able to show that Eusebius's reconstruction of early church history is "defective" (28). Bauer's own method is not able "to offer a satisfactory reconstruction" of that history either, because it "lacks sufficient sensitivity for the way in which diverse elements can be united into a non-contradictory unity" (29). Secondly, Bauer has not proved convincingly that heresy was not only early but strong as well (28).

To argue for this second criticism, Robinson proposes that not every geographical area Bauer has discussed is really useful for the confirmation of Bauer's thesis. Robinson limits the scope of inquiry by two criteria (41): 1) we can expect a result that is more than mere hypothetical reconstruction only if we have "extensive literature" in the early period within a geographical area; 2) the question of orthodoxy and heresy has to be addressed in that area "in a useful way".

b. *Places not suitable for the Bauer Thesis*

On the basis of these criteria T.A. Robinson argues that most of the cities or areas Bauer has studied do not provide sufficient evidence upon which he could firmly build his thesis. For example, Edessa provides "the least literary evidence" (45). With regard to the Marcionite heresy in Edessa, Robinson makes a strong point: Marcion's message is more likely to have appealed to a "catholic" Christian audience than to pagans (49-50). Robinson asserts (51): "We may say that in order to sustain itself, Marcionism required a Christian audience rooted in its Jewish heritage". Consequently, the very appearance of the Marcionite heresy in Edessa is an argument for the presence of some form of orthodoxy which Marcion's followers may have intended to change or re-form.

Robinson (52) also argues against Koester's proposal according to which the original form of Christianity in Edessa was not Marcionism but a non-orthodox Thomas tradition. Robinson's main counter-arguments are the following. Firstly, from the presence of the *Gospel of Thomas* in Edessa or in the Osrhöene in the late second century does not follow that the document was composed in that area (54). Secondly, the fact that the Manichaeans of that area regarded the *Gospel of Thomas* highly only indicates "that the Gospel was *known* in the Osrhöene by the middle of the third century. It indicates nothing about the locale of origin of the *Gospel of Thomas* nor does it indicate the date of the composition of the Gospel" (55). Thirdly, the precise character of the *Gospel of Thomas* is still a matter of dispute (57). Since it may have gone "through a number of editions", the fact that it was known in the second half of the second century does not help us to have an insight into the nature of early Christianity in that area.

As an example of using the criterion that the question of orthodoxy and heresy has to be addressed in an area if we want to have an insight into the character of early Christianity in that area, I think that Robinson has succeeded in refuting Bauer's case for Corinth. Firstly, Robinson argues that we cannot simply suppose that the Corinthian situation in the time of Paul was the same as the situation some forty years later when 1Clement was addressed to the Corinthians (70-71).

Secondly, if we view 1Clement in itself, there is nothing "that would indicate a theological issue was at the heart of the conflict" (71). Robinson argues that the dispute in Corinth was over the relationship between the "young" and the aged (75). He proposes that there was a "second or third-generation discontent": certain young people wanted to gain "positions of authority" (76). It is not necessary to "add a theological dimension to this dispute" (77). Thus I agree with Robinson's conclusion that the problem reflected in 1Clement "is not clearly enough a theological one ... to make the area of Corinth attractive for working out the questions of the orthodoxy/heresy debate".

Robinson carries out a similar criticism of Bauer's choice of areas concerning Egypt (59ff), Rome (77ff), (Jerusalem (85ff), which is Strecker's suggestion as an area for the discussion in the second edition of Bauer's work), and Antioch (87ff). It is important to note with Robinson (see e.g. 91) that it is not the making of hypothetical reconstructions which is criticised in Bauer's work. What is problematical in Bauer's enterprise is the thesis concerning early and strong heresy. The evidence, and the hypothetical reconstruction, are not strong enough to bear the thesis built upon them.

c. *The best test case: Ephesus*

On the basis of the criteria mentioned above, T.A. Robinson argues that Ephesus and western Asia Minor are areas in relation to which we may fruitfully test the Bauer Thesis.

Robinson points to the widely held view that "numerous writings of the [New Testament] canon reflect an Asia Minor context" (97). This geographical area made an important contribution "toward the development of a monarchical church structure, which came to be universally accepted in the Christian church" (100). These two phenomena played "a key role in drawing lines between the orthodox and the heretic". The "astounding" amount of literary evidence (101) together with the fact that much of this evidence "addresses the question of orthodoxy and heresy" (102) make Asia Minor the best candidate for testing the Bauer Thesis (see also 121).

Robinson makes the following strong points against the thesis of Bauer that there was an early and strong heresy in western Asia Minor.

1) Robinson (125, 130) first attacks Bauer's hypothesis that there was an alliance in the seventies in the first century between anti-gnostic Pauline Christians who lived in that area and Jewish Christian "immigrants" who moved there from Palestine after the destruction of the Jerusalem temple. This hypothesis supports Bauer's thesis in as much as it posits a gnostic heretical presence against which that alliance occurred. However, it also creates a problem for Bauer: the emergence of such an alliance would "indicate an early ... sense of 'orthodoxy' for a significant segment of the church" (139).

2) Robinson (145) then points to the weakness of Bauer's argument that the seer of the Apocalypse did not address other churches of the same area because he would not have had authority there. As another possibility, Robinson argues that "the Apocalyptist was limited by his peculiar message". He does not find Bauer's other argument strong either; according to this argument the reason why Ignatius did not address certain churches was that in those places the "heretics controlled the church" (151). Robinson argues that the seven Ignatian letters had an "occasional nature" (154). They all had a

more or less direct connection with the church at Smyrna (155, 157), so that they may even be called a "*Smyrnaean* corpus of the Ignatian letters" (156). Thus one cannot prove the presence of strong heresy by pointing to churches to which the seer of the Apocalypse and Ignatius did not write (see also 161).

3) Finally, Robinson argues against Bauer's proposal that the very fact that the "monarchical office" was introduced in western Asia Minor "suggested widespread heresy in the area" (163). Robinson claims that (170):

> Bauer's view that the orthodox were weak does not do justice to the strength that the orthodox seem to have had, for they apparently were able to push through a decision radically altering the structure of power in their favour, so that the chief authority came to rest in the hands of one of their own members.

Furthermore, Ignatius not only supported the office of the bishop, but also that of the presbytery (175). Bauer's thesis is made highly unlikely on the basis of the evidence that "for Ignatius, the presbytery was basically free of error and clearly in harmony with the bishop" (176). Thus it is unlikely that the heretics could have controlled the presbytery against which the authority of the bishop would have been affirmed by a minority orthodox group.

Thus Robinson concludes that "it is the catholic community, not the gnostic, that represents the character of the majority in western Asia Minor in the early period (and this seems not to be any different for the later period)" (203). If this conclusion is right, then it will have wider implications for the whole of the Bauer Thesis (204):

> The failure of the Bauer Thesis in western Asia Minor is not merely one flaw in an otherwise coherent reconstruction. The failure of the thesis in the only area where it can be adequately tested casts suspicion on the other areas of Bauer's investigation.

In this section I have summarised some points of T.A. Robinson's detailed study which support my criticism of Bauer. Let me now summarise the main results of this whole chapter.

6. Conclusion

In this chapter I have discussed some of the major challenges brought against the distinction between canonical and non-canonical writings. The majority of these challenges are in relation to the problem of distinguishing between orthodoxy and heresy.

I have briefly discussed the general thesis that historians have no right to distinguish between canonical and non-canonical writings, because they have to deal with all available evidence. I have affirmed that it is true that historians have to analyse all evidence in relation to their field. However, I have argued that the evidence may call for the acknowledgement of certain groups of writings as distinct from other writings or groups of writings. In the following chapter I shall discuss the question whether or not the New Testament canon has to be recognised by historians as a group of writings that stands apart from other writings because of historical phenomena.

I have examined the major thesis of Walter Bauer that in some geographical areas the earliest form of Christianity was one that was regarded as heresy from the point of view of second century (and later) orthodox Christianity. I have concluded that Bauer has not proved his thesis convincingly. In this criticism I have found support in a thorough examination of the Bauer Thesis by T.A. Robinson. He has shown that the Bauer Thesis proves to be indefensible in the area of western Asia Minor - an area from where we have sufficient evidence for the discussion of orthodoxy and heresy. Robinson's work also suggests that the Bauer Thesis could be even less convincingly based on the discussion of areas about which we have little evidence. Thus the traditional view may be maintained that heresy was later than orthodoxy.

Since Helmut Koester has revived and developed the Bauer Thesis, I have discussed Koester's theses in some detail. Concerning the question whether or not the Synoptic Gospels were known to the Apostolic Fathers, I have argued that Koester wants to build too much on the mechanical usage of a criterion: in his opinion, the introductory formulae would show whether or not a reference to "synoptic" type traditions was made as a reference to Scripture. I have acknowledged that Koester has a strong case. His thesis may be a plausible one. However, I have tried to show that the evidence may also be explained in a way that the thesis may be maintained: the Apostolic Fathers may have known the Synoptic Gospels.

Should Koester's thesis turn out to be right, my thesis would only lose one possible supporting argument for showing that the formation of canonical collections (for example, that of the Gospels) started very early. My case for justifying the enterprise of New Testament theology would not be ruled out.

I have discussed the theses of Koester in which he argues for trajectories that include early heretical views alongside orthodox ones. In his opinion, what was later labelled heretical grew out of traditions and genres which were as early as those adopted by the orthodox. This means that we should abandon the differentiation between orthodoxy and heresy. The difference between the two groups is simply that orthodoxy "won" and rejected later what was in fact a parallel phenomenon to itself from the earliest periods onward.

Here again we have met a strong case. The fragmentary character of the evidence makes it possible to fill in the line of the trajectories in more than one way. I have argued that Koester's trajectories are not compelling. The view may be maintained that the earliest traditions were all, or largely, orthodox. It may, however, be true that orthodoxy made use of non-Christian forms and genres. Some of these genres were of a nature that lent itself to speculative meditations and developments. Some of these later developments were rejected as heretical by the orthodox, who kept the continuity from the earliest periods of the tradition.

Thus it is a justifiable enterprise to differentiate between developments of traditions that were in line with the earliest forms of the tradition and those that were not. Just as there may be a valid historical distinction between orthodox and heretical ideas, there may be a valid distinction between the writings, or groups of writings, of the orthodox and the heretics. We may argue for the distinction of a canon in our historical enterprise, the theology of the New Testament.

In the following chapter we have to answer further major challenges brought against the case for confining the enterprise of New Testament theology to the New Testament canon. While doing this we may also find some positive arguments for focusing on the canon in a historical enterprise.

Chapter Three

Can the Canon Be Justified?

1. Introductory remarks

In the previous chapter I have argued for the justification of the distinction between early Christian groups which held "orthodox" views and those which held "heretical" ones. This distinction may be made by the historian if he finds that early Christians also made that distinction, even if they did not use this terminology at a very early stage. I have argued that if Christian groups, orthodox or heretical, set apart certain writings which were regarded by them as Scripture, then the historian will be justified in studying the content of any particular group of writings in contra-distinction from other writings or groups of writings.

In this way I have theoretically prepared the way for examining the historical questions: Did the early Christians have a canon? When did the Christian community develop their canon? Can the enterprise of New Testament theology justify the first part of its name? In other words: Can a historian justify the study of the theological content of the New Testament canon?

a. On methodology

In this chapter I shall turn to major arguments which have been put forward for and against the canon of the New Testament. My procedure has to include two types of arguments. On the one hand, I have to examine arguments in relation to the reconstruction of the history of the development of the New Testament canon. This we may call the study of the "external" evidence. On the other hand, I have to examine the questions: What did the early Christian authors think of the authority of their writings? What did they think of the relationship of their own writings to other early Christian writings? This study has to rely on the contents or implications of the writings themselves. The arguments brought forward from the writings may be referred to as the examination of the "internal" evidence.

In the first two chapters we have discussed challenges to the enterprise of writing a New Testament theology in one way only. We have looked at the challenges from the point of view of whether or not they are compelling. From now on the discussion takes a two-way direction. We shall continue to encounter further challenges and discuss their strengths and weaknesses. However, I shall make an attempt to look at the evidence from the point of view of how my thesis can be substantiated by positive arguments.

In accordance with the nature of this thesis, these arguments can only be dealt with by way of examples. To deal with all the arguments would mean to carry out an exegetical study of the whole New Testament. This would go far beyond what I can actually achieve within the limits of this thesis. A detailed study of our theme would involve what can only be done in exegetical commentaries and in actual attempts at writing New Testament theology. However, some examples of the sort of facts on which one may build a New Testament theology have to be given during the course of this chapter. Since the theses I put forward in the following are formulated in a general way, I do acknowledge that they would need more proof than the exemplifying treatment here provided.

b. On the discussion of Theodor Zahn's contribution

In this chapter I frequently refer to arguments of Theodor Zahn. His analyses of the evidence in relation to the canon are, in my opinion, unduly neglected. He has completed one of the most detailed summaries of the history of the canon, if not *the* most detailed one.[1] We may find it helpful to refer to his views in some of the sections of this thesis.

It goes without saying that one has to be careful when adopting some of his views. On the one hand, his writings come to us from around the turn of the century. We have to take into consideration new evidence - and the development of scholarship - which has emerged since his time.

On the other hand, nineteenth century scholarship may have had methodological procedures which are not acceptable today. For example, Wilhelm Schneemelcher (1991a, 19) warns us in connection with Zahn's and Harnack's discussions that their "controversy makes it clear that we can scarcely do justice to the process of the formation of the canon on the basis of preconceived categories".

We also have to bear in mind that Zahn's work may be said to have had "an apologetic tendency" (Schneemelcher, 1980, 23). This does not have to

---

[1] See his contribution to the numerous volumes of *Forschungen zur Geschichte des neutestamentlichen Kanons und der altkirchlichen Literatur*, 1881-1900.

mean that we cannot use his studies as a starting point. However, we have to draw criticisms of him developed by other scholars and some further arguments of others into the discussion.

Acknowledging these due cautions I draw into the discussion some of Zahn's arguments, because I think that he has provided us with valuable work not only in terms of collecting the available evidence, but also in regard to his detailed argumentation for a possible reconstruction of the history of the canon.

2. Is the canon a late decision of the church?

William Wrede has challenged the restriction of New Testament theology to the canonical writings. He has affirmed that (1897, 11; ET: 1973, 70-71):

> The statement that a writing is canonical signifies in the first place only that it was pronounced canonical afterwards by the authorities of the second- to fourth-century church, in some cases only after all kinds of hesitation and disagreement.

From this he concludes that "anyone who accepts without question the idea of the canon places himself under the authority of the bishops and theologians of those centuries". This means that the church created the canon by the decision of certain "governing theologians and bishops"; and their decision "cannot be decisive for us" (1909, 138-139). Räisänen summarises the final consequence of this view when he affirms that it is "arbitrary" to limit the scholar's work of interpretation to the New Testament canon (1990, 100).

Wrede builds his challenging thesis on the historical evidence that we do not have a canon agreed on by all parts of the church during those centuries. He is also right in pointing to the usage of the term "canon"; we have only late evidence of the term being used to determine the list of the books belonging together as the second part of the church's Scripture alongside the Old Testament.

However, these two correct observations do not necessarily lead to the conclusion that the New Testament canon is a rather late decision of the church. With a similar criticism Robert Morgan remarks that it is "by no means obviously true" that the acceptance of the "idea of the canon" equals putting oneself under the authority of the early church leaders (1973a, 3).

Wilhelm Schneemelcher (in a general introductory article of the revised edition of the *New Testament Apocrypha*) affirms that the first attestation of the term "canon" for the Bible is in the middle of the fourth century, in Canon LIX of the Council of Laodicea (1991a, 10). He also points to the well-known fact that the first appearance of the list of the twenty-seven books we have today in our New Testament canon dates from 367, the 39th Festal Letter of Athanasius of Alexandria.

However, Schneemelcher argues the case for saying that the collection of these twenty-seven writings "was not created by any decree of Church government, but grew together in a long process" (33). He argues in the following way.

In 4Macc 7,21 (and also in Philo) κανών is used "in the general Greek sense": it is "the rule, the precept, indeed almost the law" (p.10). In the New Testament (Gal 6,16; 2Cor 10,13.15.16) the word "is probably used with the meaning of 'norm, rule of conduct, standard' ..." (p.11; we may add that in 2Cor the meaning may be also in connection with the "field" God has assigned to Paul for his ministry, see RSV). In the second half of the second century the term is "more frequently employed [in the church], and especially in the phrases κανὼν τῆς ἀληθείας and κανὼν τῆς πίστεως". Schneemelcher proposes that "the term canon as a designation for the Church's Bible was suggested by the history of its meaning within the Church" (12). On the basis of the evidence he concludes that (11): "The word κανών presented itself as a designation that could express unmistakably what ecclesiastically was now [i.e. in the second century] obligatory".

In this thesis I also propose that we should not simply use the term "canon" in the sense of "list". Rather, we should use the term "canonical" for writings which were regarded as being on the same level as the Old Testament Scripture by the early Christians. At this stage I simply note that we may use the term "Scripture" here with due caution for "in neutestamentlicher Zeit war die Heilige Schrift keine für alle Kreise des Judentums identische Größe" (Hübner 1990, 44). I shall also have to discuss the question: What was the ("Old Testament") Scripture of the early Christians?

In another context, Zahn has put forward an argument that may be also used against the view that the creation of the canon was a "decision" of certain church leaders. In volume II.1 (1890) of his *Geschichte des Neutestamentlichen Kanons* (1888-1892) he discusses the lists of the canonical writings. On the basis of the varied orders of the books Zahn comes to the conclusion that (383):

... die Zusammenfassung der ntl. Schriften zu einem sinnlich sich darstellenden Ganzen im kirchlichen Altertum nicht ein Gegenstand kirchlicher Berathungen und Satzungen, sondern Sache der Buchhändler, der Schreiber und ihrer Arbeitgeber gewesen ist.

On the basis of these points of Schneemelcher and Zahn, I conclude that Wrede's affirmation in question is not convincing. It does contain correct historical observations, but from those it does not follow that the canon of the New Testament is a late decision of the church. It is, rather, necessary to examine the complex process which led to the final result of our twenty-seven book New Testament canon. In this thesis our aim can only be that of examining key arguments in relation to this historical process. When I retain the name "canonical" in this context, it simply refers to the process during which the New Testament writings became part of the "list" of the canon. I shall also have to discuss what factors contributed to the "canonical process" at the end of which we have the list of the New Testament canon.

3. Some aspects of the history of the New Testament canon

In his article on the process of the canonisation ("Kanonisierung") of the New Testament, W.G. Kümmel points to J.H. Semler's work, *Abhandlung von freier Untersuchung des Kanons* (1771/75), as a starting point from which it has been a matter of scientific inquiry "wie es zu der Begrenzung des NT auf 27 Schriften gekommen ist" (1957a, 1131). According to Kümmel's summarising note, Semler has shown that "die schließlich anerkannte Sammlung das Resultat einer durch verschiedenartige Einflüsse und Entscheidungen bestimmten längeren Entwicklung gewesen sei". I have argued in the previous section that these "decisions" were not simply the decisions of certain late synodal meetings. However, it is true that during the process of canonisation "decisions" were involved. Our problem is that it is difficult to trace those decisions to particular individuals, or even groups, at particular times.

a. The difficulty of reconstruction

Kümmel formulates the problem we have to face in our inquiry into the history of the canon in this way (1957a, 1131):

> Weil aber zur Aufhellung dieser Geschichte außer den ausführlichen Darlegungen des Eusebius von Cäsarea nur vereinzelte Angaben der Kirchenväter und schwer datierbare Kanonsverzeichnisse zur Verfügung stehen, läßt sich diese Geschichte nur in großen Zügen und, besonders was die inneren Triebkräfte anbetrifft, nur vermutungsweise aufhellen.

In spite of this warning, a certain confidence developed during the 1960s concerning what we may know about the history of the canon. The major monograph of H.F. von Campenhausen, *Die Entstehung der christlichen Bibel* (1968) may be regarded as an expression of a consensus of opinion of that era. Ernst Käsemann (1970a, 9) affirmed with reference to that work that:

> Über die Entstehung und Geschichte des neutestamentlichen Kanons sind wir vortrefflich informiert.

W. Schneemelcher (1980, 22) does not share Käsemann's confidence. Schneemelcher rather agrees with a statement of Lietzmann that the history of the canon is one of the most complicated parts of church history. Lietzmann made that remark in 1907. It seems that there remain many controversial points in the history of the canon up to our present day.

Zahn's work is no exception from Kümmel's remark concerning the necessarily hypothetical character of any attempt in this area of study. However, Zahn's analyses of the evidence and his proposals concerning the major stages of the history of the canon may be the starting point of our present discussion.

b. *From later to earlier sources*

In the first volume of his *Geschichte des Neutestamentlichen Kanons* (1888-1892) Zahn asserts that it is only from the beginning of the third century onwards that we have sufficient material about changes - additions and omissions - in connection with the question, which books belonged to the New Testament (vol. I.1: 1888, p.1). Consequently, Zahn adopts the method of searching backwards from the later to the earlier (2). He first discusses the period in which one can establish data with reasonable certainty. Then he moves to earlier periods. This working method is combined with another methodological thesis of Zahn: he looks in earlier periods for views that differ from what he has found in the later periods which are better attested with evidence.

I have not met any major challenge to the method of moving from later sources to earlier ones.[2] I can agree on it in general terms. I think it is a good method to describe the situation of an age for which we have sufficient evidence and then to look for indications of changes in earlier periods. If we arrive at a negative result in looking for changes, this may support the case that there was no substantial change in the canon.

However, we have to bear in mind that we have very little evidence from earlier periods in which we have to search for witnesses of a change. Our results will not be more than hypotheses - as Zahn himself acknowledges (1888, 2). Since any attempt to reconstruct the history of the canon in the first two

---

[2] I note that F. Overbeck had also proposed this method in 1880; see 1965, 72.

centuries is bound to be hypothetical, the hypothetical character of this particular method should not discourage us from using it.

Zahn asserts that in the last two decades of the second century and in the first decade of the third century we find rich sources for research (3). The situation of the church and the validity of the New Testament writings were reasonably stable and established ("wesentliche Gleichmässigkeit und Abgeschlossenheit") by that time. We have to discuss in another section the implications of the qualification "wesentlich" ("essential"). Harnack, who prepared a major critical answer to Zahn's work, accepted this period as a starting point (1889, 6). I also accept the general statement that the period in question is a suitable starting point.

According to Zahn, in this period two major controversies have to be taken into consideration in relation to the history of the canon: the dispute over the correct time of celebrating Easter; and the Montanist movement (1888, 3). With regard to the first, Zahn affirms that the controversy did not involve differing views about the content of the canon. Rather, a question was answered differently on the basis of "einem örtlich beschränkten kirchlichen Herkommen und einer dadurch beherrschten verschiedenen Auslegung der Evangelien". Zahn argues that none of the parties involved in the dispute changed their opinion concerning the New Testament, or even a part of it, during or after the discussion.

Concerning the Montanists, Zahn argues that the fact that they produced their own sacred writings does not mean that they did not acknowledge the fact that the church had its sacred writings. The Montanists thought their writings superseded those of the church, i.e. "die beiden älteren Testamente. Aber indem man das behauptete, bekannte man sich zu diesen" (20). It is true that over against the view of the Montanists the catholic church emphasised the limits of the New Testament canon. However, it is important to see that the Montanists did not intend to change the canon of the church or to add their writings to the writings of the church (21). Their new revelation required a new set of sacred writings. By this point Zahn (12) answers Harnack's argument according to which the Montanist movement could not have emerged had there been an agreed authoritative canon in the church. Zahn emphasises that the church's controversy against the Montanists has not changed the contents of the canon of the church in the period A.D. 170-220 (p.22).

Zahn further argues against the view that the Montanist movement could not have emerged had there been a strong presence of a New Testament canon by pointing to the fact that there is not a long period between the Montanist movement's origins and Irenaeus's activity. In Zahn's opinion, the movement started around A.D. 156 (p.4). Maximilla, the last Montanist prophetess, died around 179 (p.8). Irenaeus wrote "his only main work that exists today" in the time of bishop Eleutherus (A.D. 174-189) i.e. around the time of the death of Maximilla (p.13). Irenaeus's work shows a high authority of the New Testament canon (12). Since there is no "Zwischenzeit" between Irenaeus and the beginnings of the Montanist movement, during which time the canon may have reached that authority (12), Zahn concludes that (13):

> ... alle ... Vorstellungen von einem plötzlichen Entstehen oder Auftauchen oder Anerkanntwerden des neutestamentlichen Kanons in irgend einem Zeitpunkt der zweiten Hälfte des zweiten Jahrhunderts das Gegentheil der handgreiflichen Wirklichkeit sind.

In my opinion, Zahn's conclusion is in agreement with a general historical observation: historians generally look for precedents, causes, or roots in connection with new historical phenomena. Sudden changes in history require a very strong influence or reason. Thus Zahn's conclusion may be right. However, it has to face another major objection from a somewhat earlier period. Historians point to Marcion's activity as one that evoked a "sudden", quick answer on the side of the catholic church: the formation of the New Testament canon. We have to turn to this thesis next.

c. *The role of Marcion in the history of the canon*

Von Campenhausen summarises a widely accepted view when he affirms that in the middle of the second century the situation of the church became "critical" because of the emergence of "false teachers" and "sects" (1970, 115-116). It was "urgent" that the catholic church should do something "wenn der Name Christi noch etwas bedeuten und das Christentum im religiösen Synkretismus der Zeit nicht untergehen sollte" (116). Marcion produced his own canon. With reference to Marcion, von Campenhausen asserts:

> ... und erst im Gegenschlag gegen dessen Kanon und in der Auseinandersetzung mit ihm entsteht dann auch in der Großkirche verhältnismäßig schnell die Vorstellung und dann auch der klare Umriß unseres heutigen "Neuen Testaments".

This position corresponds with the thesis of A. Harnack "in modifizierter Form" (Schneemelcher, 1980, 24). However, it has not been accepted by all critical scholars. For example, H. Braun's following affirmation may be used as an argument against the view that the church created the canon as an answer to Marcion's canon (1962, 311):

> Marcions zweiteiliger Kanon hat die offizielle kirchliche Entwicklung, d. h. die
> Autorität von Kyrios *und* Apostolos, zwar beschleunigt, aber nicht überhaupt erst
> eingeleitet; hier ist Harnacks These zu modifizieren.

Schneemelcher has argued that the pre-history ("Vorgeschichte", "Vorstufen") of the emergence of the New Testament "spricht eher gegen die über-
ragende Bedeutung Marcions" (1980, 37). He concedes that it is probably
not possible to reach a definitive decision on this matter. I accept this caution
that the sources may be explained in different ways. However, I point briefly
to Zahn's argumentation in relation to our question without implying that his
contribution could solve the problem.

Zahn makes the following key moves:

1) Marcion's time is the last period of the canon of the church which is in
clear light (vol. I.2: 1889, 586). Marcion held that the message of the gospel
was distorted (650). This distortion had happened already in the time of Paul
(593, 652). Marcion fought against the Christian tradition and against the
Scripture of the church, but from that it can be seen that he did acknowledge
what was the canon of the church (595, 626ff, 637ff, 653, 663, 671).

Although I acknowledge that this is not an overall convincing argument, I
think it is a good point.

2) Marcion used a Gospel text of "Lukan type". This text had already been
influenced by the Gospels of Matthew and Mark. Consequently, these three
Gospels had to be there in the practice of the church decades earlier: ca. in
the beginning of the second century (675).

This point is a highly controversial one. The interrelationship of the Synoptic Gospels is still hotly debated, involving opposing views with regard to
the questions: Which Gospel used which? Did they use one another at all? If
they did, did they use the versions which we have today?[3]

3) Although Marcion used Luke, Marcion's Gospel differs from Luke's
Gospel. The majority of differences are due to Marcion's theological interests
(704). It was Marcion who made the changes. We do not need the hypothesis
that Luke was edited by a "catholic" church member after Marcion's day
(713).

The reconstruction of Marcion's canon is notoriously difficult since we do
not have his works but only references to them.[4] With the caution due to a
hypothetical reconstruction I leave the possibility open that this point of Zahn
may be right.

To summarise this section, we may say that the emergence of Marcion's
canon does not compel us to hold that the church did not have a canonical

---

[3] As a recent presentation of the major hypotheses see e.g. Dungan (ed.) 1990.

[4] Cf. Harnack's attempt at a reconstruction of Marcion's *Antitheses*, 1921.

process already in progress prior to Marcion's time. There is still room for looking for traces of a canonical process in the earlier periods, a process which led later to the formation of the canon as a list of books.

4. On the reasons behind the canonical process

If we tentatively accept Schneemelcher's point, quoted in the previous section, that the pre-history of canonisation does not make it likely that Marcion's canon evoked the catholic church's answer of forming a canon, then we have to say more about this "pre-history". The main reason why Schneemelcher had to acknowledge that rival theories can be argued in relation to Marcion's role in the history of the canon is that scholars give different reasons for the emergence of the canon, or even for the emergence of the idea of forming a canon.

Zahn proposed that the key factor in the formation of the New Testament canon was the fact that writings were read in worship services. He affirmed that (1888, 83):

> Nicht eine vorgefaßte Meinung von dem unterscheidenden Charakter bestimmter Schriften, nicht ein Dogma von der Inspiration der apostolischen Schriftsteller hat das NT der Kirche geschaffen und den einzelnen Büchern den Eintritt in diese Sammlung erschlossen oder versperrt, sondern umgekehrt, die thatsächliche Anwendung und die durch das Herkommen begründete Geltung der Schriften im Leben und insbesondere im Gottesdienst der Kirche hat sie mit dem Nimbus der Heiligkeit umgeben und hat die Vorstellungen von einem übernatürlichen Ursprung und von einer alle sonstige Literatur weit hinter sich lassenden Würde derselben erzeugt.

I think that the second part of this thesis is historically very likely. It is probable, indeed, natural to think, that the usage of the writings in Christian worship gave those writings the character of holiness, and distinguished them from other literature. However, the thesis, as it stands, is not without problems.

The question arises: Why does Zahn connect the second part of the thesis with the first? Why does he have to reject the idea of inspiration playing a role in the process of canonisation? He does not give any reason for this juxtaposition of the two theses. The first part is perhaps meant to defend his thesis against the charge that he operates with dogmatic terms, perhaps even anachronistic terms. This may be expressed in a remark made by Zahn in the same context (83): "Nicht ein Kapitel der Dogmengeschichte gedenke ich zu schreiben, sondern ein Stück der Geschichte des kirchlichen Lebens und insbesondere des christlichen Cultus". This qualification will be justified if it simply refers to a necessary distinction between systematic theology and a historical enterprise.[5]

However, the juxtaposition of the two theses may prove to be wrong if Zahn means that the usage of writings in worship is the only reason why they became canonical. Zahn seems to imply this, and for that he is rightly criticised by Harnack. Harnack (1889, 9) shows that in Zahn's statement, quoted above, the term "durch das Herkommen" is problematical: "Aber dieses Herkommen muss doch einen Ursprung genommen und eine Ursache gehabt haben".

Harnack points to an earlier work of his where he had argued that the creation of the New Testament canon did have certain preceding steps ("Vorstufen"). He summarises his results in this way (19):

> Ich habe in meinem Lehrbuch der Dogmengeschichte gezeigt, wie die antignostische "apostolische" regula fidei auf dem apostolischen Kerygma, die "apostolische" Schriftensammlung auf den Herrnworten, den apostolischen Anweisungen und der pneumatischen Schriftstellerei, das "apostolische Amt" der Bischöfe auf den Attributen der Apostel, Propheten und Lehrer und auf anderen uralten Vorstellungen beruht.

Schneemelcher holds that it is an important characteristic of Harnack's thesis "daß er die Entstehung des Kanons des Neuen Testaments und der christlichen Bibel in die gesamte kirchen- und dogmengeschichtliche Entwicklung einzuordnen versucht" (1980, 23). However, he criticises Harnack's thesis of "early Catholicism" which Harnack builds on these quoted observations: "... die Entstehung der sog. altkatholischen Kirche ist wohl nicht mehr durch den Aufweis der drei konstitutiven Elemente (Amt, *regula*, Kanon) hinreichend zu erfassen".

I think that we do not have to make an "either - or" decision concerning Zahn's and Harnack's theses. Both have strengths and weaknesses. We may adopt Zahn's observation as one contributing element in the formation of the New Testament canon: the usage of writings in worship played a role in those writings' becoming a part of the canon. The fact that this may only be *a* role and not *the* role can be seen in the fact that there were writings, other than those in our New Testament, which were at one time read in worship and later not included in the canon. We have to return to this problem later. Harnack may be right in pointing to theological reasons which may have lain behind the formation of the canon. This observation may be adopted from his thesis, even if one does not follow him in his reconstruction of "early Catholicism".

---

[5] See my first and last chapters.

In my opinion, Schneemelcher offers a way out of the "either - or" impasse of the Zahn - Harnack controversy. His general theses in this context are the following (1980, 46):

1) The New Testament grew out of the usage of certain writings in different congregations. Schneemelcher adds a further important argument:

> Von hier aus ist noch einmal zu betonen, daß die Bildung des neutestamentlichen Kanons hineingehört in den Prozeß der Fixierung der Jesustradition und der Weitergabe der apostolischen Überlieferung durch die über die Welt zerstreuten Gemeinden.

This point has the advantage of retaining Zahn's proposal as indicated above. This point also rightly acknowledges the important role that was played by the aim of keeping old traditions in second century Christianity. This aim was achieved by reading and copying writings that became the canon.

2) The reception of the "Old Testament" as Scripture by Christianity played a role in the formation of a solid collection of Jesus tradition and apostolic tradition.

I think that this point may be a good correction of Zahn's thesis concerning the early Christians' view on "inspiration". Even if the early Christians may not have had a doctrine of inspiration with regard to their own writings, they may have had a view of the inspiration of the "Old Testament". This view in turn may have played a role in how they regarded their own writings. I shall return to this point in another section.

3) Schneemelcher rightly points to the problem created by the phenomenon of diversity of opinion among early Christians concerning the question: Which books should be read in worship? However, he offers a twofold answer. a) He points to the possible difference between the historical thinking of our time and that of the early Christians: "Die vielfachen Differenzen hinsichtlich des Umfangs werden zwar am Ende des 2. Jh. empfunden, haben aber offensichtlich nicht das Gewicht gehabt, das man von modernen Gesichtspunkten aus vermuten möchte". b) Referring to this point, he puts forward a good argument concerning the role of the "rule of faith" (a question we return to in the following chapter): "Das aber hat doch wohl seinen Grund darin, daß die Vielfalt an der *regula fidei* gemessen wurde und alles, was damit vereinbar war, ertragen wurde".

4) The New Testament canon grew out of "innerkirchlichen Motiven (Festlegung der echten und wahren Tradition)". In the context of keeping the true tradition we may take account of the presence of impulses from outside the catholic church: "Marcion und Gnostiker haben die Entwicklung gefördert, weil sie die Kirche zwangen, 'wahre' und 'falsche' Tradition zu unterscheiden".

This point has the advantage of drawing a distinction between the views, "Marcion is the cause of the creation of the New Testament", and "The struggle with heretics played a role in the formation of the canon". I have argued against the former. With Schneemelcher, I can accept the latter.

5) The canon as a list was closed later than the third century. However, "Der Kanon ist um die Wende vom 2. zum 3. Jh. grundsätzlich vorhanden". Later, in the time of the Constantinian Empire, the church "hat auch hier das vollendet, was in den vorhergehenden Jahrhunderten im Ansatz angelegt war" (47).

In the remaining part of this chapter I shall make an attempt to present arguments which support this thesis of "early beginnings" (or origins) of the canon.

5. The role of the Old Testament in the formation of the New Testament canon

As we have seen in the previous section, Schneemelcher has put forward the proposal that the Old Testament played a role in the formation of the New Testament canon. We have to investigate what that role of the Old Testament may have been.

As a clarification of the terminology we have to note with Plümacher that the term Old Testament "findet sich bei den neutestamentlichen Schriftstellern naturgemäß noch nicht (frühestens bei Melito von Sardes ...)" (1980, 9). For convenience's sake I use the term here simply as referring to the writings which were taken over from Judaism by the early Christians as their Scripture, or γραφή. It is disputed among scholars what books belonged to these Scriptures, but it is generally agreed that *there were* Jewish writings which were regarded as Scripture by the early Christians. As James Barr has put it in relation to the Old Testament, around the time of the writing of the New Testament books (1983, 61): "The existence of authoritative holy scripture is beyond doubt, but we do not know exactly what it comprised ..." (see also 41). Thus I use the term "Old Testament" without making an attempt to define the exact list of the writings this term refers to.

It is appropriate to note at this point that I shall not refer separately to the Hebrew Bible and the *Septuagint* in the course of my discussions. It has been argued on the basis of recent studies that "we can no longer *automatically* reckon with the idea of a larger 'Alexandrian canon'" (Barr 1983, 56). We shall see below how the status as "Holy Scripture" of certain writings of the Hebrew Bible was still disputed during the course of the first Christian century. Hübner argues the same with regard to the *Septuagint* (1990, 56):

Das Anwachsen der Zahl der Hagiographen sollte man sich also am besten als kontinuierlichen, im einzelnen aber nicht verifizierbaren Prozeß vorstellen, der auch im 1. Jh. n. Chr. immer noch fließend war. Somit dürfte die Frage nach der Existenz eines festen alexandrinischen Kanons griechischer heiliger Schriften noch weniger angemessen sein als die nach dem palästinischen Kanon der Biblia Hebraica.

The evidence from Qumran may support this view. Emanuel Tov has pointed out that there were different text types of the "Hebrew Bible" preserved alongside one another in Qumran (1992, 114-117). Some Hebrew texts are close to the *Septuagint* texts (for example, in the case of the book of Jeremiah, 115). With regard to the whole collection of texts in Qumran, Tov emphasises that "we possess no information regarding the role of these texts in the sect, or their use, if at all, in the daily life of the sect" (101). This negative result, nevertheless, leaves room for the hypothesis that different texts of the same book may have been regarded as "canonical" in different groups of Judaism - or even within one group of Judaism.

In accordance with these insights, when I use the term "Old Testament", I refer to writings which were regarded as Holy Scripture around the time of the writing of the books of the New Testament, irrespective of the question whether they were written in Hebrew (or Aramaic) or in Greek. Further, when I use the term "Old Testament" I acknowledge that we do not know precisely which writings belonged to the circle of Holy Scripture of the Jews at that time.

a. The Old Testament quoted in the New Testament

E. Plümacher asserts a widely held view when he writes in an article on the question concerned (1980, 9): "Die Haltung des Urchristentums gegenüber den Heiligen Schriften des Judentums ist von Beginn an dadurch bestimmt, daß es an diesen Schriften als überkommener Autorität festgehalten und sie intensiv benutzt hat". According to Plümacher, the quotations of the Old Testament in the New Testament together with allusions and reminiscences "läßt sich freilich die Behauptung wagen, daß keine der alttestamentlichen Schriften im Neuen Testament ganz ohne Spuren geblieben ist" (12). It is worth looking briefly at the ways the Old Testament is used in the New Testament. As a summary, Plümacher asserts that: "Die neutestamentlichen Schriftsteller zitieren das Alte Testament nicht, um ihre Schriftkenntnis zu zeigen, sondern aus sachlichen Gründen".

He exemplifies these "grounds" in the following way. One general reason why the Old Testament is quoted is that it is used as an argument. For Paul, the Old Testament is "voll der Zusage des eschatologischen und nun offenbar gewordenen Heils" (16).[6] Another major type of quotation is to point out that something foretold in the Old Testament is fulfilled in the New Testament (e.g. Matthew, p.17).

Plümacher points to the significant fact that even those New Testament authors who have critical remarks concerning the Law - or the "Old Testament" - make positive use of the same. For example, concerning John's Gospel he (18) takes up a phrase of H. Braun and speaks about "Vergleichgültigung" of the Old Testament. However, the same author of the Fourth Gospel, for whom the Old Testament is insignificant ("bedeutungslos") in relation to paraenesis, *can* make positive use of it: "in 12,13-15; 19,24.28f.36 hat er traditionelles, in der Passionsgeschichte heimisch gewordenes Material benutzt und es z. T. sogar wie Mt mit Erfüllungsformeln versehen". Concerning Hebrews, Plümacher asserts that its author shows "wie man trotz Bestreitung der Weitergeltung des alttestamentlichen Gesetzes ... die Schrift sogar in ihren gesetzlichen Passagen positiv verstehen konnte". I do not attempt to discuss this seeming paradox here. It is sufficient for my thesis to note the positive "proof-text" ("Schriftbeweis", Plümacher, 15) character of the Old Testament.

The phenomena in connection with the Old Testament being quoted in the New Testament have often been noted by scholars. However, most scholars do not attach any significance to these phenomena in relation to the question of the New Testament canon. In my opinion, the reason for not relating the Old Testament references in the New Testament to the canonical process of the latter is that there seems to be a consensus of opinion that we can only see signs of the canonical process from the second half of the second century on. Schneemelcher puts this consensus of opinion in this way (1991a, 18):

> For the result of such a survey [i.e. that of the sources] is that before Justin we cannot speak of 'canonical' status for individual books of the NT. Certainly there is evidence for knowledge of, and even citations from, individual books of the later NT. But these facts simply show that the process of the putting into literary form and fixation of the Jesus tradition and of the 'apostolic teaching', begun in the 1st century, has continued.

In disagreement with this view, I put forward the hypothesis that the writings which were later called the New Testament were regarded as having some kind of a "canonical" status earlier than the second half of the second century.

As one argument in support of this thesis I propose that the Old Testament quotations in the New Testament may have had another reason - beside the

---

[6] See also the use of Genesis in Galatians.

"proof-text" one - namely, that the New Testament authors intended to put another canon alongside that of the Old Testament. In other words, they wrote with a canonical awareness; they wrote, what we may term as, a "second canon".

In order that it may be tenable, this thesis has to answer several challenges. It also has to be supported by arguments. These require to be considered in separate sections. Since I have already made a proposal which concerns the Old Testament, it is appropriate that we discuss matters in relation with the Old Testament first.

b. Problems concerning the canonisation process of the Old Testament

In relation to the "Old Testament" we find similar problems as in the case of the New Testament canon. We have very little evidence which would inform us about the history of the canonisation of the Old Testament. In the following I shall rely on studies which summarise the main views in our day, published in the third volume of the *Jahrbuch für Biblische Theologie* (1988).

aa) The problem of "Jabne"

The main problem in relating the canonisation of the New Testament writings to that of the Old Testament books is that the evidence permits us to speak about a canonical Old Testament only very late: later than the period when most of the New Testament writings were probably written. From the time when the thesis was put forward by H. Graetz in 1871 (see Stemberger, 1988, 163) up until recently it was widely held that "der palästinische Kanon der Juden erst Ende des I.Jh.s auf der Synode von Jabne festgelegt worden ist" (Kümmel, 1957a, 1131). Günter Stemberger has summarised recent arguments against this consensus by asserting "daß es eine 'Synode' von Jabne im eigentlichen Wortsinn nie gab" (1988, 163). He argues that the term "synod" draws together in one point of time decisions which were in reality made during a long period, ca. between the destruction of the Jerusalem Temple in A.D. 70 and the Bar Kokhba revolt in 132-135. He also points to the fact that the decisions of the Rabbis in this period did not prevent the later uncertainties and disputes about which books should belong to the Holy Scriptures of the Jews (163, 173). He further rejects the view that an anti-Christian polemic may have played a role in the decision of the Rabbis during that period in Jabne (163-164, 173).

Hans Hübner accepts these points in general (1990, 46-47). However he proposes important qualifications. Concerning the question whether Qohelet and Canticum were "endgültig" received as Holy Scripture, he argues that "nach der *Intention* der damals an der Entscheidung von Jamnia Beteiligten die Frage definitiv entschieden werden sollte" (47). He makes the following key moves:

1) It is true that in the relevant passage of the Mishna, *Jad* III,5, the discussion is only about Qohelet and Canticum. However, the discussion was in some connection with the question of the whole canon, because "hier anscheinend die im Blick auf ihn [i.e. the canon] noch offenen Fragen als entscheidungsreif angesehen wurden" (47).

2) It is also true that the terms "canon", "canonical" are later. Their use here is anachronistic. However, the important thing is that to Qohelet and Canticum the same "dignity" is ascribed as to the other writings which belonged undisputedly to the Holy Scriptures. *Jad* III,5 writes concerning these two writings that "they make the hands unclean" (p.46). Since in the same context in the Mishna it is stated that "Alle Heiligen Schriften ... verunreinigen die Hände", this means in Hübner's view "daß die beiden Bücher in Relation zu den übrigen Büchern der Heiligen Schrift gestellt und folglich unter dem Gesichtspunkt der *ganzen* Heiligen Schrift diskutiert wurden" (p.47).

On this basis we may conclude that the process of canonisation of the Old Testament was not completed by the end of the first century A.D. However, we may argue the case that a process of canonisation of the Old Testament was going on - perhaps even approaching its end - during that century. This seems to be what we can say with reasonable certainty about the matter. We may add two further qualifications to this overall view. These further arguments are attempts at going further back in time in our search for the origins of the Old Testament canon.

bb) *"Zusammen-Denken" before "canonisation"*

Magne Sæbø has examined the difficult problem of when and how the change took place "von der - vorwärts ausgerichteten - *Traditionsgeschichte* zu der - im wesentlichen rückwärts blickenden - *Kanongeschichte*" (1988, 116). He applies the term "Zusammen-Denken" in a historical sense to an important "Prozeß in der alttestamentlichen Überlieferungsgeschichte" (121). Pointing in an exemplifying way to the historical work of the Deuteronomist (121-122), the introductory words of Jeremiah (122-123), and the beginning of the "Solomon collection" in Prov 10,1-10 he makes a summarising statement concerning the historical, prophetical and wisdom traditions of the Old Testament (127-128):

... die lange und komplexe *Überlieferungsgeschichte*, von der die hebräische Bibel ein so vielgestaltiges Zeugnis ablegt, eine sehr lebendige und wandelbare

Größe war, die nur durch eine in mehrfacher Weise vereinheitlichende Sammlung und Deutung die schließliche Letztgestalt der Bibel erreicht hat; und *durch diese Sammlung und Deutung zieht sich als roter Faden ein umfassendes theologisches Zusammen-Denken.*

Sæbø points to an evidence where we can clearly see that the "change" mentioned above had already taken place. Qoh 12,12-14, the "epilogue" to the book, stands in tension with 11,9 - and other parts of the book (p.131). However, it is striking that "Man hat nicht mit 'Korrekturen' in das Corpus des Buches eingegriffen, sondern solche nur am Ende des Buches angefügt". Sæbø draws the conclusion that for the person who added the "epilogue" the book was already "closed". The activity of this editor was "dieses Buch nun in ein literarisch größeres Ganzes, in eine Sammlung von autoritativen Schriften, *einzuordnen* und es mit diesem - wenn nötig - möglichst zu *harmonisieren*". Only from this period onwards can we speak about a "canonical consciousness".

Sæbø rightly warns against the dangers of using the term "canonical" in a wide sense - i.e. with reference to a theological meaning which may be late (117). He rather wants to understand this term as a literary and historical one. It is helpful for my thesis that he has established a time of "canonical consciousness" in relation to the Old Testament. This time is earlier than the time of the writing of the books of the New Testament. Sæbø describes the theological "Zusammen-Denken" as "die notwendige Bedingung und Vorbereitung des Kanons" of the Old Testament (129). In this way he traces an activity which is earlier than the time of the "epilogue" to Qohelet. He does not suggest calling this activity a "canonical" one - that is why he introduces a new term.

cc) Authority and canon
Sæbø makes another important remark which belongs in this context. He points to the relationship between "authority" and "canon" (129-130). When the epilogue to Qohelet testifies that the book was regarded as closed and was intended to be incorporated in a collection of sacred writings, this also means that the tradition-material of those sacred writings is "im wesentlichen festgelegt und begrenzt worden" (131). Concerning this wider collection of sacred writings, Sæbø affirms: "als 'Heilige Schrift' trägt es zudem in sich selbst eine Autorität, die nun die personal begründete Autorität einzelner Schriften überhöht". Thus it is right to connect the terms "canon" and "authority" (129). However, Sæbø makes the fine distinction (129-130): "... der Kanon meint Autorität. Autorität braucht aber umgekehrt nicht Kanon zu bedeuten". It is important that he ascribes the same role to "authority" as he

does to the phenomenon of "Zusammen-Denken": it is a "notwendige Bedingung für die Entstehung eines Kanons" (130).

Sæbø's remarks are helpful for my thesis from the following points of view: 1) I should like to argue that a process similar to that of what he describes as "Zusammen-Denken" was going on in the process of the writing of the New Testament: an activity of handling traditions which were regarded as "sacred". 2) There was a "canonical process" going on prior to the time of the writing of the New Testament books. Although there were disputes over the question what books should belong to the collection of Holy Scripture, there was also a consciousness that there existed a circle of sacred writings which *was* Holy Scripture.

The other argument I refer to in this context is more controversial: it is more hypothetical.

dd) Early canonisation of the Old Testament?

B.S. Childs has put forward some arguments in favour of the possibility that the canonisation of the Old Testament may have ended earlier than the period of the rabbinic discussions in Jabne. Childs's name is by now generally connected with the term "canonical approach". His general contribution to the relationship between the canon and biblical theology will be discussed in some detail in the final chapter of my thesis. Here we are only concerned with his arguments in support of an early dating of the Old Testament canon. His key arguments are the following (1988, 17).

1) Josephus' work, *Contra Apionem*, is generally dated around A.D. 93. In this work (I,38) Josephus asserts that there are twenty-two books in the Holy Scriptures of the Jews. Josephus probably reflects here traditions earlier than the time of his writing. Perhaps he learnt these traditions when he was a member of the Pharisaic group, as early as ca. A.D. 56-57. It is also significant that Josephus does not say that Jabne played an important role in the formation of the canon. In this way "stützt Josephus einen Zeitpunkt für den Abschluß des hebräischen Kanons, der weit vor dem der Zerstörung Jerusalems liegt".

We have to note that the argument derived from silence has a certain risk factor. However, these remarks of Childs are plausible.

2) Childs notes the difficulty which arises out of the fact that we have only unspecific references to the third part of the Old Testament until the end of the first Christian century. The Prologue to the book of Jesus the son of Sirach, or *Ecclesiasticus*,[7] mentions the "law", "the prophets" and "the other books of our fathers". Lk 24,44 refers to "the law of Moses", "the prophets",

---

[7] I note that Childs's text here refers to *"Ecclesiastes"*, which must be a misprint.

and "the psalms". We may add that the law and the prophets are referred to together elsewhere in the New Testament, but it is true that this passage in Luke is the only place where there is a three-part type reference to the Old Testament in the New Testament (Plümacher 1980, 10).

Childs, however, argues (on the basis of studies of T. Swanson and R. Beckwith) that "die Entstehung der *Ketubim* (Schriften)" should be understood "als eine spätere Abspaltung innerhalb der nichtmosaischen Sammlung der *Nebi'im* (Propheten)" (1988, 17). Thus the three main parts of the Old Testament canon may not necessarily have been formed one after the other in the way reflected in the emergence of the evidence of a three-part division. The separation of the third part within the second part (referred to above) may not have been related to the disputes concerning the closing of the canon.

This hypothesis may be disputed, but it is significant that Childs could point out that the traditional view about the development of the three main parts of the Old Testament canon is also disputed (17). The very fact that there are books other than the law and the prophets mentioned - together with the law and the prophets - in *Ecclesiasticus* and in Luke, may point to the existence of the three-part Old Testament canon in the time of the writing of the New Testament.

3) Childs points to the fact that there is only a small number of occurrences of quotations from the Old Testament "apocrypha" in Philo, Josephus and in the New Testament (p.17). However, we may add that a "small number" of such pieces of evidence is enough to make it disputable to argue that "das pharisäische Judentum habe eine feste Form der Schrift besessen". This observation of Childs is helpful for his thesis, but - in itself - far from being decisive.

4) Childs's last, and in his opinion the strongest, argument emerges "von der Geschichte der Festlegung des Masoretischen Textes" (18). The evidence from the scrolls from Qumran suggests that approximately by A.D. 70 the Masoretic Text had reached "ein hohes Maß an Stabilität". This observation is confirmed by Tov who affirms that (1992, 187): "The lower limit for the period of the development of the biblical text can be fixed at the end of the first century CE, for the biblical text did not change greatly beyond this point in time". From this fact Childs concludes that: "Der Text eines Buches wäre nicht festgeschrieben worden, hätte es nicht bereits selbst kanonischen Status erlangt" (1988, 18).

Childs's further evidence in this same context may also be helpful. He not only points to the stable text of the Masoretic Bible, but also to "protolukianische" and "prototheodotische" revisions of the Greek Septuagint (18). These revisions were undertaken in order to bring the Greek translation into agreement with the "normative" Hebrew text. If these hypotheses can be established, then Childs could powerfully argue that the conservation of "revised" texts may point to the fact that those writings were canonical.

To sum up, these arguments may point to a canonisation of the Old Testament earlier than the end of the first Christian century. However, Childs himself acknowledges that the evidence is not compelling. He can only speak about a "relativ festen Zahl von Büchern" and a "zunehmend festgelegten normativen Text". The terms "relativ" and "zunehmend" point to the tentative nature of Childs's thesis.

To summarise this section, I have found the following results helpful for my thesis. 1) The Christian community of the first century possessed certain writings which were regarded as Holy Scripture by the Jews of the time. The "law" and "the prophets" were definitely canonised by that time and there were other sacred writings which were either canonised or on their way to canonisation. These "Writings" became the third part of the Old Testament either prior to the first Christian century or during that century. 2) The early Christians lived in a time when there was a process of canonisation of certain Old Testament books going on; and in a time by which many of the Old Testament books had reached a canonised status among the Jews.

These observations make room for the hypothesis that the early Christians undertook a process of canonisation of their own writings very early. This hypothesis would be strengthened if we found that there were people before or at the time of the early Christians who engaged in a process of producing sacred writings which were meant to be canonical, but not part of the Old Testament canon. To put it in the form of a question, Were there Jews before the first Christian century who were in the process of forming a "second canon" alongside the Old Testament canon? We may find an example of this activity in the Qumran community.

6. Excursus: The status of the Temple Scroll

In 1977 Yigael Yadin published the text of a scroll which is marked as 11QT and called the Temple Scroll. It seems that we have only two manuscript copies of this document (Brooke 1989a, 14). In the introductory volume, which he added to the text of the scroll, Yadin put forward the thesis that the author of the scroll - "and, *a fortiori*, the members of the sect" - regarded the Temple Scroll "as a veritable Torah of the Lord" (1983, 392). He gives the following arguments.

1) The *Tetragrammaton* is written in the document in the square script which is used throughout the scroll. This is usual in other "canonical" writ-

ings found at Qumran. Yadin remarks that "many Qumran scribes used the palaeo-Hebrew script when writing the Tetragrammaton in commentaries and scrolls of which the contents, even in their eyes, were not 'canonical'" (392). However, Yadin adds that this rule is not applicable one hundred per cent, because "the Tetragrammaton was written in the square script in several copies of the *peshers* and in similar books from Cave 4". We must note that this latter qualification means that this argument is not compelling in itself.

2) The author of the Temple Scroll quotes long sections of the Pentateuch "changing their grammar to the first person ... He also phrased many supplementary laws in the first person" (71). However, Yadin notes that this phenomenon is "one of the principal characteristics of certain pseudepigraphical works as well" and it "may be found in several sections of the Pentateuch itself" (71-72). He also notes that in cols. XIII-XXIX, in commands related to the festivals and their offerings, the author refers to God in the third person (p.72).

Stegemann holds that this latter phenomenon indicates that this section is based on a "separate literary source" which was used by the author of the Temple Scroll (1989, 136). Although Stegemann disagrees with Yadin on the status of the Temple Scroll (as we shall see below), this observation of his may strengthen Yadin's argument, because it gives a good reason for what would be an exception weakening Yadin's point.

3) In my opinion, a further good argument Yadin develops is the observation that the author of the Temple Scroll "edits" the commands of the Pentateuch. For example, (col. LXVI, p.73): 1) the author merges commands "either by quoting virtually verbatim or by combining the passages into a single flowing text"; 2) he omits "misplaced pentateuchal commands"; 3) he harmonises duplicate commands (e.g. col. LXVI:8-11, pp.74ff); 4) he introduces "modifications and additions" which are "designed to clarify the halakhic meaning of the commands" (77ff, quote from 77).

4) Yadin further asserts that the "most distinctive characteristics of the scroll" are the "supplementary sections" where we can find commands which follow the style of the biblical commands, and are spoken by God himself (e.g. "the Laws of the Temple"; the "Statutes of the King"; the "Laws of the Festivals and Their Offerings"; the "Sanctity of the Temple City and the Laws of Cleanness and Uncleanness", pp.82ff).

In my opinion these observations do point to striking phenomena in this Qumran document. The question arises, In what relationship does this document stand to the Pentateuch in Qumran? In a popular version of his study of the Temple Scroll Yadin called the scroll an "additional Torah" (1985, 78).

He also affirmed more conclusively his view, a view he had already cautiously suggested in his 1983 book, that (1985, 229):

> [the Temple Scroll] was in fact the basic 'Torah' of the Essenes, and was referred to by them as the Book of *Hagu* - which had to be 'meditated upon' and in which all had to be 'instructed' - or as the Second Torah, a Book of the Second Law which had been revealed only to the sect, and which was considered by them accordingly as 'canonical'.

Going even further than Yadin did, Ben Zion Wacholder has put forward the thesis that "the fragments can be properly perceived only as presenting a new and superior Torah that reveals, its author claimed, what was still unrecorded in the Mosaic books" (1983, 31). Wacholder has suggested that the Temple Scroll may be the "precursor of other Qumranic literature" (203). He claims he can show that other Qumran literature is dependent upon "the Qumranic Torah" - as he calls 11QT (p.202).

Wacholder argues that Zadok, who discovered this *Sepher Torah*, was the Teacher of Righteousness (203). Wacholder suggests tentatively that the Teacher of Righteousness may have been not only the discoverer but the author of the scroll (211). Being the founder of the community, he adopted the name *Moreh* which pointed to his own role as similar to that of Moses who taught the Jewish nation (cf. Ex 4,12; 24,12). He also called himself *Zedeq* because this was a variant of Zadok, and it also referred to "righteousness in the eyes of God" (228-229). Wacholder concludes his monograph on the Temple Scroll by affirming that "Zadok did not claim mere equality with Moses; he sought superiority. The Torah of Moses was ephemeral, Zadok's eternal" (229).

We must note that Wacholder's thesis is highly controversial. For example, Hartmut Stegemann has argued that "the Temple Scroll was not intended to supersede the canonical books of the Pentateuch ..., but [it is] a sixth book of the *Torah*, supplementing the Pentateuch and with the same level of authority" (1989, 127). He holds that "there is no specific connection at all between the Qumran community and the composition of the Temple Scroll". Contrary to the view of Yadin, Stegemann asserts that "there is not one mention of the Temple Scroll's existence in any of the other Qumranic writings".

In view of these counter-arguments, we have to be cautious with Yadin's and Wacholder's bold theses. However, there may be at least one further piece of evidence in favour of their interpretations. This evidence is even acknowledged by Stegemann. He remarks that one copy of the Temple Scroll "was written about the middle of the first century BCE by a member of this Qumran community" (pp.143-144). The other scroll, the one published by

Yadin, is generally dated somewhat later: its "paleographical date is probably within a generation of the turn of the era" (Brooke 1989a, 14).[8] Stegemann acknowledges that this scroll was used by members of the Qumran community "in such an intensive manner that it had to be repaired" (144). In my opinion, these remarks do not support Stegemann's own view that the Temple Scroll may have had a similar fate to those scrolls which were brought to the community by new members, deposited in the library, and "read by nobody any longer" (143).

Thus with due caution I conclude that the Temple Scroll is open to different explanations. Perhaps Brooke is right when he remarks that "any scholarly consensus about it will be at least another ten years in the making" (1989a, 19). In this situation I find it hard to build new hypotheses on the Qumran evidence. What may be still possible, is to find plausible explanations of the Qumran writings, and then build tentative hypotheses on them. These hypotheses may have to face attacks from other corners of scholarship. Yadin and Wacholder have completed very thorough works with arguments. I think, even if there are other solutions possible on the basis of the evidence, their solution is a possible one, too. My conclusion is that the possibility of the existence of a group which thought that they had a "second Torah" points to the possibility that the New Testament writers could regard their time as a time for a new canon.

7. From authoritative writings to canon

When I argue that a "canonical" awareness in relation to the Old Testament writings points to the possibility of a similar process in relation to the writings which later became our New Testament, then I have already started to approach one of the most significant problems for my thesis, the problem of the canon. It has been asserted by many scholars that the New Testament authors did not intend to write "canonical" works. Wrede has summarised this idea in this way: "No New Testament writing was born with the predicate 'canonical' attached" (1897, 11; ET: 1973, 70). We may see an example of this statement when Wrede affirms that Paul did not think of himself as an "author" (1909, 10). He could not think of the idea of the "publication" of his letters, otherwise he would have written only "open letters".

---

[8] We have to note that: 1) in the same context Brooke warns about the relative reliability of all palaeographic datings; 2) according to Tov (1992, 106), with the aid of a new version of the carbon 14 test, 11QT is dated "between 97 BCE and 1 CE".

As another characteristic example, we may refer to Hübner who affirms on the basis of the way the New Testament uses the Old Testament, that (1990, 38): "Die *neutestamentlichen Autoren verstanden sich*, wenn sie sich auf Aussagen der Schrift stützten, wenn sie also Schriftzitate zum Zwecke des Schriftbeweises heranzogen, gerade *nicht als biblische Autoren*". In this context Hübner argues that the New Testament authors understood themselves only as interpreters of the Old Testament.

The view that the New Testament authors did not understand themselves as writers of canonical books is compelling at first sight. As we have already seen, the term "canon" in the sense of a defined "list" of books is later than the time of the writing of the books which have become our New Testament. Hübner is right when he points to a due caution in relation to our usage of the term Old Testament with reference to the time of the New Testament (1990, 43): "Genaugenommen ist die Rede vom Alten Testament im Neuen anachronistisch, auch wenn wir heute im theologischen Stenogramm vom Alten Testament im Blick auf die neutestamentlichen Autoren sprechen".

However, the challenge put to the justification of a canon goes further than this. This challenge does not only concern the anachronistic language. Scholars like Hübner hold that the authors of the New Testament writings did not in any sense intend to write Scripture. It is this latter challenge I turn to in the following sections.

a. The "hidden" writings

In the previous section we have discussed the possibility that the Temple Scroll in Qumran was regarded as Scripture. We may tentatively extend this argument by pointing to the importance of secret teaching among the Qumran community and to the new "canonical" writings referred to in 4Ezra.

aa) "Secrets" in Qumran

Among the tasks of the "Master" in the Qumran community, G. Vermes also mentions that "he was not to dispute with 'the men of the Pit' and not to transmit to them the sect's teachings" (1987, 4). Vermes points to 1QS IX,16-17 where we read (p.75):

> He [i.e. the Master] shall conceal the teaching of the Law from men of falsehood, but shall impart true knowledge and righteous judgement to those who have chosen the Way. He shall guide them all in knowledge according to the spirit of each and according to the rule of age, and shall thus instruct them in the mysteries of marvellous truth that in the midst of the men of the Community they may walk

perfectly together in all that has been revealed to them. This is the time for the preparation of the way into the wilderness ...

Although in this quotation the term "teaching of the Law" may refer to the content of the Mosaic Law itself, it is also possible that the term refers to the teaching about the Law. The passage as a whole suggests that the "mysteries" the community was instructed in were teachings other than the Old Testament itself. These were mysteries which were "revealed" to the community. These teachings may have been related to Old Testament writings, but they were teachings distinct from the Old Testament Scripture.

In this context Yadin's proposal may be helpful. As we have seen, he argued that references in the Qumran documents to the Book of *Hagu* may have referred to the Temple Scroll (1985, 229, quoted above). For example, in the Damascus Rule, at the end of the twelfth and the beginning of the thirteenth column, we read the following (Vermes 1987, 97):

> Those who follow these statutes in the age of wickedness until the coming of the Messiah of Aaron and Israel shall form groups of at least ten men, by *Thousands, Hundreds, Fifties, and Tens* ... And where the ten are, there shall never be lacking a Priest learned in the Book of Meditation; they shall all be ruled by him.

We have to note that the reference to the Book of *Hagu* (or as Vermes translates the term, "Meditation") is problematical. There is no document among the Qumran scrolls that would be labelled with this term by the scholars. It is possible that it refers to the Mosaic Law. In our quotation Vermes has indicated with italics a reference to Ex 18,25. However, in the same context the Damascus Rule goes on to say that a Levite may substitute a Priest with one exception: "... should there be a case of applying the law of leprosy to a man, then the Priest shall come and stand in the camp and the Guardian shall instruct him in the exact interpretation of the Law". It is possible that the "interpretation" is not simply an oral teaching, but it is written in a document of the community, the Book of Meditation.

Thus, taking up Yadin's lead, I propose that the Book of Meditation may be part of the particular teaching of the Qumran community which they kept secret from outsiders.

We find further references to the "mysteries", which were treasured in Qumran, in the Thanksgiving Hymns. Vermes affirms that it is one of the fundamental themes of the scroll that (1987, 165): "The sectary thanks God continually for ... his gift of insight into the divine mysteries". For example, in 1QH V,24-26, in the ninth hymn according to Vermes's divisions, we read (pp.179-180):

> The members of my [Covenant] have rebelled and have murmured round about me; they have gone as talebearers before the children of mischief concerning the mystery which Thou hast hidden in me. And to show Thy great[ness] through me, and because of their guilt, Thou hast hidden the fountain of understanding and the counsel of truth.

It would be of help if we knew whether or not this hymn was written by the Teacher of Righteousness himself. This cannot be decided conclusively.[9] However, if it was written by the Teacher of Righteousness, then the significance of the hymn would be greatly strengthened. In any case these words would be understood best as those of a leader of the community, even if this leader is not the Teacher himself. We have to note that the term "mystery" which was hidden in the person who wrote the hymn may refer to oral teaching or knowledge. However, it may equally refer to written teaching.

With these examples I cautiously raise the possibility that the Qumran community may have regarded some of their own teachings - perhaps even writings - as something so precious that only they could share. These teachings were revealed only to them. As in the case of the Temple Scroll, I tentatively propose that these teachings were for them as sacred as the sacred Scriptures of the Old Testament which they also treasured.

This hypothesis would be strengthened if we found historical parallels to the idea that certain writings had to be hidden; and that those writings were regarded as Scripture by the community who treasured them. We may have evidence for this phenomenon in some of the pseudepigraphical writings of the intertestamental period.

bb) Fourth Ezra
The book generally included among the Apocrypha of English Bibles under the title 2Esdras is often referred to in Latin manuscripts as the Fourth Book of Ezra. Although the earliest copies we have of 4Ezra date from later centuries of the Christian era, it is widely held among scholars that the central part of the book, chapters 3-14, originates in the late first century A.D.[10] 4Ezra was most likely composed in Hebrew, then translated into Greek (Stone 1990, 1). Unfortunately we have only versions which are "either secondary or tertiary to the Greek" (8).

Two passages are of great importance for our study. The first comes after the interpretation of the fifth vision (out of seven) where it is declared that only Ezra was worthy to learn the secret, i.e. the interpretation of the vision (12,36). In 12,37-39 we read (p.372, following the RSV translation):

---

[9] See e.g. Vermes 1987, 165.
[10] See e.g. B.M. Metzger's introduction to 4Ezra in Charlesworth 1983, 517-518.

Therefore write all these things that you have seen in a book, and put it in a hidden place; and you shall teach them to the wise among your people, whose hearts you know are able to comprehend and keep these secrets. But wait here seven days more, so that you may be shown whatever it pleases the Most High to show you.

Michael Stone in his commentary on 4Ezra points to the significance of the fact that it is in this context that Ezra is called a prophet for the first time in the book (12,42, p.34). Ezra accepts a new role here: the role of a comforter. It is in this new role that he receives revelations (p.373). As Stone puts it: "Now Ezra has experienced visions basically like those of other apocalyptic seers, and he must therefore transmit them as secret knowledge".

Stone emphasises that the element of writing and/or hiding visions - or of transmitting writings for future generations - "is to be found at the end of a number of other apocalyptic visions" (372). He points, for example, to Dan 12,4.9, 1Enoch 81,6 and 82,1, 2Enoch 47,1 and 48,6-7.

The crucial question for our study is: Why did (some of) these people hide their visions as secret teaching for later times? One widely held answer to this question is formulated by Zahn in this way (1888, 124): "Weil die Verfasser [i.e. the apocalyptists] ihre Schriften unter den ehrwürdigsten Namen der grauen Vorzeit ausgehen ließen, hatten sie das Bedürfnis, den Widerspruch zwischen ihrem Anspruch auf höchstes Altertum und ihrem verspäteten Erscheinen zu erklären". Stone accepts this possibility, but he cautiously points to other possibilities when he writes (372): "... at the very least the function of such material is authenticating but ... these ideas may also arise from the nature of the tradition in which the author is immersed".

Although Stone himself does not explicate what these traditions may be, I propose that 4Ezra may be evidence of a tradition according to which there were times, probably the "end times", when new sacred writings had to be added to the existing Scriptures.

This interpretation may be strengthened by the other passage in 4Ezra, chapter 14. In vv.19-22 Ezra asks God that he may send his Holy Spirit into Ezra so that Ezra may write down the things which were written in the Law that had been burned. This he wishes to do in order that "those who wish to live in the last days may live" (v.22, Stone 425). In v.26 God orders Ezra, when he has finished writing down what God tells him, to make certain things public and "deliver" other things "in secret to the wise" (Stone 428). Then for forty days Ezra dictates to five scribes what God gives him to "understand" (vv.37-43). In vv.44-48 we read (p.437):

> So during the forty days ninety-four books were written. And when the forty days
> were ended, the Most High spoke to me, saying, "Make public the twenty-four
> books that you wrote first and let the worthy and unworthy read them; but keep
> the seventy that were written last, in order to give them to the wise among your
> people. For in them are the springs of understanding, the fountains of wisdom and
> the river of knowledge." And I did so.

The twenty-four books are generally understood to be the "canonical" books
of the Hebrew Bible (see e.g. Stone 439). Stone affirms that this "figure is the
traditional Jewish number" of the books of the Bible, although Josephus has a
different figure, twenty-two books, in *C.Ap.* I,38 (p.441). Although there is
no reference here to the hiding of the other seventy books, there is a clear
separation of them from the twenty-four. Although we do not know what
these seventy books were, Stone affirms that the "regnant view is that the
seventy books are apocalyptic works like 4 Ezra" (441). He cautiously raises
the possibility that the book of 4Ezra itself may be included in this group of
"esoteric scriptures" (439). For our study it is significant that they "contain
saving knowledge".

Stone has pointed to a "structural element" in 4Ezra which expresses a
relationship between Ezra and Moses (p.35). If we add up all the days of
"fasting or abstention" from vision 1 to vision 6, we find that the total is
forty. In vision 7, which includes the revelation of the ninety-four books, Ezra
fasts another forty days. Thus this latter revelation is "parallel to the revelation of eschatological secrets in the first six visions".

If this argument is right, then we have a "double revelation" in 4Ezra: both
what he had received during the first six visions and what he received during
the seventh vision, i.e. the ninety-four books are revelations that elevate Ezra
to the same level as Moses. As Stone has put it (35):

> ... the revelation in the final vision makes Ezra truly a new Moses: it moves him
> from being a prophet to being equal to the greatest of the prophets.

I acknowledge that I have extended Stone's lines slightly further than he himself would have drawn them. However, I conclude that it is possible to argue
that 4Ezra refers to a Jewish tradition, which existed during the time when
the New Testament writings were written, that God's revelations concerning
the end times had to be written in secret books. These books were meant to
be on the same level as the "canonical" Holy Scriptures of the Jews, and thus
formed a "second canon".

b. The sacred writings of the "heretics"

We may go one tentative step further in establishing the historical possibility that a religious group may have produced its own Scripture. We have already seen in the preceding chapter that some Christian groups that were later labelled heretics produced and treasured sacred writings which were different from the Old Testament Scripture, but were regarded as Scripture by them. Three groups of this kind may be worth mentioning again, this time with the emphasis on the relevance of their writings to our present discussion.

1) We have seen that Marcion produced a Gospel ("'gereinigten' Lk") and a collection of ten ("ebenfalls 'gereinigten'") Pauline letters (Schneemelcher 1980, 36). We have seen that according to one view (von Campenhausen 1968, 174; ET: 1972, 148): "Idee und Wirklichkeit einer christlichen Bibel sind von Markion geschaffen worden, und die Kirche, die sein Werk verwarf, ist ihm hierin nicht vorangegangen, sondern - formal gesehen - seinem Vorbild nachgefolgt". I have argued against this view, but I have left the possibility open that Marcion's "New Testament" may have played some role in the formation of what we now call New Testament, even if the process of "canonisation" may have begun prior to Marcion's time.

Whether or not one accepts the view I have followed, on the basis of both this view and that of von Campenhausen, it is significant for my thesis that Marcion did produce a collection of writings which was Scripture for him and his followers. As von Campenhausen has put it (1968, 175; ET: 1972, 148): "Markions ganze Verkündigung will in einem neuen Sinne 'neutestamentliche', biblische Theologie sein, d.h. sie gründet sich ausschließlich auf den Kanon, den er geschaffen hat". This affirmation remains true in spite of the fact that Marcion had rejected the Old Testament for "dogmatic reasons" (Schneemelcher 1980, 36).

2) We find a similar situation in relation to the Montanist movement. Whether or not Zahn is right in arguing that the Montanists' canon presupposes the existence of the orthodox Christian canon, the important fact is that the writings of the Montanists were regarded as "Holy Scriptures" by them (cf. e.g. 1888, 20). Zahn may be exaggerating when he writes that the Montanists produced "ein drittes neuestes Testament" (21). However, I think he puts forward a good argument when he affirms that (21-22):

> Gerade diese rasche, der neuen Offenbarung [i.e. that of the Montanists] Schritt für Schritt auf dem Fuße folgende Anfertigung neuer hl. Schriften zeigt, wie fest zur Zeit der montanistischen Bewegung das Ansehen und die Macht der Bibel in der Kirche begründet war. Eine Offenbarung ohne Beurkundung in hl. Schriften galt den Montanisten wie den Katholiken als unhaltbar, oder war vielmehr für Alle ein unvorstellbares Ding.

3) The third group we have already mentioned in the previous chapter is the community around the figure of Bardesanes. W. Bauer has pointed to the fact that Bardesanes wrote his own Psalms (1964, 34). He also had his own congregation with its own place of worship and order of service. Bauer affirms that Bardesanes' congregation used its own "Scripture".

These three examples are from a period later than the writing of the books of the New Testament, so they can only be used with due caution as argument in my thesis. However, they point to the possibility that different Christian groups may have developed their own sacred writings, their own "canonical" Scripture. The formation of their own Scripture may have played an important role in expressing their identity. It was through their "canonical" writings that they could show in what way they differed from other groups.

At this point it is appropriate to raise a possible objection to my hypothesis. It may be asked, do I not simply side with the winning orthodox group of Christians when I argue for the justification of the enterprise of New Testament theology focusing on the New Testament canon? As an answer to this question I affirm that from the examples in this section I only claim that there were groups in Christianity who developed their own canonical writings. The orthodox group was one among several groups who did so.

I do acknowledge that "canons" other than the New Testament may be examined with the aim of summarising their theology. For example, a historian may set himself the task of writing a theology of the Marcionite canon. I also argue, however, that the canon of the orthodox can be chosen as a field of studying the theology of a particular group of Christians.

Against the view that a historian cannot justify the limitation of his study to a "canonical" group of writings, I argue for the thesis that there is a legitimate historical distinction between canons of different religious groups. It goes without saying that someone writing a New Testament theology has to study all available material that gives insight into a particular group's theology. However, the historian may chose to study the orthodox Christians' theology. If he does so, he can justify the separation of certain writings from other writings on the basis of how certain groups separated their own writings from the writings of other groups.

c. Writing with authority

It is a significant phenomenon that many scholars, who argue against speaking about a New Testament canon in any sense prior to the fourth century, do acknowledge that - at least some of - the writings which later became our

New Testament did have some kind of an authoritative status very early on: perhaps already not long after they were written. These scholars make a sharp distinction between the terms "authority" and "canon".

Although James Barr makes the following point in relation to the Old Testament, many scholars would hold a similar view in relation to the New Testament as well. It is worth quoting his statement in our context because of its clear formulation (1983, 8):

> Considerable strata of that which we now read as our Old Testament were already in existence, and were developing [*sc.* prior to the time of the Deuteronomic movement (p.7)]. These included the authoritative national-religious traditions, and these would in due course become more fixed in form, be written down, and achieve the status of what later came to be called 'scripture'. But, central and authoritative as these traditions were, they still differed in many ways from the later idea of 'scripture'.

It is important to note that Barr differentiates between the terms "scripture" and "canon". For him, canon should only be used in the sense of "list". In the context of the views of Protestant orthodoxy Barr gives the following definition of canon: "the list which defined which books lay within the scripture ..." (2). This seems to be his own usage as well (see e.g. 41, 49, 75, 79). However, in the above quotation the term "scripture" is sharply distinguished from the term "authority"; consequently it relates to the issue I wish to raise in this section.

I should like to argue that there is a closer link between the authoritative character of a writing and the final "canonisation" of that writing than most scholars assume.

Before turning to my arguments it is appropriate to mention that Barr also distinguishes between the significance of persons about whom certain writings are written and the significance of those writings themselves. For example, he affirms (47-48):

> It no longer makes sense to speak of the authority of the Bible as if it meant the authority of the written documents, quite apart from the persons and lives that lie behind them. Authority must belong to both: certainly to the books, but not only to the books. Romans is authoritative because St. Paul is authoritative, and still more the Gospels have authority because of Jesus Christ, the person and his life, of which they tell.

It is these challenges I turn to in the following sections.

aa) *The significance of "writing"*
James Barr has argued that from the fact that the Old Testament had an "enormous importance" for the New Testament one should not conclude that

"the New Testament faith was from the beginning - or indeed within the main body of the existing New Testament - designed or destined to be a scriptural religion in the way in which by that time the religion grown out of the Old Testament had become a scriptural religion" (1983, 11-12). He has also pointed to the fact that Jesus "never even casually told his disciples to write anything down"; he did not command "the production of a written Gospel" (12).

I note that Barr acknowledges the "enormous importance" of the Old Testament for the New; he is simply not willing to attach any significance to it in the context of the formation of the New Testament writings as authoritative writings. I have already proposed that we may use the importance of the Old Testament as an argument for the possibility that the New Testament writings were meant to be on a similar - or equal - level with the Old Testament. I have put forward this argument on the basis of the historical phenomenon that around the time of the writing of the books of the New Testament there was, or at least may have been, an activity going on which may be seen as writing a "second canon" alongside the "canon" of the Old Testament.

Barr's argument from the silence concerning Jesus' command to commit to writing what he had said or done is somewhat weakened by Barr's own remark that (12):

> It is possible ... to theorize that writing was, in fact and in the culture, more important than is actually expressed in the Gospels, and that it was tacitly understood that as much as possible must be committed to writing.

Barr himself disapproves of this possibility. However, we may find little pieces of evidence that writing was important even in the context of certain New Testament books.

For example, in the book of Revelation we find the command, "Write!", on more than one occasion. For example, in 21,5 we read (RSV): "And he who sat upon the throne said, 'Behold, I make all things new.' Also he said, 'Write this, for these words are trustworthy and true.'" Commenting on this verse, P. Prigent also points to other verses in Revelation where we find a command to write (1981, 330):

> Jusqu'ici l'ordre d'écrire avait été donné par un ange sans doute en 1,11; par le Christ en 1,19; par une voix céleste anonyme en 14,13 et par un ange en 19,9. Nous approchons de la conclusion, c'est Dieu lui-même qui intervient maintenant pour mandater le voyant en authentifiant les révélations qu'il a reçues.

The command given by angels, Christ, and God to write down revelations may be a further evidence for the historical phenomenon that some early

Christians thought they had to write authoritative writings, perhaps even "sacred writings" on the level of the books of earlier revelations, i.e. the Old Testament. M. Karrer's argument in his monograph entitled *Die Johannes-offenbarung als Brief* seems to point in this direction, too. He writes in relation to the command to "write" letters to the seven churches in Rev 2-3 (1986, 160-161):

> Nicht zufällig geraten sie [*sc.* these letters] mit der Füllung der Botenformel durch Hoheitsprädikate dabei besonders in die Nähe der Prophetenbriefe: Wie jene betonen sie die sie tragende göttliche Autorität, die sie gemäß der schriftstellerischen Beauftragungskonzeption der Apk freilich neu christologisch zuspitzen.

Here I note the argument concerning the possibility that some of the apostles may have thought they were writing with an authority with which the prophets had written. I shall return to this point below in the context of the greeting formulae of the apostolic letters. It may be also worth pursuing the other suggestion in Karrer's quotation: "Christology", i.e. reflection on the belief that the Messiah had come, may also have played an important role in the fact that Jesus' words and deeds were committed to writing.

As another example of the awareness of the importance of writing, we may think of the ending(s) of the Fourth Gospel. In Jn 20,31, the author of the Gospel summarises the reason why he wrote (RSV): "... but these are written that you may believe that Jesus is the Christ, the Son of God, and that believing you may have life in his name". In Jn 21,24, the community which first treasured the Gospel confirms the authority of the writing (RSV): "This is the disciple who is bearing witness to these things, and who has written these things; and we know that his testimony is true".

We have already seen in the context of the "hidden writings" that there was a command to write in the context of some apocalyptical writings. These may be referred to as evidence here. I simply refer to that section of my thesis because of its relevance to our present discussion.

Barr himself affirms that although it was "not intended by Jesus himself or, in the early stages, by his followers" (1983, 13), some time after the events "it turned out to be desirable for many reasons that the story of Jesus should be written down" (12-13). Barr does not name these reasons. I propose that the idea that the Messiah has come may have been (one of) the most important among these reasons. We have to discuss this suggestion in some detail.

bb) The records of the words and deeds of Jesus
If Jesus was held to be the Messiah by the early Christians, that would have been a major reason for them to record what they could collect from Jesus'

sayings and from the stories about him. This possibility is in connection with one of the most debated themes in New Testament scholarship, the theme of the Messianic consciousness of Jesus.

The theme of the Messianic consciousness of Jesus may be summarised in the way A. Loisy put it: it is "the question as to what Jesus believed Himself to be and declared that He was" (1903, 98). The answers to this question - or questions, for it has two parts, - may be classified in three groups: 1) Jesus thought he was the Messiah and he did say so; 2) Jesus did not say he was the Messiah, because he did not think he was; 3) Jesus did not say he was the Messiah, but he did think he was and he acted accordingly.

The first answer is represented by, for example, H.J. Holtzmann. Holtzmann, who called the Messianic consciousness of Jesus "das Hauptproblem der neutest. Theologie" (1911, 295), held that Jesus not only acted in the consciousness that he was the Messiah (examples on pp. 299ff, 305), but also professed to be the Messiah (from the confession of Peter at Caesarea on) in the sense of the apocalypse of Daniel (p.331).

A great representative of the second answer is Rudolf Bultmann. In his view, Jesus did not think and did not say he was the Messiah (1984, 26ff). We must add that Bultmann emphasised that he did not speak about a distinction between "the historical Jesus and Christ" (1967, 448). He argued that: "The Christ of the kerygma is not a historical figure ... Whereas the kerygma, which proclaims him, is a historical phenomenon". Bultmann made a clear distinction between "Jesus als reiner Mensch aufgetreten wie ein Prophet und Lehrer" (1954, 265) and the proclamation of the early church ("Urgemeinde") which called him the Messiah (266).[11]

The third answer is argued by J.C. O'Neill. He holds that "Jesus never used any title of himself and that it would have been blasphemy had he called himself Messiah" (1984, 103). This "silence of Jesus", however, did not mean that he did not think of himself as being the Messiah. He acted like the Messiah had to act, for example, when he went up to Jerusalem "as God's Son, sent by his Father to sacrifice himself for mankind" (58). O'Neill has pointed to the following quotation of Origen for a clear expression of this third "answer":[12]

> We may also notice that it was a habit of Jesus everywhere to avoid speaking about himself. That is why he said: 'If I speak of myself, my witness is not true.'

---

[11] I note that this answer seems to be the one most widely held by New Testament scholars. For example, in a survey of twentieth century scholarship on biblical theology, H.G. Reventlow (1983, 51) quotes Grundmann as expressing a consensus of opinion: "Kein Zeugnis der Evangelien bietet einen unanfechtbaren Beweis für ein messianisches Bewußtsein Jesu".

[12] J.C. O'Neill 1995, 118, reference to Origen: *Contra Celsum* I,48, H. Chadwick's transl., 1953, 45.

[n.8: John v,31] And since he avoided speaking about himself, and wanted to show that he was Christ rather by his deeds than by his talk, on this account the Jews say to him: 'If thou art the Christ tell us plainly.' [n.9: John x,24]

It is not necessary at this stage of my thesis to enter into a detailed discussion on these answers. For my thesis, each of these answers allows for the argument that the authors of the New Testament writings (at this point we have, of course, primarily the Gospels in our view) held they were recording the words and deeds of the Messiah. This must have given a high authority to their writings in their own eyes and in the eyes of the early Christian readers of these writings. I note here that the theme of the Messianic consciousness of Jesus has to be discussed in more detail in the following chapter where we examine the diversities within the theology of the New Testament.

We may have to meet one further possible counter-argument in our present context. It may be argued that one may distinguish the level of authority the early Christians attributed to the New Testament writings on the basis of how one answers the question concerning the Messianic consciousness of Jesus. If Jesus thought he was the Messiah, and if his disciples knew he thought he was, then it is possible to argue a strong case that Jesus' words and deeds were recorded in writings that were meant to be as authoritative and "sacred" as the words and deeds of Jesus, the Messiah, were. In this case the authority of the writings "derives" from the Messiah.

However, if Jesus did not think he was the Messiah then one may argue that the writings of the New Testament have only the character of a writing of proclamation of the early church. In this case the authority of the writings does not derive from the Messiah, but from the early church's proclamation of the Messiah.

Even if we accept a differentiation in the level of the authority in this way, that does not rule out my thesis that the New Testament authors did intend to write authoritative writings: writings about the one whom they believed was the Messiah.

cc) Apostolic authority

In a recent article on "The Picture of the Apostle in Early Christian Tradition", W.A. Bienert has summarised the significance of the concept of the apostle in the following way (in Schneemelcher, 1992, 5): "The question of the *primitive Christian apostle concept* is closely connected with that of the origin of the Christian Church and the beginning of its offices and norms of faith". Accordingly, it may be fruitful to discuss this concept in the context of my thesis. We turn briefly to the question, What grade of authority does the term "apostle" contain?

In attempting to answer this question, we encounter a difficulty in tracing the origins of the New Testament usage of the term "apostle". F. Agnew calls the emergence of the term an "enigma" of New Testament scholarship (1976, 49). He argues on the basis of late (8th century A.D.) evidence that the term "was used in secular vocabulary both in the sense, messenger, and in the more significant sense, commissioned agent" (50-51). He argues that the very lateness of the evidence for the profane usage makes it probable that it was known in New Testament times with a profane meaning, because "it is difficult to think that it could have arisen after the Christian usage had so clearly won the day" (53).

Against this view Bienert emphasises that even in Agnew's examples from the late papyri "the meaning 'authorised agent' is latent"; and this use is "rooted in the ancient oriental law regarding messengers (cf. e.g. 1Sam. 25:40f.; 2Sam. 10:1ff.)" (p.6). With regard to these Old Testament "roots", Bienert further affirms that the "ideas about emissaries" are not only "characteristic for the political and legal life of Israel", but also for the religious life, "and here above all for prophecy (cf. e.g. Is. 6:8)" (p.7).

Bienert briefly mentions another hypothesis with disapproval (6): Schmithals proposed "to derive the apostle concept from Jewish or Jewish Christian Gnosis". Bienert asserts that Schmithals's proposal is "largely hypothetical", because its "basis in the sources is inadequate". Bienert affirms that Schmithals's thesis "has met with almost unanimous rejection".[13]

The general trend of scholarship seems to trace the origins of the term to the Jewish notion of *shaliach* (e.g. Bühner 1990, 143-144). The main argument for this thesis is that "*shaliach* is the direct representative of the one who sends him and can in that person's place act in a way that is authoritative and legally binding" (143). However, Bühner himself acknowledges that "the so-called institution of the *shaliach* does not describe a particular historical institution, ... therefore, the NT term 'apostle' cannot be traced back historically to the sending out of specific *sheluchim* of the Jewish community" (145).

Bienert affirms that this "conviction that the Christian apostle concept goes back directly to the Jewish institution of the *shaliach* ... has proved untenable" (1992, 7). He gives two main reasons:

a) as a designation for a particular office-bearer with an official commission, the term *shaliach* is attested in Judaism only after the destruction of the Second Temple (after A.D. 70) ... b) ... the *shaliach* as a rule is given a clearly delimited and temporally restricted commission ... On the other hand, he has no divine

---

[13] See a similar affirmation in Hahn 1974, 55.

commission for preaching or even for mission, which for the early Christian apostolate and particularly for Paul is one of the characteristic attributes.

J.C. O'Neill has argued that (1984, 93): "The word behind ἀπόστολος in the Greek may well not be שָׁלִיחַ but מַלְאָךְ, translated ἀπόστολος rather than ἄγγελος in order to mark the fact that these are men and not heavenly beings". Agnew (50, n.7) mentions an observation of Cerfaux which may support this view: "The word *aggelos*, which would normally have been used to denote someone sent, already had a specific and definite meaning, 'angel'". However, we have to add that the meanings of these terms show a greater variety. On the one hand, *mal'ak* can be used both for angels and human beings in the Old Testament. On the other hand, the "angels" (ἄγγελοι) of the congregations in Revelation (1,20 then 2,1, 2,8 etc.) were probably men.

I think that although we cannot derive the term "apostle" from the term and institution of the *shaliach*, we may see the verb *shalach* in the background of the formation of the content the term "apostle" holds. Bienert emphasises that "in the LXX the verb ἀποστέλλειν appears at more than 700 places instead of the Hebrew *shalach*" (7). It is worth mentioning that in some places the verb *shalach* is used together with the noun *mal'ak* (e.g. 2Chron 36,15, Isa 42,19). The subject of the verb *shalach* can be not only man, but also God (e.g. Gen 45,5: Joseph "sent" by God to Egypt). Moses was sent by God to Egypt from the burning bush (Ex 3,12f). In Jer 7,25 we read (RSV): "From the day that your fathers came out of the land of Egypt to this day, I have persistently sent all my servants the prophets to them, day after day". The prophets Ezekiel (3,6) and Zechariah (2,12f) were also "sent" by God. On this basis I propose that the "sending" of the Old Testament prophets may be in the background of the concept of "apostle".

To strengthen this proposal one may argue that there is an analogy between the prophets' role in proclaiming God's word and the apostles' role in proclaiming the gospel. For example, F. Hahn emphasises that "die Propheten mit der Ausrichtung des Wortes Gottes beauftragt worden sind" (1974, 70). Pointing to Isa 61,1, where the verb *shalach* occurs, Hahn affirms (p.71): "... [es] steht fest, daß die von Jes 52,7 und 61,1 herkommende Tradition von der Verkündigung der eschatologischen Frohbotschaft auf das neutestamentliche Verständnis des Evangeliums entscheidenden Einfluß ausgeübt hat ..."

Summarising the content of the gospel which was preached by the apostles, Bienert also affirms the authority which was involved in that preaching activity (in Schneemelcher, 1992, 15):

The event of Easter is not accessible in any other way than through the testimony of the apostles ... The risen Lord himself selected his messengers - not only from the circle of his disciples, as the example of Paul shows - invested them with power through the gift of his Spirit, and sent them into the world. The apostles ... are messengers of salvation, bearers of divine revelation (cf. 2Cor.12:1ff.; Mt.16:17), and they vouch for the truth of their message with their own persons ...

To sum up, I think it is sufficient for our present purpose to say that the term "apostle" may have come from the Old Testament background of the verb *shalach* and the noun *mal'ak*. The fact that it did not come from the post-Biblical *shaliach* does not mean that the apostles did not share the authority of the one who sent them. On the contrary, we may argue that their authority was similar to the authority of the Old Testament prophets also in the phenomenon that it was bestowed on them for a life time, and not only for individual occasions, to preach God's revelations.

dd) Apostolic letters

In a recent article, Helmut Koester has argued for the case that the "oldest Christian documents ..., namely, the letters of the apostle Paul" are "political instruments" (1991, 357). Koester affirms:

> It is not difficult to classify these letters within the traditional categories of ancient epistolography. These early Christian letters are neither private correspondence nor writings in which the letter format is used for the dissemination of philosophical or theological ideas to a wider public. Their format reveals that they belong to the genre of the administrative and official letter, that is, the most secular genre of the epistolary literature.

Koester points to the fact that in the administration of the Roman Empire "correspondence was the most important instrument for the regulation and adjudication of the affairs of the vast and often distant provinces". Koester rightly points to the similar phenomenon that the apostolic letters address the "affairs" of the community the letters are sent to (358).

However, I would argue that it may be anachronistic to speak of a "secular" genre in the context of the Roman Empire where even the administrative aspects of life - for example, the status of the Emperor - had a certain religious character. I think that we may complement Koester's observation concerning the "official" character of the apostolic letters with an argument put forward by Klaus Berger.

Berger has examined the introductory and ending *formulae* of apostolic letters. He has found that - "gattungsmäßig" - these are parts of speeches of blessing ("Segensworte") (1974, 191). For example, the term χάρις is not simply a substitution for the general Greek greeting, χαίρειν, "sondern hat eine eigenständige Funktion als Segensgut in einem als Segensrede formulierten Briefanfang" (201). Berger also argues that in the Hellenistic letter style ἀπό points always to the sender of the letter (202). Consequently, "Der Apostel, der den Segenswunsch ausspricht, erscheint ... nur als dessen Übermittler, und ... ist gewissermaßen Gott zum 'eigentlichen' Absender geworden".

Berger further points to the relationship among the "Gattungen" of letter, testament and apocalypse (207ff). His arguments in this context also confirm what we have already seen with regard to the significance of the activity of writing (217):

> Daß der Lehrer seine Worte, die er letzten Endes nicht von sich selbst hat, speziell schriftlich niederlegt, wird auch im Rahmen einer besonderen theologischen Wertung der Schriftlichkeit selbst beurteilt ... Ist es aber ein Offenbarungsempfänger oder ein Apostel, der schreibt, so ist das Aufschreiben eine Weise der Übermittlung dessen, was er empfing ...: ... hier gilt Schriftlichkeit als besonders reine, getreue, ... zuverlässige und dauerhafte Weise der Mitteilung von Offenbarung.

Berger concludes that the letter of an apostle is "verbindliche, auf Gott zurückgeführte schriftliche Apostelrede" (219). If this argumentation is right, then it will follow that the writings of the apostles had a very high grade of authority.

We may add that an apostle as a "mediator" of revelation may be well aware of the difference between the level of authority of his own view and of that which he received from God or Jesus. We may, nevertheless, note that even in the context where Paul differentiates between what the "Lord" says (1Cor 7,10) and what he himself says (1Cor 7,12), he applies the following expressions of his own authority (RSV): "This is my rule in all the churches" (v.17); "I give my opinion as one who by the Lord's mercy is trustworthy" (v.25); "in my judgment ... And I think that I have the Spirit of God" (v.40).

We may find some further evidence of the consciousness of this authority. For example, in 1Thess 2,7 we read (RSV, vv.6b-7): "... though we might have made demands as apostles of Christ. But we were gentle among you, like a nurse taking care of her children." Pointing to this verse, and to two others, Schnackenburg affirms that Paul's major contribution to the understanding of apostleship is that "he connects the consciousness of apostolic authority (cf. 1Thess.2:7; 2Cor.10:8; 13:10) and the charismatic preaching in which Christ makes himself known" (1970, 303). 2Cor 13,10 may support particularly my present proposal that the writing of an apostle carries the weight of the apostolic authority which I have already argued for (RSV):

"I write this while I am away from you, in order that when I come I may not have to be severe in my use of the authority which the Lord has given me for building up and not for tearing down."

Without going into much exegetical detail, one further example is worth mentioning. In the introductory sentences of Romans we may find pointers to an awareness that Paul's writing is in some sense related to the writings of the Old Testament prophets. For example, in Rom 1,2, the term ὁ προεπηγγείλατο may express that when Paul is writing he is used by God to declare the fulfilment of promises made long before. The reference to διὰ τῶν προφητῶν αὐτοῦ may indicate that Paul stands in the line of the prophets in as much as there is a connection between a promise and its fulfilment. We have to note, however, that the question of the scheme "promise - fulfilment" is still much discussed in scholarship.[14] Nevertheless, in view of the expression ἐν γραφαῖς ἁγίαις in the same verse, one may argue that if a promise made by God was recorded in a sacred writing, then the witness of the fulfilment of the promise may also claim to write sacred writing. If to write about the Son of God meant to write sacred writing in the "Old Testament", then it should also mean the same in the new era (v.3). It is difficult to say whether or not Paul intended this inference. I argue that he may have had this in mind, because it is the same "gospel" which Paul is called to preach that had been promised "beforehand through the prophets in the holy scriptures" (vv.1-2).[15]

ee) Objections

Having argued for the case of a high authority of the apostles in early Christianity, we have to consider some objections which arise in connection with the role of apostolic authority in the "canonical process".

1) I have pointed to some passages which may be interpreted as evidence of an awareness of apostolic authority. However, the objection may be raised that the examples of the Pauline letters may not be extended to other parts of the New Testament. It is certainly true that my arguments here are being put forward only by way of example. It has to be exegetically examined what authority the individual New Testament writings claimed.

---

[14] See e.g. the survey by Reventlow 1983, 49ff. Cf. also O. Hofius's thesis: "Insbesondere wird deutlich: ... daß im Blick auf das Alte und Neue Testament durchaus ein Zusammenhang von Verheißung und Erfüllung wahrgenommen werden kann ..." (1995, 201).

[15] Another passage with a similar possible inference is Heb 1,1f. Cf. Hofius's affirmation: "Als sinnvoller Ansatz- und Ausgangspunkt für die angemessene Bestimmung des Verhältnisses der beiden Testamente zueinander darf der theologische Fundamentalsatz Hebr 1,1.2a gelten ..." (1995, 196).

My examples may be used as arguments, however, not only for the Pauline epistles, but for other writings which were thought of by the early Christians as having been written by apostles. Bienert summarises views in early Christianity about the authorship of the canonical Gospels in the following way (in Schneemelcher, 1992, 17):

> The apostles Matthew (=Levi) and John, who was identified with the 'beloved disciple', are indeed considered the authors of the Gospels of Matthew and John, but for Mark and Luke the title is not affirmed. They are simply described as companions and associates of the apostles, Mark as the associate of Peter and Luke as the companion of Paul.

It may be argued that "apostolic authority" may not only have applied to apostles, but also to people who were closely "associated" with apostles.

2) These proposals may partly answer the previous objection, but they also raise another one. Modern scholarship has come to question the view of early Christians concerning the authorship of New Testament writings in the case of many of the New Testament books. How do these results of scholarship relate to the "canonical process", and especially to the end of that process, to the New Testament canon as a "list"? To put this question in another way, What shall we do if we find that the "criteria" of the early Christians were not fulfilled; if, for example, they were wrong in holding a writing to be of apostolic origin?

This is an important question. In a way it is also related to the question of *Sachkritik*, or content criticism, which may be exercised by the modern scholar: a question which will emerge in my final chapter.

Different answers may be given to this question. It may be argued that if we find that a certain writing was not written by an apostle, and it is probable that it has become authoritative - and later, canonical - on the basis that it was thought that it was written by an apostle, then this result of scholarship will make the validity of speaking about a canon problematical. The New Testament canon as a "list" may not be justified, because it is a result, at least in part, of mistaken judgements concerning the origins of certain writings.

However, this proposal may be answered by two other lines of arguments. On the one hand, it may be argued that whether or not a "criterion" of canonicity was used in a right way by the early Christians, certain writings have become authoritative. Once these writings have reached a canonical status and have retained that status throughout history, the canon has become a historical fact. This is not challenged by the result of modern scholarship that the "criterion" was used wrongly. Christopher Tuckett argues along similar lines when he points to the phenomenon that more commentaries are written, for example, on 2Peter than on the Epistle to Diognetus, although, according to him, "many would argue" that the latter "is of about the same date as 2Peter and of considerably greater theological value". He affirms (1992, 11):

> ... we can recognize and accept this fact of canonicity without ourselves subscribing to the belief system for which these texts form a canon. We do not have to be Christians to acknowledge the fact that 2Peter and other texts do form a canon for the Christian Church.

Another possible argument against the objection in question may be that of affirming that at this point we are not concerned with the end result of the canonical process, but with the process itself. If our historical inquiry finds that apostolic authority played a role in the process during which certain writings have become authoritative and - later - canonical, then we shall be justified in pointing to the historical phenomenon of certain writings' becoming part of an authoritative, "canonical", group of writings. This section of my thesis has this as its aim and nothing more.

3) The other objection may be raised that it was not only the New Testament writings that claimed apostolic origins. As, for example, Bienert points out (26):

> It is ... not only the writings which later became canonical that refer to the apostles as authorities in questions of doctrine and church practice; Marcion and the gnostics also appeal to them ... Gnostic interest was directed to the apostles above all as bearers of divine revelations and mysteries, which the risen Lord was held to have imparted to his disciples after his resurrection and which then - by way of oral transmission from teacher to disciple - could become tradition.

As Bienert rightly affirms, there were writings other than our New Testament writings which bore the names of apostles as their authors.[16] However, Bienert himself points to the phenomenon that there was some way of differentiation concerning these writings among the early Christians. He remarks in addition to what we have quoted from him above (26): "Over against this [i.e. Gnostic traditions which were claimed to be based on oral traditions of the apostles] the Church tradition from Irenaeus on increasingly relied on the written tradition of the oldest historical witnesses".

It is appropriate to affirm in the context of these possible objections, what I aim at with the arguments developed so far in this chapter. The example of the "open" character of the Old Testament aims to show that in as much as there may not have existed a "closed" Old Testament canon at the time of the

---

[16] See e.g. his reference to the Gospel of Peter, and the Gospel of the Twelve, p.17.

writing of the New Testament books, it is also clear that there existed a group of Old Testament writings that had the status of Holy Scripture. The arguable presence of disputes over some writings did not make it impossible for the Jews to regard a group of their writings as having the authority of Scripture, or to use the later term, as being "canonical".

In a historical analogy I argue for the case that certain writings, which later became our New Testament, may have had the authority of Scripture even though there were other writings which were disputed. When I argue for the possibility of a "canonical process" of the New Testament writings in the first two Christian centuries, I do acknowledge the fact that certain writings achieved their authoritative, "canonical" status later than others. This openness of the New Testament "canon" in the first two (or three) Christian centuries, however, does not make it impossible to argue for the thesis that a "canonical process" was going on in these centuries. My arguments point to the historical probability of this canonical process, and to certain concrete factors of it.

It is also appropriate to mention here that the apostolic authority of certain writings was probably not the only "criterion" on the basis of which certain writings became authoritative and, later, canonical. When I argue for the case of the significance of this factor, I acknowledge that it is only one factor which played a role in the "canonical process".

Although no completeness may be aimed at in this thesis in this context either, it is necessary to discuss at least some writings as examples from the point of view of how they did or did not become part of the New Testament canon. It is this question to which we turn next.

8. Some examples of the "canonical process"

At this point it is important to repeat that I define the term "canonical process" as a process during which certain writings acquired an authoritative status and were regarded as being on the same level of authority as the Holy Scriptures of the "Old Testament". In as much as this process led to the final result that certain writings became canonical in the sense of being part of a "list" of sacred writings, we may use the term "canonical" to describe this process.

a. Early authoritative writings

It has long been widely held that some writings of our present New Testament were regarded as having a very high status of authority at an early stage in the history of the church while other writings of our New Testament were problematic for a long time, perhaps until the end of the second century, or even later.

Let us turn to the writings which were regarded as authoritative (sacred?) writings at an early stage. In this section it is worth referring to some nineteenth century scholars to indicate that significant discussions on these matters have been going on for about two hundred years. Scholars of the last century have pointed to phenomena and to problems which are still much discussed, and not yet decisively solved. One of the scholars of the previous centuries, whose ideas have been influential ever since, is Friedrich Schleiermacher.

aa) Collections of writings

Schleiermacher lectured on introductory matters (*Einleitung*) twice: in 1829 and in the winter of 1831-32. G. Wolde published the second series of lectures and only referred to the first series of lectures where they were more detailed or differed from the later ones (1845, XVI). In this work we find Schleiermacher's hypothesis that there were probably two collections under the titles τὸ εὐαγγέλιον and ὁ ἀπόστολος respectively (59). The former title referred to the four Gospels, the latter to the writings of Paul.[17] According to Schleiermacher, the collection of Pauline letters was enlarged first by the addition of three catholic epistles (James, 1Peter, 1John), then of the remaining four.

Zahn reached similar results. He affirmed that at the end of the second century there was a group of basic writings ("Grundstock") accepted by all churches: the four Gospels, thirteen letters of Paul, and Acts (1888, 430). Apart from the Syrian church, other letters belonged to that basic circle in wide parts of the church: 1Peter, 1John, Revelation and perhaps Jude (432).

The view of "collections" may be supported by the manuscript evidence. Most of the manuscripts that contain more than fragments only, indeed, more than one book, are later than the time of the emergence of the canon as a "list" (fourth century). However, this may be seen as an argument for the likelihood that collections that were copied after the time of canonisation probably existed as collections prior to the time of canonisation. K. Aland and

---

[17] It is worth noting that the terminology is that of Marcion, although Marcion understood fewer writings under these terms, as we have seen earlier.

B. Aland (1987, 78) have summarised the numbers of manuscripts in which we have separate collections of, for example, the four Gospels, Acts and the Catholic letters, the Pauline letters. We also have combinations of these groups. Revelation stands alone in some manuscripts, but it can stand together with the other groups (see also Table 4, Chart 4, p.83). We have to note that the "sequence of the New Testament writings varies in the manuscripts, not only in the order of the four groups of writings themselves but also in the order of the writings within each group" (79).[18]

I think it is a likely hypothesis that there existed shorter collections which later together formed the whole canon. I think that it is also important to see that these collections may also have been regarded as Scripture, or being "canonical". We may at this point cautiously argue against Wrede who stated that the early Church did not have and did not even intend to have a "collected NT" prior to ca. A.D. 150 (1909, 130). Against this statement I propose that the church may have intended to have, at least, collections of parts of the later New Testament. However, we also have to acknowledge that the "Grundstock", which is argued for by Zahn, may have been different in some parts of the church.

It may also be worth advancing the hypothesis toward the possibility of more, even shorter, collections. For example, the Pastorals may have been a collection before the thirteen letter Pauline corpus was put together. K. Aland's and B. Aland's following remark, based on the manuscript evidence, may support this proposal (1987, 79): "The Pauline corpus represents a cumulative development from smaller collections, raising additional problems with its expansion to include the deutero-Pauline letters".

Zahn pointed to the phenomenon that in the *Hypotyposes* of Clement of Alexandria Paul's letters to the congregations are discussed in books 4 and 5, whereas the "private letters", i.e. the Pastorals and Philemon, are dealt with in book 7 (book 6 expounds the Acts) (1888, 272). Zahn proposed (271): "Es ist sehr möglich und für einige Theile der Kirche sogar sehr wahrscheinlich, daß die 4 Privatbriefe auch äußerlich eine Gruppe für sich bildeten ..."

Although - at least some of - the catholic epistles may be disputed to have belonged to the "Grundstock", it is worth considering that they may have formed a collection. Zahn argued that 2John and 3John may have been attached to 1John also in those cases where only 1John is referred to, but due to the shortness of these letters they were not quoted (209ff).

---

[18] For a recent discussion of the manuscript evidence see D. Trobisch 1996, especially the chapter entitled "Reihenfolge und Umfang in den Handschriften" (pp.35-68).

bb) The adoption of the codex

It is worth mentioning that the emergence of the codex made it possible that certain writings could be bound or "published" together. C.H. Roberts and T.C. Skeat have affirmed that "it is impossible to believe that the Christian adoption of the codex can have taken place any later than *circ.* A.D. 100 (it may, of course have been earlier) ..." (1987, 61). Unfortunately, we do not have any manuscripts from the first century (and we do not have any autographs), but on the basis of the fact that Christians used the codex form in the second century, we may hold that "Christians adopted the codex for their writings from the outset" (45).[19]

Roberts and Skeat affirm that there is no direct evidence for seeing a connection between the adoption of the codex and the development of the canon (62). In particular, it is "very difficult to trace any possible link between the Four-Gospel Canon and the adoption of the codex" (64). The main reason for this is that "both during and after the second century, Gospels continued to circulate individually or in smaller groups or in conjunction with other books of the Bible" (65). However, they affirm that it would have been "technically possible" to include our four Gospels in one codex. The same applies to the Pauline letters which "form a body considerably shorter than the Gospels" (66). However, it is only from the third century that we have an example of a codex of the Pauline letters, the Chester Beatty codex.

Acknowledging the fact that we do not have early evidence, it is significant for my thesis that the possibility existed for early Christians to put collections of writings into one codex already at the end of the first century, or perhaps even earlier.

To sum up, Schleiermacher has a good argument for the view that the longer collections were probably late, because otherwise there would not have been so many uncertainties with regard to the inclusion or omission of individual writings (in Wolde, 1845, 61). However, it is possible to hold that there existed short collections in the earlier period. These writings were gathered into collections because they were treasured as authoritative (perhaps sacred) writings.

b. Disputed writings

Schleiermacher argued that the term ἀντιλεγόμενα in Eusebius must refer to the fact that these writings were not accepted in all churches rather than to

---

[19] Trobisch has re-affirmed this thesis more recently (1996, 31): "Es handelt sich bei neutestamentlichen Handschriften von der äußeren Form her von Anfang an um Bücher, nicht um Rollen".

the doubts concerning their authors. His main argument in favour of this affirmation is that the Epistles of Barnabas and Clement were probably regarded as written by these authors, yet they were put into that category (45). This is a good argument. However, it has to be added that it is probable that different factors or different combinations of factors may have played a role in what was accepted and what was not, in the case of each individual "disputed" writing.

Schleiermacher himself pointed to this. Although he held that the main condition for a writing to become canonical was that it had to contain "true doctrine" ("ächte Lehre", 39), he affirmed that there were two significant factors in the formation of the canon. On the one hand, the churches collected writings which were authentic witnesses to the true doctrine. On the other hand, they brought into harmony the collections of writings which were in use in worship. These two aspects were often in opposition to one another (66). Some writings were accepted into the canon for one reason although it was surrounded with doubts with regard to the other (67). We may add that these two reasons may coincide in certain cases: writings may have been read in worship because they were regarded as containing a true doctrine.

aa) Hebrews

With regard to Hebrews, Franz Overbeck argued in 1880 that its "canonisation" could be achieved only at a time and place "wo man wenig genug vom Hbf. wusste, um ihn als das gelten zu lassen, als was er in den Kanon gedrungen ist, nämlich als paulinischen Brief" (1965, 69).

Zahn argued, in my opinion convincingly, against Overbeck in relation to Hebrews (1888, 300-301). Zahn acknowledged that in Alexandria Hebrews was regarded as a letter of Paul, and it was canonical (300). In Rome, Carthage and Lyons Hebrews was not regarded as Pauline nor was it part of the canon. However, there was no dispute over it among the oriental and occidental churches (against Overbeck, Zahn 301, n.1). Nor is it true that Hebrews was only accepted into the canon where by mistake it was regarded as a letter of Paul (302). There were churches where it was held to have been written by Barnabas, yet regarded as canonical (301-302).

It is rather likely that the usage of the letter in worship alongside Pauline letters contributed to the emergence of the view that it had been written by Paul (302). Zahn also pointed to the fact that individual theologians in the West did read and refer to Hebrews (e.g. Irenaeus, Tertullian) (300). In his opinion it is likely, that although Hebrews influenced the theological ideas and modes of speech ("Redeweisen") in the same way as did the biblical writings (300), it was more and more "forgotten about" in the West during the second and third centuries (301).

bb) James, 2Peter

This debate between Overbeck and Zahn may help us to recognise another important element in the canonical process: the different views that were possible among churches in different geographical areas with regard to the same writing.

Schleiermacher argued that the collections of various geographical areas were compared. Gradually the contents of the collections became the same (in Wolde, 1845, 62). I agree with him in that it is important to acknowledge the probability that with the travelling of Christians the "canons" of different areas may have influenced one another (65, 73).

Another example of this phenomenon may be James which was not canonical in the West at the time of the Muratorian Canon (Zahn 1888, 323), yet it was accepted in the Greek speaking Orient (325).

2Peter presents a major difficulty for seeing it in a canonical process. It was not regarded as canonical at the end of the second century (Zahn 1888, 312ff). However, Zahn pointed to the interesting phenomenon that Jude, a close "relative" of 2Peter, was widely accepted as sacred writing at the same time (319ff). It is notoriously difficult to establish what was the relationship between these two writings. If 2Peter is later than Jude, then we may cautiously raise the possibility that Jude's firm status may have played a role in the reception of 2Peter: at least first among circles which held that the warnings concerning judgement in Jude were of great significance.[20]

cc) Writings rejected

We also have to address briefly another phenomenon. There were writings which were used in worship at an early stage at least in parts of the church, but disappeared from the canon later.[21] Zahn affirmed that this showed that at the end of the second century those writings of the apostolic era - to use this phrase in its widest sense - which were regarded as useful for the building up of the church did belong to the circle of sacred writings (1888, 365).

Zahn pointed to the fact that the Muratorian Canon excluded the Shepherd of Hermas from the apostolic writings because the Shepherd was written after

---

[20] It is worth noting with K. Aland and B. Aland that the third Bodmer papyrus, P^{72}, "which dates from the third/fourth century ... contains the letters of Peter and Jude as a single collection of writings" (1987, 87). This codex, however, contains non-canonical writings, too. Trobisch has shown that the codex was put together from more than one earlier codices, but he also affirms that: "Die neutestamentlichen Schriften sind von der gleichen Hand angefertigt" (1996, 49). I further note here that the only explicit quotation in the New Testament from the "Old Testament apocrypha" is in Jude, in vv.14-15: 1Enoch 1,9 (see H.F.D. Sparks 1989, 174).

[21] Zahn discusses, for example, the Shepherd of Hermas, 1888, 326ff; the Letter of Barnabas, 347ff; the letters of Clement, 351ff; the Didache, 360ff.

the apostolic period (117). Zahn argued that there was no canon yet but there was an awareness of a "canonical time" ("eine kanonische Zeit") (116).[22]

Zahn argued in regard to this time factor in the canonical process by affirming that the idea of apostolicity in early Christianity was connected with the conviction "daß sämtliche Theile des überlieferten NT's von Aposteln und Genossen der Apostel verfaßt und somit zuverlässige Urkunden der Apostelzeit, insbesondere der apostolischen Predigt und Überlieferung seien" (449).

However, this time factor cannot be regarded as crucial in the case of all the writings. On the one hand, 1Clement is generally dated around A.D. 96, or, "not much later than 100 A.D." (K. Lake in *The Apostolic Fathers*, vol. 1, 1985, 5). Thus it may originate from a period in which some scholars would date some of the New Testament writings (e.g. John's Gospel, 2Peter, the Pastorals).

On the other hand, although the Shepherd of Hermas itself was not accepted by the author of the Muratorian Canon, this work "empfiehlt ... die private Lektüre des 'Hirten' (Zeile 77: *ideo legi eum [sc. Pastorem] quidem oportet)*" (Brox 1991, 56). The Shepherd of Hermas enjoyed "Hochschätzung ... Autorität und Gewicht" by other Christians even later than the end of the second century (71). This may be seen in the fact that the Codex Sinaiticus from the fourth century contains it (more exactly a portion of it) "hinter dem Barnabasbrief im Anschluß an das NT eingeordnet" (13). Whether or not this expression of "authority" meant that the Shepherd was regarded as canonical, remains an open question. In opposition to the view of other scholars, Brox does not think that the Shepherd's presence in the Codex Sinaiticus means that it held canonical status (71).

To sum up, we may say that some of the writings of our New Testament were accepted as having high authority very early on, perhaps around the turn of the first century or earlier, for example the four Gospels, and (at least some of) the letters that were attributed to Paul. Some other writings, for example some of the catholic epistles, were accepted later. There were other writings that were regarded as precious reading at an early stage, perhaps in the beginning of the second century, but were not included later in the canon. The decisions of "inclusion" or "exclusion" may have been based on different "criteria" in the case of the individual books - and perhaps even in different geographical areas. Although we have very little evidence from the first two

---

[22] Zahn dated the content of the Muratorian Canon around A.D. 200, see e.g. 1890, 12-13. This dating is also shared by Schneemelcher, 1991a, 34. For arguments in support of a fourth century dating see A.C. Sundberg 1973, L.M. McDonald 1996. Recently, G.N. Stanton (1996) has answered the main arguments for a fourth century dating and has argued himself for a second century date for the Muratorian Fragment. I find his arguments convincing.

centuries, we may find pointers to the phenomenon that a canonical process was going on; for example, decisions were made concerning what should be read in worship. There may have been going on a process of comparing the authoritative writings of different regions - and some regions may have convinced others to include or exclude certain writings from their reading list of the services of worship.[23]

9. On the genre of the New Testament writings

In the same tentative way as I have argued for the case of historical analogies concerning a canonical process of the Old Testament and a "second canon" of certain apocalyptic writings and also for the authority of apostolic writings, we may finally consider an argument from a formal point of view. We shall examine briefly how the genres of the various New Testament writings relate to the genres of other early Christian literature.

a. *Overbeck on the origins of Patristic literature*

In 1882 Franz Overbeck published an article entitled "Über die Anfänge der patristischen Literatur".[24] This article is of significance from two points of view. On the one hand, its author is a critical scholar who affirmed, concerning his own aims, with a reference to F.C. Baur's influence on him (1981 = 1903, 3-4):

> Was ich mir von seiner historischen Kritik des Urchristenthums zu assimiliren vermochte beschränkte sich stets auf die, wie mir freilich schien, vollkommen siegreiche Erstreitung seines Rechts, das Urchristenthum rein historisch, d. h. wie es wirklich gewesen, darzustellen, gegen die damalige theologische Apologetik oder die Prätention der Theologie ihm dieses Recht zu verlegen.

This concentration on a "kritisch-historischen Verständniss des Christenthums" (8), without the bias of a theologian (cf. 188), makes Overbeck's work a significant witness in our study.

On the other hand, the article in question does not simply deal with the Patristic literature, but it compares Patristic literature with what we find in the New Testament. In this way the article is a significant contribution to our

---

[23] For an excellent summary of the main data in relation to the formation of the "Christian biblical canon" see L.M. McDonald 1995.

[24] Here this work is referred to from a reproduction by Benno Verlag, no date.

present subject, the inquiry concerning the distinction of the New Testament canon from other early Christian literature.

Overbeck's thesis is that the New Testament writings cannot be taken as the origin of Christian literature (1882, 16). The church's teaching on inspiration points in this direction (16-17):

> Der Satz, daß mit dem Neuen Testament die christliche Literatur nicht anfängt, hat einmal das Urteil der ganzen Kirche für sich, wenn diese den neutestamentlichen Schriften die Entstehung aus göttlicher Eingebung, aus Inspiration des heiligen Geistes ausschließlich zuspricht und damit zwischen dem Neuen Testament und der sonstigen christlichen Literatur eine Schranke zieht ...

This first argument seems to be powerful. However, the question arises, When did the church first attribute inspiration to the New Testament? If we speak about the "New Testament", Overbeck's affirmation must refer to a time when we already had a recognisable canon. In the context of my thesis, Overbeck's argument may be complemented by the qualification that we may rather speak of (some of the) New Testament writings, i.e. about a time when these writings did not yet form a canonical "list". Even then we may use Overbeck's argument by pointing to the early Christian awareness of "inspiration", as it is expressed, for example, in 2Pet 1,20f and in the fact that 2Peter seems to presuppose that Paul's letters were read in congregations as "other scriptures" were read (3,16f). This latter interpretation is supported by Barr. He affirms with reference to 2Pet 3,16 that for the author of 2Peter "the Pauline letters were already by implication classed as γραφαί" (1983, 25).

Overbeck next affirms that the Church Fathers did not think of the apostles as their forerunners in writing literature (1882, 18). The Church Fathers thought that they were no longer taking ("schöpfen") "aus der Quelle apostolischer Schriftstellerei". This argument may be upheld even against Koester's point.[25] The presence of credal elements in the New Testament and in the writings of the Apostolic Fathers does not overrule this distinction the Fathers themselves maintained between the New Testament and their own writings.

Overbeck's key argument is based on a comparison between forms in the New Testament and in the Patristic literature. This comparison shows that there is a gap ("Scheidung", 1882, 18) between these two kinds of literature (18-19), and "... daß es zwischen beiden Literaturen ... literarhistorisch keinen Zusammenhang gibt". Overbeck has two main lines of arguments.

1) On the one hand, he affirms that there are forms in the New Testament which are the same in all periods of Christian literature, but these are not real

---

[25] See my second chapter, section 4.d in relation to Robinson-Koester, 1971, 272-273.

literature ("gar nicht im eigentlichen Bereich der Literatur", 19). For example, the apostolic letters belong to this category. Overbeck argues that "einem jeden Literaturwerk ist die schriftliche Form für seinen Inhalt wesentlich". In the case of a letter the writer only writes because of the distance; the writer could just as well share his message orally. "So schrieb auch Paulus an seine Gemeinden nur um ihnen schriftlich zu sagen, was er ihnen mündlich gesagt hätte, wenn er jedesmal an Ort und Stelle gewesen wäre". It is worth noting here that this argument does not weaken that of K. Berger according to which a letter of an apostle is "a binding apostolic speech in written form - originating from God" (1974, 219). The possible "oral" character of a message contained in a letter does not lessen the authority of the content.

According to Overbeck, the addressees of a letter also distinguish it from any other work of literature (1882, 19-20). Letters are written to concrete addressees (20). The addressees of a work of literature are "ein ideales Publikum", unknown to the author. Overbeck acknowledges that "Briefe wohl zum Ansehen von Büchern zu gelangen ... vermögen" - as it is the case with the letters of the New Testament. He adds, however, that this phenomenon is "ein nachträgliches Erlebnis, das gerade mit ihrer ursprünglichen Absicht und der eigenen Form dieser Schriftstücke nichts zu tun hat" (21).

Although Overbeck rightly points to the fact that letters were written in the Christian congregations also after the time of the New Testament letters, he also affirms that "es wird ... niemandem in den Sinn kommen, diese so entstehende reine Gelegenheitsschriftstellerei der alten Kirche literaturgeschichtlich aus der apostolischen abzuleiten ..." (21). We may add that we may distinguish between the letters of apostles and later letters on the basis of the introductory formulae - as we have seen above in the thesis of Klaus Berger. Berger affirms that although there are "Nachahmungen des apostolischen Briefstiles" at the beginning of some later letters (1974, 190, n.4), nevertheless "gilt der z.B. von Paulus verwendete Briefeingang als typisch 'apostolisch'" from a very early period on.[26]

It may be appropriate here also to point to the phenomenon that (at least some of) the letters of our New Testament were read in more than one congregation, and not only among the immediate addressees (cf. e.g. Col 4,16).[27]

---

[26] Berger refers, for example, to "Ign. Trall tit", 1974, 190, n.4.

[27] Cf. the thesis of D. Trobisch, who argues that Paul even "edited" some of his letters. On the basis of the examples he examined he writes under the heading "Autorenrezensionen von Einzelbriefen" (1989, 119): "Die überwältigende Mehreit der betrachteten Briefsammlungen, die aus tatsächlich geführten Korrespondenzen entstanden, gehen in ihren Anfängen auf Briefausgaben zurück, die der Autor selbst veranlaßt hat. Auch bei den Paulusbriefen halte ich die älteste Form des Röm, 1Kor, 2Kor, Phil und 1Thess für das Ergebnis einer Autorenrezension."

2) On the other hand, Overbeck argues that there are forms of books in the New Testament which belong to real literature, but are not continued in later periods (1882, 19). The Gospels, Acts, and the Apocalypse belong to this category, and perhaps the Catholic Epistles (23). The Catholic Epistles do not belong to the genre of the letters discussed above, because their addressees are characterised with an "unbestimmte Allgemeinheit" (22). The Gospels and Acts are not history books in the sense that they might be called the beginning of the writing of church history (24). It is a misleading term when people call these books the "historical books" of the New Testament. They have to be distinguished from the "Wurzeln der Kirchengeschichtschreibung". The Patristic literature does not attempt to take up and continue the "historical theme" of the Gospels and Acts (25). The Shepherd of Hermas is not a real example of the genre of the New Testament Apocalypse because of its later origin (27).

Overbeck affirms that the apocryphal writings with the names of the genres of the Gospel, Acts and Apocalypse are not a real counter-argument, because they originate outside the period of the New Testament literature of these genres. The apocryphal writings may make claims of "uralten" origins; nevertheless this claim is a "fiction" (23; see also 29).

Overbeck calls the writings of the New Testament "Urliteratur" (29). According to him, when in the second half of the second century A.D. the canon began to take shape, this phenomenon meant the end of the Early Christian literature (29-30). The consequence of the formation of the canon is summarised by Overbeck in this way (29):

> ... am Kanon der neutestamentlichen Schriften hält Jedermann unter uns den Totenschein der Literatur, von welcher hier die Rede ist, in der Hand. Als mit der Aufstellung der Sammlung der in dem Neuen Testament verbundenen Schriften als der allein gültigen schriftlichen Urkunde der Anfänge des Christentums ... durch ausschließliche Privilegierung des (wirklich oder vermeintlich) apostolischen Zweiges der christlichen Urliteratur der Kanon des Neuen Testaments entstanden war, so lag in diesem Vorgang ... an sich selbst die formelle Beurkundung der Tatsache, daß die Quellen, aus denen diese Urliteratur ihr Leben gesogen hatte, versiegt seien und sie [i.e. the "Urliteratur"!] ihr Ende erreicht habe.

According to Overbeck, the period of Patristic writings begins with the apologists (from A.D. 130 on, p.43). They made use of the forms of profane literature, because they did not write for Christians (45, 47). This may be called the "elementary school of Patristic literature" (47). From Clement of Alexandria on we find Patristic writings which made use of forms of profane literature, although they were written for Christians (49ff).

To sum up, Overbeck distinguishes between Early Christian "Urliteratur" and Christian literature. The latter is not a continuation of the former, which means that they are not simply different periods of the same historical development. The Early Christian literature had to die (!) before a writing like, for example, that of Clement of Alexandria could possibly come into existence (67). The connection between the two kinds of literature is that the New Testament canon became the norm for the Patristic literature (69).

If this thesis is right, then we have found an argument based on form to distinguish the New Testament from other early Christian writings. It has to be noted that Overbeck's thesis has not found widespread support. For example, Schneemelcher affirms that although Overbeck is right in distinguishing between "primitive literature" (*Urliteratur*) and "Christian literature" (1991a, 53), nevertheless "'primitive literature' in part continued" in the apocrypha "from the point of view of the history of *Gattungen*". According to Schneemelcher, the apocrypha "do not belong to the 'patristic literature' ..., but represent a separate category alongside, and in continuation of, the 'primitive literature'" (54).

Schneemelcher's counter-thesis may be understood as one related to Koester's thesis concerning the origins of "heresy".[28] However, whereas Koester argued on the basis of smaller units of genres, Schneemelcher argues on the level of genres of whole writings. Consequently, it is appropriate that we consider the main New Testament genres and the genres of the apocrypha in some detail.

b. *The Gospel genre*

It has been long discussed in scholarly debates whether or not the genre of the four canonical Gospels is a unique Christian creation. In a recent doctoral thesis R.A. Burridge has argued afresh for the thesis (which was widespread in the nineteenth century) that the genre of the canonical Gospels may be derived from the Graeco-Roman biography (1992, 240). The conclusion of his thesis is that "a wide range of similarities have been discovered between the gospels and Graeco-Roman βίοι; the differences are not sufficiently marked or significant to prevent the gospels from belonging to the genre of βίος literature" (242-243).

Burridge acknowledges that "Acts and the gospels may be related genres" (246). However, he goes on to affirm that "Luke's gospel itself shares the same family resemblance as the other three gospels". From Burridge's thesis it seems to follow that the real question is not whether or not the gospel

---

[28] I have already argued against the latter in my second chapter.

genre is a Christian invention, but whether or not the four Gospels belong together - and can be distinguished from other early Christian Gospels.

In his thesis Burridge accepts many of the results of the 1982 Tübingen Symposium on the gospels (see Stuhlmacher 1983). He agrees on the following views (243). I.H. Marshall argued that the pattern of "Q" as an alternative pattern to the Gospels was not followed by Luke and Matthew (1983, 293). Marshall argued with due caution that if Q ever existed it might be seen as analogous to the "Gospel of Thomas which understands itself as a collection of sayings of Jesus". Marshall then affirms that "Luke ... deliberately rejected the Q-type of composition for one that was broadly similar to that of Mk". I have already mentioned that the Q hypothesis is still much debated. It is worth noting, however, that on the basis of this widely held hypothesis the common features of the canonical Gospels stand out in contra-distinction to some other "Gospels": the Gospel of Thomas and "Q".

Burridge (243) also approves of J.D.G. Dunn's conclusion (1983, 338-339) that: "For all its differences from the Synoptics, John is far closer to them than to any other ancient writing ..." Dunn emphasises that although the author of the Fourth Gospel presents detailed discourses of Jesus, "the Evangelist did not elect to present a document consisting solely of the discourses or sayings of the redeemer (we may contrast gnostic equivalents like Gospel of Thomas, Thomas the Contender and Pistis Sophia)" (339).

In the collection of the papers of the same *symposium* Robert Guelich argues for the thesis that our canonical Gospels "do stand without adequate parallel in form and content in the literary world" (1983, 216). Consequently, "The [canonical] Gospels constitute a literary genre". It is significant for my thesis that although Guelich and Burridge disagree on the question of the uniqueness of the genre of the canonical Gospels, they both differentiate between the canonical Gospels and the apocryphal Gospels. Concerning some of the apocryphal Gospels Guelich asserts that (215):

> ... many of these 'gospels' come to us in name only, since their content exists only in scattered citations, if at all. Consequently, the literary evidence remains so fragmentary that one can hardly make adequate comparisons.

Concerning the *Gospel of the Nazaraeans* and the *Gospel of the Ebionites* Guelich affirms that they "appear to be variants of Matthew's Gospel" (215, n.201). In his opinion, "The *Secret Gospel of Mark* clearly relates to Mark and the *Gospel of the Hebrews* may reflect influence from all four Gospels" (*ibid.*; see also Burridge 249).

Burridge affirms concerning the *Gospel of Thomas*, the *Gospel of Truth*, the *Gospel of Philip* that they have a "pattern of generic features" that is different from the canonical gospels (250). Other writings that "concentrate on one part of the story of Jesus" do not share "the family resemblance of the four canonical gospels" (for example, the *Protevangelium of James*, the "infancy gospels" and the "passion gospels"). Burridge classifies these writings as a later "stage of reinterpretation and sophistication away from the basic generic pattern of βιοι Ἰησοῦ" (250; see also Guelich 216).

We have been concerned here with formal observations, but it has to be added that the question of form and content belong together. As D. Dormeyer concludes in his survey on the "Gospel as a literary and theological genre" (1989, 194):

> Form und Inhalt Evangelium gestalten sich gegenseitig ... Gattungsgeschichte ist Theologiegeschichte und umgekehrt ist Theologiegeschichte Gattungsgeschichte.

In summary, I think we may argue that whatever the origin of the genre of the canonical Gospels may be, they may be differentiated from other Gospels on a formal basis, on the basis of genre. This proposal leaves room for the existence of earlier stages of the Gospels we now have and for the existence of Gospels which may have been closely related to our canonical Gospels. We have seen some examples of this possibility above (e.g. the *Gospel of the Nazaraeans*). We may add that the *Memoirs of the Apostles* mentioned by Justin Martyr may belong to this group, irrespective of the decision whether one holds that it is a reference to our canonical Gospels (so e.g. L. Abramowski 1983, 341, 353), or that the term may refer to another Gospel the content of which was so closely related to our canonical Gospels that the *Memoirs* could be "given up" by the later church, since they thought the "canonical" Gospels contained everything the *Memoirs* contained.

c. The other New Testament genres

aa) Letters
We have already seen arguments advanced in relation to the distinct character of the New Testament letters. In as much as the genre of the letter is not a distinctively New Testament genre, we have seen arguments (mainly in connection with our discussion of Berger's and Overbeck's theses) that the "apostolic" letters held a high authority. We have also seen the argument that letters of the Patristic period did not claim to be a "continuation" of the apostolic letters.

bb) "Acts"

Concerning the apocryphal "Acts" von Campenhausen affirms that (1968, 249; ET: 1972, 214): "Sie sind nicht geschaffen, um mit der kanonischen Apostelgeschichte des Lukas zu konkurrieren". With regard to those "Acts" which were ascribed to Paul, von Campenhausen points out that although they had certain "success", nevertheless "sie noch zu Lebzeiten ihres wirklichen Verfassers als Fälschung entlarvt wurden" (249-250; ET: 214).

Von Campenhausen remarks that the inclusion of the genre of Acts in the New Testament "canon" was not without "dangers" (250; ET: 214). The Manichaeans and other "sects" made use of "ein ganzes Corpus von Apostelakten". These were rejected in the "catholic literature" from Eusebius onward.

In the "Introduction" to the second volume of the *New Testament Apocrypha* (which was edited by himself), Schneemelcher emphasises that the relation of the literature of apocryphal Acts "to the canon cannot be described in a single sentence, but must be clarified for each individual document separately" (1992a, 3). This work has to be done, but it goes beyond the limits of my thesis. Here it may suffice to quote Schneemelcher's summarising statement from the same context, where he affirms that the apocryphal Acts of apostles "are not shaped after the pattern of the canonical Acts, even though knowledge of it cannot be excluded".

cc) Apocalypses

The genre of the apocalypse is not a specifically Christian one. According to Ph. Vielhauer and G. Strecker, the early Christian movement, "especially the Palestinian and hellenistic-Jewish Christian wing", took over literary documents from the Jewish Apocalyptic and "'christianised' them by means of a rewriting of varying kinds and intensity" (1992a, 558-559). Christianity also took over the literary form of the apocalypse from Jewish Apocalyptic "and produced numerous works of its own in this genre" (559).

Concerning the only canonical apocalypse, the "Revelation of John", Vielhauer and Strecker affirm that "it shows a close relationship to Jewish Apocalyptic in form and in materials, but ... it reveals the not inconsiderable influence of Christian features on the accepted tradition" (1992b, 583). In spite of these phenomena, they assert that Revelation "is unique even among the Christian apocalypses, especially since important elements of Jewish Apocalyptic are lacking (e.g. wisdom *ex eventu*, the sealing of the revelations)".[29]

---

[29] To this last remark we may add that Revelation speaks about the opening of seals (e.g. 5,2.5.9; 6,1 etc.), rather than about sealing.

Within the limits of this thesis I cannot make a comparison between Revelation and other early Christian apocalypses. It may suffice to note with von Campenhausen that although there were other writings of the same genre in early Christianity, in the second half of the second century "hatte die Krise bereits eingesetzt, die dem unkontrollierten Wachstum des Neuen Testaments und ganz besonders dem apokalyptischen Schrifttum Halt gebot" (1968, 257; ET: 1972, 221). According to von Campenhausen, the "canonisation" of Revelation was not an answer of the catholic church to Marcion, since the latter did not include any apocalypse in his canon (255; ET: 219). Consequently, "Man brauchte hier also keinen rechtgläubigen Ersatz zu schaffen". Without reopening the discussion we have already led over the role of Marcion and the Montanist movement in the formation of the New Testament canon, it is important to see that von Campenhausen holds that the "new prophecy" of the Montanist movement was not acceptable to the catholic church (cf. 257; ET: 221). He affirms concerning the Montanist movement (258; ET: 221): "Es sind alte prophetische und apokalyptische Traditionen im Stile der kleinasiatischen Johannes-Offenbarung, die hier fortwirken und plötzlich eine massive und jähe Aktualisierung erfahren". The rejection of this "apocalyptical" movement by the catholic church may be seen as an indication that they distinguished between Revelation and other apocalyptical literature, in spite of possible similarities in terms of "genres".

It may be worth noting that Zahn argued that Revelation was regarded by the early Christians as the boundary of the New Testament "canon", because John, who was believed to be its author at least in Asia Minor, was considered to be the apostle who outlived his fellow apostles (1888, 116). With reference to Rev 22,18 Zahn affirms that the "Montanist" Tertullian as well as the "anti-Montanist" Irenaeus could refer to the end of Revelation "als die Grenzmarke der hl. Schriften des NT's" (115).

To sum up, in as much as Revelation is not the only representative of the genre of the apocalypse in early Christianity, one may argue for the thesis that (at least a part of) early Christianity recognised it at an early stage, perhaps around the middle of the second century, as the only "apocalypse" in the form of a book which they received as authoritative - and later as a book among the "canonical" writings.

10. Conclusion

In this chapter I have discussed arguments in relation to the question whether or not the historian can find justification for the distinction of the canonical writings among all the available early Christian literature.

Our discussions have repeatedly encountered the difficulty that we have very little evidence from the earlier stages of the history of the writings that later became canonical. Yet I have argued that we can trace a "canonical process" at least in a hypothetical, tentative way.

With Schneemelcher I have argued against the view that the New Testament canon was an answer of the church to the challenge put to them by Marcion's canon. Marcion, and the struggle with other "heresies", may have played a role in the formation of the canon of the catholic church: these struggles may have given impulses to identify what the catholic church believed and adhered to. However, these impulses only strengthened what was already going on in the church: a process that was elevating certain writings to a high level of authority. This level was the same as that of the "Old Testament" Scripture.

I have argued that the canonical process of the Old Testament provides us with a historical analogy to the formation of the New Testament canon. Most probably, the Old Testament canon was not yet fixed at the time when the books of the New Testament were written. However, some books of the Old Testament were "canonical", and were regarded by the early Christians as Scripture.

We have some evidence from the intertestamental literature that some Jews before and during the first Christian century were producing "canonical" writings which were outside the other "canonical" group of writings which they also revered. I have cautiously raised the possibility that there may have been a tradition among Jews to write a "second canon", a canon which is put to the side of the existing "canon" when the end-time approaches. The Temple Scroll in Qumran and the seventy books, apart from the already canonical twenty-four, in 4Ezra may be in connection with this tradition.

We have seen that it is difficult to establish criteria according to which the church received a Christian writing as authoritative. I have argued that different factors may have been decisive in the case of the individual writings. Diversities in different geographical areas were possible. Later on, however, collections of different regions may have influenced one another; the collections may have been harmonised.

Apostolic authority played a significant role in the writings' becoming "canonical". Writings which were held to have been written by apostles, or associates of apostles, were read in congregations during worship. Even letters which were originally written to one particular congregation, or, indeed to an individual, were circulated to others. The apostles' letter conveyed to the churches God's blessing and message, God's "revelation".

We have seen that it is understandable that the tradition about the one whom the early Christians believed to have been the Messiah would be committed to writing. Apostolic writings, and especially writings recording traditions about the arrival of the Messiah, may have claimed the high authority of the status of a "second canon".

The question arises, Can a historian make a distinction among writings which claim to be of apostolic origin and/or relate to the traditions of the Messiah? We have considered some formal arguments, although with the necessary qualification that matters of content cannot be avoided in this context either. The early church most likely made certain distinctions on the basis of both content and form.

I have argued that although the genres of the books of the New Testament were not "unique" to one group of Christianity, the historian can nevertheless find evidence that points to differentiation within early Christianity itself. In as much as a historian finds that a group of Christians separates its writings from the writings of another group of Christians, the historian is justified in making the distinction between "canons". The New Testament, through a lengthy process of perhaps two or three hundred years, emerged as a canon of one part of Christianity. Some parts of the New Testament may have been regarded by the early Christians as having high authority, even possibly a "canonical" status, prior to the time when the canon was established. Thus, already with regard to the canonical process that led to the New Testament canon the historian may make distinctions among the early Christian literature. The study of the origins of the canon affirms that the canon can be justified.

In this chapter formal aspects have had a prominence. We have to ask the question, however, Do we find support for the canon in its content? Is there a unity within the theological content of the New Testament? It is this question we turn to in the next chapter.

Chapter Four

What Does Theological Diversity Mean for New Testament Theology?

1. Introduction

a. "New Testament"

In the previous chapter we have surveyed major problems which arise when a historian distinguishes a canon from other writings (or canons) in early Christian literature. Having argued that the distinction between "canons" may be justified, I have prepared the way for justifying a historian's decision to study the theology of one particular group of early Christians. As we have seen, this one particular group may be chosen from more than one group, because it seems to be the case that more than one group of Christians had its own "canon".

It is, therefore, legitimate that a historian may choose to focus his attention on the group of Christians that has emerged as "orthodox". To put it in a way that may be an answer to Wrede's challenging statement we have seen earlier: the term "New Testament" in the name of the enterprise of New Testament theology may be justified (1897, 79; ET: 1973, 116).[1]

b. "Theology" defined

Wrede's challenging statement also refers to the other part of the name "New Testament theology", i.e. that of "theology". We have already discussed the point that to a large extent Wrede's (and Räisänen's) attack on "theology" is a matter of definition. Wrede argued against the dominance of "doctrine"; Räisänen argues against "theology" as something secondary to the "experience" of the early Christians.[2] I have proposed that the matter of definition may be solved if we understand doctrine and theology as broad terms.

---

[1] See the Introduction to my thesis.

[2] See as a recent re-affirmation of this point in his article, "The Law as a Theme of 'New Testament Theology'" 1992, 252-277, especially 265.

What Räisänen calls "experience" is closely connected with the theological thoughts and arguments of the early Christians. I have argued that, for example, worship, which is closely related to experience, cannot be separated from theology. Theology is not secondary to experience in the sense that it could be separated from it and studied separately. Since experience is in an inseparable relationship with theology, I have argued that we may retain the term "theology" in the broad sense: everything that is related to the early Christians' belief in God. Their religious experience is included in this term.

Scholars may hold differing views concerning the role of doctrine in religious experience. Even if it is not held to be the most important element in religion, but only one important element, it is still possible to argue that the study of doctrine may play an important part in the study of early Christianity.

We shall consider some more problems related to questions of definitions and terminology in the last chapter. In this chapter we turn to another problem which is related to the second part in the name "New Testament theology".

c. *"Theology" as expressing unity of views*

There is a strong challenge put to the enterprise of New Testament theology by a large number of scholars who argue that there is no theological unity in the New Testament. For example, when Räisänen argues for the "second stage" of the study of early Christianity, what he calls "actualizing, i.e. ... the present-day significance of his [the exegete's] historical findings", he affirms that this actualizing "would not result in a theology 'of' the early Christian sources, for these sources contain divergent theological standpoints" (1990, 137). By this Räisänen implies that due to these divergences it is not possible to summarise the theology of the early Christians; therefore this summary should not even be attempted. It seems that in this context by "sources" Räisänen means the New Testament (see n.2, p.200).

Räisänen's reference to the diversity of the theological standpoints in the New Testament seems to be a summary of the dominant view of scholarship of our day. It is significant that Räisänen points to Dunn as a scholar "from a 'conservative evangelical' background" (82) who "has done scholarship a great service in emphatically drawing attention to the issue of diversity" (83).

The question arises, Does diversity in the New Testament make it impossible to maintain the enterprise of studying *the* theology of the New Testament? To put this question in another way, Are the *theologies* in the New Testament divergent to such an extent that we can no longer speak about the *theology* of the New Testament? In this chapter we discuss challenges that are in connection with this major challenge, that there is no unity in the theology of the New Testament.[3]

2. Development in early Christianity

The differences between theological viewpoints in the New Testament - or, with Räisänen's term, the "diversities" - are often discussed in terms of major "theologians" in the New Testament. For example, scholars compare the theology of Paul, John, or that of the author of Hebrews. Another possibility is to compare writings, for example, the theology of the individual Gospels. However, it may be a better starting point for our present inquiry to discuss a general view which does not simply relate to individual authors and/or writings, but argues a wider thesis, the thesis that there was a development of doctrine in early Christianity.

This thesis argues that if we want to learn about early Christianity, we cannot simply turn to the New Testament as our source for the inquiry, because for the most part the New Testament contains a picture that is later than the earliest period of the Christian movement. From the time of Jesus - and from the time of the first period of the Christian congregations - to the time when our New Testament writings were written, the theology of the early Christians underwent a change. This thesis argues that we have to reconstruct the development of this change in early Christianity.

If there was a major change (or, indeed, more than one major change) in early Christianity, then it might be argued that one cannot summarise the theology of the New Testament. Rather, one can only attempt to report the development of early Christian theology (or, theologies).

The roots of this thesis may lie (in modern times) in the work of the Deists, or, at latest in the work of the Enlightenment scholars.[4] The very idea that the picture we have in the New Testament is a "distorted" picture of early Christianity - a picture which has to be restored - may go back to much earlier times, for example, to the teaching of Marcion in the second century. However, for the purpose of our thesis it is not necessary to go back to the roots of this thesis. We may start our discussion with one of the most influential proponents of this thesis, Ferdinand Christian Baur (1792-1860).

---

[3] Cf. the title and subtitle of K. Berger's recent work (1995[2]): *Theologiegeschichte des Urchristentums: Theologie des Neuen Testaments*.

[4] See e.g. J.C. O'Neill's reference to Semler and Thomas Morgan in a similar context, 1991a, 120-121.

a. F.C. Baur's thesis

In the first chapter, in the context of the justification of studying doctrine in New Testament theology, we have already summarised some of Baur's views that are relevant in this section as well. Therefore, it may suffice here to point to his ideas from the point of view of their connection to our present discussion, namely, Baur's thesis concerning development in early Christianity.

Baur's posthumously published *Vorlesungen über Neutestamentliche Theologie* (1864) contains in the form of a summary what he had written earlier in more detailed works. I focus here on his *Vorlesungen*.

aa) Building on the consensus of his day
Baur builds his own thesis largely on the scholarship of others in his day - and on the scholarship of previous generations that had reached certain results by his time. In the first section of his *Vorlesungen*, where he summarises the history of the discipline of New Testament theology, he affirms that in this discipline the aim is "die Grundsätze der historischen Kritik in ihrer ganzen Strenge zur Anwendung zu bringen" (25). This criticism results in the fact that one can no longer accept that all the epistles in the New Testament "man ... auch für eine ächt apostolische Schrift halten kann". One has to distinguish even between authentic and inauthentic ("ächten und unächten") Pauline letters.

In Baur's opinion, only Galatians, 1Corinthians, 2Corinthians, and Romans were written by Paul (39). These are the "Hauptbriefe" of the apostle; and these are the oldest writings of the New Testament canon. Someone summarising the Pauline doctrine ("Lehrbegriff") can use only these four letters as a source (40).

bb) Method and structure
Baur has put his own methodological principle in this way (42-43):

> Je weniger sich eine charakteristische Verschiedenheit der Lehrbegriffe verkennen lässt, um so geneigter wird man sein, auch eine grössere Zeitferne zwischen den sie betreffenden Schriften anzunehmen, und je wahrscheinlicher der spätere Ursprung so mancher Schriften ist, um so weniger kann die Verschiedenheit der Lehrbegriffe befremden.

On the basis of this principle, he summarises his own result of historical analysis in a way that presents a classification of the New Testament writings in periods. These periods, in turn, provide the structure of Baur's *Vorlesungen* (42):

Es lassen sich ... drei Perioden mit verschiedenen Lehrbegriffen unterscheiden. In der ersten stehen sich die Lehrbegriffe des Apostels Paulus und des Apokalyptikers Johannes gegenüber, in die zweite gehören die Lehrbegriffe des Hebräerbriefs, der kleinern paulinischen Briefe, des Petrus- und Jacobusbriefs, der synoptischen Evangelien und der Apostelgeschichte, in die dritte die der Pastoralbriefe und der johanneischen Schriften.

Baur seems to concentrate on one key element in establishing similarities or differences between doctrines. This element is the view of a particular author about the relevance of the Old Testament (see e.g. 132, 230).

cc) From opposition to harmonisation of "Lehrbegriffe"

According to Baur, the four main epistles of Paul show that "der Paulinismus" is "der entschiedenste Bruch des christlichen Bewusstseins mit dem Gesetz und dem ganzen auf dem alten Testament beruhenden Judenthum" (128).

As we have seen, for Baur there is only one other New Testament writing that belongs to the first period to be discussed in a New Testament theology: this is Revelation, "welche, da sie unmittelbar vor der Zerstörung Jerusalems im Jahre 70 geschrieben ist, den schicklichsten Endpunkt für die erste Periode gibt" (40). In contrast to the Pauline "Lehrbegriff', Revelation relates closely to Judaism (207). The "Judaism" of Revelation, however, has to be qualified: "Nur ist es nicht das gesetzliche mosaische Judenthum, sondern das selbst schon geistigere Elemente enthaltende prophetische, das hier in einer eigenthümlichen Verbindung mit dem Christenthum erscheint".

Thus, there is a fundamental difference ("Gegensatz") between the "Lehrbegriffe" of Paul and Revelation (230). This fundamental difference is bridged in some of the other New Testament writings. For example, Hebrews stands mediating ("vermittelnd") between those two. Concerning Hebrews Baur affirms(231): "Auf der einen Seite verhält sich das Judenthum zum Christenthum rein negativ, auf der andern ist alles, was das Christenthum als absolute Religion ist, an sich, ideell auch schon im Judenthum enthalten".

The inauthentic "smaller Pauline" letters do not share with the authentic four letters "was zum Charakter eines paulinischen Briefs gehört" (40). They lack "das ächte Gepräge seines [i.e. Paul's] Geistes". The "Lehrbegriff' of the "smaller Pauline" letters, with the exception of the Pastorals, stands very near to that of Hebrews (256).

James, on the other hand, presents an opposition that is directed at the very heart of the Pauline doctrine (277). Rom 3,28 is contrasted with Jas 2,24.

The two "Petrine" letters stand near to the Pauline doctrine, however, (287): "Der Lehrbegriff dieser Briefe ist überhaupt ein vermittelnder, eklektischer, katholisirender, in welchem daher verschiedene, zu einer neutralisirenden Einheit verbundene Elemente zu unterscheiden sind". Acts is also characterised by a harmonising element; its aim is to show a "harmonious relationship" between Paul and Peter (331).

These examples show that Baur's thesis may be presented in the Hegelian terms of "thesis, antithesis, synthesis". For example, E.E. Ellis in the Foreword to H. Harris's book, *The Tübingen School*, points out the "Hegelian dialectic in his [i.e. Baur's] postulation of a Pauline party (*thesis*) in conflict with a Petrine party (*antithesis*) whose opposition began to be reconciled (*synthesis*) in the letters of James and 1 and 2 Peter" (1990, xii).

Baur's thesis has been influential ever since. Although it started to be criticised in his own century, it has also found followers up to the present.[5]

dd) Criticism of Baur's "picture" of early Christianity

We may summarise the major criticisms Baur's thesis is confronted with in the following way.

1) E.E. Ellis has pointed to the problematical character of Baur's exegesis of passages that are crucial for his thesis. For example, referring to Baur's 1831 article entitled "The Christ party in the Corinthian Congregation", Ellis affirms that (1990, xiv):

> In the 'Christuspartei' he accepted without question and without exegetical analysis that 1 Corinthians 1:12 refers to *parties* divided over *theological* issues even though the text speaks only of an *ethical* problem of *individuals* (*hekastos*) bickering and boasting about who had baptized them.

2) In relation to the study of the Gospels, Baur's name is associated with the term "tendency criticism". Robert Morgan has pointed out that Baur "examined the theological *tendency* of each Gospel, and in this respect anticipated redaction criticism" (1991, 66). However, Morgan adds that Baur lacked "twentieth-century sophistication in distinguishing within each Gospel between the traditions inherited by the evangelist and all the 'redactional', or editorial, modifications of this material" (66-67).

3) Robert Morgan affirms that "Baur did not force his history into a 'Hegelian' pattern of thesis-antithesis-synthesis" (1991, 71). Morgan partly approves of the thesis of Baur, but only with the qualification: "Baur had been right to emphasize the conflict between Paul and some Jewish Christians" (72). However, Morgan adds that: "By making this conflict the key to the whole development, Baur failed to give due weight to other factors".

4) It is widely held today that we may attribute to Paul more than the four letters ascribed to him by Baur. For example, in addition to the four "Haupt-

---

[5] Cf. Ellis's reference to G. Lüdemann, in Harris 1990, xv.

briefe" referred to by Baur, Hans Hübner regards as "authentic" also 1Thessalonians, Philippians and Philemon (1993, 30).

5) Horton Harris has made a distinction between Baur's "theological perspective" and "historical perspective". The former "concerns the theological presupposition ... that no supernatural intervention in history could be demonstrated" (1990, xxiii). The latter "was Baur's own historical framework, which he constructed on the supposition of a bitter and long-lasting antagonism between Pauline and Jewish Christianity" (xxiv). Although it is possible to accept the former without accepting the latter, nevertheless "one could not logically accept Baur's historical viewpoint without also accepting the theological presuppositions on which it was based".

Harris has argued that if Baur's "historical perspective was erroneous" - and in Harris's opinion it was - then "one may ... *postulate* that Baur's erroneous historical viewpoint was the consequence of an erroneous theological viewpoint" (xxvi).

b. The problem of the dating of the New Testament writings

We have already seen that F.C. Baur used the late date of the New Testament writings as an argument for postulating a development in the theological ideas reflected in those writings. Although Baur's dating of New Testament writings is related to his overall "picture" of early Christianity, because of its general significance, the question of dating is worth discussing separately at some length. This aspect of Baur's thesis may be criticised in the following way.

aa) Circular arguments

Baur seems to argue his case for establishing development in doctrine somewhat inconsistently. On the one hand, he proves that theology must be developed by arguing the sources are unhistorical and therefore late. For example, he argues that we do not have Jesus' teachings from a direct source, but from the writings of the New Testament authors (1864, 21). Critical scholarship has established that the latter are not eye-witnesses of Jesus. There is a period ("Zwischenraum") between the events and their writing. According to Baur, this is a period "... in welchem so Vieles dazwischen liegen kann, wodurch der ursprüngliche Thatbestand mehr oder minder verändert worden ist".

On the other hand, he proves lateness by arguing from the existence of a developed theology. For example, the Gospel of John is late because the theology in it is developed (22): "... je höher die Entwicklungsstufe des christlichen Bewusstseins ist, welcher ein so ausgebildeter Lehrbegriff angehört [*sc.* that of the Evangelist John], um so grösser muss auch der Zeitunterschied gewesen sein, welcher ihn von der Person Jesu trennte".

As it stands, it is a circular argument. It may be argued that this "circle" is methodologically unavoidable, but then the hypothetical character of the results has to be noted.

bb) Baur's dating of New Testament writings

We may also note that Baur's dating of many of the New Testament writings in the second century is not widely held today. Although theses concerning very early dates remain controversial[6], only a very few scholars would date only very few books of the New Testament in the second century.

It is true that the majority view of present-day scholarship with regard to dating the New Testament writings does not refute the thesis of "development". However, scholars have to argue that the developments they posit had to take place in a shorter period of time.

We may further note, by way of examples, that the dating of Revelation and Mark plays a significant role in Baur's reconstruction of the history of early Christian "Lehrbegriffe". We have already mentioned the place of Revelation in Baur's picture. It is not widely accepted today that Revelation (in the form we have it) is as early as Baur proposed.

Concerning the Gospels, Ellis (1990, xiii) has pointed to an observation of Karl Barth: Baur "saw the Jewish-Christian Matthew ... and the Gentile-Christian Luke as oppositions that were overcome in ... Mark, [which] was an earlier form of the Johannine unity". This quotation refers to the fact that Baur held the view of the priority of Matthew. Although this view is still held by a group of scholars today[7], others support the view that Mark was earlier.[8]

As a general criticism we may refer to Robert Morgan's point which argues that "different strands coexisted in early Christianity" (1991, 72). Consequently, there is no need "to string out the development" in early Christian doctrine; and there is no need to "place the Gospels in the second century" as Baur did.

To conclude, we have to note that the majority of scholars put most of the New Testament writings in the first century and yet maintain some form of a "development thesis". It is significant that they have to argue theses for sud-

---

[6] Cf. e.g. J.A.T. Robinson 1976, 352: his list displays a pre-70 date of each New Testament writing; and J. Wenham affirms with regard to the Synoptics: "all three are probably to be dated before 55", 1991, p.xxii.

[7] See e.g. Dungan (ed.) 1990, 125ff.

[8] *Ibid.*, 3ff.

den and quick changes in the theology of early Christianity. To give justification for a sudden change may be problematic. We can see an example of this problem in our next section. At this point I emphasise that any attempt at New Testament theology has to take the arguments concerning the "development theory" seriously. If there is a major development within the theology of the New Testament writings, then it may be argued that the enterprise of New Testament theology cannot be maintained. At most one can aim at describing that theological development with its differences.

c. "The Proclaimer became the Proclaimed"

The formula - which has become a slogan by our day - that "the Proclaimer became the Proclaimed" is a short formulation which wants to point to the significance of the difference between the earthly Jesus' teaching and the early church's teaching about Jesus. We find this formula clearly coined in Bultmann's *Theologie des Neuen Testaments*. Concerning the relationship between Jesus and the preaching of the early church ("Urgemeinde") he affirms (1984, 35): "Aus dem Verkündiger ist der Verkündigte geworden". In as much as this thesis concerns the relationship between the two teachings, that of Jesus and that of the early church, the content of the thesis originates in works of scholars which addressed this relationship. Thus it is worth looking at Bultmann's thesis as well as at the thesis of some of his predecessors.

In the previous chapter we have already pointed to the connection between the thesis discussed in this section and the problem of the "Messianic consciousness of Jesus". Inevitably this latter theme has to be drawn into the present discussion as well.

aa) H.J. Holtzmann
Although Holtzmann held that Jesus professed to be the Messiah[9], he also prepared the way for the thesis in question with some of his remarks.

Holtzmann affirmed that it was the messiahship ("der Messianismus") of Jesus that led to the formation of a new religion in which "the teaching of Jesus has been developed or transformed into the teaching about Jesus" (1911, 295). Holtzmann not only held that "the teacher himself became the object ("Gegenstand") of teaching", but he even risked affirming that "under certain circumstances" the teacher (Jesus) became "the object even of his own teaching" (296). Holtzmann used this distinction even in the structure of his *Lehrbuch*. At the end of the section on "The Proclamation of Jesus" he led on

---

[9] See e.g. 1911, 299ff, 305, 331.

to the subsequent section by the following transition: "Haben wir bisher die Lehre Jesu behandelt, so gelten unsere weitere Betrachtungen der Lehre von Jesus als dem Christus" (420).

Holtzmann probably did not think that the idea of distinguishing between the teaching of Jesus and the teaching about Jesus would lead in a direction where it could become a counter-argument against the unity of the theology of the New Testament. Holtzmann noted that Wrede found that distinction "rein literarisch und unzulässig" and that J. Kaftan and M. Kähler neglected ("Bemängelung") that distinction by over-emphasising the post-Easter character of the Christ-traditions (420, n.1). Perhaps Holtzmann could not see at that time that his own distinction had paved the way to views similar to that of Kaftan and Kähler: views which did not affirm a connection between the life of Jesus and the early church's claim that he was the Messiah.

bb) Alfred Loisy

Although Loisy wanted to "analyze and define the bonds that unite" the gospel and church in history (1903, 3), in my opinion he also argued for the thesis that may be labelled with the later formula of Bultmann: "the Proclaimer became the Proclaimed".

Loisy defended elements of Christian belief by showing their connection with the New Testament. However, this connection goes back only to the early Christian tradition, as it is expressed by the Gospels, and to Paul. The connection does not go back directly to Jesus. Loisy affirmed that "we know Christ only by the tradition, across the tradition, and in the tradition of the primitive Christians" (13).

It is a paradoxical phenomenon that Loisy's assertions were made in order to defend the church and at the same time his very assertions confirm a distinction between Jesus and the post-Easter church. For example, Loisy's famous statement that "Jesus foretold the kingdom, and it was the Church that came" was originally made in order to argue that "the law of life" also applies to Christianity (166). The law of life is "movement and a continual effort of adaptation to conditions always new and perpetually changing" (166). However, the statement itself announces a gap between Jesus and the early church in as much as it implies that Jesus did not intend to form a church, yet the church came into existence.

It is significant that even at places where Loisy seemed to connect later church developments with Jesus, he immediately added the element of the earliest church tradition to the teaching of Jesus. For example, he affirmed that: "The systematic definition of the dogma is in relation to the systematic definition of Redemption, but the ideas which supported these definitions existed before them in Christian belief, and their evolution has its starting point in the gospel of Jesus and apostolic tradition" (201). In a similar way Loisy linked the following elements in one flow: "The ancient dogmas have their root in the preaching and ministry of Christ, and in the experiences of the church, and their development in the history of Christianity and in theological thought: nothing else was possible" (215).

Perhaps the example, which comes closest to the content of the formula discussed in this section, is Loisy's view concerning the development of worship in early Christianity. His starting point in the relevant chapter of his book was the following: "It may be said that Jesus, in the course of His ministry, neither prescribed nor practised any external rite of worship which would have characterized the gospel as religion" (230). Acts 2,22-36 and Matt 28,18-20 show the way in which after Easter "Christian consciousness represented the founder of Christianity, following all that Jesus had Himself proclaimed of His coming glory" (252). Thus Christianity very early became "the worship of Christ, and it is a probable supposition that this worship preceded in some way, sustained, and inspired the work of Christian thought on the person of the Redeemer" (253).

Loisy's arguments challenge New Testament theology at more than one point. We have to discuss issues raised by him in later sections of this chapter. For example, we have to discuss the relationship between Jesus' teaching and the other parts of the New Testament. It is particularly the last point of Loisy we have mentioned above which presents a strong challenge to the unity of the theology of the New Testament. If Jesus did not encourage, or call for, any "worship" of his own person in any sense, how do we account for the fact that his person started to be "worshipped" very early on among his followers?[10]

cc) Rudolf Bultmann

Bultmann held that from among the Son of Man sayings in the Synoptics only those are authentic sayings of Jesus which relate to the future coming of the Son of Man (see e.g. 1984, 31-32). Although the "Parusieweissagungen" in this group are "ursprüngliche Jesusworte" (31), these speak about the Son of Man in the third person (32). Bultmann concluded that "in den Worten, die vom Kommen des 'Menschensohnes' reden, ist gar nicht daran gedacht, daß dieser 'Menschensohn' in Person schon da ist und erst durch den Tod entfernt werden muß, um dann vom Himmel wieder kommen zu können" (31). This means that Jesus thought the Son of Man would come in the future and that he held the two figures (himself and the Son of Man) to be distinct (8).

---

[10] For this argument I am indebted to Professor J.C. O'Neill. Cf. also the Introduction of J.C. O'Neill's recent monograph, 1995, especially pp.2-3.

Concerning the teaching of Jesus, Bultmann affirmed that "Nicht das Was, sondern das Daß seiner Verkündigung ist das Entscheidende" (1954, 265). Jesus called men to decision "angesichts der hereinbrechenden Gottesherrschaft" (1984, 8). Jesus' call is "Gottes letztes Wort vor dem Ende". Here we simply note the famous and much discussed "that" ("daß") without following up the contribution of the post-Bultmannian school concerning the "what" ("was").

Bultmann argued that: "Die Urgemeinde hat ... die Verkündigung Jesu wieder aufgenommen ... Er, früher der Träger der Botschaft, ist jetzt selbst in die Botschaft einbezogen worden, ist ihr wesentlicher Inhalt" (1984, 35). After Easter the early church called Jesus the "Messiah" (27). Bultmann concluded: "Der Verkündiger muß zum Verkündigten werden, weil das Daß seiner Verkündigung ja das entscheidende ist, seine Person, aber nicht seine Persönlichkeit ..." (1954, 266).

Although Bultmann seemed to be arguing for a radical thesis that Jesus did not proclaim himself but the early church proclaimed him to be the Messiah (see e.g. 1984, 35), he also introduced a notion which softened the radicality of the thesis. Bultmann spoke about a Christology that was implicit in Jesus' teaching. In his article on the Christology of the New Testament he affirmed that Jesus' call to decision implied a Christology (1954, 266). It is difficult to understand what Bultmann means by this affirmation, because he does not expand on this "implicit Christology". He says in a rather concise way (1967, 457):

(Wohl aber) kann man sagen, daß *Jesu Auftreten und seine Verkündigung eine Christologie impliziert,* insofern er die Entscheidung gegenüber seiner Person als dem Träger des Wortes Gottes gefordert hat, die Entscheidung, von der das Heil oder das Verderben abhängt.

We have seen that, for Bultmann, Easter is the decisive point for New Testament theology. This can also be seen in his exegesis of Synoptic passages which seem to present Jesus as Messiah already in his earthly lifetime. For example, the confession of Peter in Mk 8,27-30 and the story of the transfiguration of Jesus in Mk 9,2-8 are characterised by Bultmann as "von Markus in das Leben Jesu zurückprojizierte Ostergeschichte" (1984, 28). In connection with the Matthaean parallel to the first of these two passages Bultmann affirms (1961, 277):

... der Auferstandene spricht Mt 16,17-19 zweifellos; und ist die Vermutung richtig, daß Mt 16,17-19 ursprünglich den Schluß der Bekenntnisszene gebildet hat, so kommt in ihr auch zum Ausdruck, daß das Ostererlebnis des Petrus die Geburtsstunde des Messiasglaubens der Urgemeinde war.

Easter is of crucial significance for Bultmann's theology, because he did not hold that Jesus thought he was the Messiah. It is Easter that provided Bultmann with an answer to an objection he was aware of, namely, the argument that "der Glaube der Gemeinde an die Messianität Jesu ... sei nur verständlich, wenn sich Jesus selbst als Messias gewußt und sich - wenigstens den 'Jüngern' gegenüber - als solchen ausgegeben habe" (1984, 27). To this objection Bultmann answered: "... ebenso möglich ist es, daß der Glaube an Jesu Messianität mit und aus dem Glauben an seine Auferstehung erwachsen ist".

The exegesis of the numerous passages Bultmann built his thesis on cannot be discussed here. However, it is appropriate to examine at least one verse which is a key verse for Bultmann - and for many other scholars who hold the thesis that "the Proclaimer became the Proclaimed".

d. An exegetical excursus: Acts 2,36

Bultmann expressed a view which is widespread among scholars of the New Testament when he affirmed that Acts 2,36 shows "daß man in der ältesten Gemeinde die Messianität Jesu von seiner Auferstehung ab datiert hat" (1984, 28). This is such a widespread view that most scholars do not even discuss the possibility that the verse may mean something else.

Most scholars argue that Acts 2 is a composition of the author of "Luke-Acts". For example, Ernst Haenchen asserts that "Peter's speeches go back to Luke himself" (1971, 185). However, scholars generally agree that there are traditions in Peter's speech at Pentecost earlier than the writing of Acts. According to Martin Hengel, in Luke's redactional work the titles in his terminology "have been chosen deliberately" (1979, 104). Hengel asserts: "In Acts 2.36, as in Rom. 1.3f., there are hints at an archaic adoptionist christology: through the resurrection God has made Jesus *kyrios* (Ps. 110.1) and *christos*, 'Lord' and 'Anointed'" (p.104).

Jürgen Roloff also holds that Acts 2,36 is an old tradition (1988, 60). That the verse is not Lukan can be seen in the fact that it contradicts Luke's own Christology. For Luke Jesus was the Anointed One and Lord already in his earthly life (see e.g. Lk 2,11; 3,22; 4,18). In Acts 2,36 Luke gives place to an older idea "derzufolge Jesus erst auf Grund der Erhöhung zum Christus und Herrn geworden ist". Haenchen argues along similar lines. However, he notes that "Luke had no intention, in verses 22, 33, 36, of outlining an older Christology" (1971, 187). Luke "understood traditional statements in terms of contemporary doctrine".

Let us briefly examine the question anew: Does Acts 2,36 mean that according to early Christians Jesus was made Messiah at his resurrection? Or, to put it in another way, Did the early church believe that God "adopted" Jesus as his "son" through Jesus' resurrection?

aa) The origin of the term "Lord"

There is a disagreement among scholars with regard to the origin of the term κύριος. The majority of scholars seem to argue for a Hellenistic background of the term. Roloff argues that it is an anachronism to show Peter at Pentecost as one interpreting Joel 3,5a as applying to the "Lord Jesus". Peter must have spoken in Aramaic whereas that interpretation was only possible later, on the basis of the Greek *Septuagint* (1988, 55).

However, Hengel, who maintains a Hellenistic origin of the term (1979, 103), points to evidence in Qumran "that *mare* was also used in Palestinian Judaism in the absolute form as a designation of God" (105).

R.F. Zehnle rejects the possibility that the term κύριος would come from "the *mar*-title of the Aramaic-speaking church" (1971, 69). His argument is that "the only known milieu for *mar*-sayings is the eschatological expectation of the Aramaic-speaking community; Acts 2:36 certainly does not fit into this milieu" (69).

J.C. O'Neill suggests a way out of the difficulties by affirming on the one hand that: "The title κύριος for Jesus originated in the Aramaic-speaking Church"; and on the other hand that: "The way the title is used in Acts, however, shows that the author was writing when the Aramaic origins had long been forgotten" (1961, 129).[11]

I agree about the view that the Aramaic-speaking early Christian community worshipped Jesus as "Lord". One may argue that the little evidence we have[12] does not exclude the possibility of a wider use of the *mar*-title. It may also be argued (against Zehnle) that Peter might have regarded his speech at Pentecost as an "eschatological event".

However, the origin of the term in itself does not answer the question whether or not Acts 2,36 is an evidence for an adoptionist Christology. We can only distinguish levels of likelihood of this theory. If the "Hellenistic" origin thesis were right, then the adoptionist theory would be more likely, because the lateness of the title might correspond with the slowness of Christians to see God's Messiah in Jesus. If the "Aramaic" origin theory were right, then it would be less likely that Acts 2,36 expresses an adoptionist view, because

---

[11] I note that the chapter on the titles is omitted from the revised edition in 1970, see p.xi.

[12] 1Cor 16,22, Did 10,6; cf. also Rev 22,20.

there is only a short period "available" to posit the development in the Christology of the early Christians. If Acts 2,36 is a record of a real speech of Peter at Pentecost, then the adoptionist theory will be even less likely. One may argue that Peter confessed Jesus to be the Messiah in Jesus' earthly life (although this is highly disputed), so he may have made that application of Joel 3,5 and Ps 110,1 to Jesus at Pentecost. Here I can only speak of levels of likelihood, because much depends on exegetical decisions with regard to the Gospel material.

bb) The term "Messiah"

It is widely accepted that the term "Christ", "Messiah", is used as a title in Acts 2,36.[13] However, it is one of the most hotly debated issues in New Testament scholarship: When and by whom was the term first applied to Jesus? Two quotations may indicate the divergence of opinions with regard to one and the same passage: Mk 8,27ff. Roloff affirms: "Der irdische Jesus hatte diesen in starkem Maße mit irdisch-politischen Implikationen belasteten Titel weder für sich beansprucht, noch dessen Anwendung auf ihn durch seine Anhänger toleriert" (1988, 60). Rudolf Pesch holds: "Daß Jesus als von Gott durch Zeichen und Wunder als Messias ausgewiesen gilt, entspricht der alten Überlieferung in Mk 8,27-30" (1986, 127). Pesch adds with a reference to a quotation in Peter's speech in Acts 2: "Die Messianität Jesu ist den ersten Zeugen Voraussetzung zum Verständnis seines (sühnenden) Todes und der Theo-Logik seiner Auferweckung, für die sich in Ps 16,10 ein Anhaltspunkt finden ließ" (127).

cc) The term "made"

It is interesting that very few of the commentators discuss the translation possibilities of ἐποίησεν. Most of the scholars take it with the most obvious first meaning as "made". However, this is not the only possibility. Pesch suggests: "'Machen' kann in 36 das schöpferische Auferweckungs- und Erhöhungshandeln bezeichnen, wie die Christen nach Eph 2,10 als mit Christus Auferweckte und in den Himmel Versetzte Gottes *poiäma* sind" (128).

We may add that "made" may mean "made known". It does not necessarily express the idea of coming into existence the first time. This possibility is present in texts where somebody appoints or installs somebody else in an office. ποιέω seems to be able to carry this meaning even in a absolute usage, i.e. without the addition of the phrase that would express "in" what somebody was "installed" or "appointed". For example, in 1Kg 12,6, LXX, (1Sam 12,6) Samuel's reference to God's action probably has the meaning, God

---

[13] See e.g. Zehnle 1971, 68.

"appointed" (so e.g. RSV) Moses and Aaron (as leaders): "μάρτυς κύριος ὁ ποιήσας τὸν Μωυσῆν καὶ τὸν Ααρων ..." In Mk 3,14 ποιέω most likely means that Jesus "ordered", "appointed" (RSV), perhaps "chose" the Twelve: "καὶ ἐποίησεν δώδεκα [οὓς καὶ ἀποστόλους ὠνόμασεν] ἵνα ὦσιν μετ' αὐτοῦ καὶ ἵνα ἀποστέλλη αὐτοὺς κηρύσσειν ..." (NA²⁶).

In both cases one may argue that the subject, God and Jesus, respectively, knew beforehand whom he would appoint or install in an office at a certain point of time. For God, Moses and Aaron were "leaders" before they actually became leaders. For Jesus, the Twelve were his chosen apostles even before he called them to himself.

It is worth noting that by Athanasius the term ἐποίησεν was taken in Acts 2,36 with the meaning "He [i.e. God] manifested Him [i.e. Jesus]".[14]

dd) Towards a solution

In my opinion a solution of our problem may be achieved if we do not isolate verse 36 from its context. This does not mean that we decide the question whether verse 36 is "Lukan" or whether it contains earlier tradition. If we think of the passage as Peter's speech (at least in its origins), then it will be natural to view verse 36 in the context of his speech. If the "speech" is the work of the author of Luke-Acts, then it will be more probable to think that the author intended a climax in verse 36 than to think that he did not see a contradiction between the material he was using and his own knowledge from elsewhere.

I think it is more likely that the author did not think he was using adoptionist material. I would argue that the following observations may point in this direction.

In relation to the Old Testament background of the passage, Johannes Munck (1986, 18) pointed to the quotation of Ps 16 (LXX 15) in Peter's speech in Acts 2,27: "It is at any rate difficult to disregard that God ... would not let his *Holy One see corruption* or let him leave his *soul in the kingdom of the dead*". It may be argued that this Psalm quotation, applied to Jesus, suggests that Jesus was Messiah even prior to the resurrection.

G. Schille (1984, 114) not only thinks that the term "Messiah" in Acts 2,36 is an "association" with the quotation of Psalm 16, but he holds that the term "Lord" in Acts 2,36 refers to the other Old Testament quotation in the passage: Ps 110 (LXX 109). Referring to this Psalm, Schille affirms: "Der

---

[14] Athanasius' second oration against Arianism, section 12; in English: in Newman 1881, 263; in Greek: in Bright 1873, 80: "... ἐν μέσῳ ὑμῶν ἐποίησεν, ἴσον τῷ εἰπεῖν, ἀπέδειξε". I am indebted to Professor J.C. O'Neill for the references to 1Sam 12,6, Mk 3,14 and Athanasius. Cf. also O'Neill 1995, 16-19.

Psalm redete als Krönungshymnus vom Eintreten Gottes für seinen Gesalbten gegen dessen Feinde. Die erste Christenheit hat das auf Christus bezogen" (p.114).

Pesch (1986, 124) even tries to prove that connection by translating the καί before κύριον (and not only the one between the two titles):

> Petrus zieht die Schlußfolgerung aus dem Schriftbeweis für die Erhöhung Jesu; mit sicherer Gewißheit soll (und kann) "das ganze Haus Israel" erkennen, daß Gott diesen Jesus "auch zum Herrn" (von dem Ps 110,1 spricht) gemacht hat ...

I note that the exegesis of Psalm 110 is highly controversial. Scholars emphasise that the new king was always "adopted" by God at the king's enthronement.[15] However, one may argue that the person of the new king was often foreseen by God or even predetermined by him prior to the actual enthronement. God presented to the nation at the enthronement the one whom he had already regarded as king. Mowinckel's words leave this interpretation as a possible one (1956, 63):

> Anointing was an act which first and foremost ratified the king's status as the chosen of Yahweh, and as duly installed ... That one of the king's sons (usually the eldest) whom Yahweh had designated by an oracle was conducted in solemn procession to the holy place, where the ceremony took place 'before Yahweh'.

Hans Conzelmann (1963, 30) points to Acts 4,25f where Psalm 2 is quoted. He argues that the combination of the terms "Lord" and "Messiah" in Acts 2,36 was evoked by their usage in Ps 2. However, we have to note that the difficulties mentioned above with regard to Ps 110 apply also to Ps 2.

Here I briefly point to the problem of the term "I have begotten" in Ps 2. It is clear that it cannot be taken literally not only because of the subject, Yahweh, but also because of the fact that the enthronement does not happen to an infant. It is possible that the term means: today "I present you"; "I lead you forward into the public".

As another Old Testament reference we may note that Acts 2,30 alludes to 2Sam7,12ff. Mowinckel (1962, I.63) sees in this Old Testament verse a connection to Pss 110 and 2:

> ... it is the style and content of such anointment oracles that furnish the material which the tradition used when, in the legend of Nathan, it makes Nathan pronounce such promises to David. The historical core here is that Yahweh's covenant with the king and his 'decree' at the anointing was expressly understood to be a renewal of 'the favours promised faithfully to David' and of the covenant with him.

---

[15] See e.g. S. Mowinckel 1956, 78; for a brief discussion of some aspects of Psalm 110 (and of Ps 2) see P. Balla, 1995, 21ff and 56ff.

In my opinion the expectation that the Messiah should come from the descendants of David does not favour the "adoptionist" view. The idea is more probable that God knows who his Messiah will be (from the descendants of David) even before the Messiah appears than the idea that the Messiah will appear as any other human being and that then God will adopt him. In this latter case the Davidic descent would lose its importance.

Apart from the Old Testament allusions in Acts 2, there are other phrases in that chapter that deserve our attention in this context.

Munck (1986, 18) pointed to Acts 2,22: "... God vouched for Jesus by *powerful deeds*". The reference in this verse is made to Jesus' earthly life. If the "powerful deeds" may be seen as a reference to "messianic" deeds, then this verse may be an argument against the "adoptionist" reading of verse 36.

Finally, Acts 2,23 may be an argument against the adoptionist view when it affirms with regard to Jesus: τοῦτον τῇ ὡρισμένῃ βουλῇ καὶ προγνώσει τοῦ θεοῦ ἔκδοτον (NA[26]). Although it is difficult to determine at what point did God appoint and know beforehand that Jesus would be "delivered up", it is sufficient for the present argument to note that these terms refer in this context to a time prior to Jesus' resurrection.

To sum up, there seems to be evidence in the context of Acts 2,36 that this verse is not likely to reflect an adoptionist Christology. It rather speaks of an "enthronement" where by his resurrection Jesus is shown to the "public" what he always had been in God's view. In this sense of "Inthronisation" I agree with Pesch (1986, 128):

> In 36 scheint noch die in der von Paulus Röm 1,2f aufgenommenen Tradition bezeugte alte Christologie von der Inthronisation des auferweckten Messias als Menschensohn und Gottessohn durch. Der von Gott als Messias beglaubigte Jesus ist durch seine Kreuzigung nicht widerlegt worden, sondern seit seiner Auferweckung als "Herr und Messias" in die ihm zukommende Machtstellung zur Rechten Gottes eingesetzt worden.

It may be worth pointing out that whereas Hengel saw in both Acts 2,36 and Rom 1,3f hints at an adoptionist Christology (see above), Pesch does not find an adoptionist Christology in either of these two passages. We may note in this context that Cullmann calls Rom 1,3f a "confessional passage" (1963, 291). He holds that this passage is a "very old" confession "further developed" by Paul. Cullmann argues (292):

> Jesus is the 'Son of God' from the beginning. At least this appears to be Paul's understanding when in v.3 he makes 'Son' the subject of the whole two-part confession. But since the resurrection, the eternal divine sonship manifests itself ἐν δυνάμει; the Son of God becomes the *Kyrios*.

This line of argument may support Pesch's understanding of both Acts 2,36 and Rom 1,3f. These passages do not have to be understood as showing traces of an adoptionist Christology.

Thus Acts 2,36 should not be taken with the surface meaning as "God 'made' Jesus Messiah at Jesus' resurrection". Rather, it should be understood as Athanasius long ago had understood it (Newman 1881, 263-264):

> ... the Father has *made* Him Lord and King in the midst of us, and towards us, who were once disobedient; and it is plain that He who is now displayed as Lord and King, does not now begin to be King and Lord, but begins to show His Lordship, and to extend it even over the disobedient.

Accordingly, Acts 2,36 should not be called upon as evidence for the view that there is such a turning point at Easter in early Christian "theology" that a New Testament theology could only discuss the theology of the early Christians "after Easter".[16]

e. Summary

Within the limits of my thesis it has only been possible to point to the significant challenge of a "development thesis" for the enterprise of New Testament theology. We have also seen that the "development thesis" is not one without difficulties. The main problem that has to be dealt with if New Testament theology is to be justified can be summarised in the following questions: Did "theology" develop in early Christianity?; If it did, are the developments of thoughts in the New Testament of such a character, that later developments differed antagonistically from earlier stages?; Is it true that these earlier stages were concealed by the later ones in such a way that we have a "distorted picture" of early Christianity in the New Testament?

In this section I have looked at an influential example of the "development theory", F.C. Baur's thesis. We have found that in as much as many scholars would follow his ideas in some form, his thesis has been modified by many scholars and rejected by some. In my opinion, it is an interesting phenomenon that although many of Baur's particular results are now generally being held to be wrong, his overall picture of development seems to be widely followed. On the basis of the above criticisms I raise the question: How far can the de-

---

[16] For a detailed discussion of this theme see also the chapter entitled "A Basic Assumption in Modern New Testament Christologies" in J.C. O'Neill's recent monograph, 1995, 7-22. I am grateful to Professor O'Neill for allowing me to use his manuscript even before it was published.

tails of a reconstruction be modified and the reconstruction still be held to be valid? With due carefulness I tentatively ask, May it not be the case that we have reached a stage in New Testament scholarship when the idea of antagonistic oppositions in early Christianity, reconciled in early Catholicism, may be given up?

3. Jesus and Paul

Any attempt to maintain that there is a unity in the theology of the New Testament has to consider the relationship (at least) between the major figures or authors of the New Testament. One large field in the study of these relationships is the problem: Is there a continuity between the teaching of Jesus and that of Paul?

Scholars have pointed to points of connection as well as to points of difference between Jesus and Paul. We may exemplify these points by some earlier and some more recent studies.

a. Loisy on the relationship between Jesus and Paul

Loisy affirmed that it was the apostle Paul who "laid the foundations of Christian dogma" (1903, 182). There are certain points where Paul's teaching differs from that of Jesus. The most notable are the following.

1) In the teaching of Jesus eternal life "is not the possession of God by man through faith, but the possession of the kingdom in the life to come, the life that is unending" (198). Consequently, "the gift of immortality is not yet conceived as a ransoming, a restoration of humanity" in the teaching of Jesus. Paul sets forth immortality to be "an effect of the mediation and sacrifice of the 'heavenly man' Christ" (199).

2) Jesus did not teach any "doctrine of sin and justification" (207). In Jesus' teaching there are two conditions of entering the Kingdom: a) "faith in the Divine mercy and in the coming kingdom"; b) repentance (208). Paul added to the gospel in as much as he developed a "theory": the dogma of grace. Loisy adds that this dogma of grace is "an interpretation ... of the theology of the heavenly kingdom" which "was made necessary by the circumstances in which the gospel was perpetuated". He concludes that the dogmas and their development have "their root in the preaching and ministry of Christ" (215).

b. The thesis of Johannes Weiss

Weiss affirmed that there is a "fundamental difference between the religion of Paul and the type of religious life which was originally created by Jesus" (1909, 72). However, he argued that "the faith of Paul" is connected to "the historical personality of Jesus". Weiss founded his latter thesis on the exegetical argument that Paul must have known Jesus during Jesus' earthly life (23; also 29).

The former thesis is similar to what we have also seen in Loisy's work: according to Weiss, the fundamental difference between Paul and Jesus lies in the fact that for Paul Jesus is an object of religious worship (3), while Jesus never claimed a place in the devotion of his followers (5).

Weiss argued that even if one is prepared to accept that Jesus thought he was the Messiah, still there will be a gap ("Sprung") between the "messianic consciousness" of Jesus and the faith of Paul in Christ (3). Jesus could not have expected a "cult" directed to his own person. Jesus probably thought of himself as a "Führer der Menschen zum Heil", but he could not have thought of himself as a "Stück des Heils selber". In Paul, "Die sakramentale Vereinigung mit dem erhöhten Herrn, das 'Leben in Christus' sind Formen einer Religion, in der Christus nicht mehr die Stellung des prophetischen Offenbarers Gottes oder des menschlichen Heilsmittlers, sondern der Gottheit selber einnimmt" (4). This is a *novum* in comparison with the proclamation of Jesus.

Apart from this fundamental difference, Weiss referred to some other differences as well, although in his opinion these may be regarded as "eine Bereicherung unsrer religiösen Lebensquellen" rather than as a problem (72). Weiss pointed to the following differences of this kind.

1) The doctrine of Paul on redemption is a point of difference between Jesus and Paul. Jesus spoke neither about his pre-existence, nor about his death as one being of a substitutionary effect ("stellvertretende Wirksamkeit", 7). He may have thought his death would be a necessary sacrifice, but it was a *novum* that Paul saw salvation to be based on the self-sacrifice of Jesus (6). We may note here again the similarity between this view and the view of Loisy mentioned above.

2) Weiss argued that there are differences between Paul and Jesus in terms of their "world picture" ("Weltanschauung", 32). He marshalled points of difference which are due to the Hellenistic background of Paul (32ff, e.g. vocabulary; "Wertschätzungen", etc.). Other differences are due to the Rabbinic background of Paul (38ff, e.g. Paul feels there is a need to prove statements about certainty concerning salvation with arguments, 40).

3) The Pauline question: "Works or faith?" is missing in Jesus' proclamation (46).

4) The "ethics" of Paul (60ff) is different from that of Jesus. For Jesus, the moral change in man is a condition ("Vorbedingung") of entering the Kingdom; for Paul, new life is effected by God's acts, for example, the pouring out of the Spirit (60-61). Jesus uttered "Forderungen ... als verstünde es sich von selbst, daß wer sie hört, sie auch tun werde" (61). Paul did not trust that man can do good. However, Weiss adds that Paul also used "ethical imperatives" (62). This is due to the "after effects" of an "ethical impulse" from Jesus, that was taken up by the early church.

Without entering discussion with these arguments we may observe how much depends on exegesis of certain passages. Scholars differ in their reconstruction of what Jesus may have thought about himself; they also differ in their reconstruction of what Paul may have meant. Thus it is highly problematic to achieve reliable results as regards the comparison between Jesus' teaching and Paul's doctrines. Yet anyone attempting a New Testament theology cannot avoid addressing these issues. Here we can only point to them. I should like to highlight only two points in this context.

I think that a key - and highly controversial - question is whether or not Jesus may have expected that his followers should direct "worship" toward his person. The majority of scholarship seems to share Weiss's view on this matter. J.C. O'Neill in a paper answering Maurice Casey's book, *From Jewish Prophet to Gentile God*, rightly affirms that (1992, 196): "Unless Jesus knew himself to be God incarnate, we can hardly treat him as such; it would be very odd to worship someone who would have repudiated that worship". The question arises, Can we find evidence that Jesus may have expected this worship, or does the church worship Jesus contrary to Jesus' intentions? New Testament theology has to address this question.

It is also important to raise the question whether or not the difference amounts to a contradiction. For example, Weiss affirmed with regard to the differences of the ethics of Paul and that of Jesus (62): "Es wird niemals gelingen, diese Zeugnisse einer übernatürlichen Ethik [*sc.* that of Paul] und die Forderungen der Bergpredigt in eins zu arbeiten".

However, in a major recent textbook on the ethics of the New Testament, Wolfgang Schrage has neither refuted nor substantiated claims like that of Weiss. Schrage finds the following relationship between Jesus and Paul (1988, 172): "The starting point and basis for Paul's ethics is the saving eschatological event of Jesus' death and resurrection". Schrage affirms that although "Paul does not quote the actual words of the Lord verbatim", nevertheless there are "many points of agreement" between the sayings of Jesus and Paul's ethical teaching (210). He concludes that "it is certainly true that for Paul the authority of the earthly Lord is not simply made irrelevant by Easter".

c. Eberhard Jüngel's contribution

In a book that contained his doctoral thesis (under a different title), Jüngel affirmed as a starting point that "the theology of Paul is grounded in the kerygma of Jesus Christ" (1962, 6). Accordingly, he formulated his main question in this way: What is the relationship between Jesus' proclamation ("Jesu Verkündigung (gen. subj.)") and the proclamation of Jesus Christ ("Verkündigung Jesu Christi (gen. obj.)")?

Jüngel has carried out a detailed examination of the Pauline doctrine on justification and of the proclamation of Jesus. His main concluding points show areas where the proclamation of Jesus and the proclamation of Paul are related.

1) The main factor in "eschatology" is not the expectation of the imminent end, but the view that one is determined by the eschaton (265). Jesus' ideas of the Kingdom are expressed in the parables in this sense: "God is near to history". The eschatological phenomenon of the Kingdom determines the whole proclamation of Jesus. The "righteousness of God", on the other hand, is an eschatological phenomenon which determines the whole Pauline theology (266).

If I understand him correctly, Jüngel's main thesis is that "Kingdom" and "righteousness" are different "language-events" ("Sprachereignisse") which carry the same meaning at different times to different audiences (cf. 273). He affirms that there is a "time difference" ("eine temporale Differenz") between Jesus and Paul: for Jesus, the present is determined only by the near future; for Paul, the present is viewed from the perspective of the past in the light of the future (272). The reason for this difference is a simple one, namely, "daß Paulus auf ein Ereignis zurückblickt, welches es ihm möglich macht, in Jesus das Eschaton als dagewesen zu behaupten" (273).

In a similar way, Jüngel speaks of a language difference ("sprachliche Differenz", 282) with regard to Jesus' term, "Kingdom", and Paul's term, "righteousness". This "Sprachwechsel" is in connection with the above mentioned "Zeitwechsel".

In this way Jüngel points to differences as well as relations between a theme of Jesus and a theme of Paul which are, in the opinion of the majority of scholars, central to Jesus and to Paul. In my judgement, the relationship established by Jüngel between "Kingdom" and "righteousness" is more weighty than the difference, because the difference is due to the fact that Paul's doctrine is later than Jesus' preaching. The time difference accounts for the language difference.

2) The other main point of Jüngel has a twofold character, too. Here again we find a theme that has both points of difference and relationship between

Jesus and Paul. This is the theme we have already encountered more than once in the above discussions of other scholars. Jüngel affirms that "Jesus selbst hat keinen Glauben an sich gefordert" (276). However, his activity ("Verhalten") did provide a point of contact ("Anhaltspunkt") for the faith of the first congregations (277). Jüngel affirms that "Jesu Verhalten selber Glauben *gewährte*".

The death of Jesus meant a certain withdrawal ("Entzug") of Jesus which made a theology necessary, because this withdrawal necessitated a history of explication of faith (280). With reference to this "necessity" Jüngel argues that: "So kam es zum Sprachereignis der paulinischen Rechtfertigungslehre". The resurrection bears witness ("bezeugt") to an identification of the eschaton with the historical Jesus (281).

In conclusion, Jüngel affirms that Jesus' proclamation has an implicit Christology, while the Pauline doctrine on justification has an explicit Christology (283). The relationship between the two is summarised by Jüngel in this way: "Sowohl das Sprachereignis der Verkündigung Jesu als auch das Sprachereignis der paulinischen Rechtfertigungslehre weisen auf das eschatologische Ja Gottes zum Menschen als das beide Sprachereignisse ermöglichende extra nos der Sprache Gottes".

Jüngel's thesis is formulated in a somewhat complex theological language. It is not possible to go into detail here with regard to the way he defines his theological terms. It should suffice here to point out that his conclusions do point to a connection between Jesus and Paul that does not support a thesis which would describe the teaching of Jesus as one in contradiction with that of Paul.

Without pursuing this matter in any further detail, it is worth noting that more recently A.J.M. Wedderburn has argued in several articles (e.g. 1985, 1988) in favour of a "similarity" between Jesus' and Paul's "message and practice" (1989a, 13).[17] Wedderburn rightly affirms that, if these similarities can be shown, then "that may ... force one to postulate the channels by which Paul inherited these shared patterns" (14).

To sum up, the justification of the enterprise of New Testament theology calls for a study of the great voices within the New Testament. New Testament theology, however, is only challenged if the result of the comparison between the great figures in the New Testament, or between authors of the various New Testament books, would show that these figures represent opposing theologies. We have examined one of the major pairs of comparison, the teaching of Jesus and that of Paul. I think we may affirm that the differences are not of the nature that would compel us to conclude that there was a contradiction between those two teachings.

---

[17] See also further articles by Wedderburn and others in this 1989 volume.

4. Should the teaching of Jesus be part of New Testament theology?

a. Bultmann's statement

One may see a certain logical connection between some points discussed so far in this chapter and the question whether or not Jesus' teaching should be part of a New Testament theology. For example, if one accepts Bultmann's thesis that we can speak about Christian faith only after Easter, when the kerygma of the crucified and risen Jesus Christ emerges (1984, 2), then one has to follow Bultmann's whole line of argument: since New Testament theology "besteht in der Entfaltung der Gedanken, in denen der christliche Glaube sich seines Gegenstandes, seines Grundes und seiner Konsequenzen versichert" (1-2), it follows that Jesus' proclamation is not part of a New Testament theology; it belongs to the presuppositions ("Voraussetzungen") of New Testament theology (1).

This argumentation is based on two key statements. On the one hand, it has to prove that Easter is the starting point of Christian faith. In other words: only when the Proclaimer became the Proclaimed can we speak about the beginning of the theology of the early Christians. We have already seen that this thesis may be challenged. It cannot be made a firm starting point for the other thesis that Jesus' teaching should not be part of New Testament theology.

On the other hand, Bultmann gives a brief definition of New Testament theology as a part of his argumentation. His definition speaks only about the description of the "thoughts" of the early Christians concerning their belief. This definition implies that Bultmann understands theology as "reflection". I have already argued that the enterprise of New Testament theology should define theology in such a way that theology should include "experience" as well as "reflection", because the latter is inseparable from the former.[18]

Here it may suffice to note with Räisänen that (1990, 40): "In accordance with the fundamental emphases of dialectical theology the term 'religion' does not appear at all" in Bultmann's discussion of Jesus' teaching. I have proposed that what is understood under the term "religion" by the history-of-religion school may be fruitfully understood as "theology" in the context of a New Testament theology (chapter one). The terms "religion" and "theology" should not be separated from one another.

Thus we may say that we only have to exclude Jesus' teaching from New Testament theology if we accept Bultmann's two main points. These points, as we have seen, are not without problems.

---

[18] See my first chapter.

b. An inconsistency in F.C. Baur's work

Baur affirmed that although the teaching of Jesus constituted the original form in which Christianity emerged as a new religion, nevertheless this original form differed sharply "von einem dogmatisch entwickelten Lehrbegriff" (1864, 122). Jesus' teaching may be referred to as "a teaching that expresses itself in the form of universal principles" ("allgemeinen Princips") (123). Paul's teaching represents a dramatically different form ("eine ... wesentlich verschiedene Gestalt") of Christianity. It is the death of Jesus that provided Jesus' person with the significance it had for Christianity.

If there is such a difference between the teaching of Jesus and that of Paul, then one might argue that the teaching of Jesus should not be part of a New Testament theology. At this point Baur came near to becoming a predecessor of Bultmann's thesis, as discussed above. Baur did not make that move of excluding Jesus' teaching from his New Testament theology. However, we have to note that there is a certain inconsistency in his dealing with this issue.

Baur first states that the teaching of Jesus naturally forms the "first period" of development of thought that ought to be discussed in New Testament theology (39). When he begins his discussion on Jesus' teaching, he does affirm it belongs to New Testament theology, but he distinguishes Jesus' teaching from the rest of the New Testament development of doctrines (45). When he begins his discussion on Paul, he gives it the heading "first period" (122). Here he calls the period of Jesus' teaching "die Urperiode". This corresponds to the division of his table of contents where Jesus' teaching is in the first section ("Abschnitt"); and the second section, the teaching of the apostles, is divided in three periods (pp.Vff).

In this way, Jesus' teaching *is* dealt with in Baur's New Testament theology; however, Jesus' teaching is at the same time *separated* from the theology of the early Christians. Baur's struggling with this problem may be seen in some way at least as paving the way for Bultmann's radical thesis.

We have to note that Baur's "inconsistency" may reflect that the question whether or not Jesus' teaching should belong to New Testament theology presents us with a difficult problem. Let us discuss briefly a few more examples of how scholars have grappled with this problem.

c. Hans Conzelmann

It is significant to note that Conzelmann has not included the teaching of Jesus in his *An Outline of the Theology of the New Testament* as a separate heading (1969). However, he draws a careful distinction between the theme of the "historical Jesus" and the teaching of Jesus. He affirms that the former "is not a theme of New Testament theology" (xvii). In his opinion, a New Testament theology should rather discuss the question, How does Jesus determine church, faith and theology? Conzelmann attempts to answer this question "by discussing the teaching of Jesus (including the problem of his understanding of himself) within the framework of the section on the synoptic gospels" (xvii-xviii).

In this way Conzelmann seems to agree with Bultmann in that Jesus' teaching should not form the first part of a New Testament theology. Conzelmann does not even present a short section on the proclamation of Jesus at the beginning of his *Outline*, whereas Bultmann did place a few pages on "Die Verkündigung Jesu" at the beginning of his *Theologie des Neuen Testaments*. Nevertheless, Conzelmann differs from Bultmann in as much as he discusses the Synoptic Gospels - which do not receive a separate treatment from Bultmann.

Conzelmann acknowledges that his *Outline* is indebted to Bultmann's work "in a number of places" (xv). Nevertheless, it is significant for my thesis that Conzelmann differs from Bultmann in his view about the "basic problem" of the enterprise (xviii):

> The basic problem of New Testament theology is not, how did the proclaimer, Jesus of Nazareth, become the proclaimed Messiah, Son of God, Lord? It is rather, why did faith maintain the identity of the Exalted One with Jesus of Nazareth after the resurrection appearances?

Conzelmann affirms that there are different ways in which this identity, or continuity, is maintained in the New Testament. It is significant, however, that in Conzelmann's opinion "the identity itself remains. Where it is surrendered, we have the separation into orthodoxy and heresy, and the conflict between them."

We may briefly note that Conzelmann's thesis may be viewed as an indirect support for the result of our inquiry into the question of "orthodoxy and heresy". According to Conzelmann's argument, this question arises when the above "identity" is surrendered. This implies that the view of "identity" was the earlier Christian view; and deviations from it were regarded as "heresy".

To sum up, I note that in Conzelmann's work we may find a post-Bultmannian conception of New Testament theology which does find some place for Jesus' teaching in the enterprise of New Testament theology, albeit through the discussion of the "Synoptic kerygma" (97ff), and, within that section, through the discussion of the Synoptic Gospels.

d. *Some earlier works: Wrede, Holtzmann*

It may be worth noting that prior to the time of Bultmann, in the history-of-religion school, it was not seen as necessary to exclude the teaching of Jesus from New Testament theology. For example, Wrede affirmed that (1897, 61; ET: 1973, 103): "The first main theme of New Testament theology is *Jesus' preaching*".

Wrede did not feel the need of justifying his statement. In the same way we find no discussion of reasons why Jesus' teaching should be part of New Testament theology in Holtzmann's work (1911). He simply discusses "Jesus und das Urchristentum" as the first part of his *Lehrbuch*; and within it "Die Verkündigung Jesu" (159ff) - after the description of contemporary Judaism.

e. *Some recent contributions: Jeremias, Käsemann, Goppelt, Morgan*

Wrede and Holtzmann, who wrote before Bultmann, did not see the problem which was highlighted by Bultmann. It may be of interest to look for "answers" in writers who knew Bultmann's work and nevertheless maintained that Jesus' teaching should be part of New Testament theology in a more direct way than in Conzelmann's conception.

aa) *Joachim Jeremias*
Joachim Jeremias has completed only the first volume of his *New Testament Theology*. This volume is entirely devoted to "The Proclamation of Jesus". It is surprising that Jeremias, who published his work in 1971, after Bultmann's *Theologie des Neuen Testaments* (1948-1953), does not reflect on his decision to discuss Jesus' teaching in a New Testament theology.

bb) *Ernst Käsemann*
Käsemann has not written a "New Testament theology"; nevertheless he has contributed to the matter under discussion. Having initiated the "New Quest" of the earthly life of Jesus in a (by now classical) programmatic lecture (1953),[19] he explained in an article (1972-73) why he holds that Jesus' teaching should be included in a New Testament theology. As a starting point he raises the question "whether New Testament theology ought not methodologically to begin with" Paul (243), since we do not have any "uniform and steady development of the whole Church" prior to Paul's time (242). He affirms, however, that even if we start with Paul, we have to "work backwards and forwards from him to the other divergent movements" (243).

---

[19] Published also in *Exegetische Versuche und Besinnungen*, 1960, 187-214.

Käsemann then goes on to assert that it was an "inconsistency" on the side of those scholars who emphasised the real humanity of Jesus to "hold the earthly Jesus to be no more than a presupposition and not a constitutive part of a New Testament theology" (244). Käsemann acknowledges that Jesus was not a "theologian". Nevertheless, he adds that:

> ... the discipline of New Testament study has to do not only with theologians but with early Christian preaching in general. This preaching becomes an ideology when the Nazarene can no longer be identified, and if it is a matter of debate whether he remains the measure of all dogmatics and Church organisation.

We note that Käsemann does not use the term "Jesus' teaching" in this context. He affirms that the "identity of the Nazarene is defined by the Cross, more than by anything else" (244). Nevertheless, we may infer from these quotations that Jesus' teaching is also part of the means by which we can "identify" him. Consequently, Jesus' teaching also should form a "constitutive" part of a New Testament theology.

cc) Leonhard Goppelt

Leonhard Goppelt includes "Jesu Wirken in seiner theologischen Bedeutung" as the first main part in his *Theologie des Neuen Testaments* (1985, 52ff). He discusses in a separate section "Die Frage nach dem Ansatz der Neutestamentlichen Theologie" (54ff). He first asserts (56):

> *Zur Bildung christlicher Gemeinden und damit zu einem Weiterwirken Jesu kam es nach den frühchristlichen Überlieferungen ausschließlich durch das Osterkerygma; dieses ist der Ansatz der Neutestamentlichen Theologie.*

Goppelt gives the following reasons for the inclusion of Jesus' teaching in a New Testament theology in spite of the assertion that the Easter-kerygma is the starting point of a New Testament theology. 1) The Easter-kerygma was extended "backwards" to the earthly Jesus already in the early church, in order to make the Easter-kerygma understandable (57). 2) Even in the application of the Easter-kerygma to the situation of the early Christian congregations the Easter-kerygma is "vom Erdenwirken Jesu her gefüllt" (58). Although Paul mentions "nur vereinzelte Logien" of Jesus (56), nevertheless one can discern "Jesusüberlieferung" behind the theological explication of the kerygma in Paul (58).

Goppelt concludes (58): the "Grundlage" of the Easter-kerygma was "das Berichten über das Erdenwirken Jesu". Accordingly, if we want to present the theology of the New Testament in accordance with the structure of the theology of the New Testament, then we should start our treatment with the question of the earthly Jesus.

Goppelt gives a further reason for the inclusion of Jesus' teaching in New Testament theology. He argues that the phenomenon that the "Weiterwirken" of Jesus is due to a message of his resurrection is unparalleled in the antique world (61-62). From this he draws the conclusion that the New Testament stories of the resurrection can only be understood from their own context and should not be set aside as "zeitbedingtes mirakelhaftes Denken" (62). If this is accepted then the crucial question is: "Ist das Erdenwirken tatsächlich der sachliche - nicht etwa der psychologische - Grund des Osterkerygmas?" This consideration leads to the proposal that it is appropriate from historical reasons "die Darstellung der Ntl. Theologie mit der des Wirkens und Weges Jesu zu beginnen".

Goppelt concludes that in as much as it is true that the Easter-kerygma is the "Ansatz" of New Testament theology, this Easter-kerygma should not be separated from its "transsubjektiven Begründung"; and the "Weiterwirken" of Jesus should not be separated from its "Ausgang" (62).

I find these arguments convincing. I think we may develop this line of argumentation even one step further. It may be argued that Jesus' teaching ought to be included in a New Testament theology in order to provide a basis for a comparison with the theology of the early Christians, so that we can examine the question: In what way did the early Christians relate their belief to Jesus of Nazareth? This argument has the advantage that it does not say beforehand whether or not Jesus' teaching is in unity with the theology of the early Christians. It simply affirms that we need to describe something if we want to compare it with something else.

It is worth emphasising in this context that Goppelt deliberately does not use the term "historical Jesus" when he considers the question how should Jesus (or, Jesus' teaching) be included in New Testament theology (58). Goppelt argues: "Das 'rein historische' Bild Jesu ist nicht zugänglich; es ist zudem theologisch belanglos (2Kor 5,16)". Goppelt has concluded:

> *Die Ntl. Theologie aber fragt nach Jesus, wie er sich den Nachfolgenden in den Erdentagen darbot, und das ist auch der Jesus, der geschichtlich weiterwirkte.*

dd) Robert Morgan

This emphasis corresponds to an important distinction made by Robert Morgan. Morgan (1987) holds the view that a description of the historical ministry of Jesus should not be made a substitute for Christology in New Testament theology (194). He argues against the inclusion of a summary of the "historical Jesus" in New Testament theology by affirming that: "A historical description of Jesus admittedly falls short of Christian confession because it mentions neither the Incarnation (in the broad Christian sense of a claim that Jesus represents God finally and uniquely) nor the Resurrection (vindication by God)." Morgan's aim is to integrate "modern historical knowledge of Jesus into New Testament theology" (192). He wants to achieve that aim by: a) retaining "the evangelists' own Christological frameworks" (198); b) including in that framework "good historical information" which is not speculative (199).

On the basis of this argument we may affirm that in New Testament theology we are not concerned with a reconstruction of the "historical Jesus". Nevertheless, Jesus' teaching may be argued to be a necessary part of New Testament theology if we are to understand the Christology (or, at least, the origins of Christology) in the New Testament.

We have seen that the question of whether or not Jesus' teaching should be part of a New Testament theology is still a matter of debate among scholars. One view may be summarised in Räisänen's words: "if you restrict yourself to the canon, you should take seriously the fact that the teaching of Jesus as reconstructed with critical methods is not an issue there" (1990, 61). However, arguments may be developed for the inclusion of Jesus' teaching in a New Testament theology.

To sum up, we may say in a generalising way that those scholars who think that "theology" in the New Testament started "after Easter" would exclude Jesus' teaching from New Testament theology. We have also seen that scholars who maintain that Jesus' teaching should be part of New Testament theology do see some connection between Jesus' teaching and the theology of the early church. To that extent, our question under discussion in this section remains tied up with the wider question whether there is a unity in the theology of the New Testament. The term "Jesus' teaching" may be understood in a wide way: "the way Jesus influenced his followers". In as much as this influence can only be established by historical methods, New Testament theology is not simply interested in the "historical Jesus", but rather in Jesus as the "originator" of the Christology of the early Christians, for example, that of the evangelists.

5. The thesis of contradictory theologies in the New Testament writings

It has become a widely held view among scholars of both the Old and the New Testaments that because of the diversities expressed in various parts of the Testaments one cannot speak about *the* theology of either of the Testaments; rather one should speak about the *theologies* of the Old or of the New Testament. Manfred Oeming has summarised this view in the following way (1986, 50):

> [Andererseits] wird gerade durch eine immer feinere Wahrnehmung der biblischen Stimmen deutlich, daß 'die Bibel' alles andere als eine einheitliche, geschlossene Theologie enthält, sondern eine Vielzahl von Theologien, die je für sich zu betrachten sind: ... eine Theologie Jesu, eine Theologie der Logienquelle, des Markus, des Matthäus, des lukanischen Doppelwerkes, des Johannes, des Paulus, der Deuteropaulinen, des Hebräerbriefes, der Pastoralbriefe, der Apokalypse.

Oeming affirms summarisingly that the differences of the biblical witnesses make "die innere Zusammengehörigkeit fraglich" (50-51). There are numerous examples of this "difference" given in works of New Testament scholars. It may suffice to point to the most widely held ones through the example of two (by now classical) articles of the not too distant past.

The following articles of Ernst Käsemann and Herbert Braun summarise the main themes in which scholars claim to have found contradictory theologies in the New Testament. The articles sometimes simply state their theses. In some cases they refer to biblical passages as underlying arguments. Because of the great number of passages and theories involved, I cannot discuss the arguments in detail. However, I shall try to point to the direction my arguments would go in a detailed discussion.

a. Käsemann's points

The article entitled "Begründet der neutestamentliche Kanon die Einheit der Kirche?" summarises the most important variations in the proclamation of the New Testament. These variations ("Variabilität") cause Käsemann to answer his question in the title in the negative (1970b, 124).[20]

aa) The explications of Jesus' "sonship"
Käsemann affirms that none of the writers of the canonical Gospels had known the historical Jesus (124). They believed in the exalted Lord first; and they saw the incarnation in the light of the exaltation. All these writers belong to the "Hellenistic" church. The Hellenistic Christians applied the title "Son of God" to Jesus.

According to Käsemann, the Gospel writers differ in their explication of this "sonship" (125). Mark depicts Jesus in the terms of the Hellenistic

---

[20] The article was originally read as a paper in 1951.

"theios anthropos". Matthew sees in Jesus the "second Moses". Luke speaks of Jesus' birth as the birth of a divine child, the Saviour of the world, in the terms of Hellenistic myths. John sees in Jesus the Revealer, because Jesus as the Logos was there with the Father from the beginning. Käsemann affirms in summary that: "Ein theologischer Aspekt läßt in unsern Evangelien den incarnatus modifiziert verkündigen".

Käsemann does acknowledge that all the canonical Gospels affirm the divine "sonship" of Jesus. To that extent, we may say they do share a common theology. However, Käsemann goes on to add that: "Das allen gemeinsame Bekenntnis zur Gottessohnschaft Jesu wird ... mit Hilfe einer jeweils der Umwelt entnommenen Anschauung verschieden expliziert" (125). The question arises, In what way can these explications be said to be contradictory?

bb) Gospels criticising traditions
Käsemann affirms that the story of Jesus' baptism in Mark shows that at an early stage the Christology of the church was an adoptionist one (125). Rom 1,4, Acts 2,36, Heb 1,5 show the same. I have already argued against this thesis by pointing to some exegetical arguments in relation to Acts 2,36. Here we are concerned with Käsemann's re-affirmation of this thesis from the point of view of the additional thesis that in the four Gospels we find modifications of one another as well as modifications of the traditions used by the Gospels.

Käsemann affirms that Mark did not agree with the adoptionist Christology, so he criticised it (125). In a similar way Matthew and Luke criticised Mark where their theology did not agree with that of Mark.[21] The Fourth Gospel uses traditional material in a critical way. For example, in 4,48; 6,26; 20,29 Jesus' miracles are symbols for the Evangelist whereas in their original setting they served as "Glaubenslegitimation" (126). Käsemann affirms that "die Differenzen in unsern Evangelien und sogar die abweichende Auswahl des Überlieferungsstoffes sich weithin aus der verschiedenen theologisch-dogmatischen Haltung der Evangelisten erklären".

It is a real challenge to the unity of New Testament theology if it can be shown that at an early stage a part of the church held an "adoptionist" Christology. However, I think that the passages referred to as evidence for an adoptionist view can be interpreted in another way. As I have done in an excursus on Acts 2,36 earlier in this chapter, I would argue that those passages mean that God revealed, announced, made publicly known what had been true prior to that moment: that Jesus has to be honoured as God's own Mes-

---

[21] Käsemann's examples: changes in Matthew over against Mk 5,27ff; change in Luke over against Mk 8,33, 1970b, 125.

siah (or Son). The passages do not necessarily mean that Jesus became the Messiah at the resurrection, and that he was not the Messiah prior to the resurrection.

The thesis of the Evangelists' changing or modifying the material of each other is in connection with another general thesis, the Two-Document-Hypothesis. We have already seen that this widely held, perhaps consensus-view is challenged by some scholars.[22] Here I point briefly to one argument which has been employed against the above hypothesis. J.C. O'Neill calls it an "unlikely hypothesis" that "scribes, collectors, and editors deliberately changed words of Jesus or accounts of his deeds or added to them or subtracted from them" (1991b, 484). O'Neill argues that the words and deeds of Jesus, who was held to be the Messiah, "would have been regarded from the start as holy". Curses and warnings against changing any of the words of sacred books (for example, like those in Rev 22,18f), may have been also the "rules the evangelists and their predecessors were most likely to have followed".

Thus the thesis that the Evangelists have thoroughly modified the theology of one another shares the problematic character of the thesis that they used and fundamentally changed the works of one another.

cc) Variations in the kerygma

Käsemann argues that it was only a minority of early preaching Christians who committed their message to writing (128). The variations in the kerygma of the early church must have been even more numerous than what was transmitted by the church. Käsemann adds that even in our canon the variations not only bear witness to tensions but also to "irreconcilable theological oppositions" ("unvereinbare theologische Gegensätze"). Käsemann lists a number of them. For example, although according to Mk 7,15 Jesus denies that man can be made unclean by things "from the outside" ("von außen her", 128), it can be seen by critical analysis that "die palästinische wie die hellenistische Christenheit das Jesuswort im übrigen Kapitel mit kommentierenden Zusätzen umgeben hat" (129). These changes include a limitation of the polemics: Jesus is shown to turn only against Rabbinism which "den eigentlichen Gotteswillen mit seinen Sonderauflagen und seiner Kasuistik verdeckt".

Käsemann asserts that the early church did not simply continue the teaching of Jesus: the church also altered it (130). Käsemann gives another example where a general radical statement of Jesus was softened by the church: Mk 2,27 (129). Jesus wanted to attack and to abolish Jewish cultic and purification laws. The church could not live with this freedom: they wanted to return to a "christianised Judaism" (129).

---

[22] See e.g. Dungan (ed.) 1990.

Without going into details I simply note here that this view belongs to a highly debated area of present-day scholarship: Did Jesus contradict the Old Testament law (or its contemporary interpretation)? As regards the "variations" in the canon, as pointed to by Käsemann, they do need careful exegetical studying. I note here how closely exegetical decisions are linked with wider views, for example, that of denying the unity of the theology of the New Testament.

Turning back to Käsemann's starting point, I do accept the general argument of Käsemann, that what we have in the canon is not the whole picture of the early church. It is also probable that opinions not in agreement with the "orthodox" views were not preserved. However, we have to study the evidence we have. This argument from silence cannot be made a decisive one in the discussion of the theme of our present chapter.

dd) Paul and James
Käsemann holds that Luther was right in affirming that the doctrines of justification in Paul and in James are "theologically irreconcilable" (130).

Since this is one of the most "famous" examples of contradictions in the New Testament, I shall summarise my own line of argument on this matter in a short, separate section further below.

ee) Acts and Galatians
Käsemann holds with regard to the apostolic mission of Paul that Acts is affirming what Paul is denying in Gal 1 (130).

It is a notoriously difficult question of New Testament scholarship how to establish the historical facts from Acts and Gal 1. However, historical contradictions are not necessarily theological contradictions. I would put the question to Käsemann's thesis: In what sense do Acts and Paul reflect a contradictory *theology* with regard to the apostolic mission?

ff) Eschatology
Without giving any example of the differences, Käsemann asserts (130): "Es ist mir unbegreiflich, wie man die Eschatologie des 4. Evangeliums und der Offenbarung ausgleichen will". Probably, he has in mind the thesis, that the Fourth Gospel originally had an eschatology in terms of the "present", and this view was then combined with a futuristic eschatology by a later editor, whereas Revelation has a futuristic eschatology. This view (represented also by Bultmann) is also repeated by Braun, as we shall see below. This view first raises the question of how reliable our work of separating "sources" in the Gospels is.

My general question here would be: Are different views of eschatology necessarily contradicting? How would early Christians holding different views about eschatology have related to one another's views - even if these differences included an understanding of "present" or "future" eschatology? Would they have seen in them mutually exclusive beliefs in God (or in what God would "do" in the final days)?

gg) Early Catholicism

Finally, Käsemann affirms that there are parts of the canon which do not belong to the early church ("Urchristentum"), but to "early Catholicism" (130). For example, the Spirit becomes the "Spirit of Office" in 2Peter, the Pastorals and Acts - a view different from the "Geistlehre" expressed by Jesus, Paul and John.

In conclusion Käsemann asserts that the New Testament canon shows that it does not simply stand between Judaism and Catholicism, but has elements of both in it (131). The canon does not prove the unity of the church. On the contrary: the canon affirms the plurality of denominations (131). However, Käsemann adds that the canon is the Word of God when the canon is and becomes "gospel". The gospel does affirm the unity of the church (133).

The fact that the canon incorporates material from Judaism and early Catholicism is not a challenge for my thesis. I do not think we have to hold that the whole of the teaching of Jesus is uniquely new. Jesus' teaching does not have to be "free" from Judaism.

It may be true that the church moved toward institutionalisation. However, one may argue that institutionalisation may have been unavoidable. In itself this phenomenon is not wrong. The question to be addressed is: Is there a continuity between the doctrine of the institutionalised form and the doctrine of the previous period? I also note that the characteristics of "early Catholicism" do not necessarily prove lateness.

It may also be possible to argue that the movement toward institutionalisation was not simply a later development, but the continuation of certain "institutions" in the early period. For example, if we argue that the circle of the Twelve around Jesus was a historical phenomenon, then it may be argued that the Twelve represented the twelve leaders of the twelve tribes of Israel. This may have been an "organisation" of the early Christians who understood themselves as living in a messianic era.[23] 1Cor 15,4 may be a piece of early evidence of a tradition concerning the "Twelve". We shall see another argument for the thesis that some kind of "organisation" is likely to have existed

---

[23] The term "organisation" could be defined as a "community with some identity markers". I am grateful to Professor Gerd Theissen for this comment.

in earliest Christianity when we discuss the *nomina sacra*: the early existence of a set of sacred words points to the likelihood of an organised Christianity which established certain rules.[24]

My general view about Käsemann's "no" to the question in his title is that his thesis does not dissolve the canon. Plurality in opinions may well remain within the boundaries of a canon. New Testament theology has to discuss the question: What is the point at which tensions and divergences become contradictions? I propose that the thesis may be maintained: The "denominations", to use Käsemann's term, may adhere to one Christian canon: They may agree in their theology to the extent that they do not want to exclude one another as heretics.

b. Herbert Braun's arguments

Braun has argued that the New Testament does not have a unified view concerning some of the most important themes of it. In an article entitled "Hebt die heutige neutestamentlich-exegetische Forschung den Kanon auf?" (1962, 310-324) he lists the following themes.[25]

aa) The teaching about the law

Braun asserts that Jesus radicalised the demands of the Torah. Jesus' radicalism went beyond the boundaries of the Torah in the following areas (315): denial of any possibility of an oath; denial of retaliation; command to love one's enemies; prohibition of divorce; command to leave one's possessions; ritual purity is an indifferent matter; one's neighbour is more important than observing a cultic day.

Paul is not dependent on Jesus' teaching in Paul's doctrine on justification: Paul uses a different vocabulary (315). However, Paul and the Fourth Gospel agree with Jesus' polemic against the claims of the pious.

Paul's doctrine on justification is not followed by later parts of the Synoptics (315). Matthew adds to Luke's material in relation to the Beatitudes. According to Braun, this shows "a naive, moralising recommendation of Torah-piety" (315-316).

Paul's views are also modified in Hebrews, Acts and the Pastorals (316). James does not attack Paul himself, but a paulinism that is dangerous in James' view.

As we have seen, this highly controversial issue was also raised by Käsemann. Much depends on how one describes Jesus' view about the law. Any

---

[24] See below in the thesis of C.H. Roberts.

[25] The article was first published in 1960.

comparison stands or falls with the question: How does one describe the view of the various New Testament authors, and that of Jesus, about the law?

bb) Eschatology

Braun holds that Jesus thought that the final judgement, the coming of the Son of Man and the "breaking in" of the Kingdom would come in his own generation's time (316).

Paul shared this view, but he also held that salvation is present, because God accepts sinners. Braun refers to 2Cor 6,2: "Behold, now is the acceptable time; behold, now is the day of salvation" (316).

Braun argues that the delay of the parousia caused a modification in two respects. a) The date of the parousia is prolonged into the distant future (some Synoptic sayings; Acts; 2Peter). b) The futuristic time-factor is completely abandoned: "judgement and resurrection occur now, in the hearing of the Word" (John and 1John, but with glosses which make these writings conform to the "official" view expressed under point a) above; p.316).

Jesus' view about the Kingdom is highly debated among scholars. The following questions are notoriously difficult to answer: Was the Kingdom understood by Jesus in a purely futuristic sense?[26] If so, did he refer to an imminent future, and, consequently, was he wrong? In what sense are different views about the eschaton "contradictory"?

cc) The teaching on church and offices

According to Braun, Jesus did not envisage the foundation of a church, nor did he plan to introduce office-bearers to lead congregations (316). Originally the number of apostles was not a fixed one (317). When James, the brother of Jesus, became the leader of the Jerusalem church, the church became institutionalised on a Jewish pattern. This later institutionalisation was said to have started in an earlier time, although this was not the case. Acts balanced earlier tensions between Paul and the first apostles. Braun sums up the divergence in this way: "Die Lehre des Neuen Testamentes von Kirche und Amt ist dadurch bestimmt, daß die Leitung vom regulierenden zum konstituierenden Faktor wird" (317).

These themes are in connection with the process which led to "early Catholicism": the doctrine became static (2Pet 1,12; Jud 3; "healthy teaching" in the Pastorals, p.317).

My arguments here would be similar to those I have proposed in connection with Käsemann's thesis concerning Judaism and early Catholicism in the New Testament.

---

[26] A recent argumentation for answering this question in the affirmative can be found in J.C. O'Neill's 1993 article.

dd) Christology

Braun holds it is most likely that Jesus did not proclaim himself to be the Messiah. A basic paradoxical phenomenon of the New Testament is that the one who radicalised the Torah was also the friend of the tax-collectors and of the sinners (317). The significance of Jesus lies both in his teaching and his deeds (317-318). The Easter-faith of the church put an emphasis on who Jesus was. This was the way they wanted to express that Jesus' deeds had a lasting validity even after the cross (318).

The kerygma about the resurrection is expanded by the stories about the empty tomb and the Ascension (318). The dignity of Jesus is put into the narratives of his earthly life (e.g. birth stories, baptism of Jesus). Jesus' deeds were depicted in "metaphysical categories of being". Christology in the New Testament was originally an expression of an event, but already in the New Testament Christology develops into a doctrine.

This view about the development of Christology may be called a consensus of the scholarship of this century. However, it has to be emphasised that it is built on hypotheses in the case of many of its parts. These hypotheses have to be examined as to their (levels of) probability. Since I have already discussed aspects of Jesus' messianic consciousness in other parts of my thesis, I point here only to two crucial questions: Did Jesus *think* he was the Messiah?[27] I deliberately refer to Jesus' messianic *consciousness* and not to the question whether or not he *said* he was the Messiah. If Jesus thought he was the Messiah, then it is probable that in some way he did encourage his disciples to think of him as Messiah.

The other controversial matter is: Is it true that Jesus was elevated to the dignity of a deity only by later generations? and, Is it true that this happened on Hellenistic soil? These questions have not been answered in a conclusive way by New Testament scholarship.

ee) The sacraments

Braun argues that baptism on Jewish soil was a bath of purification for the forgiveness of sins. On Hellenistic soil it became a participation in Jesus' death and resurrection, based on a mystery pattern (318).

The Lord's Supper on Jewish soil was a table-fellowship connected with the expectation that the Messiah would come soon. On Hellenistic ground it became φάρμακον ἀθανασίας (318). Braun adds that the Fourth Gospel

---

[27] Cf. the seventh chapter of J.C. O'Neill's monograph (1995, 115-135). The title of the chapter is the same as that of the whole book: "Who Did Jesus Think He Was?" Here O'Neill argues that Jesus did think he was the Messiah, he also acted as Messiah, but because of a "legal ruling" he was precluded from saying so (see especialy pp.134-135).

does not present the Last Supper as an initiation of the practice of the Holy Communion (319).

Without entering the debate whether or not Braun's theses are right concerning the sacraments, I argue that the usage of ideas of different background would not necessarily prove that their *theology* of the sacraments were contradicting one another. Christians of Jewish and those of Gentile origin may have referred to the same content even when using a different language. The wider question arises in this context: How does one reflect on the relationship between words and meaning, language and content?

ff) Braun's summarising point

Braun has summarised his results in a pointed way: "Das Neue Testament - so stellt es sich heraus - hat in zentralsten Stücken weder eine Aussage-Einheit hinsichtlich der tatsächlichen Vorgänge noch eine Lehr-Einheit hinsichtlich der Artikel des Glaubens" (314).

With regard to the unity of descriptions of events I think that it may be an unrealistic expectation that all the reports should say the same. Differences in detail do not prove that they did not speak of the same event.

With regard to the unity of doctrine I would argue that first one has to consider the question: What may have been the articles of the faith of the early Christians? Then one can look at the question: Were the differences to which Braun points so great as to mean that those who held different opinions would have held a different "confession of faith"? We shall return to these questions later in this chapter.

To conclude, in some cases the theses of Käsemann and that of Braun are based on particular interpretations of biblical passages which may be challenged. Other interpretations of those passages may be possible.

In other cases the differences they point to are not of a depth that would put one group into the position of "heresy": thus out of the canon. Differences are not necessarily contradictions. Early Christians may have been aware of differing opinions without thinking that those who held those opinions could not share the fellowship of the same faith - at least in its most basic elements. We shall have to address this question in connection with possible "credal elements" in early Christianity. Here we note once again that the various interpretations of the evidence (and the hypotheses developed) seem to have a direct bearing on the question whether or not one may maintain that there is a unity in the theology of the New Testament.

c. On the relationship between "law and gospel" (with an excursus on Eph 2,15)

One major example of a theme - in relation to which it is often argued that there are contradictory views within the New Testament - is the question about the relationship between the "law" and the "gospel". Scholars point to passages which seem to prove that the "orthodox" early church had opposing views about the validity of the Old Testament Law for Christians. Scholars argue that in the opinion of some Christians the New Testament gospel meant that the Old Testament Law was not valid any longer. If this is true, then this view of the early Christians will stand in antagonistic contrast to, for example, Matt 5,17, where Jesus is reported to have said (RSV): "Think not that I have come to abolish the law and the prophets; I have come not to abolish them but to fulfil them".

There are many passages brought into the discussion. In this thesis we may examine two of them by way of examples: one in an exegetical excursus and the other only briefly.

aa) Excursus: Eph 2,15
Räisänen has summarised his understanding of Eph 2,14ff in the following way (1987, 83): "The author states very clearly that 'the law of the commandments in precepts' (ὁ νόμος τῶν ἐντολῶν ἐν δόγμασιν) has been destroyed by the death of Christ, so that the separating wall between Jews and Gentiles has been torn down". Räisänen asserts that the author of Ephesians "makes the law without reservation the object of καταργεῖν" (205).

As I have presented a longer argumentation in an article (1994), I shall focus here on my key points in proposing that we should understand Eph 2,15 in a different way.

It is generally agreed that vv.14-18 form a unit.[28] These verses stand out from their surrounding context. The main characteristics which set apart vv.14-18 as a unit are its form, its theme and its vocabulary. The "we" style in vv. 14 and 18 marks the boundaries of the unit as opposed to "you" in vv. 13 and 19.[29] The whole section of vv.14-18 has one theme: "he is our peace".[30] Some words occur only here in the epistle.[31] Some are rare in the New Testament.[32]

---

[28] E.g. Westcott 1906, 36; Schlier 1965, 122.

[29] So, for example, Schnackenburg 1982, 104, 106, 111.

[30] See e.g. Schlier 1965, 123; many scholars share this view of the unity of theme.

[31] E.g.: two of three words used in the description of the law in v.15: νόμος and δόγμα; τὰ ἀμφότερα; τὸ μεσότοιχον τοῦ φραγμοῦ; ἔχθρα.

[32] E.g. ἀποκαταλλάσσω only here and in Col 1,20.22; δόγμα only six times in the New Testament, but only here and possibly in Colossians with reference to the Old Testament Law.

In as much as we can emphasise the unity of verses 14-18, we can also affirm that this unit fits into its immediate context. We have to note that words and topics related to those of this unit also occur in the passages which precede and follow vv.14-18: "flesh" in v.11; "far" and "near" in v.13; "blood" in v.13; "alienated from the commonwealth of Israel" in v.12; "no longer strangers" in v.19; "Spirit" in v.22; "without God" in v.12; "dwelling place of God" in v.22.

Because of the fact that vv.14-18 are related to their context by ideas and also by grammar ("he" at the beginning of v.14 refers to "Christ" at the end of v.13), I suggest that we should regard vv.14-18 as an integral part of the chapter.

If we accept this working hypothesis as a starting point, then it will be worth looking at the wider context that surrounds vv.14-18, in order to gain help for the interpretation of our crucial passage.

Firstly, I should like to emphasise the significance of the preceding section: Eph 2,11-13.

In v.11 the readers are addressed as "Gentiles". They have to compare their present situation with that of the past. In the present they are "near" (v.13). In the past they were "far". The antithesis is most likely based on Isa 57,19 which verse is referred to in Eph 2,17.[33]

It is interesting to note that in the Isaiah passage those who are far as well as those who are near are Israelites. In Isa 57,19 it is not mentioned that those who are far would become people who are "near" (unlike in Eph 2,13). Most probably the Jews in the diaspora and those who are at home in Jerusalem are addressed. They all have sinned (Isa 57,17), but God offers them peace.

Schlier mentions that later "far" and "near" have expressed an antithesis between Proselytes and Israelites and also between non-Jews and Jews. He refers to Nu R 8 (149d) where the Gibeonites are those who are "far" and Isa 57,19 is quoted in application to them (1965, 122).

J.A. Robinson pointed to Deut 4,7 to show that Jews felt privileged over against other nations in that the Jews "had God 'so nigh unto them'" (1903, 61). I note that in the same context the Law is mentioned as a reason for Israel to feel distinguished among the nations (Deut 4,8).

We may say that the author of Ephesians has in mind a unified church made up of Gentile Christians together with Jews who are in the right relationship with God, because they repented from their sins (Isa 57,15). Both these groups are now "near" to God.

My key argument is that the past of the addressed Gentiles is compared with the past of the Jews and described as lacking those benefits which the

---

[33] See e.g. Westcott 1906, 36; Lincoln (1990, 138) sees a reference to Isa 57,19 only in v.17, but not in v.13.

Jews possessed. Commentators discuss the elements of the comparison but they usually cannot see its significance. In this comparison the Jews are referred to in positive terms. It almost seems as if the writer would say: "Look what privileges you have been without, because you did not belong to the chosen people". J.A. Robinson argues in support of this view: "The Jew, and the Jew alone, was nigh to God. And hence it followed that to be nigh to the Jew was to be nigh to God ..." (1903, 61).

Schlier argues that "law" is not mentioned in the list of the privileges of the Jews. He affirms that: "Die Verheißung und nicht das 'Gesetz' ist das Lebensprinzip Israels" (1965, 120).

Against this affirmation I argue by pointing to Rom 9,4 where in a similar list of Jewish privileges "the giving of the law" is mentioned. Schnackenburg can even see "eine Reminiszenz an Röm 9,4" here (1982, 110).

I suggest that v.12 is a positive argument in the hand of the author: the benefits of Israel are real benefits. One can feel sorry if one does not share those benefits. The fact that the Law is not mentioned here does not mean that the Law was not regarded as a benefit by the author.

I propose that the reason for the inclusion of this comparison here may be the view of the author about Israel. About this view my suggestion may be summarised tentatively as follows.

There is a part of Israel which understood and followed God's will in the right way. They repented from their sins, consequently God had promised peace to them. They had "privileges" in the past (v.12): Christ (as a promise in the past); commonwealth (i.e. the fellowship of the chosen ones); covenants of promise (the plural probably referring to the covenants of Noah, Abraham, Moses etc.); hope (for eternal life); and God (the only one true God, and a relationship based on what God himself revealed to them).

Following the development which had evolved after the time of Isa 57,19, the author of Ephesians calls these Jews those who are "near". These benefits were valid in the past and are still valid for Jews in the time of the epistle. These Jews, who have a right relationship with God, are now Christians. The author of Ephesians is most likely one of them. They share these benefits with Christians of Gentile origin.

To summarise what I have found up to this point, I affirm that the context would not lead us to expect a condemnation of the ("Old Testament") Law as such.

Secondly, let us examine the expression for "Law" in v.15: "the law of commandments *contained* in ordinances" (AV).

One group of scholars hold that our expression is a pleonasm: the three-part term simply means Law, because, as Lincoln has put it, this "lengthy formulation ... is characteristic of the style of Ephesians" (1990, 142).

Another group take ἐν δόγμασιν as a qualification: the phrase limits the meaning in which the Law is thought of here.[34]

For example, Schlier, who holds that the letter was written by Paul, argues that it is a characteristic feature of Paul in this letter to express himself in a precise way (1965, 125). Schlier points to examples where Paul uses "commandment" (Rom 7,8ff, 13,9; plural only in 1Cor 7,19). However, I have to note that in none of these cases do we have a genitival connection between law and commandment. On the other hand, it may also be significant that in all these cases Paul refers to the "commandment(s)" in a positive way.

Schlier holds that τὸν νόμον τῶν ἐντολῶν refers to the Mosaic Law: the law consists of commandments. ἐν δόγμασιν qualifies "commandments" and consequently the whole phrase. This qualification means that the commandments appear as "fordernde Einzelverordnungen" (125). This refers to that side of the Law which "awakens sin" and "creates the curse of death". This casuistic-legalistic law, which misuses the Torah, is abolished (126).

Gnilka, who holds that the letter was written by a disciple of Paul, argues that the present form of vv.14-18 is a re-formation of an earlier Christ-hymn.[35] He thinks that the three-part genitival form is the work of the author of the epistle. This form has replaced a simpler form (1982, 140). The formulation "corresponds to the style of the letter" and also wants to express the "unbearable burden" which the Law presents (141).

Mitton unfolds the meaning of the three components of the phrase as follows (1976, 106): "The whole Mosaic law consisted of broad commandments (like the Ten Commandments), and these were then elaborated in numerous precise regulations (the oral tradition of the Pharisees)".

I have not found any place in the *Septuagint*, Philo, Josephus and the New Testament where δόγμα would qualify the Law in a similar way to Eph 2,15.[36] The term νόμος ἐντολῶν does not occur in this genitival form in the *Septuagint*, in Philo, in Josephus or in the New Testament. The term δόγμα does not occur in the Pentateuch. It appears in 3 and 4 Maccabees, Daniel (Theod.), Philo and Josephus frequently. Very often it refers to imperial decrees.[37] According to W. Bauer (1979, 201), it refers to the Mosaic Law e.g. in 3Macc 1,3, Philo *Gig.* 52 and *Leg.All.* 1,54f, Josephus *C.Ap.* I,42.

It seems that although δόγμα was not used in connection with the Mosaic Law in the Pentateuch, it could be used in that connection in the first century

---

[34] I have to note that the term which is crucial for this interpretation, ἐν δόγμασιν, does not occur in P[46] and vg[ms]. I would argue that the "omission" is due to scribal error.

[35] See e.g. his excursus, 1982, 147ff.

[36] Thesaurus, 1986, together with Ibycus CD-ROM at New College, Edinburgh.

[37] In this sense in the New Testament in Lk 2,1, Acts 17,7, Heb 11,23 textual variant.

A.D. Thus it may have been available for the author of Ephesians as a term in the context of the Mosaic Law.

Because of the fact that the author of Ephesians often uses synonyms and long structures it is worth looking for possible parallel constructions. I have found that in all cases where a noun, a noun in the Genitive, and a noun with the preposition ἐν follow each other, one can say that: the three nouns are not synonyms; or, even if the meanings are related, there is a qualified, new meaning of the structure as a whole. Thus the phrases, which occur in a similar construction, are not pleonasms.[38]

Thirdly, let us attempt to find an answer to the question: Is the law abolished according to Eph 2,15a?

As we have seen, the uniqueness of the three-part term in connection with the Law makes it impossible to argue for its meaning from parallel material. I propose that we should understand v.15a from its context.

I have argued from the closer context that the Law may be thought of as a part of the privileges the Jews had and which the Gentile Christians are reminded of as among the things they had missed before they came to accept Jesus Christ (v.12).

From the wider context of Ephesians I also argue that it is not likely that the Law is spoken of here in completely negative terms. Lincoln mentions an argument which he thinks does not rule out his interpretation that the Law is spoken of here in a negative sense. However, this argument supports the probability of my "non-negative" reading of the Law here. In Eph 6,2 the author of Ephesians refers to one of the Ten Commandments "for secondary support for his own paraenesis" (1990, 143): "the first commandment with a promise" (ἐντολὴ πρώτη ἐν ἐπαγγελίᾳ, NA[26]).[39]

To sum up, I argue that it is not the whole Law of Moses which is referred to as "abolished" in Eph 2,15. I agree with Macpherson who held that it is the "ceremonial law" which is abolished according to Eph 2,15 (1892, 216). Macpherson argued: "If the apostle had intended the law generally, he would simply have called it the law ..." (217). This is a simple argument in itself: it may or may not be true. However, the style of the author and the context suggest to me that Macpherson may be right: the three-part term does not mean the Law as such, but the Law with certain qualifications.

---

[38] See e.g. Eph 1,17; 2,7; 4,19; 5,26.

[39] We must note that 2Cor 3 may present a difficulty. In v.7 the glory on Moses' face is called καταργουμένην ("fading", RSV) - the same root which is used in the sense of "abolish" in Eph 2,15. In 2Cor 3,11 the neuter τὸ καταργούμενον is used but not explained in other words. I would argue that even if it refers to the service of the letter, i.e. the Law, there is a comparison between something glorious and something even more glorious. Without exegeting 2Cor 3 here, I propose that the Law is not simply spoken of in negative terms there.

These qualifications are summarised by scholars in the following ways. Schnackenburg argues from the context that those parts of the Law are abolished which erected a wall between the Jews and the Gentiles: circumcision, laws of purification, and laws in connection with meals (1982, 115).

Mitton's list of the aspects in which the Law is abolished further includes: "methods of slaughter of animals, sabbath behaviour" (1976, 106).

Although Col 2,16ff is a very difficult passage, and there is a controversy among scholars with regard to the question about its background, J.A. Robinson's argument is worth mentioning here: the author of Ephesians "uses parallel language" to that of this Colossians passage (1903, 64). Col 2,14 mentions δόγμα in the plural.[40]

Col 2,20 uses the same root in a verbal form. According to J.A. Robinson, the author of Ephesians asks "of those who seemed to wish to return to a modified system of external prohibitions: 'Why are ye still ordinance-ridden?' And at the same time he explains his meaning by examples of such ordinances: 'Touch not, taste not, handle not'" (64).

M. Barth mentions two further possible interpretations. Although he disapproves of these possibilities, I can accept them, because of the reason why I accept the previous proposals, i.e. they are in connection with a "qualified" meaning of the Law. M. Barth summarises these other possibilities in the following way. a) "Eph 2:15 may well allude exclusively to those additional rabbinic teachings which were added as a 'fence' around the law after the formation of Israel's Bible" (1984, 288). b) "The formula 'the law ... the commandments ... in statutes,' may serve the purpose of identifying the law with a sentence of death. In this case only a specific function of the law is meant: its role in bringing knowledge and an increase of sin, and in inflicting a curse and death upon man" (289).

I conclude that only those regulations of the Mosaic Law which separated the Jew from the non-Jew are not valid for the Gentile Christians.[41]

bb) Rom 10,4

This verse is often taken by scholars to mean "Christ is the end of the law".[42] Robert Badenas has re-examined the meaning of this verse in a recent thesis (1985). He has argued that law in this verse means "Torah as it stands for Scripture: the OT" (148). He has presented the following arguments in favour of the thesis that the term "law" in this verse is used in a positive sense.

---

[40] Though omitted in minusc. 1881 and in Chrysostom.

[41] I note that Cranfield in an excursus of his *Romans* vol. 2 in ICC (1979) and M. Bouttier in his 1991 commentary arrive at the same conclusion.

[42] E.g. Käsemann 1980, 273.

1) Badenas points out "that nowhere else in his writings does Paul quote the OT so frequently as in Romans, and nowhere else in Romans does Paul quote the OT so frequently as in chs. 9-11" (90). The reason for this is probably that Paul "wanted to prove from all the Scriptures the total agreement of the revealed word on the point he wished to make" (91).

2) Badenas emphasises the importance of the insight that Paul's main theme in chapters 9-11 is what Paul explicitly stated in 9,6: "Has the word of God failed?" (93). Paul's three main answers are (94): 1) "the inclusion of the Gentiles ... is not contrary to the divine promises nor unjust"; 2) Israel's rejection of Christ comes from the "misunderstanding of God's purposes as revealed in the Scriptures"; 3) Israel's failure is "only partial and temporary".

Badenas argues on the basis of this context that in 10,4 Paul cannot say that Christ has abolished the Torah, if it is Paul's main argument here to prove "that the word of God's Torah has not failed (9.6)" (114).

3) Badenas holds that the main theme of Romans is "that salvation has always been by grace through faith" (36, 116). He refers especially to chapter 4 (also p.149). This would render improbable that Paul meant in 10,4 that Christ is the end of the Law as a way of salvation (35).

I think it is methodologically appropriate to argue for a meaning of 10,4 which is coherent with the context. 10,4 as it stands shows no indication of not being related to its context.

Badenas has also examined the use of τέλος in Biblical and cognate literature (chapter 2 of his thesis). His conclusion is that the "basic connotations" of the term are "directive, purposive, and completive" (79). τέλος with the Genitive is generally used to indicate "result, purpose, outcome, and fate". τέλος νόμου generally indicates "the purpose, fulfilment, or object of the law".

Paul uses τέλος in a "teleological" sense, in the majority of the thirteen occasions he uses the term. On three, perhaps five, occasions he uses the term in a temporal sense, but these "instances appear in eschatological contexts" (79). Badenas holds that it is more likely that Paul used the term in Rom 10,4 in the teleological sense. If someone wishes to hold a different opinion, he or she has to prove Paul made an exception from the general Hellenistic usage and his own general usage of the term (see 79, 114).

Without exegeting the passage, I affirm that I incline toward the view that τέλος means "goal" in Rom 10,4. However, I think that the real question is not whether or not τέλος may have a temporal sense. Even if we take the sense "goal" in the context of running a race (so Badenas 115), we may say that the person who reaches the goal has finished his running. His race has come to an end.

In my opinion the more important question is whether or not the Law is spoken of here in negative terms. I take the meaning of "goal" here to express something positive about the Law. In as much as the Law points to Christ (Badenas 147), Christ has not put an end to the Law.

In conclusion, I present tentatively my view about the Old Testament Law. The Law was given by God. It taught righteousness in the sense that those who live their lives in faith and trust in God are fulfilling the righteousness God requires. Those who lived by faith had to be open to God's new revelation in time. At a certain point in time God revealed that he accomplished the salvation of humanity in Jesus Christ. From that point on he required from those who trust in him that they should believe in Jesus as Saviour. The Law taught righteousness as life in faith. In this way the Law prepared those who followed it to accept Jesus as Christ.

We should emphasise that we have discussed only two of the passages involved in the "law and gospel" theme. The question of the law and the gospel is only one of many which are in connection with the problem of the unity of the theology of the New Testament. We have seen again how much depends on exegetical decisions. I hope to have shown that some key passages which are often referred to as evidence to prove that there are contradictory theologies in the New Testament are open to different interpretations. Any attempt at writing a New Testament theology has to discuss these, and many similar, passages.

d. Lack of contradiction

Having shown the problematic character of some of the major areas where scholars argue for the presence of contradictions, it may be worth adding one more area of discussion in this context. There are writings in the New Testament which seem to have originated in rather different circles. Once scholars establish the main characteristics of the theology of those circles, it may be possible that we find lack of contradictions in writings where we may have expected a contradiction because of the different thinking of their authors. This "lack of contradiction" may positively support the results of our study under the preceding points: the thesis of contradictory theologies in the New Testament may be further weakened.

We may mention here two examples. Our first example comes from 1John and Romans. It is often argued that Paul's letters and 1John show a different style. They differ in their technical terms. It may be the more striking, then, to find that there are similarities in them, even in relation to the terms they use.

For example, 1Jn 2,2 says (RSV): "and he is the expiation for our sins, and not for ours only but also for the sins of the whole world". G. Strecker sees in the term "expiation" (ἱλασμός) "urchristliche Begrifflichkeit" (1989, 93). Although the term only occurs here and in 1Jn 4,10 in the New Testament, Strecker holds that it is related to the term ἱλαστήριον. He affirms that this latter term in Rom 3,25 is probably part of a baptismal tradition (94). Klauck refers to Rom 3,25 as a "pre-Pauline tradition originating in Hellenistic Jewish Christianity" (1991, 108). He holds that the author of 1John uses in 2,2 "an older Christological formula" which is "near" to the pre-Pauline tradition of Rom 3,25.[43]

e. On the contradiction between Paul and James concerning the theme of "faith and works"

Our second example comes from the area of the notoriously difficult problem of the relationship between Paul and James. At a first glance some sentences in Paul and James seem to say the direct opposite. For example (RSV), James 2,14.17.24 says: "What does it profit, my brethren, if a man says he has faith but has not works? Can his faith save him? ... So faith by itself, if it has no works, is dead ... You see that a man is justified by works and not by faith alone".

Rom 3,28 affirms: "For we hold that a man is justified by faith apart from works of law". Gal 5,4-5 states: "You are severed from Christ, you who would be justified by the law; you have fallen away from grace. For through the Spirit, by faith, we wait for the hope of righteousness".

Acknowledging the difficulty that lies in the "Paul versus James" problem, I indicate to some possible lines of argument against the thesis that these statements testify to contradictory theologies.

1) There are other sayings in Paul which affirm a view (in relation to this subject) that is similar to that of James, (and vice versa). For example, Rom 2,13 says: "For it is not the hearers of the law who are righteous before God, but the doers of the law who will be justified". James 1,25 affirms: "But he who looks into the perfect law, the law of liberty, and perseveres, being no hearer that forgets but a doer that acts, he shall be blessed in his doing".

---

[43] We may note that both Strecker and Klauck attribute the similarity between the term "expiation" used in 1John and in Romans to an early tradition which was handed down in the form of a "formula" ("Formel": Klauck 1991, 108; cf. "Tauftradition": Strecker 1989, 94). We shall see the significance of early traditional formulae for New Testament theology later in this chapter.

2) James may not speak about works which obtain righteousness in themselves, but about a righteousness where faith and works are in close relationship. Faith is necessary for righteousness; and there is no faith which cannot be shown by one's works. I would argue that James 1,3 should be regarded as an introduction to the whole letter. James 1,3 suggests that the letter will speak about works as things which test one's faith. James 1,21ff may be another argument in this context, if we accept that the "word" mentioned there is in some relation to "faith in Christ".

3) The "ethical parts" of Paul's letters (e.g. Romans chs. 12ff) contain much material which show that "works" cannot be missing in a Christian's life.

4) We may add that irrespective of the question who wrote Ephesians, it is striking that Eph 2,8 and Eph 2,10 can stand so near each other without any indication of worry on the side of the writer that these would be contradictory sayings.

To sum up, in my opinion Paul does not say that man is justified by faith alone; and James does not say that man is justified by works alone. Both of them say that faith in Christ together with works, which are in harmony with that faith, characterise a righteous man's life. If this conclusion is right, then it may have some bearing on the question of "canon within the canon": the opposition between Paul and James does not have to compel us to a certain decision concerning a canon within the canon.[44]

Having shown - by way of examples - that the view that there are contradictory theologies in the New Testament is not without problems, and that it may be challenged, I now turn to some positive (and tentative) arguments in favour of the thesis that there may have been a theology shared by the early Christians - at least in its most basic points.

6. Is there a centre to the New Testament?

There have been numerous attempts in scholarship to show that there is a central theme in the New Testament which is shared by many of the New Testament authors.

---

[44] This theme - so important for Martin Luther and many Lutheran theologians up to the present day - will recur in the next chapter.

a. Hasel's survey

G.F. Hasel (1978) has surveyed the major proposals in the following way.

- R. Bultmann and H. Braun suggest anthropology (144). In relation to Bultmann, Hasel uses the term "kerygmatic anthropology". Braun's emphasis is summarised by Hasel as "theological anthropology" (148). We may note that the Christological content of the kerygma was essential for Bultmann's enterprise.

- G. Ebeling points to Christology "in its That": the fact *that* it is expressed. On the other hand, Christology is variable in the *way* it is expressed - "in its How", 147.

- F.C. Grant argues that there is unity in the presentation of the view of God, of his revelation, of salvation, of the finality and absoluteness of Christ (148).[45]

- O. Cullmann (from the 1950s on) has worked out the theme of "salvation history" (149).

- O. Loretz, F.C. Fensham have emphasised the significance of "covenant" (154).

- H. Seebass points to the "rulership of God" (154).

- G. Klein holds that the idea of the Kingdom of God is central (154).

- G. Fohrer highlights the rule of God and communion between God and man - as a dual concept (154).

- W.C. Kaiser sees the centre in the term "promise" (154).

- W. Künneth sees it in the resurrection of Jesus Christ (154).

- B. Reicke points in general terms to the Christ-event (155).

- W. Beilner affirms two basic aspects: the proclaimed Jesus as the Christ and the "locus" of that proclamation, the existence of the church (157).

- F. Mussner describes the centre as the gospel of the dawn of the eschatological saving time in Jesus Christ (158).

- W.G. Kümmel also highlights a twofold aspect: The fulfilment of God's promise about final salvation begins in Jesus Christ; God sets us free when we encounter him in the Christ-event (159).

- E. Käsemann and W. Schrage return to the "Lutheran" emphasis: the message of justification of the godless (160). We have to note that Käsemann holds the view of "a canon within the canon".

- U. Luz holds that the theology of the cross is central (162).

---

[45] Although it may be said that "unity" is not the same as "centre" in Grant's opinion.

b. *Reumann's summary*

John Reumann (1991) summarises the major proposals concerning a centre to the New Testament in the following way (he does not always name the holders of the various opinions): Jesus, the prophet from Nazareth, revealed as Christ and Lord (28); the gospel (29); love, in the full biblical sense of *agape* (30); the kerygma (C.H. Dodd) (30); theology of the word (cf. G. Ebeling) (31); God's plan of salvation, including *shalom* - peace, well-being, wholeness with God (31); the time of salvation, the new age, eschatology (32); faith (32-33).

Reumann himself points to a "surface similarity" among the twenty-seven documents: their chronological nearness. Because of the fact that many New Testament writings are close to one another in time, there is a "certain commonality in dates and interests" within the second and third generation of Christianity (27-28).

This latter remark already leads us away from the attempts to name one "centre" and points to another direction: instead of finding the centre to the New Testament in one expression, it may be more promising to investigate in more general terms what unites the witnesses in the New Testament. Let us refer briefly to three examples.

c. *The contributions of Cullmann, Dunn and Thüsing*

O. Cullmann concluded his study on the confessions with the claim that the divine Sonship of Jesus Christ and his dignity as *Kyrios* were the "two essential elements in the majority of the confessions of the first century" (1949, 57). There are, however, confessions where the first is lacking, while "the resurrection and the exaltation are never lacking". Thus it is "the present Lordship of Christ, inaugurated by His resurrection and exaltation to the right hand of God, that is the centre of the faith of primitive Christianity" (58).

J.D.G. Dunn affirms that there is a "common element" in the different proclamations in Acts, Paul and John (1991, 29). He lists the following three elements of the *"core* kerygma" - as his own "abstraction" (30): 1) "the proclamation of the risen, exalted Jesus"; 2) "the call for faith, for acceptance of the proclamation and commitment to the Jesus proclaimed"; 3) "the promise held out to faith".

Dunn also finds that there is a "unifying strand" in the New Testament kerygmata (32) and in the tradition of earliest Christianity (76). In a summarising way he makes the following affirmation (369):

That unifying element [i.e. the unifying strand] was the unity between the historical Jesus and the exalted Christ, that is to say, the conviction that the wandering charismatic preacher from Nazareth had ministered, died and been raised from the dead to bring God and man finally together, the recognition that the divine power through which they now worshipped and were encountered and accepted by God was one and the same person, Jesus, the man, the Christ, the Son of God, the Lord, the life-giving Spirit.

W. Thüsing offers a detailed examination of the possibility of finding a continuity between Jesus Christ and the "theologies" contained in the New Testament. Thüsing summarises his own programme as follows (1981, 15):

Die jetzt begonnene Arbeit versucht also, die Vielzahl verschiedener neutestamentlicher "Theologien" auf das zurückzubeziehen, was allein die Möglichkeit bietet, eine letztgültige Einheit zu finden: auf die "Ursprungsstrukturen" des christlichen Glaubens, das heißt: auf die theologischen Strukturen von Botschaft, Wirken und Leben Jesu von Nazaret und auf den theologischen Kern-Gehalt des Glaubens an seine Auferweckung.

d. Conclusions from the survey

From this brief survey two major conclusions may be drawn for our discussion. On the one hand, the survey may be seen as producing a "negative" result. If there are found so many "centres" to the New Testament, we may rather argue that none of the proposals has sufficiently solved the problem. Scholars have mutually found that the other scholars' proposals concerning a centre have not succeeded in finding the theme that would be central to all strata of early Christian tradition and/or to each one of the New Testament writings. None of these centres may be called *the* centre to the New Testament.

On the other hand, all these "centres" are powerfully argued by their proponents. These centres can often be found in various strata of the early Christian tradition and in many of the New Testament documents. We may turn this result into a "positive" one. We may argue that these "centres" may point to important themes which may have played some significant role in (at least part of) early Christianity.

This calls us to examine a possible thesis: Was there a "creed", at least in some form, in early Christianity to which all "orthodox" Christians adhered?

7. Did the early Christians share a "creed"?

a. Problems

The attempt to answer our present question leads us to problems similar to the ones we have found in relation to the canon. These problems may be summarised as follows.

1) We do not have early examples of fully developed creeds. In a recent article (1984) on confessions of faith in the early church, A.M. Ritter has pointed to the fact that even at the time of Irenaeus (p.403) and Tertullian (p.405) the *regula fidei* did not have a fixed wording. Ritter affirms that the church in the first two centuries had "eine substantielle Bekenntniseinheit ohne Bekenntnis*formel*, ohne ein normatives, im einzelnen wie im ganzen verbindliches Lehrbekenntnis oder Symbol" (405).

2) We have little evidence to rely upon as regards the first Christian century. For example, writing on the "Einheit und Vielfalt neutestamentlicher Theologien", Ulrich Luz has re-affirmed in connection with the early church ("Urchristentum"): "Deutlicher als je zuvor ist uns bewußt, wie wenig wir hier wissen" (1983, 143). We have to reconstruct hypothetically possible elements of early creeds. This enterprise is bound to remain tentative.[46]

3) It is widely held among scholars that we should not even look for "creeds" in early Christianity, because it is not likely that early Christians would have formed creeds from the earliest times on. Frances Young has summarised this consensus of opinion in this way (1991, 1-2):

> Christianity arose within Judaism: as has so often been said, Judaism is not an orthodoxy, but an orthopraxy - its common core is 'right action' rather than 'right belief' - Judaism was not the source of Christianity's emphasis on orthodoxy, and has formulated its 'beliefs' only in reaction to Christianity.

b. Methodology

My method in discussing our present theme is similar to what I have attempted in connection with the canon. I start from Ritter's affirmation that

---

[46] It is worth noting, however, that U. Luz himself lists "*Das Bekenntnis*" among the "Einheitsfördernde Kräfte" in the early church (1988, 65ff). He writes in connection with 1Cor 15,3 (p.67): "Der Text zeigt uns jedenfalls klar, daß es in der Kirche sehr früh gemeinsame Bekenntnistexte gegeben hat ... Natürlich fällt im ganzen Neuen Testament auch auf, wie verschieden diese alten Bekenntnisformeln im einzelnen formuliert sind ... Aber es gibt keine Gründe, die darauf schließen lassen, daß es irgendwo ein Christentum ohne formulierte Bekenntnisse gegeben hat".

we have certain "Bekenntniseinheit" in the second half of the second century, although we do not have one dominating "Bekenntnisformel". Working "backwards" in time, I examine some proposals concerning the origins of the later creeds. In doing this, I fully acknowledge the hypothetical character of any possible "results".

Within the limits of this thesis, I cannot attempt to find in Judaism parallels to the significance of creeds in Christianity. I can only point to the fact that Old Testament scholars put forward arguments for the thesis that certain Old Testament passages may have served as "credal" statements in Israel. Deut 6,4, the *Shema*, may be argued to be a credal statement that played a key role in Israel's life even around the time of the New Testament.

In the present context of my thesis, my tentative argument would be that orthopraxis and orthodoxy may not have to be separated in such a sharp way as it is done by Frances Young. Even if we acknowledge that schools around rabbis may have had differing rulings on certain matters, even then it may be argued that there were limits to the divergence of opinion. Whether or not the rabbis had "creeds", they still may have had a "theology" that required a certain allegiance. The rabbis may have had their "heretics", too.

Having pointed briefly to the problematic character of the thesis that "Christianity is the only major religion to set such store by creeds and doctrines" (Young 1991, 1), I turn to the theme of credal elements in the New Testament.

c. The thesis concerning a development of credal elements

It seems to be the most widely held view among scholars that the credal elements in the New Testament underwent a development: they grew from more simple forms to more complex forms. For example, K. Wengst has summarised the early stages of "Bekenntnisbildung" (1984, 397) in the following way (398):

> Voraussetzung aller Aussagen ist der grundlegende Glaube, daß Gott Jesus von den Toten auferweckt hat. Von daher wird Jesus als messianischer König und Gottessohn geglaubt, der alsbald als Richter und Retter kommen wird; von daher wird sein Tod reflektiert und als heilvolles Handeln Gottes begriffen; von daher wird er als gegenwärtiger Herr über alle Mächte bekannt.

There is a strong case for the thesis of a development of credal elements into a creed or creeds.[47] The more important arguments are as follows.

---

[47] I note that creeds may have been different in Eastern churches and in the West, as Lietzmann argued, 1962, 212.

1) There is a variety of forms of the credal elements in the New Testament. For example, Lietzmann classified the credal elements in this way (1962, 230ff).

- Simple Jesus-creeds where it is stated that Jesus is Lord, or, the Son of God: 1Cor 12,3; Rom 10,9; 1Jn 4,15; Acts 8,37. These formulas were later developed into the ΙΧΘΥΣ formula.
- A Christ-creed, styled in a wider way: Rom 1,3; 2Tim 2,8; 1Cor 15,3ff; 1Pet 3,13-22; Phil 2,5-11 (cf. also Ign. Eph 18,2; Ign. Trall 9; Ign. Smyrn 1,1-2).
- A two-membered creed referring to God and Christ: 1Cor 8,6; 1Tim 6,13; 2Tim4,1.
- The three-membered creed that has become dominant: Matt 28,19; 2Cor 13,13.

With regard to Lietzmann's classification I would argue that the passages referred to by him under the various classes do not simply come from books which would correspond in their order of date to the stage of the development of the passages in question. For example, Romans is referred to both under "simple Jesus creeds" and under the more developed Christ-creed. The three-membered confession is argued to be late by the logic of the development by expansion. However, 2Corinthians may not be a very late letter of Paul.

The end of the Gospel of Matthew may be material formed by the early church. However, the saying as it stands is attributed to Jesus, about whom many scholars would agree that he spoke about the Spirit of God; and at least some scholars would argue that he believed God was his "Father". Thus a "trinitarian" saying, whether or not it was ever uttered by Jesus, can well be thought of in the time of Jesus.

Another difficulty in Lietzmann's classes is presented by the texts under the heading "a Christ-creed styled in a wider way". On the one hand, this group precedes the last two, because it is "one-membered" in the sense that it only deals with Christ. On the other hand, it might be argued on the basis of the same logic that it must be even later than the three-membered formula, because it has many detailed statements about Christ.

If we look at the passages in Ignatius, the classification of Lietzmann becomes even more problematic. Ign. Eph 18,2 has a specific reference to the Holy Spirit in connection with the conception of Jesus. Ign. Trall 9,2 affirms that it was "his Father" who raised Jesus from the dead. Ign. Smyrn 1,1 calls Jesus "God's son". It also refers to the baptism of Jesus by John which could remind the readers of the Holy Spirit even without mentioning it. Thus it may be argued either that these passages do not belong to a class which only mention Christ, or that even if they were referring to only "one article" they could still presuppose a trinitarian background. Lietzmann's thesis is inconsistent at this point, because it both suggests that the "one article" type Christ-creed is early, and at the same time it is mainly attested by "late" evidence, i.e. Ignatius.

My argument against the development thesis would be the possibility that confessions of different types ("classes") may have existed parallel to each other, and are not necessarily representing the various stages of a development in time. To put this argument in a more modest way: even if the actual wording of the confessions may have grown ("developed") in time, the content of the longer confessions may have existed very early, even in the time of the "simpler" forms.

This view is supported by Cullmann's observation. He pointed to the fact that "formulas of one, two, and after a certain date three articles, contemporaneous and alongside one another, are attested from the earliest time" (1949, 36).

However, he does maintain a development thesis by arguing that there was not only one line of the development, but certain parts developed parallel with others. Cullmann suggested that there were simultaneous causes which were responsible for the origin of the confessions (18ff): 1) baptism and catechumenism;[48] 2) regular worship (liturgy and preaching);[49] 3) exorcism;[50] 4) persecution;[51] 5) polemic against heretics.[52] Cullmann affirmed that the same confession may have been used on different occasions (33).

The main thesis of Cullmann is that: "Proclamation of Christ is *the starting-point of every Christian confession*" (39). During the earlier part of the development of the creeds, the first and the third article of the Credo were also brought into connection with the second: their mention was justified "in a Christological way" (52, cf. also 62).

Cullmann's efforts indicate that even if one wants to hold onto the development thesis, one will have to modify it thoroughly in comparison with Lietzmann's thesis. His emphasis on the "parallel" existence of credal elements may be called in as a support for my thesis.

2) Another argument affirms that the canon, which was being formed from the middle of the second century onward, was too large "to serve as rule of

---

[48] Cf. Acts 8,36-38 where the eunuch's confession of faith is "one of the most ancient confessions of faith which we know", p.20.

[49] E.g. Phil 2,6-11 was "composed for the worship of the primitive community", p.22.

[50] Cf. Acts 3,6, pp.24-25.

[51] Cf. 1Tim 6,13; Cullmann argues that also 1Cor 12,3 can be explained against this background, pp.28-29.

[52] Cf. 1Jn 4,2; 1Cor 8,6; 1Cor 15,3-8, p.32.

faith. In view of the richness of this compilation and the multiplicity of the writings there assembled, the essential content had to be extracted" (Cullmann 1949, 11). This is the reason why a creed was to be formed.

This argument, however, may only apply to the later confessions. It cannot be used as a reason for the emergence of the "credal formulae" which are there even in the "early" and "undisputed" letters of Paul. If one holds that the later confessions developed or, at least, grew out of the earlier credal elements, then this thesis of Cullmann will become even more unlikely. At most, this thesis may point to one factor among others which led to the emergence of late and long confessions.

At this point it may be appropriate to refer to Lessing who held the opposite view. On the basis of his study of the "Church Fathers in the first four centuries" (in Chadwick, 1956, 64), he listed among the points concerning the *regula fidei* the following (62):

> 1. The content of the Creed is called by the earliest Fathers *regula fidei*. 2. This *regula fidei* is not drawn from the writings of the New Testament. 3. This *regula fidei* existed before a single book of the New Testament existed ... 11. In accordance with the *regula fidei* even the writings of the apostles were judged. The selection from their writings was made according to the degree of their agreement with the *regula fidei*, and writings were rejected according to the degree of their disagreement with it, even though their authors were, or were believed to be, apostles.[53]

A further argument may be that even if we attribute a significance to creeds, we could not claim that we have found the basic theology of the early Christians, because some affirmations which may have been important for the first Christians are not there in the creeds. For example, the Apostles' Creed does not mention the teaching of Jesus or the "Pauline doctrine of justification by faith" (Cullmann 1949, 12).

Cullmann's observation is right with regard to important statements of faith not being there in fully developed later creeds. Other "items" may be added to the list which "are missing" from the Apostles' Creed and yet may be argued to have been important for the church from early times on.[54]

However, we cannot say that only those "articles" which we now have in the Apostles' Creed may possibly have been parts of earlier confessions. Hypothetical reconstructions of early creeds support this point. However closely they resemble the creeds we now know, they do contain elements which "are

---

[53] I am indebted for this reference to Professor J.C. O'Neill.

[54] The relationship between Israel and the church may be one example. Other examples are given by E. Best: "ethical or experiential material" is not contained in the historic creeds, 1986, 8.

missing" from the Apostles' Creed or from the Niceno-Constantinopolitan Creed. Two major examples of such reconstruction are appropriate to be cited.

A. Seeberg reconstructed an early creed ("Glaubensformel") as follows (1966, 85):

Ὁ Θεὸς ὁ ζῶν, ὁ κτίσας τὰ πάντα, ἀπέστειλε τὸν υἱὸν αὐτοῦ Ἰησοῦν Χριστόν, τὸν γενόμενον ἐκ σπέρματος Δαυείδ, ὃς ἀπέθανεν ὑπὲρ τῶν ἁμαρτιῶν ἡμῶν κατὰ τὰς γραφὰς καὶ ἐτάφη, ὃς ἠγέρθη τῇ ἡμέρα τῇ τρίτῃ κατὰ τὰς γραφὰς καὶ ὤφθη Κηφᾷ καὶ τοῖς δώδεκα, ὃς ἐκάθισεν ἐν δεξιᾷ τοῦ θεοῦ ἐν τοῖς οὐρανοῖς ὑποταγεισῶν αὐτῷ πασῶν τῶν ἀρχῶν καὶ ἐξουσιῶν καὶ δυνάμεων, καὶ ἔρχεται ἐπὶ τῶν νεφελῶν τοῦ οὐρανοῦ μετὰ δυνάμεως καὶ δόξης πολλῆς.

For example, the references to David, to the resurrection appearances, and to the coming with the clouds are not parts of later creeds; and yet they may be argued to belong to the earliest traditions - as "credal elements".

Lietzmann reconstructed the following "archetype" of confessions in the East (1953, 112):

I believe in one God, the Father, the Almighty,
    the creator of everything visible and invisible;
And in one Lord Jesus Christ, the only begotten Son of God,
    Who was born from the Father before all the Aeons,
        through whom everything came into being,
    Who became man, suffered, and rose on the third day,
        and ascended into heaven,
        and who will come in glory,
        to judge the living and the dead;
And in the holy Ghost.

In this reconstruction the reference to the time "before all the Aeons" may be an example of an early tradition which is missing from later creeds.

On the basis of the examples, I would argue that reconstructed credal elements may have formed parts of the "basic theology" of the early Christians, irrespective of the fact that these elements are not there in later creeds.[55]

---

[55] We have to note one major reason why any reconstruction of an early creed has to remain on a hypothetical level. The various credal statements are preserved in diverse parts of the New Testament writings. None of the New Testament writings contains all the elements. In as much as this very fact may be an argument for the widespread attestation of credal statements, this same fact calls for caution when we argue that the credal statements were part of a creed. C.F. Evans summarised our problem in a pointed way (1956, 25): "When the various strands of the New Testament are separated, and each is examined on

To sum up, I point to one significant result of the reconstructions discussed above. In as much as scholars disagree about the stages of developments of creeds, their work points to the phenomenon that the early Christians did live in a creed-forming age. If this is true, then it may be argued that the early Christians adhered to these "credal elements". I would argue for the thesis that the early Christians may have had a "basic theology" which is expressed in these credal elements.

d. An argument from the "external evidence"

We may find an argument in favour of the thesis that there was a theological unity at an early stage of Christianity in the study of *nomina sacra* by C.H. Roberts. Roberts has pointed to the remarkable phenomenon that "a strictly limited number of words, at most fifteen", are abbreviated in Greek and Latin (biblical as well as non-biblical) religious writings (1979, 26). Roberts classifies these words in three groups (p.27): four words, Ἰησοῦς, Χριστός, κύριος, θεός, "the abbreviation of which in their sacral meaning may be said to be invariable"; three words, πνεῦμα, ἄνθρωπος, σταυρός, "of which the contracted form is found relatively early and relatively frequently"; eight words, πατήρ, υἱός, σωτήρ, μήτηρ, οὐρανός, Ἰσραήλ, Δαυείδ, Ἰερουσαλήμ, of which "the contraction is irregular".

Roberts argues that the abbreviations have a Christian origin (34). He affirms that behind the list of the abbreviated words "lies a quite unmistakeable, if implicit, theology" (41). Roberts points out that "the *nomina sacra* found in our earliest papyri have a strongly Jewish flavour" (45). He emphasises that "the system of *nomina sacra* presupposes a degree of control and organization". Jewish Christianity may have followed the example of the synagogue concerning "the great care taken in writing and preserving the rolls of the Law" (46). Roberts argues that the Christian invention of abbreviating the *nomina sacra* may have originated in the Jewish Christian community of Jerusalem, "probably before A.D. 70" (p.46).[56]

We must note that Roberts attributes significance to words that are not included among the *nomina sacra*. On the basis of the omission of words such as λόγος, σοφία, αἷμα, ἄρτος, οἶνος, σάρξ, σῶμα he argues that the list of abbreviated words may have been created at a very early stage and in

---

its own in relation to its historical and doctrinal background, ... the question becomes pressing whether and in what sense the New Testament is a unity from within ..."

[56] Here I point again to the argument, significant for my thesis, that some kind of "organisation" may have existed in early Christianity.

an "area where Pauline and Johannine influence had not penetrated" (40). Whether or not so much may be attributed to these "omissions" as Roberts suggests, his conclusion is significant for my thesis (46):

> ... the *nomina sacra* may be plausibly viewed as the creation of the primitive Christian community, representing what might be regarded as the embryonic creed of the first Church; the four primary terms (as they later became) together with πατήρ, σταυρός, and πνεῦμα represent the beliefs common to all Christians, some of the others the particular Jewish strain in the Jerusalem church.

If Roberts is right in seeing "a summary outline of theology" (47), or, "theology implicit" (72) in the *nomina sacra*,[57] then his thesis may be called in as a support for my thesis concerning the early origins of a creed - and of early Christian theology.[58]

To conclude, I tentatively propose that early Christianity's theology can be found in the "credal elements" of the New Testament. These credal elements may be seen as short articles of a creed. If the early Christians adhered to creed-type short summaries of their belief, then it may be argued that this adherence formed a unity among them.

It has to be added that this unity in the "basic theology" of the early Christians may have left room for a variety of opinions on certain individual matters of faith. The variety of expression of faith does not mean that the holders of the varying views would not have shared a "basic theology". They need not have regarded one another as holding contradictory views as long as they adhered to the belief expressed in the "credal elements".

8. Conclusion

In this chapter we have surveyed major challenges that are brought against the enterprise of New Testament theology from the point of view of the second part of the name of the enterprise, i.e. "theology".

My thesis is that New Testament theology should be understood as an enterprise describing the theological content of the New Testament - and thus "*the* theology" of the group of Christians that produced the New Testament canon.

This thesis is challenged by the view that there was a development in the theology (or theological thought) of early Christianity. This development is

---

[57] For a recent study of the evidence for the *nomina sacra* see D. Trobisch 1996, 16-31.

[58] I note my indebtedness to Mr D.F. Wright, New College, Edinburgh, for calling my attention to the work of Roberts.

said to have resulted in views which were differing to such a degree that the beginning and the end of the development may be seen as opposing theological viewpoints.

I have argued that the development thesis, which is widely affirmed by scholars, is largely based on a certain understanding of some New Testament passages. As an example, I have tried to show that Acts 2,36 should not be taken as an expression of an adoptionist Christology among early Christians. In this context I have examined the thesis that Jesus, the Proclaimer, had become Christ, the Proclaimed - after Easter. I have tentatively argued that if we understand verses like Acts 2,36 in a non-adoptionist way, we may find that Easter does not have to be seen as such a turning point (or even starting point) in early Christian theology as it is proposed, for example, by Bultmann.

I have also pointed to criticisms which have been raised against one major expression of the development thesis, F.C. Baur's theory.

We have discussed one major example of comparisons between "theologies" within the New Testament. I have found that the views of Jesus and Paul may not be diverging to such an extent as has often been suggested.

I have argued for the view that Jesus' teaching should be part of a New Testament theology by referring to two major reasons. On the one hand, Jesus' teaching may form a part of New Testament theology if we find that Jesus' teaching is not in contradiction with other theological views expressed in the New Testament. On the other hand, even without this condition, one may argue that Jesus' teaching will have to be presented first if one makes an attempt to compare it with other theologies in the New Testament.

The enterprise of New Testament theology, as I should like to define it, faces a major challenge from the side of those scholars who argue that there are contradictory theologies in the New Testament. Although the thesis concerning contradictory theologies is worth discussing on its own, it is important to point out that in the case of many of its sub-theses and arguments it is in connection with the "development thesis" mentioned above.

To discuss the themes which are argued to have developed in New Testament times, or to contradict one another, is an enormous enterprise. Perhaps it may be part of a New Testament theology or an exegetical work in preparation for a New Testament theology. As an end result it may well turn out to be impossible to find a basic theology the New Testament authors all shared. Then one can attempt only to write the *Theologies* of the New Testament or even a *History of the Development* of the Theologies of the New Testament.

This exegetical task cannot be carried out within the limits of my thesis. One possible method for the exegetical analysis may be that of gathering the theological statements of the New Testament writings. Then one may hypothetically suggest a summary of those statements which seem to be widely shared. One may examine the content of the individual New Testament writings in comparison with that summary. This comparison may be followed by an examination: Do the New Testament writers agree upon that summary?, and, Why do they not mention all parts of the summary?[59]

A second aspect of the examination may be added. One may point out the lack of contradiction in writings where we may have expected a contradiction because of the different thinking of their authors or of the circles from which the writings have emerged.[60]

I have only attempted to give some examples of this exegetical side of the enterprise of New Testament theology. On the one hand, I have argued that one may point to statements in the New Testament which, it may be argued, stand out from their context as earlier traditions. Reconstructed "credal formulae" may be an argument for a shared basic theology in New Testament times.

On the other hand, I have pointed to the problematic character of some of the major theses concerning (alleged) contradictory theologies in the New Testament. I have proposed that even one of the most famous cases where one may "expect" to find contradictions, the views of Paul and James on "faith and works", may not necessarily be an example of irreconcilable oppositions.

On the basis of the examples of lines of arguments I would follow, I tentatively conclude that the enterprise of New Testament theology may be justified with regard to the "theology" element of the enterprise. There may have existed a basic, creed-type theology to which all those Christians adhered, whose writings are gathered in the New Testament. Their allegiance made it also possible for them to express their belief in different ways, because they all thought - about themselves and the others - that they are within the boundary of that "creed" that may (at least partly) be reconstructed by us from "credal elements" in the New Testament.

---

[59] This latter question may often be answered by the primary aim of the individual writings, and by their *Sitz im Leben*.

[60] I am indebted to Dr. D.L. Mealand, New College, Edinburgh, for the suggestion of this "double criterion".

Chapter Five

The Main Characteristics of the Enterprise

In the preceding chapters we surveyed the major challenges that have been mounted against the enterprise of New Testament theology. I have argued against these challenges by pointing out that they are either not conclusive even if we accept them, or that they are based on an interpretation of the evidence that may not be the final word in the history of interpretation: other interpretations may be argued for. I have also attempted to show, in most cases in a tentative way, that we may put forward arguments for theses other than those favoured by those who question the possibility of the enterprise.

By these two types of argumentation I have aimed to support my thesis that the enterprise of New Testament theology may be justified. I have prepared the way to say something about the general matter: If New Testament theology as an enterprise may be maintained, what should the main characteristics of the enterprise be?

In this last chapter of my thesis I shall discuss questions relating to definitions, presuppositions, and the aims of the enterprise of New Testament theology. Some of what follows may be seen as harvesting the fruits of the work accomplished so far - but some sections rely on arguments not discussed as yet. First I shall discuss some major themes briefly; and I shall present my proposals concerning the enterprise of New Testament theology. Then I shall re-affirm my theses in the course of a brief discussion of some recent contributions to the enterprise.

1. Defining the enterprise

We have found on more than one occasion that much depends on how we define key terms related to our study, such as, for example, theology, religion, experience. As I have already argued in the first chapter that I would use the terms religion and experience in a wide sense, it may suffice here to expand only on the most crucial term for our study, that of "theology".

We have seen that both Wrede and Räisänen use the term "theology" in a twofold sense. For Wrede, theology may mean, on the one hand, the doctrines of the early Christians. It is probably in this sense that Wrede affirms (1897, 34; ET: 1973, 84): "... the discipline has to lay out the history of early Christian religion and theology". On the other hand, theology also means "systematic theology" - or, in Wrede's term, "Dogmatik". It is against the controlling function of "Dogmatik" that Wrede emphasises the historical character ("streng geschichtlichen Charakter") of New Testament theology (1897, 8; ET: 1973, 69).

We have also seen how Räisänen distinguished between "early Christian thought", to which he added in brackets: "or theology, if you like", and a "theological 'reflection on the New Testament'" (1990, xviii).

These two usages of the term "theology" are most helpfully summarised by Gerhard Ebeling. He affirms concerning the term "biblical theology" (1963, 79):

> It can mean either 'the theology contained in the Bible, the theology of the Bible itself', or 'the theology that accords with the Bible, scriptural theology'.

We can find an example of the distinction, which shows how the author was aware of the significance of that distinction, in Schlier's work on "Pauline theology". In the preface to his book entitled *"Grundzüge einer paulinischen Theologie"*, 1978, he clearly distinguishes between the theology of Paul and a Pauline theology. In this book he attempts to write the latter, presupposing the former (7). The theology of Paul for Schlier means the historical reconstruction of Paul's theology from his letters. A Pauline theology is a theology which is influenced by the kerygma of the Pauline letters, and which is explicitly dependent on the theology of Paul in terms of contents (9).

In my thesis I adopt the first meaning of the term "theology" as described by the authors above, that is, I should like to take the word "theology" in the name of the enterprise of New Testament theology to mean the theology contained in the New Testament writings, the theology of early Christianity.

If we adopt this meaning, then we can agree with those who argue for a historical character of New Testament theology, but we also have to face other challenges evoked by our decision.

2. A historical, descriptive enterprise

Wrede's call for a "purely historical discipline" of New Testament theology (1897, 8; ET: 1973, 69) has found a widespread response in our century.[1]

---

[1] We must note that it may remain a matter of discussion what we should understand under the term "purely". One may question whether a "purely" historical enterprise is possible at all.

There is widespread agreement among scholars that New Testament theology should have a historical character.

Even scholars who would not argue that New Testament theology should only have a historical character would agree that New Testament theology should have a historical character as well as some other character(s). For example, Jürgen Roloff (1994, 241) writes in his review of Peter Stuhlmacher's first volume of *Biblische Theologie des Neuen Testaments*:

> ... trotz der grundsätzlichen Feststellung, daß Neutestamentliche Theologie ihren Schwerpunkt in der theologischen Interpretation der ntl. Verkündigungsinhalte haben müsse, entscheidet sich St. bei der praktischen Durchführung für einen faktischen Primat der historischen Rekonstruktion ...

It is also significant to note with D. Lührmann (1992, 734) that since Wrede's programmatic 1897 essay the vast majority of New Testament theologies do not follow a structure based on theological concepts, but on a historical reconstruction of the development of early Christianity from Jesus to the early church. This means that the historical element dominates even works that are theologically orientated, because - in the opinion of those who hold a "development thesis"[2] - the factor of historical sequence or order has a major bearing on the theology of the authors of the New Testament.

Räisänen agrees with Wrede that "New Testament theology" should be a historical discipline (1990, 106). However, Räisänen does add the important warning that "the person of the scholar cannot be wholly bracketed out in historical work". With due caution in relation to the fact that historical reconstruction involves "interpretation" on the side of the exegete (108), he affirms that (107-108):

> There seem to be good reasons for an exegete to write a history of early Christian thought in which he clings as consistently as possible to the historical task - setting forth 'what has been' rather than 'what ought to be'.

At this point it is appropriate to affirm that I agree with those who define New Testament theology as a historical enterprise. The development of the discipline in the last two hundred years points in this direction. Morgan is right in insisting that (1992b, 691):

> Despite some impatience with the narrow vision of some historical scholarship, it seems inconceivable that any intellectually responsible theology should wish to lose the gains of the past 200 years.

---

[2] See the previous chapter.

However, if we adopt the view that New Testament theology should be a historical enterprise, we should note that we encounter some difficulties.

1) First of all, the majority of those scholars who argue for a historical character of the enterprise would hold that the historical character is unavoidable because of the fact that historians find a development in the theology of the early Christians. I have argued in other chapters that this view may be challenged on two grounds. On the one hand, I have argued that the "development thesis" is not without problems, i.e. it may not be true in the form in which many scholars would present it. On the other hand, I have argued that certain "developments" do not necessarily imply a change in doctrine to the extent that the later phase of the development would be in contradiction with the earlier phase.

2) We may mention separately (although it is often related to the "development thesis") that some of the scholars who argue for the historical character of the enterprise would conclude that the historical character excludes the theological character of the enterprise. Räisänen is the most radical representative of this opinion. He argues that it is in an ecclesial context that New Testament theology may retain an "actualizing emphasis" and "even a normative character" (1990, 107). He argues:

> Why should New Testament theology be practised in the church as a purely historical discipline ..., when the limitation to the canon already implies a theological decision?

This argument of Räisänen shows that he thinks "New Testament theology" should not be a "theological" enterprise outside a church context. The argument itself, however, may be challenged. I have argued in other chapters that the focus on the canon may be a focus evoked by a historical investigation (chapter two): it may be argued that the canon was the result of a historical process a historian can report about, without presupposing a "normative" character for the canonical writings (chapter three).

I have also argued that the "canon" is not a "theological decision" of the fourth century church (or church leaders). Consequently, to describe the theology of the New Testament does not have to involve a "theological decision" on the side of the historian.

Against Räisänen, I would argue for a historical character of New Testament theology which does not exclude the study and description of the theological content of the New Testament.

3) We shall see later that some scholars would like to define New Testament theology in terms other than "historical". These scholars agree that the historical character has to be retained; nevertheless they would argue for

other modes of enquiry that have to complement or follow the historical one. We may note that this emphasis is in some connection with a dissatisfaction with what can be achieved by a strictly historical enterprise. As an example of a call for interpretations other than the historical one, we may refer to Morgan's affirmation (1992b, 691):

> ... only the social sciences are today providing plausible (i.e. empirically tested) theories of religion compatible with its [i.e. a free biblical scholarship's] truth or claims to revelation. The future shape of critical NT theology will therefore be found here.

We shall discuss examples of these definitions of New Testament theology later. Here it may suffice to point to the fact that a decision in favour of a New Testament theology which is a historical enterprise also has to address the relationship with definitions which add new aspects to the historical one.

If we adopt the view that New Testament theology should be a historical enterprise, we shall have to adopt a rule that springs out of this decision: New Testament theology should be a descriptive enterprise. I have argued in the first chapter that no normative character of the New Testament should be presupposed in New Testament theology. This proposal is one consequence of adopting a descriptive character for the enterprise. It is appropriate here to expand on what "descriptive" means in my understanding of New Testament theology.

When I argue for New Testament theology as a (historical) descriptive enterprise, I am nearer to K. Stendahl's view than to Räisänen's view, although I agree with both of them in separating New Testament theology from systematic theological reasoning on the New Testament.

I agree with Räisänen that the "actualizing interpretation" should be regarded as a second stage after the "historical interpretation". It is also possible that a New Testament theologian would wish to engage in this second stage of the task and not to leave it to systematic theologians. However, I do not agree with Räisänen's proposal that the first stage, i.e. the historical one, could not be a "theological" enterprise. In my opinion, we can retain the term "theological" in the sense that the enterprise aims at describing the theology of (or contained in) the New Testament.

In his significant article in *The Interpreter's Dictionary of the Bible* (1962), Stendahl concluded that New Testament theology should be a descriptive discipline (422). He argued that:

> ... once we confine ourselves to the task of descriptive biblical theology as a field in its own right, the material itself gives us means to check whether our interpretation is correct or not.

As a due caution he added that the biblical texts "are not extensive enough to allow us certainty in all areas". Nevertheless, he maintained that in New Testament theology "our only concern is to find out what these words meant when uttered or written by the prophet, the priest, the evangelist, or the apostle - and regardless of their meaning in later stages of religious history, our own included".

It may be worth noting that James Barr's article in the supplementary volume of the same *Dictionary* (1976) distinguishes between Stendahl's view and the general trend of the "Biblical Theology" movement of the time of Stendahl's article. In relation to Stendahl's views Barr affirms (106):

> The high value attached to objectivity in description, the strict separation between description and systematic theology, and the critical attitude toward dumping Semitic or Hebrew categories in the lap of the twentieth century - all these were quite the reverse of the positions then generally esteemed as biblical theology.

Although Barr criticises the Biblical Theology movement of the time of Stendahl, Barr's criticism does not apply to Stendahl's programmatic views.

Räisänen's caution that the "statement that historical study is about 'what the text meant' (Stendahl) is surely somewhat oversimplified" (1990, 107) is in connection with Räisänen's right emphasis on the fact that an "actualizing concern always exists [in the historical interpreter], consciously or unconsciously" (106).

Accepting this warning, I propose that Stendahl's programme should be followed in New Testament theology: the enterprise should be a historical one; i.e. should describe what theology is contained in the New Testament.

By this decision I do not exclude the proposals that the historical character may be complemented by other characters, to which matter I return later. At this point it is only affirmed that - in my understanding of the enterprise - New Testament theology may be defined as a historical, descriptive enterprise, irrespective of the further decision whether or not we complement the historical character with other methods.

3. Is faith a requirement for carrying out the enterprise?

Our answer to the question whether or not faith is a necessary condition on the side of the interpreter depends on how we have decided on the matters discussed so far in this chapter. If a scholar defines "theology" in the name of the enterprise to refer to the theological interpretation of the scholar, then it will be a logical consequence that faith should be required from the interpreter. In the same way, faith will be presupposed if the task of New Testament theology is not that of describing the content of the New Testament, but that of conveying the truth claim made in the New Testament toward the present-day reader.

For example, Robert Morgan affirms that the discipline of New Testament theology "originated and has survived in the service of the Church's use of Scripture" (1992a, 480). This means that New Testament theology is "Christian theology" which has as its presupposition "the revelation of God in Jesus". Since Christians believe that this revelation is mediated by the "biblical *Sache* or 'content'" (483), the task of New Testament theology is "a theologically and historically responsible presentation" of that content.

I have already indicated that I do not exclude this understanding of the enterprise of New Testament theology. However, this definition has its own problems - as is clearly seen by Morgan. The main difficulty lies in tensions that "stem from its [i.e. the discipline's] combination of this religious interest with the rigorous use of the linguistic and historical methods" (480). In other words, the most difficult problem of the enterprise is to explicate the revelation of God "in ways that avoid conflict with the methods and results of the rational investigation of the Bible".

In this thesis I propose that New Testament theology may not only be defined in the way that is represented by Morgan's words quoted above, but also in such a way that we do not set it the aim of explicating God's revelation. If we adopt the descriptive character of New Testament theology, then we may agree with Stendahl also in that the "descriptive task can be carried out by believer and agnostic alike" (1962, 422).

Stendahl argues that believer and agnostic could co-operate in New Testament theology, because in their task the "meaning for the present - in which the two interpreters are different - is not involved" (422). It is even desirable that believer and agnostic should mutually criticise one another in the course of interpretation, because both have different disadvantages. The believer's faith "threatens to have him modernize the material", i.e. to apply it to the present; or, in Räisänen's term, to "actualize" it. Stendahl affirms that the agnostic does not have this temptation, but the agnostic's "power of empathy must be considerable if he is to identify himself sufficiently with the believer of the first century". The agnostic's temptation is that "distaste for meaning" may colour his descriptive work.[3]

---

[3] It is interesting to note that Peter Stuhlmacher argues against a "faith-requirement" in New Testament theology on theological grounds. He affirms that (1992, 11): "Die fides, von der das Neue Testament spricht, ist kein menschlicher Besitz, sondern Gabe Gottes. Sie kann und darf deshalb nicht zur methodischen Voraussetzung der Bibelauslegung erhoben werden."

I conclude that faith should not be regarded as a requirement for engaging in the enterprise of New Testament theology. However, we may add that an openness toward the *Sache* - or, in other words, an empathy to religious utterances - is necessary.

The proposal that faith should not be made a condition in New Testament theology is in close relationship with my view on the question, whether or not New Testament theology should be carried out in a church context. It is appropriate, therefore, to turn to this question.

4. For and in the church only?

Wrede argued against the view that a New Testament theology should be carried out as a "service to be rendered to the church" on the following basis (1897, 15-16; ET: 1973, 73). The church context of a New Testament theology could be felt in three areas: 1) "the results of research"; 2) "the way in which the material is treated"; 3) "the tasks which are set". Wrede rightly affirms that the first two should be "determined solely by the nature of the historical object". With regard to the third area he asserts that although "questions and needs of the church can be a legitimate influence", nevertheless "only in a limited sense", because the tasks of the enterprise should "come also in the main from the subject-matter".

Räisänen agrees with Wrede's view. Räisänen adds further arguments against the restriction of the enterprise to a church context. He argues that exegesis "can be pursued with the aim of providing people with means of coping with life" (1990, 95). In the case of "New Testament theology" this means: to cope "with their cultural and religious heritage". Räisänen programmatically affirms:

A synthesis directed to the wider society, to people interested in the findings of New Testament study independently of their relationship to a church, seems preferable to a church-orientated way of conceiving the task. In the context of a state university such a solution is especially natural.

Räisänen goes on to expand the circle of the "addressees" of a "New Testament theology" from society to "humankind as a whole" (96; see also 120). For example, the study of the "rise of Christianity" may contribute to world peace if it helps to make Christianity "understandable to representatives of *other traditions*" (96). This affirmation leads to the conclusion that in New Testament theology a "close co-operation with comparative religion is necessary" (97).

I fully agree with Räisänen's concern. He puts forward a programme very much needed toward the end of the twentieth century: New Testament theology and "exegesis need a global perspective" (96). I propose that we should adopt Räisänen's emphasis on this wide context of New Testament theology.

However, I cannot agree with his affirmation (made in the same section of his 1990 book) that a New Testament theology in a church context would necessarily be a task different "from a historical interpretation of the material" (96). In my understanding of the enterprise, a church context would only mean that New Testament theology would not remain on the level of a historical description, but would also call for an acceptance of the content that is described.

We may also add that even this latter possibility is an option rather than a necessity. A New Testament theologian in the church may decide to confess that he wishes to enrol in the circle of those early Christians whose theology he has described, and he may call his readers to do so.

However, this is not a necessary requirement in a church context. I would argue that in today's society, even a teacher in a church college or seminary may be respected and listened to more openly by his students if he does not carry out this final step of witnessing, but stops at describing the evidence and leaves it open whether or not the truth claim of the early Christians is accepted and followed by the present-day hearers.

I think the reason why Räisänen holds that New Testament theology in a church context is different from a historical interpretation of the material is that he also holds that the historical interpretation would not correspond to the church's teachings. To this, one may give a twofold answer.

On the one hand, the church should only benefit from learning more of the "historical truth" and should not hide from the "facts" that can be found by historical methods.

On the other hand, the results of historical research are not necessarily as far from the church's teaching as it is often held today in scholarly circles - as we have found in the course of the discussions of the previous chapters of my thesis.

At this point we have to note that a decision to adopt a historical enterprise in a church context creates a new problem. We have to accept the possibility that present-day Christian teachings may differ from what the historical inquiry into the early Christians' beliefs establishes. What happens to Christian faith in this case? To put it in another way, Does Christian faith depend on historical facts?

One possible way of answering this question is that of Bultmann: Christian faith does not depend on the results of historical inquiry. On the contrary,

Christian faith can show that it is real faith precisely in its decision not to base itself on anything else than God's grace. To base Christian faith on historical facts would be equal to basing it on a false security; this very act would be an act of unbelief.[4]

Without entering the debate which continued after Bultmann's famous article on "New Testament and Mythology",[5] I propose that Christianity may and should expose itself to a historical testing of what it claims. However, it is in part due to my awareness of these difficulties that I propose to define New Testament theology as a historical enterprise which may be - but does not have to be - carried out in a church context. To solve the problems, which may emerge for the church due to the results of the enterprise, should be the task of the church, but these possible problems should not cause New Testament theology to abandon its historical character.

5. The need to clarify one's presuppositions

The points discussed in the preceding sections may be seen as arguments for highlighting the necessity that scholars should think through what their presuppositions are in engaging in the enterprise of New Testament theology.

For example, Räisänen rightly warns us that "for all practical purposes the faith of the scholar amounts to his confidence that behind diversity a theological unity is found in the New Testament" (1990, 110). We may add that this unity is even more likely to be presupposed by scholars standing in the Calvinistic reformed strand of the Christian tradition. Lutheran scholars generally presuppose that there is a "canon within the canon".

With Räisänen (1990, 112) we may also point to another warning, made by Stendahl (1962, 422), that it is not enough to "state our bias in an introductory chapter" and think that this may be an excuse to go on "to excel in bias". Räisänen (1990, 112) proposes as a criterion for scholars (to hold their "personal prejudice" under control) the following test of *fair play*: can he do equal justice to all parties of the process he is studying"?

Robert Morgan emphasises that texts "have no rights, no aims, no interests" (1991, 7). It is the interpreters "who are the active subjects in the act of interpretation". Consequently, "the interpreters' interests are decisive in textual interpretation" (8). Morgan argues that "the study of texts is always undertaken within some larger framework" (22). This framework, "constituted

---

[4] See e.g. in Bartsch, 1964[2], 19, 41-42, 44.
[5] See the two English volumes edited by Bartsch, 1964[2] and 1962.

by interpreters' interests, determines what questions are considered important, what methods are found appropriate, and what explanations are deemed satisfying".

In the light of these observations, I agree on Morgan's emphasis that "reflection on the various uses of the Bible and on one's aims in interpreting it should precede biblical study" (21), and that "interpreters ought to clarify and declare their aims" (239).

6. The focus of the study

One of the major "aims" - that involves "presuppositions" - deserves mentioning separately. Although I summarise this theme in the one question: What should New Testament theology focus on?, nevertheless this theme is a complex one: it relates to the thesis of a "canon within the canon" and to content criticism, or *Sachkritik*.

It is much discussed in scholarship whether or not Bultmann was right in focusing his New Testament theology upon two major groups of witnesses: the Pauline and the Johannine writings. Between the first part of his *Theologie des Neuen Testaments* (1984), "Voraussetzungen und Motive der Neutestamentlichen Theologie" and the third part, "Die Entwicklung zur Alten Kirche", the central part of the work is entitled "Die Theologie des Paulus und des Johannes".

Bultmann affirms that Paul is the founder of a Christian theology (1984, 188). He argues that Paul "sieht Welt und Mensch stets in der Beziehung zu Gott" (192). Consequently, he asserts concerning Paul's writings that:

> Jeder Satz über Gott ist zugleich ein Satz über den Menschen und umgekehrt. Deshalb und in diesem Sinne ist *die paulinische Theologie zugleich Anthropologie.*

According to Bultmann, "Johannes gehört nicht in die paulinische Schule und ist durch Paulus nicht beeinflußt, sondern er ist eine originale Gestalt und steht in einer andern Atmosphäre theologischen Denkens" (1984, 361).

In spite of the radical difference between Paul and John in terms of "Denkweise und Begrifflichkeit", Bultmann can see "eine tiefe *sachliche Verwandtschaft*" between Paul and John (361). This "Verwandtschaft" includes, for example, that "bei beiden das eschatologische Geschehen als ein schon in der Gegenwart sich vollziehendes verstanden ist", and that both of them demythologise the "gnostic, cosmological dualism".

These similarities coincide with the key elements that characterise Bultmann's theology, and so they can be seen as the main reason for Bultmann's focusing upon Paul and John. As, for example, D. Fergusson has put it (1992, 103):

> The assertion that Paul and John are already engaged in demythologizing eschatological and Gnostic concepts indicates the extent to which demythologizing is an integral feature of Bultmann's theology of the New Testament.

Thus we may say that Bultmann is consistent in his own system: the beginnings of demythologising activity in Paul and in John can make them the right focus of Bultmann's existentialist interpretation. However, without going into discussion with Bultmann's thesis, we have to note that individual parts of his consistent system, as well as some of the presuppositions of the system, have been criticised.[6]

We have already seen that it may be argued that Jesus' teaching should not only be regarded as a presupposition of New Testament theology, but as an essential part of it. If we adopt this view, then it can be seen as another criticism of Bultmann's approach.

W.G. Kümmel announced in the subtitle of his *Die Theologie des Neuen Testaments* (1987) that he focuses on the "Hauptzeugen": Jesus, Paul and John. He has often been criticised for this, since it may be argued that a focus on the major witnesses should not be called "New Testament theology".

However, this may not be a justifiable criticism, because Kümmel himself acknowledged that it is necessary that in another work the theology of the remaining writings of the New Testament should be dealt with (18). His aim with his focus on the three major witnesses was "von diesen Hauptformen der neutestamentlichen Verkündigung auszugehen und sich mit ihrer Hilfe eine grundlegende Einsicht in das Wesen der neutestamentlichen Gedankenwelt zu verschaffen".

Kümmel's work may be criticised, however, on other grounds. For example, in relation to Kümmel's aim (1987, 18), "nach der in diesen Verkündigungsformen [i.e. those of the three "Hauptzeugen"] sich zeigenden Einheit zu fragen", C.K. Barrett has argued (1983, 11):

> To speak of picking out the agreements between Jesus, Paul, and John implies that there are also disagreements, or at least differences, between them ... Even to recognize that such disagreements do, or may, exist means that we are setting each of our authorities against each of the other as standard: Jesus is judged by Paul, Paul by John, and so on.

---

[6] See e.g. a well balanced recent criticism in Fergusson, 1992.

We may add in this context that it may be argued that Kümmel's focus on the main witnesses is also an example of a "canon within the canon". This criticism by Barrett may lead us to a general argument against the view "canon within the canon". If we want to stress some parts of the New Testament in distinction from others, then we shall have to face the question: How do we justify our "picking" of the part(s) that can "judge" the other parts? Or, to pose a related question, What are the criteria for exercising content criticism (*Sachkritik*)?

I propose that the view "canon within the canon" should not be adopted in New Testament theology. My main reason for this proposal is that any "canon within the canon" affirms by definition that there are different theologies in the New Testament. We cannot exclude that this may be the end-result of our carrying out the enterprise, but it should not be made a presupposition.

The issue of *Sachkritik* is related to the view of "canon within the canon", but the two may be separated in some aspects. Similarly to the need of clarifying one's aims and presuppositions in relation to the enterprise of New Testament theology, scholars have to analyse what their criteria are in content criticism. On the one hand, content criticism should not pre-judge what can be accepted as historically reliable. On the other hand, content criticism is in connection with historical criticism. As I have proposed in the first chapter - in agreement with many scholars - that historical criticism may be a necessary tool in New Testament theology, I also affirm that content criticism is unavoidable as well. Much depends on the presuppositions one's content criticism is based upon.

7. How much material should be discussed?

One final theme may be appropriate to be addressed before we turn to the proposals of some of the scholars who have written recently in connection with New Testament theology. This theme concerns the "sources" of the enterprise.

I have argued in the second chapter that a historian may find reasons to justify his focus on a "canonical" circle of writings when describing the theology of any particular Christian group. Having argued for the justification of retaining "New Testament" in the name of the discipline, it is appropriate to re-affirm at this point that I do not say that writings outside the New Testament should not be studied by the New Testament theologian.

My thesis against Wrede's and Räisänen's view is that they are wrong when they hold that the enterprise cannot justify the limitation of its scope to the New Testament canon. If it is clearly seen that I argue for the validity of a historical distinction between "canons" of different groups of Christians, then it should be added that I agree with Wrede and Räisänen in their emphasis on the significance of all available evidence. This emphasis remains a necessity in New Testament theology as a historical study.

It is in this latter, methodological sense that I agree with Wrede (1897, 58-59; ET: 1973, 101):

> If I ask what was the content and state of development of Christian belief and thought at a particular point in time, it is clear that all the material from this period is relevant to resolving the task.

We must note, however, that for Wrede this affirmation was in close connection with his understanding of the enterprise of New Testament theology. He held that it was the "development" in early Christian thought that made it impossible to focus on the "canonical" New Testament writings only. I have pointed to weaknesses of the thesis that early Christianity's theology underwent a major "development" - starting from the earliest times. Here I simply note that those scholars who hold the "development thesis" have taken up Wrede's initiative that in carrying out the enterprise we should go in time "beyond the New Testament" (1897, 17; ET: 1973, 73).

For example, Bultmann entitles the third part of his *Theologie des Neuen Testaments* (1984, 446): "Die Entwicklung zur Alten Kirche". In his discussion of the development of Christology and Soteriology (507ff) he includes the Shepherd of Hermas, the Didache, the Epistle of Barnabas, 2Clement, the Letter of Polycarp, 1Clement, and Ignatius. Wrede proposed a similar "limit" when he argued that "the border" when "new movements in the early church begin" lies *"approximately* with the transition from the Apostolic Fathers to the Apologists" (1897, 60-61; ET: 1973, 103), although he added that material from Justin may be referred to, in as much as that material may have early origins.

It may be worth noting in this context, that F.C. Baur and H.J. Holtzmann shared the view that "non-canonical" material should belong to New Testament theology; however, in practice they did not include much of non-canonical material in their New Testament theologies.

Baur affirmed that non-canonical writings are of interest in a historical presentation of the origins of Christianity (1864, 30). However, he added that the doctrine of the New Testament "ist so für sich abgegrenzt, dass ihre Kenntniss aus keiner andern Quelle als eben nur aus diesen Schriften geschöpft werden kann". Baur put his understanding of the concern of the discipline of New Testament theology in this way (33):

> Man will nur wissen, was die Schriften des neuen Testaments als Lehre enthalten, und welche Formen in ihrem Lehrinhalt durch ihre charakteristische Eigenthümlichkeit sich unterscheiden.

Holtzmann answered some of Wrede's criticisms directed against the first edition of his *Lehrbuch der Neutestamentlichen Theologie* (1897) in the second edition (1911). Holtzmann re-affirmed that he was concerned with "das klassische, schöpferische, durch die Namen Jesus und Paulus gekennzeichnete Zeitalter" of early Christianity (1911, VII). As a pragmatical argument he added that the New Testament canon has an "incomparable significance" for Christian theology; consequently the canon deserves a separate treatment (IX).

However, Holtzmann did acknowledge that even if holding to this special place of the canon, (23):

> ... kann und darf, ja muß man geradezu, um ein allseitig abgerundetes Bild zu erhalten, die übrige Literatur der ungefähr 100 Jahre, welcher die später kanonisch gewordenen Schriften angehören, wenigstens in soweit berücksichtigen, als sie die Entwickelung des christlichen Gedankens, wie solche im NT angelegt und zum Ausdruck gelangt ist, mit bedingt und beleuchtet.

Noting again my reservation concerning the thesis of "development" in New Testament thought, I conclude that this answer of Holtzmann to Wrede's criticism is also acceptable for my understanding of the discipline of New Testament theology. I affirm that in as much as we can justify the limitation of New Testament theology to the New Testament canon we have to draw on any available evidence from the era of the New Testament, and from the periods surrounding it.

These brief discussions of some of the key issues involved in the enterprise of New Testament theology do not claim to be of the depth these themes deserve. I have only pointed to what has to be addressed by scholars engaging in the enterprise. Having expressed the line I would take in these matters, I now turn to some recent contributions to the enterprise. It is natural that some of these issues will re-occur in this remaining part of our discussion.

8. The "canonical approach" of B.S. Childs

Childs's emphasis on the canon in relation to biblical theology can be found not only in his recent work, *Biblical Theology of the Old and New Testaments* (1992), but in his "*Introductions*" to both of the Testaments. He laid the foundations to his approach in numerous earlier articles as well as in an essay on biblical theology: *Biblical Theology in Crisis* (1970).

In the following, I discuss Childs's main theses and arguments on the basis of his own report on his approach in his major works. When I engage in criticism of Childs's approach, I also draw on some of James Barr's (1983) and M.G. Brett's (1991) critical points.

a. Final form

In his Old Testament *Introduction*, Childs's aim is "to describe the form and function of the Hebrew Bible in its role as sacred scripture for Israel" (1987, 14). He is more concerned with the "present form of the text" than with its earlier stages of development. He defines his usage of the term "canon" as writings which "were received, shaped, and transmitted by a community of faith" (16).[7] These were "authoritative writings of ancient Israel" (14).[8] Childs argues for the "normative theological role of the final form of the biblical text" by affirming that the final form "performs a critical function in evaluating that historical process through which Israel went in construing its history with God" (17).[9]

A key argument of Childs "for insisting on the final form of scripture" (75) is that "it alone bears witness to the full history of revelation" (76). The very existence of the "Old Testament" canon affirms that for those who created the canon "history per se is not a medium of revelation", but it is only the end result of that history which matters. Thus the canon even exercises a critical function "in respect to the earlier stages of the literature's formation" (76).[10]

I think that Childs has provided a useful contribution to scholarship with this emphasis on the canon. However, in my opinion this view raises the question: What difference do we ascribe to the writers, to those who handed on the tradition, and to the final canonisers of these writings? Childs's position seems to put the unknown people who played the final role in the process of canonisation on a higher level of authority than that of the writers or of those who transmitted and edited the writings prior to the final canonisation, in as much as the final "collectors" and canonisers chose from different lines of tradition. I would like to argue for a canonisation process which would not separate the participants of the process so much.

---

[7] See also 1984, 25-26 concerning the New Testament's canonical "process by which authoritative tradition was collected, ordered, and transmitted".

[8] See also 1984, xvii.

[9] See also 1970, 99-100.

[10] See also 1984, 38, 43.

b. Religious community

Childs emphasises the role of the community which treasured this literature as scripture. He affirms that "it is constitutive of Israel's history that the literature formed the identity of the religious community which in turn shaped the literature" (1987, 41).[11]

I agree with Childs when he points out the significance of a particular religious community in relation to the writings treasured by the community. In my opinion, this also sets limits to a general comparative history-of-religion approach, because the particular religious community, whose "canon" we study, may have characteristics that are unique to the community.

In connection with the two points discussed so far, it may be worth mentioning that Brett (1991, 19) has pointed to a contradiction between Childs's aim to interpret the final form of the text and the argument of the text's usage by the historical community of ancient Israel. According to Brett, "it is manifestly the case that ancient Israel did not use the final form of the Hebrew text since this was not stabilized, according to Childs himself, until the end of the first century CE".

However, another argument of Childs may answer this criticism. He affirms that when the "canonical process" came to an end, the final form of the fixed body of writings became authoritative and not the process itself. Later on, the new interpretations like the Targums were "set apart sharply from the received sacred text of scripture" (1987, 59).[12]

In my opinion, Childs has not been able to solve the tension between a historical analytical work that has to deal with preliminary stages of traditions and the emphasis on the final form of the canonical text. Barr affirms that Childs's "programme of canonical criticism was essentially confused and self-contradictory in its conceptual formulation" (1983, 132). Barr rightly points to an unsolved tension between the facts that Childs's approach "is in large measure not different in its framework and methods from scholarship informed by historical criticism" (132), and that Childs shows a "strong antipathy" toward "traditional criticism" (133). It is in this line of criticism that, in opposition to Childs's exclusive emphasis on the canonical approach, Brett proposes a "'pluralist' account of Bible studies" (1991, 5, see also 71).

c. Descriptive task?

In his introductory works Childs affirms that the task of the canonical analysis is to describe the shape and function of the canonical texts. Because of the

---

[11] See also 1987, 59; 1984, 22, 25; 1970, 102-103.
[12] See also 1984, 28.

descriptive character of the enterprise, faith is not assumed on the side of the reader or investigator. After the descriptive task has been accomplished, the reader may choose whether or not to identify with the perspectives of the texts (1987, 72-73; 1984, 37, 39).

We have to note, however, that in his recent *Biblical Theology* (1992) he proclaims one of his major decisions already in the subtitle of the work: it is a *Theological Reflection on the Christian Bible* he wants to carry out. He does not take biblical theology to be a purely descriptive, historical discipline, but by definition a theological reflection as well (see also 55). He is not satisfied with the definition of biblical theology as a historical discipline, because in his opinion the latter "had resulted in the dissolution of the very discipline itself" (6). Childs's definition of the task of biblical theology is: "to formulate a modern theology compatible in some sense with the Bible" (3). He agrees with Ebeling that the task of the discipline of biblical theology is to write a "modern theologian's reflection on various aspects of the Bible" (7).

However, to adopt this starting point means to exclude the possibility of a discussion with those who want to separate the descriptive and "constructive" (Childs 1992, 3) elements.

I attempt to study the theses of Wrede and Räisänen by adopting their starting points. Thus I define the term New Testament theology as the theology which may eventually be found in the New Testament and not as the theology of the modern interpreter. I adopt Childs's view concerning his introductory work: I think it is a good aim to work with an approach which can be studied or applied by anyone who wants to carry out an historical study (1984, 38).

d. "Canon within the canon"

Childs opposes the view of a "canon in the canon" (1984, 42). This follows from his emphasis on the whole of the canon. I think it is also a consequence of his disapproval of the view that first one has to establish the origin and the development of a tradition in order to be able to interpret it.

I agree with Childs that focusing on the whole of the canon may serve as a "major check" against views which over-emphasise parts of Scripture and run the risk of neglecting other parts (42).

e. Text

Childs acknowledges the need for an attempt to recover the "best" text, but he also stresses the significance of the textual history. He argues that for the canonical approach, harmonised readings in the Gospels are also important because they confirm that the "Gospel accounts were not heard as being significantly different" (1984, 187).

Textual criticism has to abandon the aim set by Hort which wants to establish the text of the original autographs. Childs follows Dahl in the affirmation that - at least with regard to the Gospels - one has to reckon with "a variety of traditions, written and oral, which competed for recognition" in the early church (1984, 525-526). The aim of textual criticism is "to recover that New Testament text which best reflects the true apostolic witness" (527). In other words, "the best received text" equals the canonical text (528).

However, there is a tension between the affirmation of a variety in tradition and the aim to recover the best received text. Childs would probably argue that this tension cannot be avoided. Childs argues that there were two "contradictory principles", both derived from "canonical" thinking, which influenced the development of the textual tradition. On the one hand, revisions and recensions sought to preserve the "best" and "oldest" text of the tradition. On the other hand, the Byzantine textual activity "sought to include the widest possible number of variant traditions actually in use by Christian communities through conflation and harmonization" (527).

Childs's own proposal for the task of textual criticism is to accept as the "outer parameter" the Byzantine, or *koine*, text which is "the best representative of the common tradition" (1984, 528, 530).

In my opinion, Childs's textual critical proposals are in harmony with his canonical approach. Childs's general picture of canonisers who freely followed their own intentions is also transferred to the copyists (or scribes). I think one might distinguish between the theological intentions of copyists which entitled them to change the texts and between the main "intention" of a copyist to preserve tradition. Both may have resulted in similar results in terms of extension of the transmitted text. But the question may be raised: How free did the scribes feel in the transmission of sacred texts?

The final form may be the "fullest" form of the *koine* text. Thus Childs holds it most precious. However, he does want to use the criteria of critical scholarship to establish earlier and better texts. He does not answer the main question: Which of the texts should be regarded as "canonical"? Or, if he has answered that we may leave open the possibility of accepting different textual traditions of the same pericope as canonical, then I would ask: What would he regard as canonical in cases where there is a disagreement in meaning or even in "theology" between existing textual variants?

f. The Bible as witness

Childs emphasises that there is a difference between looking at the Bible as "source" or as "witness". The former method is a detached phenomenological examination of the writings. The latter, which is adopted by Childs, acknowledges that the Bible points "beyond itself to a divine reality" (1992, 9). This approach is "confessional" (9). It regards the Bible as "the authoritative word of God" (8). The "community of faith" received the writings of the Bible as authoritative. This fact is an argument for accepting the idea of a canon.

With regard to these methodological decisions, I have a twofold opinion. On the one hand, I have the same reason for rejecting the authority of the Bible as a starting point as under an earlier point: I should like to be engaged in a discussion with those who cannot accept the Bible as authoritative. On the other hand, as a historian I should like to find out: What authority does the Bible claim? To accept or to reject that authority will remain a free option for the modern readers at the end of the historical enterprise.

Thus I would not regard the Bible as "witness" as a starting point in a biblical theology. The witness character of the Bible should be studied and described rather than presupposed. It may be the result of an enquiry and not the starting point in a biblical theological study. Similarly, we may find that faith played an important role in the communities which treasured the canon, but faith cannot be prescribed as a condition for studying the theology contained in the Bible.[13]

g. The Bible's subject matter

Childs affirms that for biblical theology "it is crucial that the reality of God be understood as primary" (1992, 82). Both testaments present "a witness to the one Lord Jesus Christ, the selfsame divine reality" (85).

I agree with Childs in seeing Christology as "the heart of the enterprise" of New Testament theology (for Childs: biblical theology). However, I propose to distinguish between two enterprises: 1) the study of the theology expressed in the canonical writings; 2) the Christian reading of the Bible for the sake of encountering God. New Testament theology should be the enterprise under point 1). The second enterprise is a possibility. It is the decision of Christians to approach the Bible like this. This decision cannot be forced upon or prescribed for scholars engaged in New Testament theology.

---

[13] Cf. Childs's different position: biblical theology is "faith seeking understanding", 1992, 86.

h. Two testaments in one canon

Although I try to limit my thesis to New Testament theology, it may be appropriate to mention here that for biblical theology it is a central question how the two testaments relate to each other. Childs affirms that the two testaments speak about the one "divine reality" in "dissident voices" and in "diverse ways" (1992, 85).

Childs argues that "the modern Christian theologian shares a different canonical context from the early church. The first Christian writers had only one testament, the modern Christian has two" (78). Childs affirms: "Both testaments make a discrete witness to Jesus Christ which must be heard, both separately and in concert". This thesis then defines the structure of Childs's whole book.

I think that it is methodologically useful to insist with Childs that the Old Testament "must be heard on its own terms" (78). The question then arises: Why should we presuppose that the Old Testament bears witness to Jesus Christ (e.g. 91)? I think it may be methodologically more consistent to examine the Old Testament in itself and the New Testament's understanding of the Old and then to discuss whether or not the two share the same "subject matter".[14]

Childs's major argument for seeing "discrete" witnesses in the two testaments is that "the Christian experience of the gospel as a radically new revelation of God sets its sacred writings consciously in opposition to Moses, as the representative of the old" (93). "The New Testament proclaims the new story of Jesus Christ ... The disciples had a new message to proclaim".

This emphasis of Childs leads him to be surprised at the fact that the New Testament "bears witness to the radically new in terms of the old" (93). Childs wants to solve the difficulty by affirming that the New Testament writers had "a radically new understanding of the Jewish scriptures": they had a "transformed" Old Testament.

The problem with this thesis is that it has to face the question: How did the early Christians expect the Jews to accept Jesus as the Messiah if the Christians argued from a "transformed" Old Testament? Here, I think, Childs relies too much on the widespread view that the New Testament message is in discontinuity with the Old Testament; early Christianity is in discontinuity with Judaism. This issue is related to another section of my thesis: on "law and gospel". Without entering the discussion of the relationship between the two testaments, I would argue for a closer relationship between them than Childs would hold.

---

[14] See Childs's own caution: "... the New Testament's use of the Old Testament cannot be easily reconciled with the Old Testament's own witness", 1992, 80.

To sum up, I agree with Barr's statement that Childs's general approach deserves sympathy as regards the approach's "interest in canonicity and in the final form of the text" (1983, 131). However, I also hold with Barr that the canon should not be absolutised "as an exegetical principle" (132, see also 146). Childs's canonical approach has not succeeded in becoming *the* solution to the problems of biblical theology. However, it is a significant attempt to solve the tension between historical work, which differentiates between the origins of layers in the tradition, and a theological interpretation, which emphasises the final form of the canon.

Childs's failure in solving this tension does not mean that the enterprise of New Testament theology - as I understand it - would be challenged. I argue for an enterprise in which the canonical writings are studied in order that the theology contained in them may be found. For my understanding of the enterprise the fact is important that certain writings (and traditions contained in them) had such an authority that the writings became "canonical". Earlier stages of the tradition should not be put against the final text. Rather, both of them should be studied as expressions of the theology of early Christianity.

9. Robert Morgan on biblical interpretation

Robert Morgan has reflected on problems involved in the enterprise of New Testament theology in numerous essays. The most comprehensive of them is the work entitled *Biblical Interpretation* which he published together with John Barton, the major part of the book being Morgan's work.[15]

Already the title of this book shows that Morgan's main concern in New Testament theology is the theological reflection of the modern interpreter on the biblical texts. For Robert Morgan, New Testament theology is not the description or summary of the theology of the New Testament writings or writers (1991, 73), but the theology of the person who engages in New Testament theology.[16] Since my thesis differs from this view, Morgan's understanding of the enterprise deserves careful consideration.

a. On historical work

1) In the context of discussing D.F. Strauss's *Life of Jesus*, Morgan advances the thesis that historical work on the New Testament has "an essentially

---

[15] 1991, orig. 1988, see p.vi; for a more recent discussion see his article of 1996.

[16] See e.g. 1973a, 2, 52; 1973b, 60, 88-89; 1987, 194; 1991, 167, 181.

negative function within the theological enterprise" of New Testament theology (1976-77, 244, see also 250). Historical investigation destroys "impossible or untrue theological interpretations of the text" (245, see also 249). The only "positive" function of historical investigation is in "its preliminary service in clarifying the tradition" (248-249).

Morgan sympathises with the implication of Strauss's work that historical descriptive work "cannot deliver normative theological judgements" (1977-77, 246, see also 253). In another context Morgan affirms that "historical research cannot establish Christology" (1987, 200).

We have to note that much depends on what we understand by the term "deliver" (and "establish"). On the basis of Morgan's affirmation that historical methods are "not designed to communicate religious faith" (1992a, 473), it seems that for him the term "deliver" refers to the modern interpreter's aim to convey truth claims for his readers' acceptance. If we take the term in this sense, then Morgan's statement above will be right: historical work cannot convince about the truth of theological claims made in the New Testament.

However, it may be added - and this would also be accepted by Morgan - that historical descriptive work may have to report that certain (New Testament) writings or authors claim to make normative theological judgements, if historical investigation finds it to be the case. To fail to report this would be a mistake on history's side. In my opinion, we may leave open the question whether or not the historian or the modern reader accepts those claims.

2) In his 1976-77 article Morgan was prepared to conclude from Strauss's thesis that historical reconstruction and theological interpretation should be separated (1976-77, 246, 252, 260). However, he indicated that "New Testament scholars need to renew their licence to interpret *theologically* that part of the tradition which they know best" (264).[17]

In *Biblical Interpretation* Morgan affirms concerning the relationship between historical study and theological interpretation that the values of the former do not preclude making use of the latter (1991, 179). Morgan calls for a "style of interpretation in which historical and theological interests are fused".

Acknowledging the validity of defining New Testament theology in the way Morgan does, in this thesis I argue for an enterprise that is historical in its character; that does not include the theological interest of the modern interpreter; and that is "theological" only in the sense that it is concerned with the description of the theology of the early Christians.

---

[17] Cf. also 1973a, 66-67.

b. Theological interpretation

1) For Morgan, the "Theology of the New Testament" as an enterprise or a discipline is not the description of what the New Testament writers and early Christians believed, or what their religion was (1991, 73).[18] New Testament theology is theological interpretation, "i.e. a translation intended to communicate what believers acknowledge as the transcendent subject-matter of these texts" (73).[19]

He affirms that theological interpretation is carried out in order that the tradition may be "enabled to communicate its subject-matter in a new intellectual environment" (1976-77, 246). For this aim more is needed "than what the historian *qua* historian can provide" (246, 248). Theological interpretation "should be set free from the obligation to be simply a historical discipline" (244). However, theological interpretation cannot go against historical probability (261) and plausibility (262). Historical work is useful, because without its controlling function "interpretation can become arbitrary" (1991, 182, see also 198).

Morgan points to the ambiguity of the term "interpretation": the term "may refer either to the historian's general task of making the past intelligible to the present *or* to the theologian's special interest in making it intelligible in such a way that contemporary Christians recognize it to be a more or less adequate expression of the faith which they hold" (1976-77, 247, n.2). Morgan adopts the latter sense of the term "interpretation".

As I have already affirmed in this thesis, I would rather define New Testament theology in the former sense of "interpretation" in Morgan's quotation. If we take the latter it will be difficult to see how historical investigation can be used as a control against improbable or implausible theological interpretations. If we say more than what a historian *qua* historian can say, then that statement will be out of the control of historians.[20]

2) Consistent with his emphasis on interpretation, Morgan suggests a change in the name of the discipline to *"theological interpretation of the Old and New Testaments"* (1991, 174, see also 281).

Morgan (1992a, 475) argues against the definition of New Testament theology as a discipline which describes the theology of the New Testament by affirming: a) that the New Testament does not provide "a uniform doctrinal

---

[18] See also on the Old Testament, 1991, 100.

[19] Cf. also his affirmation that "a theologian interprets the tradition for the sake of understanding and communicating his faith", 1974, 400.

[20] Cf. as an example Morgan's affirmation: "Bultmann's theological interpretation goes beyond any valid account of what is meant by 'purely historical'", 1973a, 61.

system"; b) that "belief in a God who relates to the world invokes (in principle) all human experience and knowledge, and that varies from age to age".[21]

As a possible answer to the first argument I refer to the preceding chapter of my thesis where I have made an attempt to argue that the New Testament contains credal elements that point to a basic theology of the early Christians which they generally adhered to.

My arguments for the distinction of the canon on historical grounds may be an answer to the second point.

3) It is important for understanding Morgan's emphasis on interpretation to note that he also emphasises the commitment of the interpreter to convince his reader about religious truth.[22] He rightly observes that this aim raises the problem: "how to get from historical to theological judgements" (1991, 91).

In my understanding of the enterprise, New Testament theology does not necessarily have the task of "convincing" the modern reader of the religious values of the New Testament.[23]

c. Theory of religion

Morgan affirms that from the Enlightenment onward to up until recently, the key term in the relationship between biblical scholarship and religious faith was "religion".[24] It was a useful term because it made it possible to bring forward arguments about the Bible among believers and non-believers (1991, 19, 189). It also made it possible for modern observers to speak about God (20, 32). Morgan affirms that "understanding religion is compatible with believing" (91, see also 138-139, 279).

Morgan proposes that "a theory of religion and reality" is needed in theological interpretation (1991, 232, see also 187ff, 276ff). Although he does not present his own theory in detail, he has in mind a "theory of religion which is compatible with its truth, i.e. open to the possibility that the transcendent to which it refers actually exists" (185). This theory not only reflects on "religion and reality", but also on the methods used and the knowledge gained by using the methods (281).

Morgan states that religion "can also be held to mediate some true awareness of God" (30). However, we may raise the question, How can religion mediate an awareness of God? If the problem of modern enlightened men and

---

[21] Cf. also 1973b, 88-89.

[22] Cf. 1991, 98, 179, 186, 194, 197.

[23] Cf. also Morgan 1991, 111, 259.

[24] See e.g. 1991, 18ff, 30, 39, 187, 276.

women is that they are only able to share a "man-centred thinking", why should they accept "that the truth about human existence, especially human morality and self-transcendence, is only grasped when the essential truth contained in religion is understood, and the reality of God acknowledged" - as Morgan claims (30)?

A theory of religion may be helpful in justifying a place for religious studies in modern, secular universities, but it is not needed if we define New Testament theology as a descriptive enterprise. In the case of this latter definition, we do not need a theory of religion that is "compatible" with the modern believers' "experience that their religion points them to the divine reality beyond the system of symbols" (188).

d. Literary framework

According to Morgan, "acts of God cannot be spoken of, let alone established, by historical research" (1991, 70). Since history is not capable of conveying theological judgements (cf. also 119), other approaches are needed (cf. also 123, 197-198).

According to Morgan's survey, more recent developments in biblical interpretation suggest that religious aims could be better served if one interprets the Bible in a literary framework of interpretation (see e.g. 143, 199). There may be cases where the historical aspect may even become "subordinate" to the literary one (287).

Morgan defines the literary approach in the following way (221):

> The literary frame of reference can be characterized as a shift in the focus of interest from past persons, events, traditions, literary forms, and conventions, to the now available texts and their impact upon present-day hearers and readers.

Morgan's argument in favour of the literary approach is that literature is capable of conveying religious messages for modern men (cf. 223). He points to examples which may support the view that literary methods can contribute to the religious understanding of the Bible (see e.g. 245).

I think that Morgan's differentiation between the roles and possibilities of the historical and literary approaches is established by axioms and examples rather than by convincing arguments (e.g. 70, 184). Perhaps this is inevitable, for what we can expect from our method will depend on how we define and posit its characteristics. As Morgan affirms (170): whether biblical scholarship's questions "are best organized within a historical or a literary frame of reference" will depend "on each particular interpreter's aims or priorities".

I would adopt the view that a historical framework of reference in New Testament theology may be retained for the following reasons.

1) Historical study has its own values - as it is acknowledged by Morgan himself. For example, in his conclusion Morgan affirms that historical criticism has had "positive contributions to constructive theological restatement" in as much as its "negative theological role" made theologians "restate the traditional faith" (1991, 288).

2) We have already seen historical study's function in controlling against arbitrary interpretations.[25] We may put the following argument against Morgan's opting for a literary approach: If we put the historical aspect into the background and introduce non-historical aspects into our investigation, these latter ones cannot be controlled by the former.

3) Morgan concedes that there may be occasions in theological work where "the historical framework of research co-ordinates all the methods used" (1991, 287). He also acknowledges the fact that literary methods were used alongside the historical ones even in the past (e.g. Wellhausen, 82). From these observations it follows that the historical and the literary approaches do not exclude one another. I would argue for a combination of the two approaches in the sense as it is conceded by Morgan: literary study may supplement historical criticism; history of literature is part of the historical enterprise (cf. 215).

4) I have already proposed that New Testament theology does not have to set itself the aim of convincing its modern readers that the religious truths of the New Testament are true and to be accepted. In as much as Morgan may be right that making use of a literary theory in theology may be "one way of making religious talk of God intelligible in a secular culture" (219), New Testament theology may be restricted to the description of the theological content of the New Testament.

e. Social sciences

Earlier in this chapter, we have already seen what a great significance is ascribed by Robert Morgan to the role of social sciences in the future of New Testament theology. In *Biblical Interpretation* Morgan describes the relationship between history and sociology in the following way.

There are significant differences between the two disciplines: a) "history attends to the individual and particular, sociology to what is general or typical" (1991, 139); b) history has a diachronic character, sociology has a synchronic one (139-140).

---

[25] See e.g. Morgan 1973a, 59; 1991, 182-183, 198.

Morgan affirms that these differences imply "that the disciplines are complementary" (140). Since in New Testament theology we are more concerned with the "unique" than with the "typical", it follows "that history rather than sociology should provide the framework for studying the biblical past". A "sociological theory" - that is "based on empirically grounded generalizations", for example, on "observing many societies" - may be a helpful complement by improving the picture gained in historical study.

Morgan further argues that: "Since religion is a social phenomenon, the history of religion must be social history" (140). Consequently, Morgan approves of those successors of Baur who emphasised the "non-doctrinal dimension of religion" as a correction to Baur's enterprise.

Morgan can also point to the limitations of using a social theory in biblical work. He emphasises that a "theory" is not identical with "evidence" (142). In biblical studies - where "data are sparse" - "statistical work, important in some sociology and economics, is impossible". However, sociological theory may provide hypotheses that may prove to be helpful in reaching "the best historical guesses".

In my opinion, we may distinguish between an emphasis on extending historical inquiry into the society of biblical times and the use of sociological theories based on present-day analyses of societies. Morgan makes a similar distinction "between the way historical methods have been properly enlarged by social-scientific methods on the one hand, and the hermeneutical or theological dimensions of this approach on the other" (147). The latter may help the former, but they are not necessarily to be combined. Historical work may study early Christianity's theology in a way that social aspects are also included in the historical study, without making use of present-day sociological theories.

As in the case of the literary framework, I do not exclude the possibility of complementing historical study with the use of a sociological theory in the enterprise of New Testament theology. However, in my opinion this latter extension remains an option for the scholar. Without this "complementary" approach, New Testament theology may still be maintained as a historical discipline.

To sum up, Robert Morgan's contribution to New Testament theology offers support for my challenge to Räisänen's thesis of separating historical and theological activity in New Testament theology. I largely agree with Morgan's affirmation (1974, 399):

> The amalgam of history and theology with which the New Testament confronts us can never finally be separated ... [But] the central role of New Testament historical study for the understanding of Christianity remains the analysis of certain Old

Testament, later Jewish, early Christian and pagan traditions, and the use made of them in various situations to understand and communicate the past, present and future Jesus as the revelation of God. This is the heart of New Testament theology, a historical activity of central importance for the study of the religion which centres upon Jesus Christ.

However, Morgan invites New Testament theologians to bring their own theological interest to the historical enterprise and to engage in approaches other than the historical one, for example, that of a literary theory and of the social sciences. I accept the possibility of widening the definition of the enterprise in these directions. Nevertheless, I argue in this thesis that the enterprise may remain on a descriptive level: it may set itself the aim to summarise the theological content of the New Testament.

10. Hans Hübner's "prolegomena"

Hübner has recently published three volumes entitled *Biblische Theologie des Neuen Testaments*. The whole first volume is devoted to matters to be discussed before one attempts to write a biblical theology. Hübner calls this volume *Prolegomena* (1990). In the following I summarise some of his views in his *Prolegomena* which relate to the theme in our present discussion, i.e. the characteristics of the enterprise of New Testament theology.

a. Whose theology?

Hübner understands the word "theology" in the name of the enterprise of New Testament theology to imply "a systematic-theological aspect" (1990, 13).

Hübner also raises the question which I have found important to clarify: Should biblical theology be a theology contained in the Bible, or a theology which is in accordance with the Bible (23-24)? My impression is that Hübner does not want to decide for one against the other. He does emphasise the difference between the two views, but he seems to be sympathetic to both.

Hübner's aim in his own recent biblical theology may be expressed in a footnote of his (p.28, n.60) where he states the difference between his own approach and that of Räisänen. He does so by siding with Schlier in one aspect, and distinguishing his own position from Schlier's in another:

> Ich wähle als evangelisch-lutherischer Theologe wie der Katholik *Heinrich Schlier* auch die Theologie des Neuen Testaments ... Ich möchte im Blick auf die

neutestamentliche Theologie nicht wie er [Schlier] die "historisch-philologische Methode" von einer "theologischen Methode" unterscheiden.

Hübner's second volume (1993) - on Paul's theology and on its "Wirkungsgeschichte" in the New Testament - confirms this affirmation. This volume contains the description of the theology of Paul. However, there are parts in which Hübner relates Paul's thinking to modern philosophy. For example, in an excursus Hübner discusses the problem of "Räumlichkeit" in Paul's theological thinking in comparison with the works of Heidegger, Cassirer and others (1993, 179ff).

At the end of the second volume, in a section entitled "Rückblick: Theologie, Glaube und Offenbarung" (1993, 411ff), in some respects Hübner identifies his own approach with that of Bultmann - as it is expressed in the article published as the "Epilegomena" of Bultmann's *Theologie des Neuen Testaments* (1984, 585ff). Hübner affirms that the theological thoughts of the New Testament are "thoughts of faith" (1993, 412). Furthermore, Paul's faith is "die glaubende Aufnahme der Offenbarung Gottes". From this follows Hübner's understanding of the enterprise:

> Wir werden die Theologie des Neuen Testaments als Offenbarungstheologie zu verstehen suchen und die in Jesus Christus ergangene Offenbarung Gottes theologisch so reflektieren, daß sie für uns Menschen heute zur verstandenen, nämlich *in unserem Glauben verstandenen Theologie* wird.

Before we relate to Hübner's view on this matter, it is worth mentioning another important theme in Hübner's *Prolegomena*.

b. Theology and/or theological reflection in the Bible

Related to the previous question is the problem of determining whether the biblical authors thought they communicated God himself in that they proclaimed what they believed God had entrusted them to convey, or whether they intended to write their theological reflections on God's revelation. Hübner seems not to decide this in an exclusive way either. For example, with regard to the Fourth Gospel's view on "revelation" Hübner raises the question (1990, 191):

> Ist die in Joh zu Sprache kommende Offenbarung des Offenbarers im Sinne des Evangelisten *theologische Reflexion über die Offenbarung* oder ist sie die *an den Leser gerichtete Offenbarung Gottes*?

Hübner answers this question by affirming that there is an *"innere(s) Ver-flochtensein von Theologie und Verkündigung als autoritative Weitergabe von Offenbarung"* in the Fourth Gospel.[26]

Although this affirmation appears in connection with the author of the Fourth Gospel, I think the distinction in the quotation may be applied to Hübner's own work as well. In my opinion, one of the strengths of Hübner's work is the clear distinction between: 1) "God's revelation directed to the reader"; and 2) "theological reflection about the revelation" (191).

Reflecting on the two major points discussed so far, I would argue that "God's revelation directed to the reader" may be the object of New Testament theology. However, I should like to modify this phrase of Hübner in a way that I would distinguish between a description of the subject matter of the New Testament authors (for example that they claim that God wants to address their readers) and the claim of the writer of a present-day New Testament theology that God wants to address the reader.

In my definition of the enterprise, New Testament theology records, or, "describes" what is written about God's revelation and does not attempt to convey faith to the reader. It may be added that I also hold that it is a legitimate move for the authors of New Testament theologies to state that they accept the biblical authors' claim and call the readers to do the same. However, this cannot be made a condition of engaging in the enterprise of New Testament theology.

The theological reflection of the modern theologian can be added to the descriptive task - as it is in Hübner's case (e.g. his section 1.3.3: "Systematisch-theologische Erwägungen zur Offenbarung in der Heiligen Schrift", 1990, 203ff). As I have repeatedly affirmed, I would leave it to the personal choice of the theologian to add or not to add the "second stage" (in Räisänen's terms), i.e. the theological reflection. In this thesis I argue that those who engage in a descriptive, historical enterprise of New Testament theology do not have to follow Bultmann's and Hübner's emphasis on the modern interpreter's relationship with the "Glaubensgedanken" of the New Testament.[27]

c. *Biblical theology*

Hübner distinguishes his view on the term "biblical" in biblical theology from the usage of the term by Gabler. The latter used the term "biblical" in contrast to "dogmatic" (=systematic) theology. Gabler also suggested the separation

---

[26] See a similar observation with regard to the Old Testament, 1990, 133.

[27] Cf. Hübner 1993, 412; Bultmann 1984, 586.

of the treatment of the two testaments. Hübner uses the term "biblical" to emphasise that the object of the enterprise is the whole Bible. Biblical theology seeks to understand the Old and the New Testament as a "theological unity" (1990, 14).

Hübner's main arguments for insisting on a biblical theology rather than on a separate study of the two testaments are as follows.

1) Von Rad's thesis may be right that the Old Testament is open toward the New Testament (15, 30).

2) Gese may be right in his thesis that it was with the appearance of the revelatory events of the New Testament that the process of building up the Old Testament traditions came to an end (16).[28]

3) Most of the New Testament writers use parts of the Old Testament as their arguments. They would lose their "theological profile" if we took out the Old Testament references from their works (28).

I am open to the proposal that New Testament theology should be carried out as part of a biblical theological project. Whether or not the enterprise of a biblical theology of both of the testaments is possible is a wider question than the scope of my thesis. My research is restricted to the question: Is New Testament theology a possible enterprise? The answer of Hübner, and of those who write a biblical theology, would probably be "yes". If the enterprise of biblical theology may be justified, that would add further support for the justification of New Testament theology.

d. The reception of the Old Testament in the New Testament

A major difference between Hübner and other scholars who attempt a biblical theology is in their view concerning the role of the Old Testament in the New Testament. Hübner introduces a distinction between "Vetus Testamentum" and "Vetus Testamentum in Novo receptum" (e.g. 66). He argues that not the whole Old Testament is received by the New Testament ("whole" simply in the sense of all major parts of it). Even sections of the Old Testament which are used in the New Testament may undergo a change during the course of the interpretative work of the New Testament authors (cf. 165). As an example Hübner affirms that the book of Isaiah in itself is different from

---

[28] Cf. also the recent reaffirmation of H. Gese's thesis in his article entitled "Über die biblische Einheit" (in Dohmen - Söding, 1995, 38): "Für die neutestamentliche Traditionsbildung wird durch sie selbst die alttestamentliche zu Ende und zur Vollendung geführt: das Alte Testament entsteht als solches durch das Neue Testament". (For more literature see also the list of Gese's publications to the theme of biblical theology, 1995, 44.)

the Isaiah as it is used by Paul in Romans, chapters 9-11. The latter has a "new theological quality" (67).

Hübner adds that it is significant to notice in a biblical theology of the New Testament that which is not "received" from the Old Testament by the New. He affirms: "Aber auch die Konstatierung dieser Negativa, dieser Ausblendung alttestamentlicher Gehalte gehört zur Antwort auf die Frage nach dem *theologischen* Verhältnis beider Testamente!" (29).

I think that Hübner's term "Vetus Testamentum in Novo receptum" may be helpful in certain respects. For example, it points to the important fact that the New Testament authors thought christologically (cf. 69). The Christ event became the centre for them from which and through which they looked at the Old Testament (cf. 172-173, 179). However, I do not think this thesis should be stretched as far as Hübner wants to stretch it. I have the following counter-arguments to put to his thesis.

1) It may not be true that certain texts of the Old Testament have become different when the New Testament authors used them. It may rather be the case that Old Testament texts were interpreted by Christians differently from how some or even many Jews of their day interpreted those texts. One might argue that even within Judaism a certain Old Testament text may have had different interpretations. Then we may raise the possibility that the Christian interpretation may have been nearer to one Jewish interpretation than to another.[29]

2) The fact that the New Testament authors *did not* use the whole of the Old Testament may not necessarily be used as an argument to state what the New Testament authors *did not want* to use. One may argue that the New Testament was not only meant to be an interpretation of the Old. Consequently, "silence" about certain books of the Old Testament may not have been a deliberate omission from their "theology". We may also add here that the Old Testament canon may not have been finally closed at the time of the formation of the New.[30]

3) Even if we found that certain themes were probably omitted on purpose, it is still important to know what was omitted in order to see the significance of the omission.

Thus I would argue that a biblical theologian of the New Testament has to work with the whole of the Old Testament.

---

[29] I note that not only "interpretations" of texts may have differed, but Christians may have had texts that differed from what we now know as the Masoretic Text or as the versions of the *Septuagint*. Here I refer back to E. Tov's affirmations concerning the variety of text types of the Hebrew Bible in Qumran - noted in my third chapter.

[30] See the third chapter of my thesis.

e. *Proclaimed word and written word*

Hübner rightly emphasises the importance of the stage when the tradition was orally transmitted and the gospel proclaimed prior to the time when the Gospels were written. He affirms that for the preachers among the early Christians the content of the written word of God, i.e. the "Old Testament", and the content of the proclaimed word of God (i.e. their preaching) was identical (38-39).

Hübner uses the term "Autoritätengefüge" for describing the written Old Testament, the proclamation of the early Christians, the authority of the preaching of Jesus and later the authority of the New Testament (39). It is not clear whether Hübner wants to refer to the sequence in time or to a decreasing grade of authority. It seems that he may have both in mind.

It is slightly misleading that he mentions Jesus' teaching after the early Christian proclamation. This is, however, simply due to the fact that Hübner discusses the problem in the historical order of the documents. In this case the discussion of the Synoptic Gospels (vol. 3, 1995) comes after the discussion of Paul (vol. 2, 1993). However, Hübner does seem to maintain a difference in the grade of authority at least between the proclaimed word and the written word. He affirms that (1990, 40):

> Der Grad, in dem die verkündigende Kirche - nochmals: in actu praedicationis! - an der Autorität des verbum Dei partizipiert, ist qualitativ höher als der Grad, in dem das schriftlich fixierte Wort der Schrift an der Autorität des verkündigten Wortes partizipiert.

Hübner draws the consequence that the written New Testament is secondary in relation to the proclaimed word (39-40). The authority of the written New Testament is derived from the proclaimed word, because the written word holds/keeps ("aufbewahrt") the oral word (40).

In my opinion, it is good to emphasise the existence of an oral stage of the transmission. However, it may not be a useful distinction to affirm that the written word is secondary in relation to the oral word. On the one hand, we do not live in the age of the first Christians when the oral proclamation preceded in time the written one. On the other hand, we only have access, if we have access at all, to the oral stage through the existing written documents of that proclamation (as Hübner himself contends, 42). At most, we can reconstruct the preaching of the early Christians. I cannot see any justification in calling "primary" the reconstruction we produce, and "secondary" the documents which have been transmitted to us - and are now the basis of our reconstructions.

f. Revelation

Hübner discusses at length the question: In what way can we speak about human beings being able to receive revelations from God? This is one of the important problems to be dealt with in connection with the possibility of an enterprise of biblical theology. It is also connected with the question whether one should attempt to write theology in order to speak about God or whether one should rather report and describe what the biblical authors said about God.

Hübner points very clearly to the difficult questions involved. For example, he lists the following (102):

> Wenn Gott Offenbarer ist, *was* hat er überhaupt offenbart? ... Welcher Gottesbegriff steckt dahinter? ... Wie steht es mit dem Verhältnis von dem offenbarenden Gott und dem die Offenbarung empfangenden Menschen? ... Wie kann der Mensch mit seinem durch die Immanenz bestimmten und begrenzten Verstehensvermögen erfassen, was Gott über das hinaus sagt, worauf menschliches Denken im Grunde von sich selbst kommen müßte ...?

Hübner summarises at great length the main views of the biblical authors about God revealing himself. The main result of his analysis is that "one can speak meaningfully about revelation only where the revelation is received by people" ("wo sie als Offenbarung beim Menschen ankommt", 123; see also 146, 149, 167, 172).

Hübner attempts to answer the charge that people use anthropomorphisms when speaking about God's revelation. Hübner cannot deny that. Instead he points to the fact that anthropomorphisms are unavoidable if we want to speak about God at all. He affirms (158):

> Denn wenn es *Gott* ist, der als der Offenbarer dem Menschen begegnen will, warum muß dann mit einem Postulat die Möglichkeit einer Audition kategorisch ausgeschlossen werden? Ob telepathischer Vorgang oder Audition (oder auch Vision) - so oder so muß eine "Einwirkung" des transzendenten Gottes auf ein Empfangsorgan des immanenten Menschen angenommen werden. Und in *keinem* Fall ist dabei eine "natürliche", d.h. im Blick auf Gott nichtanthropomorphe Erklärung möglich ... Die Annahme, daß Gott Person ist, zwingt zur theologischen Reflexion auf die *Möglichkeit* göttlichen Redens und menschlichen Hörens, mag auch mit dem Aufweis einer solchen Möglichkeit noch nichts über die Faktizität einer Offenbarung Gottes gesagt sein.

The last clause in this quotation of Hübner expresses a due recognition of the difference between claiming to take part in God's revelation through our theology and claiming that we summarise the revelation of God according to the authors of the Bible. Hübner further contends (205):

Ist nun von Phänomenologie die Rede, dann mag sich die Aporie melden, wie denn phänomenologisch die im Begriff der Offenbarung vorausgesetzte Kommunikation zwischen Gott und Mensch vorstellbar sei. Und sofort sei uneingeschränkt eingeräumt, daß diese Frage aufs erste nicht beantwortbar ist.

However, Hübner does seem to go beyond his own suggested limits. On the basis of Heidegger's analysis of being, and on the basis of Bultmann's and Rahner's work, he discusses the possibility of God's revelation being received by human beings (207ff). Hübner summarises his study of the philosophical analysis and his own further suggestions as follows (235):

Die existenziale Betrachtung des Angesprochen-Werdens und des Hörens hat fundamentaltheologisch den Zugang zum Offenbarungsgeschehen eröffnet. Dieser Weg a priori wurde aber erst wirklich einsichtig aufgrund der neutestamentlichen Aussagen a posteriori. Das Neue Testament ist so Offenbarung als Evangelium der Gerechtigkeit Gottes ... Das Neue Testament ist ... die Anrede Gottes an den Menschen als desjenigen, der sich als der rechtfertigende Gott kundtut und genau dadurch den Glaubenden rechtfertigt.

One may try to prove that revelations are possible. In my opinion, this goes beyond the task of a biblical theology, or a New Testament theology, as I understand it. It is, however, a great strength of Hübner's *Prolegomena* to point to the need of a discussion of revelation. A discussion of problems related to the term "revelation" may be an essential part of any attempt at biblical theology.[31]

I think that Hübner's own warning (expressed in the previous quotation) supports my view that in biblical theology one should only attempt to describe what the biblical authors say about God's revelation, rather than to claim that revelation can be received by humans, and that God - as he is revealed in the Bible - should be accepted.

To conclude, I think that Hübner's work is an example of the significance of studying the problems involved in the enterprise of New Testament theology (or in his term: biblical theology). His *Prolegomena* supports the relevance of my project. This brief discussion of his thesis may have shown that major questions in relation to the characteristics of the enterprise are still open to debate. New Testament theology may be defined in more than one way.

---

[31] Cf. also the section entitled "Theologie als Theologie der Offenbarung(en) Gottes", in Hübner's recent article (in Dohmen - Söding), 1995, 211ff. The theme of revelation is also discussed by Hübner in another article, 1994. (For more publications of Hübner, see 1995, 223.)

11. Peter Stuhlmacher's major proposals

The first volume of Stuhlmacher's recent *Biblische Theologie des Neuen Testaments* (1992) begins with a "Grundlegung" in which he discusses the task ("Aufgabe") and the structuring ("Aufbau") of the enterprise. Stuhlmacher is well aware of the objections which have been raised against the enterprise of a biblical theology (13; 30ff). Because he wants to make an attempt to carry out the enterprise, he makes his own starting point clear in a number of carefully formulated affirmations. Here I focus on his proposals in relation to the task of the enterprise.

a. *Method gained from the New Testament*

Stuhlmacher makes four basic assertions. His first assertion ("Grundsatz") is that a New Testament theology has to receive its theme and its mode of presentation ("Darstellungsweise") from the New Testament itself (2).

He acknowledges that it is not self-evident to attribute such a role to the canon. He justifies his decision concerning the canon by arguing that the criterion of "apostolicity" led to a selection of writings in a twofold way: 1) apostolicity meant a historical argument: the writings had to be early; 2) apostolicity also meant a dogmatic argument: the writings had to contain the right doctrine (p.3). By the fact of the selection the writings became the canon of the church. Consequently, biblical theology has to take seriously the "special claim" of these writings which is expressed in their canonicity (2).[32]

Stuhlmacher's statement about the twofold importance of the criterion of apostolicity may be seen as a support of the results of my study of the process of canonisation in an earlier chapter (chapter three). I agree with Stuhlmacher's affirmation (3):

> *Die Kirche hat das Neue Testament nicht einfach eigenmächtig festgelegt, sondern in einem jahrhundertelangen Prozeß von Bewahrung des Ursprünglichen und Abgrenzung gegen Sekundäres und Fremdes festgestellt.*

The proposal of letting the New Testament determine the theme and the mode of presentation of the enterprise represents a major departure from attempts at New Testament theology which work under the influence of philosophy (e.g. F.C. Baur's Hegelianism) or from categories suggested by phi-

---

[32] I note that Stuhlmacher will present his view about the process of canonisation in his forthcoming second volume (cf. p.X).

losophies (e.g. Bultmann's existentialist interpretation). I think that this starting point may be a good decision in a historical, descriptive enterprise, for which I argue in this thesis.

However, the question has to be raised: Even if we receive the theme and the mode of presentation from the New Testament, from whence shall we take our expressions with which we want to describe the theme of the New Testament? In as much as description cannot be a simple repetition of the words of the Bible, the problem of terminology arises.

b. *Claim of revelation*

In his second assertion Stuhlmacher stresses that a New Testament theology has to do justice to the historical claim of revelation of the New Testament canon.

Stuhlmacher argues that the major part of the early church (with the exception of the Marcionites) regarded the Old Testament as their Holy Scripture. The Old Testament is the most important basis of tradition for the New Testament (5).

Stuhlmacher's view at this point differs from that of Hübner. As we have seen, Hübner emphasises that for a biblical theology of the New Testament one has to draw into the discussion the Old Testament as it was received (and changed) by the New Testament. Stuhlmacher objects that this distinction would have been unknown to the New Testament writers (37). He argues that it was important for the early Christians to preach to the Jews on the basis of an Old Testament which they shared with the Jews (37).[33]

I accept this emphasis on the importance of the Old Testament for the New. It is, however, similarly important to emphasise with Stuhlmacher's fourth assertion that the message of the New Testament was primarily addressed toward the Graeco-Roman world of the first two centuries (10).

Stuhlmacher argues that the larger part of early Christianity held that the writings of the New Testament was an addition ("Zusatz") to the Old Testament (4). He acknowledges that the term "New Testament" is attested only from the works of Clement of Alexandria and Tertullian, nevertheless he emphasises the fact that the two testaments were brought into relationship with one another (5).

I agree with this line of argument. I have to note, however, that on the basis of this argument the Old Testament's claim of revelation can only be brought into

---

[33] A similar point was also made by Childs, 1992, 65. In my opinion it is a good argument.

connection with that of the New Testament from the end of the second century onwards. In chapter three, I have used a similar argument in relation to the first Christian century when I argued that (at least some of) the New Testament authors wrote with a claim of revelation similar to that of the Old Testament. If my argument there is right, then New Testament theology will have to report that claim as a claim found in the New Testament, and not only in later church history.

c. Biblical theology of the New Testament

Stuhlmacher's third assertion is the consistent application of his first two assertions: If a New Testament theology has to receive its theme from the New Testament, and if the New Testament is closely connected with the Old, then a New Testament theology has to respect the Old Testament roots of the New Testament's faith message ("Glaubensbotschaft", 5). Consequently, Stuhlmacher formulates the main thesis of his enterprise in this way:

> *Die Theologie des Neuen Testaments ist als eine vom Alten Testament herkommende und zu ihm hin offene Biblische Theologie des Neuen Testaments zu entwerfen und als Teildisziplin einer Altes und Neues Testament gemeinsam betrachtenden Biblischen Theologie zu begreifen.*

This thesis is implied in the title of Stuhlmacher's work. If I were to write a New Testament theology, I should examine this thesis in detail. This thesis does not approve of an independent enterprise of New Testament theology. However, it presupposes the possibility of a New Testament theology and even extends it to the Old Testament. This thesis implies that there is a theology in the New Testament: a theology which is also in agreement with the theology of the Old Testament.

d. Relation to systematic theology

Stuhlmacher wants to distinguish three phases of the enterprise of biblical theology which have to follow one another: historical analysis of the New Testament texts; historical reconstruction of the connection of the elements that have been analysed; an attempt to show the relevance of the reconstruction for the present in a systematic interpretation (12). The outline of a biblical theology should not be determined by dogmatic theology. The outline should be a historical one which then reaches dogmatic decisions and an assessment of the centre to the Scripture at the end (12).

Stuhlmacher himself puts the emphasis on the first two stages (30). Stuhlmacher affirms that there is no finally established basic text or tradition: one has to exegete the whole New Testament "step by step" again (30; see also 14, 34). In my thesis, I have also reached the conclusion repeatedly that the question whether or not the enterprise of New Testament theology is possible, or whether or not there is a unity in the theology of the New Testament, can only be answered on the basis of the understanding of (many) individual New Testament passages. Exegesis has to be the basis on which we answer the question put to the enterprise by Räisänen's challenge: Do we have to move "beyond New Testament theology"?

I note that - in my understanding of the enterprise - Stuhlmacher's proposal concerning the third stage does not belong to New Testament theology. A writer of a New Testament theology should not set himself the aim to "show the relevance of the reconstruction for the present". If the theology of the New Testament is described, modern readers can make up their minds whether or not they want to accept the content of that theology as authoritative for them.

It is true that the proclamation of the Gospel is the task of the church. It may be done by a New Testament theologian as well. However, for the sake of the dialogue with those who think like Räisänen, I do not want to adopt that aim as a starting point in New Testament theology. I rather agree with another definition of Stuhlmacher: "Die Disziplin 'Theologie des Neuen Testaments' hat eine geordnete Zusammenschau der wesentlichen Verkündigungsinhalte und Glaubensgedanken der neutestamentlichen Bücher zu bieten" (2).

I conclude that Stuhlmacher's attempt to write a biblical theology - after the programmatic challenge of Räisänen - suggests that the problems involved in the justification of the enterprise may be overcome. Stuhlmacher's historical approach, complemented with his emphasis on "Einverständnis" which I have referred to in my first chapter, may be seen as a support for my understanding of the enterprise as one aiming at the description of the theological content of the New Testament.

12. Conclusion

In this chapter we have considered general questions in relation to the enterprise of New Testament theology. We have returned to themes mentioned earlier (particularly in the first chapter) and discussed them in the light of the results of the central chapters of the thesis. We have also discussed some of the major recent proposals concerning the enterprise. We have seen how they relate to the view represented in this thesis.

We may summarise some general results - or rather simply impressions - gained from this overview in the following way.

1) Recent scholarship in the discipline affirms that Räisänen's radical challenge to abandon New Testament theology - and to replace it by another enterprise - is not convincing. Scholars who are aware of Räisänen's challenge nevertheless make attempts to write New Testament theologies.

2) It is also clearly visible that scholars do not hold that the enterprise may be maintained without some justification. There are weighty challenges to be answered. The engagement of scholars in methodological questions of the enterprise confirms the relevance of my thesis.

3) With Stuhlmacher I hold that most of the questions of the exegesis are still open. If one of Räisänen's main reasons for proposing to abandon the enterprise is his exegetical opinion on many New Testament passages, as I think it is, then exegetical results different from his may contribute to re-establishing the enterprise. Stuhlmacher's (and Childs's and Hübner's) own exegetical decisions cannot be examined within the limits of this thesis. Here we may only say that their recent works show that Räisänen's challenge has not succeeded in becoming the final word in the discipline.

4) Scholars argue for different ways of understanding the enterprise of New Testament theology. It seems as if more depended on decisions than on arguments: scholars may wish to choose from more than one possibility of defining the enterprise. They differ on certain points (for example Hübner and Stuhlmacher on the role of the Old Testament); and they can widely agree on others. One widely held agreement is the proposal that New Testament theology should be part of a biblical theology overarching both testaments (Childs, Hübner, Stuhlmacher).

There are scholars who propose a framework other than the historical one. Morgan, himself referring to other examples, is a representative of this group of scholars.

In as much as there are definitions different from that of mine, the plurality of opinions suggests that there is no one definitive answer to the question: What should be the characteristics of the enterprise? I hold that more than one possibility may be argued for.

However, I maintain that my thesis, too, may be justified as one possibility among several valid ones: New Testament theology can be understood as a descriptive, historical enterprise. The enterprise does not need the extension of its aim to include that of convincing its readers about the religious truth claims of the New Testament. It may also be maintained without complementing (or replacing) its historical character by others, for example, those of a theory of literature and of the social sciences.

Conclusion

We have encountered many theses and arguments in this thesis. They are so numerous that it is impossible to reflect on them here. Since I have added concluding sections to the individual chapters, it may be appropriate to try to give only an overall picture of my thesis in this final conclusion.

In this thesis I have attempted to survey major challenges that are mounted against the enterprise of New Testament theology. We have started from the well formulated challenge put forward by Wrede that there are two great areas which may be seen as problematic in the enterprise (see my Introduction). These two areas are related to the two terms in the name of the enterprise: a) the term "theology" calls for a clarification of definitions that are involved in any attempt to maintain the enterprise; b) the term "New Testament" points us to problems in connection with the canonical status of the New Testament writings.

In as much as the logical connection between the problems has made it impossible to deal with the questions under these two headings only, the five chapters of the thesis may be seen as related to these two areas: chapters one, four and five would belong under point a); chapters two and three would belong under point b).

1. "Theology"

It seemed appropriate both to start and to end our work with some discussion of terminology (chapters one and five). As regards the term "theology", we have found that it can be used with two distinct meanings.

1) The term "theology" may refer to the theology of the scholar who summarises his own reflections on the content of the New Testament. This is a good and valid usage. There are scholars, even in most recent times, who maintain that the aim of writing a New Testament theology is to give a modern theological account of the Christian faith - referring to the faith of the early Christians as well as the faith of present-day Christians (see e.g. Stuhlmacher and Hübner in chapter five). In relation to this approach I have affirmed that it remains an option for the scholar. However, with Räisänen

I would ascribe this option to a "second stage" that follows the first stage of the enterprise, i.e. the stage of a historical, exegetical study.

2) "Theology" may be used for describing the content of the New Testament. In this case it may refer in a broad sense to the thoughts of the New Testament authors and of the early church about God. I have proposed that this usage of the term should be adopted in New Testament theology.

Since this definition covers a wide range of theological opinions held by the early Christians, a further differentiation may be helpful. We may distinguish between a basic theology of the early Christians and a more detailed expression of that basic theology. We have seen some support for this distinction in connection with the discussion of the credal formulae of early Christianity (chapter four).

We have examined the relationship between definitions adopted for "theology" and the proposal of Wrede, Räisänen (and others) that New Testament theology should be a historical enterprise (chapter one).

In this thesis I have adopted, and consistently held to, the proposal that New Testament theology should be an enterprise that is historical in its character. I have acknowledged that the enterprise may be given characteristics other than the historical one, for example, a "frame of reference" drawn from the literary theories or from social sciences (see Morgan's survey and proposals in chapter five). However, I have made an attempt to meet Räisänen's challenge on its own ground: I argue for the possibility of justifying the enterprise even if we retain its historical character.

Moving beyond the question of definitions, the distinction between a basic theology and its fuller expression (or "working out") may help us in dealing with a further problem in relation to the term "theology": the problem of the diversity of the theological content of the New Testament (chapter four). If we find that a large part of early Christianity shared a basic theology, then we may remain open to a diversity in the details with which early Christians "filled in" their basic theology. The basic theology may have been expressed in short statements of a credal type.

I have tried to argue in the form of exegetical excursus that two major theses may be challenged in which early Christians are said to have held opposing views.

One of these theses affirms that a part of early Christianity held that the Old Testament Law was no longer valid for Christians of Gentile origin. I have tried to show that Eph 2,15 (and Rom 10,4) does not support this view of scholarship.

The other thesis states that a part of early Christianity held an adoptionist Christology. I have made an attempt to argue that, contrary to a widespread view in scholarship, Acts 2,36 cannot be referred to as evidence for this thesis.

I do acknowledge that there may be passages (not dealt with in my thesis) that would prove to be real contradictions. I can only claim on the basis of the material provided in my thesis that some key passages, referred to as proof of contradictions, are not convincing: they are open to a different interpretation. I also hope to have put forward some arguments in favour of the thesis that the view is more likely that the majority of the early Christians shared a basic theology than the view that we can recover from the New Testament witnesses to opposing theologies in early Christianity.

My finding that early Christianity is likely to have shared a basic theology does not only rest on the unconvincing character of arguments for contradictions and on the hypothetical reconstruction of an early Christian theology on the basis of credal formulae.

The thesis that a large part of early Christianity shared a basic theology is strengthened by my findings in relation to the question of the canon.

2. "New Testament"

I have examined the thesis of W. Bauer and H. Koester that in large parts of early Christianity, views were held that later became labelled as heretical and that in certain geographical areas these views were even earlier than the ones later regarded as orthodox (chapter two). I hope to have shown that this thesis is not based on solid evidence. I have argued that the thesis may be maintained that views later regarded as orthodox were more likely to have been the original and most widespread theological ideas of the early Christians.

I have argued that it is historically likely that Christians with different theological views formed different canons from the second century onwards (e.g. the canon of Marcion). By this argument I have prepared the way for the proposal that the orthodox part of Christianity also formed its own canon.

This proposal has enabled us to raise the question (chapter three): Can the canon be justified in a historical enterprise, or is it true that the canon can only be accepted as a legitimate limitation of the enterprise on the basis of a theological decision? Having found traces of a New Testament canon in the second century, I have attempted to show that the Christians of the first century may have written with a certain canonical awareness. Once again, I acknowledge that I have not shown this in relation to all of the New Testament writings. However, I have argued that this awareness is historically possible on the basis of the parallel (or, "analogical") canonical process of the Old Testament. I have argued in an excursus that the Temple Scroll in Qumran may provide us with such an analogy. I have also argued that the various genres of the New Testament writings may provide us with some basis upon which we may differentiate between "canonical" and non-canonical writings.

If as historians we find that the New Testament "canon" - in the form of a "canonical process" - is a historical "fact" of the first two Christian centuries (and not only a later "theological fact", i.e. a decision of the church), and if we find that the New Testament does make a high claim of authority, perhaps even that of being "canonical", then it is legitimate to look for the theology contained in the writings of the New Testament.

In conclusion, I acknowledge the "programmatic" character of some parts of my own thesis - in this being similar to those of Wrede and Räisänen. I also feel the weight of many arguments that have not been dealt with in my work.

My thesis may be summarised as an answer to the two great challenges put to the enterprise. We do not have to move beyond New Testament theology. New Testament theology can be justified in both parts of its name: the enterprise can legitimately focus on the canonical New Testament; and it can set itself the aim of describing the theology of the New Testament writings.

If the challenges can be met, and if the enterprise can be justified, then we may expect that scholars will find themselves called, not least by their historical findings, to engage in it. The present work would like to serve as an encouragement toward this goal.

Bibliography

Abramowski, L.: "Die 'Erinnerungen der Apostel' bei Justin", in: Stuhlmacher, P. (ed.): *Das Evangelium und die Evangelien*. 1983, Tübingen: J.C.B. Mohr (Paul Siebeck), pp.341-353

Agnew, F.: "On the Origin of the Term *Apostolos*", *The Catholic Biblical Quarterly* 38 (1976), pp.49-53

Aland, K. and Aland, B.: *The Text of the New Testament: An Introduction to the Critical Editions and to the Theory and Practice of Modern Textual Criticism.* (transl. by E.F. Rhodes from the 1981 German orig.) 1987, Grand Rapids: William B. Eerdmans, Leiden: E.J. Brill

Apostolic Fathers, The (The Loeb Classical Library) vol. 1 (transl. by K. Lake; ed. by G.P. Goold; reprint of 1912 orig.) 1985, Cambridge, Massachusetts: Harvard University Press, London: William Heinemann Ltd

Badenas, R.: *Christ the End of the Law: Romans 10.4 in Pauline Perspective.* 1985, Sheffield: JSOT Press

Balla, P.: "Is the Law Abolished According to Eph. 2:15?", *European Journal of Theology* 3 (1994), pp.9-16

Balla, P.: *The Melchizedekian Priesthood.* 1995, Budapest: The Faculty of Theology of the Károli Gáspár Reformed University

Balla, P.: "Does Acts 2:36 Represent an Adoptionist Christology?", *European Journal of Theology* 5 (1996), pp.137-142

Balla, P. (ed.): *Teacher, Scholar, Friend: An unusual Festschrift in honour of John Cochrane O'Neill on his 65th birthday.* 1996, Budapest: The Faculty of Theology of the Károli Gáspár Reformed University

Balla, P.: "Does the Separation of History and Theology Destroy New Testament Theology? Räisänen's Challenge", in: Balla, P. (ed.): *Teacher, Scholar, Friend: An unusual Festschrift in honour of John Cochrane O'Neill on his 65th birthday.* 1996, Budapest: The Faculty of Theology of the Károli Gáspár Reformed University

Barr, J.: "Biblical theology", in: Crim, K. - et al. (eds.): *The Interpreter's Dictionary of the Bible: An Illustrated Encyclopedia.* Supplementary Volume. 1976, Nashville: Abingdon

Barr, J.: *Holy Scripture: Canon, Authority, Criticism.* 1983, Oxford: Clarendon Press

Barrett, C.K.: "The Apostles in and after the New Testament", *Svensk Exegetisk Årsbok* 21 (1956), pp.30-49

Barrett, C.K.: *The Signs of an Apostle.* 1970, London: Epworth Press

Barrett, C.K.: "The Centre of the New Testament and the Canon", in: Luz, U. - Weder, H. (eds.): *Die Mitte des Neuen Testaments: Einheit und Vielfalt neutestamentlicher Theologie.* 1983, Göttingen: Vandenhoeck & Ruprecht, pp.5-21

Barth, M.: *Ephesians: Introduction, Translation, and Commentary on Chapters 1-3.* (The Anchor Bible) (orig. 1974) 1984[8] , Garden City, New York: Doubleday & Company, Inc.

Bartsch, H.W. (ed.): *Kerygma and Myth: A theological debate.* 2 vols. (transl. by R.H. Fuller), vol. 1: (English transl. orig. 1953) 1964[2], vol. 2: (English transl.) 1962, London: SPCK

Bauer, W.: *Rechtgläubigkeit und Ketzerei im ältesten Christentum.* (orig. 1934) (second edition ed. by G. Strecker) 1964[2], Tübingen: J.C.B. Mohr (Paul Siebeck)

Bauer, W.: *Orthodoxy and Heresy in Earliest Christianity.* (transl. from the second German edition by a team from the Philadelphia Seminar on Christian origins; ed. by R.A. Kraft and G. Krodel; 1971, Fortress Press) first British edition: 1972, London: SCM Press Ltd

Bauer, W.: *A Greek-English Lexicon of the New Testament and Other Early Christian Literature.* (transl. by W.F. Arndt and F.W. Gingrich; adaptation from the fourth edition of W. Bauer's original German work; revised and augmented by F.W. Gingrich and F.W. Danker from W. Bauer's 1958 fifth edition) 1979[2], Chicago and London: The University of Chicago Press

Baur, F.C.: *Kritische Untersuchungen über die kanonischen Evangelien, ihr Verhältniss zu einander, ihren Charakter und Ursprung.* 1847, Tübingen: Verlag und Druck von Ludw. Fr. Fues

Baur, F.C.: *Vorlesungen über Neutestamentliche Theologie.* 1864, Leipzig: Fues's Verlag

Baur, F.C.: *Paulus, der Apostel Jesu Christi: Sein Leben und Wirken, seine Briefe und seine Lehre.* (orig. 1845; second edition ed. by E. Zeller) 1866[2], Leipzig: Fues's Verlag

Berger, K.: "Apostelbrief und apostolische Rede: Zum Formular frühchristlicher Briefe", *Zeitschrift für die Neutestamentliche Wissenschaft* 65 (1974), pp.190-231

Berger, K.: *Theologiegeschichte des Urchristentums: Theologie des Neuen Testaments.* (revised and expanded edition of 1994 orig.) 1995[2], Tübingen und Basel: A. Francke Verlag

Best, E.: *On Defining the Central Message of the New Testament.* (The Ethel M. Wood Lecture 1986) 1986, London: University of London

Betz, O: "Jesu Evangelium vom Gottesreich", in: Stuhlmacher, P. (ed.): *Das Evangelium und die Evangelien.* 1983, Tübingen: J.C.B. Mohr, pp.55-77

Bienert, W.A.: "The Picture of the Apostle in early Christian Tradition", in: Schneemelcher, W. (ed.): *New Testament Apocrypha.* vol. 2: 1992, Cambridge: James Clarke & Co. Ltd, Louisville, Kentucky: Westminster/John Knox Press, pp.5-27

Boers, H.: *What Is New Testament Theology?: The Rise of Criticism and the Problem of a Theology of the New Testament.* 1979, Philadelphia: Fortress Press

Bouttier, M.: *L'Épître de saint Paul aux Éphésiens.* (Commentaire du Nouveau Testament, IXb) 1991, Genève: Labor et Fides

Braun, H.: *Gesammelte Studien zum Neuen Testament und seiner Umwelt.* 1962, Tübingen: J.C.B. Mohr (Paul Siebeck)

Brett, M.G.: *Biblical Criticism in Crisis?: The impact of the canonical approach on Old Testament studies.* 1991, Cambridge: Cambridge University Press

Bright, W. (introd.): *The Orations of St. Athanasius against the Arians According to the Benedictine Text.* 1873, Oxford: Clarendon Press

Brooke, G.J. (ed.): *Temple Scroll Studies.* (Papers presented at the International Symposium on the Temple Scroll, Manchester, December 1987) 1989, Sheffield: JSOT Press

Brooke, G.J.: "Introduction", in: Brooke, G.J. (ed.): *Temple Scroll Studies.* 1989a, Sheffield: JSOT Press, pp.13-19

Brox, N.: *Der Hirt des Hermas.* 1991, Göttingen, Vandenhoeck & Ruprecht

Bultmann, R.: *Glauben und Verstehen.* vol. 1. 1954^2, Tübingen: Verlag J.C.B. Mohr (Paul Siebeck)

Bultmann, R.: *Die Geschichte der synoptischen Tradition.* (reprint of 1931 second edition) 1961^4, Berlin: Evangelische Verlagsanstalt

Bultmann, R.: *Exegetica: Aufsätze zur Erforschung des Neuen Testaments.* (ed. by E. Dinkler) 1967, Tübingen: J.C.B. Mohr (Paul Siebeck)

Bultmann, R.: *Theologie des Neuen Testaments.* (orig. 1948-53) 1984^9, Tübingen: J.C.B. Mohr (Paul Siebeck)

Burridge, R.A.: *What are the Gospels?: A Comparison with Graeco-Roman Biography.* 1992, Cambridge: Cambridge University Press

Bühner, J.-A.: "ἀπόστολος", in: Balz, H. - Schneider, G. (eds.): *Exegetical Dictionary of the New Testament.* vol. 1: (German orig. 1978-80) 1990, Edinburgh: T & T Clark Ltd, pp.142-146

Campenhausen, H.F. von: *Die Entstehung der christlichen Bibel.* 1968, Tübingen: J.C.B. Mohr (Paul Siebeck)

Campenhausen, H.F. von: "Die Entstehung des Neuen Testaments", in: Käsemann, E. (ed.): *Das Neue Testament als Kanon: Dokumentation und kritische Analyse zur gegenwärtigen Diskussion.* 1970, Göttingen: Vandenhoeck & Ruprecht, pp.109-123

Campenhausen, H. von: *The Formation of the Christian Bible.* (transl. by J.A. Baker from the 1968 German orig.) 1972, London: Adam & Charles Black

Chadwick, H. (transl., introd. and notes): *Origen: Contra Celsum.* 1953, Cambridge: Cambridge University Press

Chadwick, H. (transl.): *Lessing's Theological Writings.* (Selections in translation with an Introductory Essay by H.Chadwick) 1956, London: Adam & Charles Black

Charlesworth, J.H. (ed.): *The Old Testament Pseudepigrapha.* vol. 1: *Apocalyptic Literature and Testaments.* 1983, Doubleday: New York

Childs, B.S.: *Biblical Theology in Crisis.* 1970, Philadelphia: The Westminster Press

Childs, B.S.: *Introduction to the Old Testament as Scripture.* (third impression of 1979 orig.) 1987, London: SCM Press Ltd

Childs, B.S.: *The New Testament as Canon: An Introduction.* 1984, London: SCM Press Ltd

Childs, B.S.: "Biblische Theologie und christlicher Kanon", in: Baldermann, I. - *et al.* (eds.): *Jahrbuch für Biblische Theologie.* vol. 3: *Zum Problem des biblischen Kanons.* 1988, Neukirchen-Vluyn: Neukirchener Verlag, pp.13-27

Childs, B.S.: *Biblical Theology of the Old and New Testaments: Theological Reflection on the Christian Bible.* 1992, London: SCM Press Ltd

Childs, B.S.: "Die Beziehung von Altem und Neuem Testament aus kanonischer Sicht", in: Dohmen, Ch. - Söding, Th. (eds.): *Eine Bibel - zwei Testamente: Positionen biblischer Theologie.* 1995, Paderborn: Ferdinand Schöningh, pp.29-34

Collingwood, R.G.: *The Idea of History.* (reprinted from 1946 orig.) 1961, Oxford: Oxford University Press

Collingwood, R.G.: *An Autobiography.* (reprinted with introduction from 1939 orig.) 1982, Oxford: Clarendon Press

Conzelmann, H.: *Die Apostelgeschichte.* (Handbuch zum Neuen Testament, 7) 1963, Tübingen: J.C.B. Mohr (Paul Siebeck)

Conzelmann, H.: *An Outline of the Theology of the New Testament.* (transl. by J. Bowden from the 1968 second German edition) 1969, London: SCM Press Ltd

Cranfield, C.E.B.: *A Critical and Exegetical Commentary on the Epistle to the Romans.* (ICC) vol. 2, 1979, Edinburgh: T. & T. Clark Ltd

Cullmann, O.: *The Earliest Christian Confessions.* (transl. by J.K.S. Reid; French orig. 1943) 1949, London: Lutterworth Press

Cullmann, O.: *The Christology of the New Testament.* (transl. by S.C. Guthrie and C.A.M. Hall from the 1957 German original) 1963^2, London: SCM Press Ltd

Dibelius, M.: "Biblische Theologie und biblische Religionsgeschichte: II. des NT.", in: Gunkel, H. - Zscharnack, L. (eds.): *Die Religion in Geschichte und Gegenwart.* vol. 1, 1927^2, Tübingen: Verlag von J.C.B. Mohr (Paul Siebeck), cols. 1091-1094

Dohmen, Ch. - Söding, Th. (eds.): *Eine Bibel - zwei Testamente: Positionen biblischer Theologie.* 1995, Paderborn: Ferdinand Schöningh

Donahue, J.R.: "The Changing Shape of New Testament Theology", *Theological Studies* 50 (1989), pp.314-335

Dormeyer, D.: *Evangelium als literarische und theologische Gattung.* 1989, Darmstadt: Wissenschaftliche Buchgesellschaft

Dungan, D.L. (ed.): *The Interrelations of the Gospels.* (A Symposium led by M.-É. Boismard - W.R. Farmer - F. Neirynck, Jerusalem, 1984) 1990, Leuven: Leuven University Press, Uitgeverij Peeters

Dunn, J.D.G.: "Let John be John: A Gospel for Its Time", in: Stuhlmacher, P. (ed.): *Das Evangelium und die Evangelien.* 1983, Tübingen: J.C.B. Mohr (Paul Siebeck), pp.309-339

Dunn, J.D.G.: *Unity and Diversity in the New Testament: An Inquiry into the Character of Earliest Christianity.* (second impression of the 1990 second edition; orig. 1977) 1991^2, London: SCM Press, Philadelphia: Trinity Press International

Ebeling, G.: *Word and Faith.* (transl. by J.W. Leitch from the 1960 German orig.) 1963, London: SCM Press Ltd

Ellis, E.E.: "Foreword", in: Harris, H.: *The Tübingen School: A Historical and Theological Investigation of the School of F. C. Baur.* 1990, Leicester: Apollos, pp.vii-xvi

Epp, E.J. - MacRae, G.W. (eds.): *The New Testament and Its Modern Interpreters.* 1989, Philadelphia, Pennsylvania: Fortress Press; Atlanta, Georgia: Scholars Press

Evans, C.F.: "The Kerygma", *The Journal of Theological Studies* 7 (1956), pp.25-41

Fergusson, D.: *Bultmann.* 1992, London: Geoffrey Chapman

Friedrich, G.: "εὐαγγελίζομαι κτλ.", in: Kittel, G. - Bromiley, G.W. (eds.): *Theological Dictionary of the New Testament.* vol. 2, 1964, Grand Rapids, Michigan: Wm.B. Eerdmans Publishing Company, pp.707-737

Fuller, R.H.: "New Testament Theology", in: Epp, E.J. - MacRae, G.W. (eds.): *The New Testament and Its Modern Interpreters.* 1989, Philadelphia, Pennsylvania: Fortress Press; Atlanta, Georgia: Scholars Press, pp.565-584

Gasque, W.W. - Martin, R.P. (eds.): *Apostolic History and the Gospel.* 1970, Exeter: The Paternoster Press

Gese, H.: "Über die biblische Einheit", in: Dohmen, Ch. - Söding, Th. (eds.): *Eine Bibel - zwei Testamente: Positionen biblischer Theologie.* 1995, Paderborn: Ferdinand Schöningh, pp.35-44

Gnilka, J.: *Der Epheserbrief.* (Herders theologischer Kommentar zum Neuen Testament, X.2) (orig. 1971) 1982³, Freiburg-Basel-Wien: Verlag Herder

Goppelt, L.: *Theologie des Neuen Testaments.* (two volumes in one; ed. by J. Roloff) (orig. 1976) 1985³, Göttingen: Vandenhoeck & Ruprecht

Guelich, R.: "The Gospel Genre", in: Stuhlmacher, P. (ed.): *Das Evangelium und die Evangelien.* 1983, Tübingen: J.C.B. Mohr (Paul Siebeck), pp.183-219

Haenchen, E.: *The Acts of the Apostles: A Commentary.* (transl. by B. Noble and G. Shinn from the 1965 fourteenth German edition; transl. revised by R.McL. Wilson) 1971, Oxford: Basil Blackwell

Hahn, F.: "Der Apostolat im Urchristentum: Seine Eigenart und seine Voraussetzungen", *Kerygma und Dogma* 20 (1974), pp.54-77

Hahn, F.: "Neue Beiträge zur Theologie des Neuen Testaments: Zu Joachim Gnilka und Klaus Berger", *Berliner Theologische Zeitschrift* 12 (1995), pp.250-268

Harnack, A.: *Das Neue Testament um das Jahr 200: Theodor Zahn's Geschichte des Neutestamentlichen Kanons (erster Band, erste Hälfte) geprüft.* 1889, Freiburg I. B.: Akademische Verlagsbuchhandlung von J.C.B. Mohr (Paul Siebeck)

Harnack, A. von: *Marcion: Das Evangelium vom fremden Gott.* 1921, Leipzig: J.C. Hinrichs'sche Buchhandlung

Harris, H.: *The Tübingen School: A Historical and Theological Investigation of the School of F. C. Baur.* (the 1975 edition with a foreword and preface to the new edition) 1990, Leicester: Apollos

Harvey, V.A.: *The Historian and the Believer: The Morality of Historical Knowledge and Christian Belief.* (American orig. 1966) 1967, London: SCM Press Ltd

Hasel, G.F.: *New Testament Theology: Basic Issues in the Current Debate.* 1978, Grand Rapids, Michigan: William B. Eerdmans Publishing Company

Hengel, M.: *Acts and the History of Earliest Christianity.* (transl. by J. Bowden from the 1979 German orig.) 1979, London: SCM Press Ltd

Hofius, O.: "Das apostolische Christuszeugnis und das Alte Testament: Thesen zur Biblischen Theologie", in: Dohmen, Ch. - Söding, Th. (eds.): *Eine Bibel - zwei Testamente: Positionen biblischer Theologie*. 1995, Paderborn: Ferdinand Schöningh, pp.195-208

Holtzmann, H.J.: *Lehrbuch der Neutestamentlichen Theologie*. vol. 1. 1897, Freiburg i. B. und Leipzig: Akademische Verlagsbuchhandlung von J.C.B. Mohr

Holtzmann, H.J.: *Lehrbuch der Neutestamentlichen Theologie*. vol. 1. (ed. by D.A. Jülicher and W. Bauer) 1911[2], Tübingen: Verlag von J.C.B. Mohr

Hurst, L.D. and Wright, N.T. (eds.): *The Glory of Christ in the New Testament: Studies in Christology in Memory of George Bradford Caird*. 1987, Oxford: Clarendon Press

Hübner, H.: *Biblische Theologie des Neuen Testaments*. 3 vols. vol. 1: *Prolegomena*. 1990, vol. 2: *Die Theologie des Paulus und ihre neutestamentliche Wirkungsgeschichte*. 1993, vol. 3: *Hebräerbrief, Evangelien und Offenbarung, Epilegomena*. 1995, Göttingen: Vandenhoeck & Ruprecht

Hübner, H.: "Offenbarungen und Offenbarung: Philosophische und theologische Erwägungen zum Verhältnis von Altem und Neuem Testament", in: Pedersen, S. (ed.): *New Directions in Biblical Theology*. 1994, Leiden: E.J. Brill, pp.10-23

Hübner, H.: "Was ist Biblische Theologie?", in: Dohmen, Ch. - Söding, Th. (eds.): *Eine Bibel - zwei Testamente: Positionen biblischer Theologie*. 1995, Paderborn: Ferdinand Schöningh, pp.209-223

Jahrbuch für Biblische Theologie. (ed. by I. Baldermann - et al.), vol. 1: *Einheit und Vielfalt Biblischer Theologie*. 1986, Neukirchen-Vluyn: Neukirchener Verlag

Jahrbuch für Biblische Theologie. (ed. by I. Baldermann - et al.), vol. 3: *Zum Problem des biblischen Kanons*. 1988, Neukirchen-Vluyn: Neukirchener Verlag

Jeremias, J.: *New Testament Theology*. vol. 1: *The Proclamation of Jesus*. (transl. by J. Bowden from the 1971 German orig.) 1971, London: SCM Press Ltd

Jüngel, E.: *Paulus und Jesus: Eine Untersuchung zur Präzisierung der Frage nach dem Ursprung der Christologie*. 1962, Tübingen: J.C.B. Mohr (Paul Siebeck)

Kaftan, J.: *Neutestamentliche Theologie*. 1927, Berlin: Verlag von Martin Warneck

Karrer, M.: *Die Johannesoffenbarung als Brief: Studien zu ihrem literarischen, historischen und theologischen Ort*. 1986, Göttingen: Vandenhoeck & Ruprecht

Käsemann, E.: *Exegetische Versuche und Besinnungen*. vol. 1. 1960, Göttingen: Vandenhoeck & Ruprecht

Käsemann, E. (ed.): *Das Neue Testament als Kanon: Dokumentation und kritische Analyse zur gegenwärtigen Diskussion*. 1970, Göttingen: Vandenhoeck & Ruprecht

Käsemann, E.: "Einführung", in: Käsemann, E. (ed.): *Das Neue Testament als Kanon: Dokumentation und kritische Analyse zur gegenwärtigen Diskussion*. 1970a, Göttingen: Vandenhoeck & Ruprecht, pp.9-12

Käsemann, E.: "Begründet der neutestamentliche Kanon die Einheit der Kirche?", in: Käsemann, E. (ed.): *Das Neue Testament als Kanon: Dokumentation und kritische Analyse zur gegenwärtigen Diskussion*. 1970b, Göttingen: Vandenhoeck & Ruprecht, pp.124-133

Käsemann, E.: "The Problem of a New Testament Theology", *New Testament Studies* 19 (1972-73), pp.235-245

Käsemann, E.: *An die Römer.* (Handbuch zum Neuen Testament, 8a) (orig. 1973) 1980[4], Tübingen: J.C.B. Mohr (Paul Siebeck)

Klauck, H.-J.: *Der erste Johannesbrief.* (EKK, XXIII.1) 1991, Zürich, Braunschweig: Benziger Verlag, Neukirchen-Vluyn: Neukirchener Verlag

Köster, H.: *Synoptische Überlieferung bei den apostolischen Vätern.* 1957, Berlin: Akademie-Verlag

Köster, H.: *Einführung in das Neue Testament: im Rahmen der Religionsgeschichte und Kulturgeschichte der hellenistischen und römischen Zeit.* 1980, Berlin, New York: Walter de Gruyter

Koester, H.: "From the Kerygma-Gospel to Written Gospels", *New Testament Studies* 35 (1989), pp.361-381

Koester, H.: *Ancient Christian Gospels: Their History and Development.* 1990, London: SCM Press Ltd, Philadelphia: Trinity Press International

Koester, H.: "Writings and the Spirit: Authority and Politics in Ancient Christianity", *Harvard Theological Review* 84 (1991), pp.353-372

Kümmel, W.G.: "Bibel II B. Sammlung und Kanonisierung des NT", in: Galling, K. (ed.): *Die Religion in Geschichte und Gegenwart.* vol. 1, 1957[3]a, Tübingen: J.C.B. Mohr (Paul Siebeck), cols.1131-1138

Kümmel, W.G.: "Bibelwissenschaft II. Bibelwissenschaft des NT", in: Galling, K. (ed.): *Die Religion in Geschichte und Gegenwart.* vol. 1, 1957[3]b, Tübingen: J.C.B. Mohr (Paul Siebeck), cols.1236-1251

Kümmel, W.G.: *The New Testament: The History of the Investigation of Its Problems.* (second impression of the 1973 first British edition; transl. by S.M. Gilmour and H.C. Kee from the 1970 German orig.) 1978, London: SCM Press Ltd

Kümmel, W.G.: *Die Theologie des Neuen Testaments nach seinen Hauptzeugen: Jesus, Paulus, Johannes.* (orig. 1969) 1987[5], Göttingen: Vandenhoeck & Ruprecht

Lake, K. (transl.): "The First Epistle of Clement to the Corinthians", in: Goold, G.P. (ed.): *The Apostolic Fathers.* vol. 1, 1985, Cambridge, Massachusetts: Harvard University Press, London: William Heinemann Ltd, pp.1-121

Lietzmann, H.: *The Founding of the Church Universal: A History of the Early Church.* vol. 2, (transl. by B.L. Woolf; first published 1938) 1953[3], London: Lutterworth Press

Lietzmann, H.: *Kleine Schriften III: Studien zur Liturgie- und Symbolgeschichte zur Wissenschaftsgeschichte.* (Ed. by Die Kommission für spätantike Religionsgeschichte) 1962, Berlin: Akademie-Verlag

Lincoln, A.T.: *Ephesians.* (Word Biblical Commentary, 42) 1990, Dallas, Texas: Word Books, Publisher

Link, Ch. - Luz, U. - Vischer, L.: *Sie aber hielten fest an der Gemeinschaft...: Einheit der Kirche als Prozeß im Neuen Testament und heute.* 1988, Zürich: Benziger Verlag

Loisy, A.: *The Gospel and the Church.* (transl. by Ch. Home) 1903, London: Isbister & Company Limited

Luz, U. - Weder, H. (eds.): *Die Mitte des Neuen Testaments: Einheit und Vielfalt neutestamentlicher Theologie.* (Festschrift für Eduard Schweizer zum siebzigsten Geburtstag) 1983, Göttingen: Vandenhoeck & Ruprecht

Luz, U.: "Einheit und Vielfalt neutestamentlicher Theologien", in: Luz, U. - Weder, H. (eds.): *Die Mitte des Neuen Testaments: Einheit und Vielfalt neutestamentlicher Theologie.* 1983, Göttingen: Vandenhoeck & Ruprecht, pp.142-161

Luz, U.: "Unterwegs zur Einheit: Gemeinschaft der Kirche im Neuen Testament", in: Link, Ch. - Luz, U. - Vischer, L.: *Sie aber hielten fest an der Gemeinschaft ...: Einheit der Kirche als Prozeß im Neuen Testament und heute.* 1988, Zürich: Benziger Verlag, pp.43-183

Lührmann, D.: "Wrede, W.", in: Coggins, R.J. - Houlden, J.L. (eds.): *A Dictionary of Biblical Interpretation.* (second impression of 1990 orig.) 1992, London: SCM Press, p.734

Macpherson, J.: *Commentary on St. Paul's Epistle to the Ephesians.* 1892, Edinburgh: T. & T. Clark

Maier, J.: *Die Tempelrolle vom Toten Meer.* 1978, München-Basel: Ernst Reinhardt Verlag

Maier, J.: "Zur Frage des biblischen Kanons im Frühjudentum im Licht der Qumranfunde", in: Baldermann, I. - *et al.* (eds.): *Jahrbuch für Biblische Theologie.* vol. 3: *Zum Problem des biblischen Kanons.* 1988, Neukirchen-Vluyn: Neukirchener Verlag, pp.135-146

Marshall, I.H.: "Luke and his 'Gospel'", in: Stuhlmacher, P. (ed.): *Das Evangelium und die Evangelien.* 1983, Tübingen: J.C.B. Mohr (Paul Siebeck), pp.289-308

Marshall, I.H.: *Jesus the Saviour: Studies in New Testament Theology.* 1990, London: SPCK

McDonald, L.M.: *The Formation of the Christian Biblical Canon.* (revised and expanded edition of the 1988 orig.) 1995, Peabody, Massachusetts: Hendrickson Publishers

McDonald, L.M.: "The Integrity of the Biblical Canon in Light of Its Historical Development", *Bulletin for Biblical Research* 6 (1996), pp.95-132

Mealand, D.L.: "The Dissimilarity Test", *Scottish Journal of Theology* 31 (1978), pp.41-50

Metzger, B.M. (transl. and introd.): "The Fourth Book of Ezra", in: Charlesworth, J.H. (ed.): *The Old Testament Pseudepigrapha.* vol. 1: *Apocalyptic Literature and Testaments.* 1983, New York: Doubleday, pp.516-559

Meyer, A.: "Bibelwissenschaft: II. Neues Testament", in: Schiele, F.M. (ed.): *Die Religion in Geschichte und Gegenwart.* vol. 1, 1909[1], Tübingen: Verlag von J.C.B. Mohr (Paul Siebeck), cols.1212-1228

Meyer, A.: "Bibelwissenschaft: II. des NT.", in: Gunkel, H. - Zscharnack, L. (eds.): *Die Religion in Geschichte und Gegenwart.* vol. 1, 1927[2], Tübingen: Verlag von J.C.B. Mohr (Paul Siebeck), cols.1074-1086

Mitton, C.L.: *Ephesians.* (New Century Bible) 1976, London: Oliphants (Marshall, Morgan & Scott)

Morgan, R. (ed., transl., and introd.): *The Nature of New Testament Theology: The Contribution of William Wrede and Adolf Schlatter.* 1973, London: SCM Press Ltd

Morgan, R.: "Introduction: The Nature of New Testament Theology", in: Morgan, R. (ed., transl., and introd.): *The Nature of New Testament Theology: The Contribution of William Wrede and Adolf Schlatter.* 1973a, London: SCM Press Ltd, pp.1-67

Morgan, R.: "Expansion and Criticism in the Christian Tradition", in: Pye, M. - Morgan, R. (eds.): *The Cardinal Meaning: Essays in Comparative Hermeneutics: Buddhism and Christianity.* 1973b, The Hague: Mouton, pp.59-101

Morgan, R.: "The New Testament in religious studies", *Religious Studies* 10 (1974), pp.385-406

Morgan, R.: "A Straussian Question to 'New Testament Theology'", *New Testament Studies* 23 (1976-77), pp.243-265

Morgan, R. - Pye, M. (transls., eds.): *Ernst Troeltsch: Writings on Theology and Religion.* 1977, London: Gerald Duckworth & Co. Ltd.

Morgan, R.: "The Historical Jesus and the Theology of the New Testament", in: Hurst, L.D. - Wright, N.T. (eds.): *The Glory of Christ in the New Testament: Studies in Christology in Memory of George Bradford Caird.* 1987, Oxford: Clarendon Press, pp.187-206

Morgan, R. - Barton, J.: *Biblical Interpretation.* (reprint of 1988 orig.) 1991, Oxford: Oxford University Press

Morgan, R.: "Theology: New Testament", in: Freedman, D.N. (ed.-in-chief): *The Anchor Bible Dictionary.* vol. 6, 1992a, New York: Doubleday, pp.473-483

Morgan, R.: "Theology (New Testament)", in: Coggins, R.J. - Houlden, J.L. (eds.): *A Dictionary of Biblical Interpretation.* (second impression of 1990 orig.) 1992b, London: SCM Press, pp.689-691

Morgan, R.: "Can the Critical Study of Scripture Provide a Doctrinal Norm?", *The Journal of Religion* 76 (1996), pp.206-232

Mowinckel, S.: *He That Cometh.* (transl. by G.W. Anderson from the 1951 Norwegian orig.) 1956, Oxford: Basil Blackwell

Mowinckel, S.: *The Psalms in Israel's Worship.* 2 vols. (transl. by D.R. Ap-Thomas) 1962, Oxford: Basil Blackwell

Munck, J.: *The Acts of the Apostles.* (twelfth printing of 1967 orig.) 1986, Garden City, New York: Doubleday & Company, Inc.

Newman, J.H. (transl.): *Select Treatises of St. Athanasius in Controversy with the Arians.* (Freely translated by J.H. Newman) vol. 1, 1881[2], London: Pickering and Co.

Norden, E.: *Agnostos Theos: Untersuchungen zur Formengeschichte religiöser Rede.* 1913, Leipzig, Berlin: Verlag B.G. Teubner

Oeming, M.: "Unitas Scripturae? Eine Problemskizze", in: Baldermann, I. - *et al.* (eds.): *Jahrbuch für Biblische Theologie.* vol. 1: *Einheit und Vielfalt Biblischer Theologie.* 1986, Neukirchen-Vluyn: Neukirchener Verlag, pp.48-70

O'Neill, J.C.: *The Theology of Acts in its Historical Setting.* (second edition, revised and supplemented: 1970) 1961, London: S.P.C.K.

O'Neill, J.C.: *Paul's Letter to the Romans.* 1975, Harmondsworth: Penguin Books Ltd

O'Neill, J.C.: *Messiah: Six lectures on the ministry of Jesus.* (reprint of 1980 orig.) 1984, Cambridge: Cochrane Press

O'Neill, J.C.: *The Bible's Authority: A Portrait Gallery of Thinkers from Lessing to Bultmann.* 1991a, Edinburgh: T&T Clark

O'Neill, J.C.: "The Lost Written Records of Jesus' Words and Deeds behind Our Records", *Journal of Theological Studies* 42 (1991b), pp.483-504

O'Neill, J.C.: "Review Article: P.M. Casey, *From Jewish Prophet to Gentile God*", *Irish Biblical Studies* 14 (1992), pp.192-198

O'Neill, J.C.: "The Kingdom of God", *Novum Testamentum* 35 (1993), pp.130-141

O'Neill, J.C.: *Who Did Jesus Think He Was?* (Biblical Interpretation Series, 11) 1995, Leiden: E.J. Brill

Origen: *Contra Celsum.* (transl., introd. and notes by H. Chadwick) 1953, Cambridge: Cambridge University Press

Overbeck, F.: *Zur Geschichte des Kanons.* (reprint of 1880 orig., Chemnitz: Verlag von Ernst Schmeitzner) 1965, Darmstadt: Wissenschaftliche Buchgesellschaft

Overbeck, F.: *Über die Anfänge der patristischen Literatur.* (reproduction of the article in: *Historische Zeitschrift* 48 (1882), pp.417-472) no date, Basel: Benno Schwabe & Co. Verlag

Overbeck, F.: *Über die Christlichkeit unserer heutigen Theologie.* (reprint of the 1903[2] Leipzig edition) 1981, Darmstadt: Wissenschaftliche Buchgesellschaft

Pedersen, S. (ed.): *New Directions in Biblical Theology.* 1994, Leiden: E.J. Brill

Pesch, R.: *Die Apostelgeschichte.* 1. Teilband: Apg 1-12 (EKK, V.1) 1986, Zürich: Benziger Verlag, Neukirchen-Vluyn: Neukirchener Verlag

Plümacher, E.: "Bibel II. Die Heiligen Schriften des Judentums im Urchristentum", in: Krause, G. - Müller, G. (eds.): *Theologische Realenzyklopädie.* vol. 6, 1980, Berlin, New York: Walter de Gruyter & Co., pp.8-22

Prigent, P.: *L'Apocalypse de saint Jean.* (Commentaire du Nouveau Testament, XIV) 1981, Lausanne, Paris: Delachaux & Niestlé Éditeurs

Pye, M. - Morgan, R. (eds.): *The Cardinal Meaning: Essays in Comparative Hermeneutics: Buddhism and Christianity.* 1973, The Hague: Mouton

Räisänen, H.: *Paul and the Law.* (revised and enlarged edition of 1983 orig.) 1987[2], Tübingen: J.C.B. Mohr (Paul Siebeck)

Räisänen, H.: *Beyond New Testament Theology: A story and a programme.* 1990, London: SCM Press, Philadelphia: Trinity Press International

Räisänen, H.: *Jesus, Paul and Torah: Collected Essays.* (translations from the German by D.E. Orton) 1992, Sheffield: JSOT Press

Räisänen, H.: "Die frühchristliche Gedankenwelt: Eine religionswissenschaftliche Alternative zur 'neutestamentlichen Theologie'", in: Dohmen, Ch. - Söding, Th. (eds.): *Eine Bibel - zwei Testamente: Positionen biblischer Theologie.* 1995, Paderborn: Ferdinand Schöningh, pp.253-265

Räisänen, H.: "The Future of New Testament Theology", unpublished manuscript of a main paper delivered at Growth Points in Biblical Studies: A Scottish-Scandinavian Conference, in Glasgow, on 3rd April 1993. I am indebted to Professor Heikki Räisänen for sending me the manuscript in May 1994. According to him, the paper is due to appear in: Jones, G. - Ayres, L. (eds.): *Studies on Christian Origins.* vol. 1, 1997, London: Routledge

Reumann, J.: *Variety and Unity in New Testament Thought.* 1991, New York: Oxford University Press

Reventlow, H.G.: *Hauptprobleme der Biblischen Theologie im 20. Jahrhundert.* 1983, Darmstadt: Wissenschaftliche Buchgesellschaft

Richardson, A.: *An Introduction to the Theology of the New Testament.* (second impression of 1958 orig.) 1961, London: SCM Press Ltd

Riches, J.K.: *A Century of New Testament Study.* 1993, Cambridge: The Lutterworth Press

Riesenfeld, H.: "Biblische Theologie und biblische Religionsgeschichte II. NT", in: Galling, K.(ed.): *Die Religion in Geschichte und Gegenwart*. vol. 1, 1957^3, Tübingen: J.C.B. Mohr (Paul Siebeck), cols.1259-1262

Ritter, A.M.: "Glaubensbekenntis(se) V. Alte Kirche", in: Müller, G. (ed.): *Theologische Realenzyklopädie*. vol. 13, 1984, Berlin, New York: Walter de Gruyter & Co., pp.399-412

Roberts, C.H.: *Manuscript, Society and Belief in Early Christian Egypt.* (The Schweich Lectures of The British Academy, 1977) 1979, London: Published for The British Academy by the Oxford University Press

Roberts, C.H. - Skeat, T.C.: *The Birth of the Codex*. 1987, London: Published for The British Academy by the Oxford University Press

Robinson, J.A.: *St Paul's Epistle to the Ephesians: A Revised Text and Translation with Exposition and Notes*. 1903, London: Macmillan and Co., Limited

Robinson, J.A.T.: *Redating the New Testament*. 1976, London: SCM Press Ltd

Robinson, J.M. - Koester, H.: *Trajectories through Early Christianity*. 1971, Philadelphia: Fortress Press

Robinson, T.A.: *The Bauer Thesis Examined: The Geography of Heresy in the Early Christian Church*. 1988, Lewiston, Queenston: The Edwin Mellen Press

Roloff, J.: *Die Apostelgeschichte*. (Das Neue Testament Deutsch, 5) (reprint of 1981 orig.) 1988, Berlin: Evangelische Verlagsanstalt

Roloff, J.: "Stuhlmacher, Peter: *Biblische Theologie des Neuen Testaments*", in: *Theologische Literaturzeitung* 119 (1994), cols.241-245

Sæbø, M.: "Vom 'Zusammen-Denken' zum Kanon. Aspekte der traditionsgeschichtlichen Endstadien des Alten Testaments", in: Baldermann, I. - *et al.* (eds.): *Jahrbuch für Biblische Theologie*. vol. 3: *Zum Problem des biblischen Kanons*. 1988, Neukirchen-Vluyn: Neukirchener Verlag, pp.115-133

Sandys-Wunsch, J. - Eldredge, L.: "J. P. Gabler and the Distinction between Biblical and Dogmatic Theology: Translation, Commentary, and Discussion of His Originality", *Scottish Journal of Theology* 33 (1980), pp.133-158

Schelkle, K.H.: *Theology of the New Testament*. vol. 3: *Morality*. (transl. by W.A. Jurgens from the 1970 German orig.) 1973, Collegeville, Minnesota: The Liturgical Press

Schille, G.: *Die Apostelgeschichte des Lukas*. (Theologischer Handkommentar zum Neuen Testament, V) (orig. 1983) 1984^2, Berlin: Evangelische Verlagsanstalt

Schleiermacher, F.: "Kurze Darstellung des theologischen Studiums zum Behuf einleitender Vorlesungen entworfen" in: *Friedrich Schleiermacher's Saemtliche Werke. Erste Abtheilung. Zur Theologie. Erster Band*. 1843, Berlin: bei G. Reimer, pp.1-132

Schleiermacher, F.: *The Christian Faith*. (transl. from the 1830 second German edition; ed. by H.R. Mackintosh and J.S. Stewart) 1928, Edinburgh: T. & T. Clark

Schleiermacher, F.: *Der christliche Glaube nach den Grundsätzen der evangelischen Kirche im Zusammenhange dargestellt (1821-22)*. (Kritische Gesamtausgabe I.7.2, ed. by H. Peiter) 1980, Berlin, New York: Walter de Gruyter

Schlier, H.: *Die Zeit der Kirche: Exegetische Aufsätze und Vorträge*. 1958^2, Freiburg: Verlag Herder

Schlier, H.: *Besinnung auf das Neue Testament: Exegetische Aufsätze und Vorträge II.* 1964, Freiburg: Verlag Herder

Schlier, H.: *Der Brief an die Epheser: Ein Kommentar.* (orig. 1957) 1965[5], Düsseldorf: Patmos-Verlag

Schlier, H.: *The Relevance of the New Testament.* (transl. by W.J. O'Hara from *Besinnung auf das Neue Testament: Exegetische Aufsätze und Vorträge II.* 1964, Freiburg: Verlag Herder, omitting chapters IV, X, XVI, XVIII-XXVI) 1968, London: Burns and Oates Ltd, New York: Herder and Herder

Schlier, H.: *Grundzüge einer paulinischen Theologie.* 1978, Freiburg: Verlag Herder

Schnackenburg, R.: "Apostles Before and During Paul's Time", in: Gasque, W.W. - Martin, R.P. (eds.): *Apostolic History and the Gospel.* 1970, Exeter: The Paternoster Press, pp.287-303

Schnackenburg, R.: *Der Brief an die Epheser.* (EKK, X), 1982, Zürich: Benziger Verlag, Neukirchen-Vluyn: Neukirchener Verlag

Schneemelcher, W.: "Bibel III. Die Entstehung des Kanons des Neuen Testaments und der christlichen Bibel", in: Krause, G. - Müller, G. (eds.): *Theologische Realenzyklopädie.* vol. 6, 1980, Berlin, New York: Walter de Gruyter & Co., pp.22-48

Schneemelcher, W. (ed.): *New Testament Apocrypha.* 2 vols. (revised English edition based on the sixth edition of the German original; English translation ed.: R.McL. Wilson) vol. 1: 1991 (German 1990), vol. 2: 1992 (German 1989), Cambridge: James Clarke & Co. Ltd, Louisville, Kentucky: Westminster/John Knox Press

Schneemelcher, W.: "General Introduction", in: Schneemelcher, W. (ed.): *New Testament Apocrypha.* vol. 1, 1991a, Cambridge: James Clarke & Co. Ltd, Louisville, Kentucky: Westminster/John Knox Press, pp.9-75

Schneemelcher, W.: "Writings Relating to the Apostles: Introduction", in: Schneemelcher, W. (ed.): *New Testament Apocrypha.* vol. 2, 1992a, Cambridge: James Clarke & Co. Ltd, Louisville, Kentucky: Westminster/John Knox Press, pp.1-4

Schrage, W.: *The Ethics of the New Testament.* (transl. by D.E. Green from the 1982 German orig.) 1988, Edinburgh: T. & T. Clark Ltd

Seeberg, A.: *Der Katechismus der Urchristenheit.* (reprint of 1903 orig., with an introduction by F. Hahn) 1966, München: Chr. Kaiser Verlag

Sparks, H.F.D. (ed.): *The Apocryphal Old Testament.* (reprint of 1984 orig.) 1989 Oxford: Clarendon Press

Stanton, G.N.: "The Fourfold Gospel", Presidential Address delivered at the 1996 General Meeting of SNTS, forthcoming in *New Testament Studies*

Stegemann, H.: "The Literary Composition of the Temple Scroll and its Status at Qumran", in: Brooke, G.J. (ed.): *Temple Scroll Studies.* 1989, Sheffield: JSOT Press, pp.123-148

Stemberger, G.: "Jabne und der Kanon", in: Baldermann, I. - *et al.* (eds.): *Jahrbuch für Biblische Theologie.* vol. 3: *Zum Problem des biblischen Kanons.* 1988, Neukirchen-Vluyn: Neukirchener Verlag, pp.163-174

Stendahl, K.: "Biblical theology, Contemporary", in: Buttrick, G.A. - *et al.* (eds.): *The Interpreter's Dictionary of the Bible: An Illustrated Encyclopedia.* vol. 1 (A-D), 1962, New York, Nashville: Abingdon Press

Stone, M.E.: *Fourth Ezra: A Commentary on the Book of Fourth Ezra.* (Hermeneia) 1990, Minneapolis: Fortress Press

Strauss, D.F.: *The Life of Jesus Critically Examined.* (transl. by G. Eliot from the 1840 fourth German ed.; first German ed.: 1835; first English ed.: 1848) 1906[5], London: Swan Sonnenschein & Co. Lim.

Strecker, G. (ed.): *Das Problem der Theologie des Neuen Testaments.* 1975, Darmstadt: Wissenschaftliche Buchgesellschaft

Strecker, G.: "εὐαγγελίζω - εὐαγγέλιον", in: Balz, H.- Schneider, G. (eds.): *Exegetisches Wörterbuch zum Neuen Testament.* vol. 2, 1981, Stuttgart, Berlin, Köln, Mainz: Verlag W. Kohlhammer GmbH, cols.173-186

Strecker, G.: *Die Johannesbriefe.* (Kritisch-exegetischer Kommentar über das Neue Testament, 14) 1989, Göttingen: Vandenhoeck & Ruprecht

Strecker, G.: *Theologie des Neuen Testaments.* (ed. by F.W. Horn) 1995, Berlin, New York: Walter de Gruyter

Stuhlmacher, P.: *Das paulinische Evangelium.* 1968, Göttingen: Vandenhoeck und Ruprecht

Stuhlmacher, P.: *Vom Verstehen des Neuen Testaments: Eine Hermeneutik.* 1979, Göttingen: Vandenhoeck & Ruprecht

Stuhlmacher, P. (ed.): *Das Evangelium und die Evangelien.* (Vorträge vom Tübinger Symposium 1982) 1983, Tübingen: J.C.B. Mohr (Paul Siebeck)

Stuhlmacher, P.: "Zum Thema: Das Evangelium und die Evangelien", in: Stuhlmacher, P. (ed.): *Das Evangelium und die Evangelien.* 1983a, Tübingen: J.C.B. Mohr (Paul Siebeck), pp.1-26

Stuhlmacher, P.: "Das paulinische Evangelium", in: Stuhlmacher, P. (ed.): *Das Evangelium und die Evangelien.* 1983b, Tübingen: J.C.B. Mohr (Paul Siebeck), pp.157-182

Stuhlmacher, P.: *Biblische Theologie des Neuen Testaments.* vol. 1: *Grundlegung; Von Paulus zu Jesus.* 1992, Göttingen: Vandenhoeck & Ruprecht

Stuhlmacher, P.: *Wie treibt man Biblische Theologie?* 1995, Neukirchen-Vluyn: Neukirchener Verlag

Sundberg, A.C.: "Canon Muratori: A Fourth-Century List", *Harvard Theological Review* 66 (1973), pp.1-41

Theißen, G. - Merz, A.: *Der historische Jesus: Ein Lehrbuch.* 1996, Göttingen: Vandenhoeck & Ruprecht

Thesaurus Linguae Graecae: Canon of Greek Authors and Works. (Ed. by L. Berkowitz and K.A. Squitier, with technical assistance from W.A. Johnson) (orig. 1977) 1986[2], New York, Oxford: Oxford University Press; Ibycus Scholarly Personal Computer CD-ROM, C version

Thüsing, W.: *Die Neutestamentlichen Theologien und Jesus Christus I.: Kriterien aufgrund der Rückfrage nach Jesus und des Glaubens an seine Auferstehung.* 1981, Düsseldorf: Patmos Verlag

Tov, E.: *Textual Criticism of the Hebrew Bible.* 1992, Minneapolis: Fortress Press, Assen/Maastricht: Van Gorcum

Trobisch, D.: *Die Entstehung der Paulusbriefsammlung: Studien zu den Anfängen christlicher Publizistik.* (Novum Testamentum et Orbis Antiquus, 10) 1989, Freiburg, Schweiz: Universitätsverlag, Göttingen: Vandenhoeck & Ruprecht

Trobisch, D.: *Die Endredaktion des Neuen Testaments: Eine Untersuchung zur Entstehung der christlichen Bibel.* (Novum Testamentum et Orbis Antiquus, 31) 1996, Freiburg, Schweiz: Universitätsverlag, Göttingen: Vandenhoeck & Ruprecht

Troeltsch, E.: "Historiography", in: Hastings, J. (ed.): *Encyclopaedia of Religion and Ethics.* vol. 6, 1913, Edinburgh: T. & T. Clark, pp.716-723

Troeltsch, E.: "Ueber historische und dogmatische Methode in der Theologie", in: *Gesammelte Schriften. Zweiter Band: Zur religiösen Lage, Religionsphilosophie und Ethik.* (reprint of 1913 orig.) 1922^2, Tübingen: J.C.B. Mohr (Paul Siebeck), pp.729-753

Tuckett, Ch.: *Reading the New Testament: Methods of Interpretation.* (third impression of 1987 orig.) 1992, London: SPCK

Vermes, G.: *Scripture and Tradition in Judaism: Haggadic Studies.* (Studia Post-Biblica, vol. 4) 1961, Leiden: E.J. Brill

Vermes, G.: *The Dead Sea Scrolls in English.* (revised and augmented edition of 1962 orig.) 1987^3, London: Penguin Books Ltd

Vielhauer, Ph. and Strecker, G.: "Apocalypses and Related Subjects: Introduction", in: Schneemelcher, W. (ed.): *New Testament Apocrypha.* vol. 2, 1992a, Cambridge: James Clarke & Co. Ltd, Louisville, Kentucky: Westminster/John Knox Press, pp.542-568

Vielhauer, Ph. - Strecker, G.: "Apocalyptic in Early Christianity: Introduction", in: Schneemelcher, W. (ed.): *New Testament Apocrypha.* vol. 2, 1992b, Cambridge: James Clarke & Co. Ltd, Louisville, Kentucky: Westminster/John Knox Press, pp.569-602

Wacholder, B.Z.: *The Dawn of Qumran: The Sectarian Torah and the Teacher of Righteousness.* 1983, Cincinnati: Hebrew Union College Press

Wedderburn, A.J.M.: "Paul and Jesus: The Problem of Continuity", *Scottish Journal of Theology* 38 (1985), pp.189-203

Wedderburn, A.J.M.: "Paul and Jesus: Similarity and Continuity", *New Testament Studies* 34 (1988), pp.161-182

Wedderburn, A.J.M. (ed.): *Paul and Jesus: Collected Essays.* 1989, Sheffield: JSOT Press

Wedderburn, A.J.M.: "Introduction", in: Wedderburn, A.J.M. (ed.): *Paul and Jesus: Collected Essays.* 1989a, Sheffield: JSOT Press, pp.11-15

Weiss, J.: *Paulus und Jesus.* 1909, Berlin: Verlag von Reuther & Reichard

Wengst, K.: "Glaubensbekenntnis(se) IV. Neues Testament", in: Müller, G. (ed.): *Theologische Realenzyklopädie.* vol. 13, 1984, Berlin, New York: Walter de Gruyter & Co., pp.392-399

Wenham, J.: *Redating Matthew, Mark and Luke: A Fresh Assault on the Synoptic Problem.* 1991, London: Hodder & Stoughton

Westcott, B.F.: *Saint Paul's Epistle to the Ephesians: The Greek Text with Notes and Addenda.* 1906, London: Macmillan and Co., Limited

Westermann, C.: "Zur Frage einer Biblischen Theologie", in: Baldermann, I. - et al. (eds.): *Jahrbuch für Biblische Theologie.* vol. 1: *Einheit und Vielfalt Biblischer Theologie.* 1986, Neukirchen-Vluyn: Neukirchener Verlag, pp.13-30

Wilckens, U.: *Der Brief an die Römer.* 2. Teilband: Röm 6-11 (EKK, VI.2) 1980, Zürich: Benziger Verlag, Neukirchen-Vluyn: Neukirchener Verlag

Williams, D.S.: "Reconsidering Marcion's Gospel", *Journal of Biblical Literature* 108 (1989), pp.477-496

Wolde, G. (ed.): *Einleitung ins Neue Testament: Aus Schleiermacher's handschriftlichem Nachlasse und nachgeschriebenen Vorlesungen.* 1845, Berlin: bei G. Reimer

Wrede, W.: *Über Aufgabe und Methode der sogenannten Neutestamentlichen Theologie.* 1897, Göttingen: Vandenhoeck und Ruprecht

Wrede, W.: *Das Messiasgeheimnis in den Evangelien.* 1901, Göttingen: Vandenhoeck und Ruprecht

Wrede, W.: *Charakter und Tendenz des Johannesevangeliums.* 1903, Tübingen und Leipzig: J.C.B. Mohr

Wrede, W.: *The Origin of the New Testament.* (transl. by J.S. Hill) 1909, London and New York: Harper and Brothers

Wrede, W.: "The Task and Methods of 'New Testament Theology'", in: Morgan, R. (ed., transl., and introd.): *The Nature of New Testament Theology: The Contribution of William Wrede and Adolf Schlatter.* 1973, London: SCM Press Ltd, pp.68-116

Yadin, Y. (ed.): *The Temple Scroll.* vol. 1: *Introduction.* 1983, Jerusalem: The Israel Exploration Society

Yadin, Y.: *The Temple Scroll: The Hidden Law of the Dead Sea Sect.* 1985, London: Weidenfeld and Nicolson

Young, F.M.: *The Making of the Creeds.* 1991, London: SCM Press Ltd, Philadelphia: Trinity Press International

Zahn, Th.: *Forschungen zur Geschichte des neutestamentlichen Kanons und der altkirchlichen Literatur.* 6 vols. 1881-1900, vols. 1-3: Erlangen: Verlag von Andreas Deichert, vols. 4-5: Erlangen - Leipzig: A. Deichertsche Verlagsbuchhandlung Nachf. (Georg Böhme), vol. 6: Leipzig: A. Deichertsche Verlagsbuchhandlung Nachf. (Georg Böhme) (vol. 1: *Tatian's Diatessaron*, 1881; vol. 2: *Der Evangeliencommentar des Theophilus von Antiochien*, 1883; vol. 3: *Supplementum Clementinum*, 1884; vol. 4: *Analecta zur Geschichte und Literatur der Kirche im zweiten Jahrhundert*, pp.247-329, 1891; vol. 5: *Paralipomena*, pp.1-158, 1893; vol. 6: I. *Apostel und Apostelschüler in der Provinz Asien*; II. *Brüder und Vettern Jesu*, 1900.)

Zahn, Th.: *Geschichte des Neutestamentlichen Kanons.* 2 vols. 1888-1892, vol. I.1: 1888, Erlangen: Verlag von Andreas Deichert; vol. I.2: 1889, II.1: 1890, II.2: 1892, Erlangen - Leipzig: A. Deichert'sche Verlagsbuchh. Nachf. (Georg Böhme)

Zahn, Th.: *Introduction to the New Testament.* 3 vols. (transl. from the third German edition by J.M. Trout, *et al.*), 1909, Edinburgh: T. & T. Clark

Zehnle, R.F.: *Peter's Pentecost Discourse: Tradition and Lukan Reinterpretation in Peter's Speeches of Acts 2 and 3.* 1971, Nashville, Tennessee: Abingdon Press

Index of Authors

Index of References

Index of Subjects